Dorr Perkins Dearborn

Happy Birthday '88

Love,

Joyce & Dad

UNDERSTANDING
R:BASE
SYSTEM V

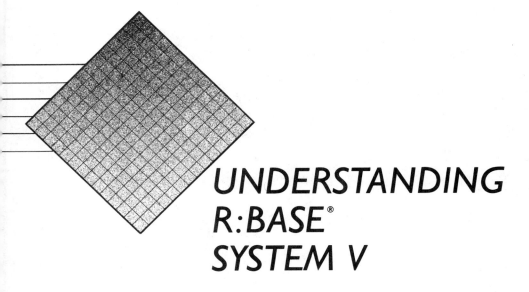

UNDERSTANDING
R:BASE®
SYSTEM V

■ Alan Simpson

SYBEX®

San Francisco ■ Paris ■ Düsseldorf ■ London

■ Cover art by Thomas Ingalls + Associates
Cover photography by Casey Cartwright
Book design by Ingrid Owen

Clout, Microrim, R:BASE 4000, R:BASE 5000, R:BASE System V, and FileGateway are trademarks of Microrim, Inc.
dBASE II, dBASE III, and dBASE III PLUS are trademarks of Ashton-Tate.
DIF is a trademark of Software Arts Products Corporation.
IBM, IBM PC, XT, AT, and PC-DOS are trademarks of International Business Machines Corporation.
Lotus 1-2-3 and Symphony are trademarks of Lotus Development Corporation.
MailMerge and WordStar are trademarks of Microsoft Corporation.
Net/One is a trademark of Ungermann-Bass inc.
Novell and Netware are trademarks of Novell, Inc.
pfs:FILE is a trademark of Software Publishing Corporation.
VisiCalc is a trademark of VisiCorp.
3Com and EtherSeries are trademarks of 3Com, Inc.

SYBEX is a registered trademark of SYBEX, Inc.

SYBEX is not affiliated with any manufacturer.

Library of Congress Card Number: 86-63745
ISBN 0-89588-394-5
Manufactured in the United States of America
10 9 8 7 6 5 4 3 2

■ *To*
SUSAN

ACKNOWLEDGMENTS

Many thanks to all the people whose skills and talents produced this book, including, in roughly chronological order, Elizabeth Forsaith, copy editing; Jim Compton, production editing; Greg Hooten, technical review; Olivia Shinomoto and David Clark, word processing; Ingrid Owen, design; Cheryl Vega, typesetting; Aidan Wylde, proofreading; and Amparo Del Rio, paste-up.

Special thanks to my literary agents Bill and Cynthia Gladstone, for keeping my writing career alive and well.

Sincere thanks to my wife, Susan, for keeping me alive and well through all the long hours and short deadlines.

TABLE OF CONTENTS

■ 10　■ MANAGING NUMBERS IN A TABLE　　195

■ 11　■ ADVANCED REPORT AND FORM TECHNIQUES　　209

■ 14 ■ VARIABLES AND FUNCTIONS 297

■ 15   ■ *THE R:BASE PROGRAMMING LANGUAGE*   *335*

■ 17 ■ USING CODELOCK   417

INTRODUCTION

R:BASE System V is the third major version of the R:BASE database-management system for microcomputers. Like its predecessors, R:BASE 4000 and R:BASE 5000, R:BASE System V is a powerful and flexible tool for storing, organizing, analyzing, and retrieving information on a microcomputer. However, the new R:BASE System V is a significant improvement over its predecessors. For the beginner, R:BASE System V is simpler and better integrated for managing and analyzing data spontaneously, without any programming.

For intermediate and advanced users, R:BASE System V offers more powerful tools for rapid development of customized business systems, including powerful report, form, and application generators. The new R:BASE also offers 70 new functions that perform a wide variety of tasks, including statistical, financial, and trigonometric calculations.

■ WHO SHOULD READ THIS BOOK

This book is written for the absolute beginner in R:BASE System V. To encourage rapid learning and complete mastery, this book focuses on practical examples of putting R:BASE System V to work immediately. Once you've learned how to manage data in R:BASE databases effectively, the book will instruct you in the more advanced topics of custom applications development, using a sophisticated accounts-receivable system as the practical example.

There are so many new features in R:BASE System V, that even readers with previous experience in R:BASE 4000 or R:BASE 5000 will be able to profit from this book. While some of the basic concepts presented in the earlier chapters in the book may seem "old hat" to experienced R:BASE users, the new R:BASE System V tools and techniques will quickly become apparent as you read on.

■ TIPS FOR TYROS

There are a few tools and techniques that you can use in your work with R:BASE that will foster your learning. First, and perhaps most important, is the simple saying

When in doubt...
Escape key out

The Escape key (labeled Esc on most keyboards, CANCEL on others) will usually allow you to escape from any jam that you might get yourself into. If you ever feel lost while working with R:BASE, press the Esc key a few times until you find yourself in more familiar territory. This is safer and easier than turning off the computer or rebooting with the Ctrl-Alt-Del keys.

Another point to keep in mind is that you can usually find additional help in R:BASE System V by looking for instructions at the top or bottom of your screen. In addition, you can almost always press the F10 key to get further help on your screen.

Finally, look for the plastic keyboard template that came with your R:BASE System V package. Place this template over the function keys (labeled F1 through F10) on your keyboard. It may not mean much to you when you first place it on your keyboard, but as you work through the exercises in this book, the template will remind you of the purpose of the various function keys.

■ STRUCTURE OF THIS BOOK

This book is designed as a tutorial, not as a reference manual. It begins with the simplest and most basic concepts and builds upon acquired knowledge and skills toward complete mastery.

The first eight chapters discuss all of the basic database-management techniques. These techniques include storing, organizing, analyzing, searching, and updating information in a database table. Chapters 9 through 12 discuss more advanced techniques involving multiple database tables.

Chapters 13 through 15 discuss the development of custom business applications with the R:BASE System V application generator and programming language. Chapters 16 and 17 bring together all the material from previous chapters and present a fully customized accounts-receivable system as an example.

Chapter 18 discusses techniques for transferring data between R:BASE System V databases and other software systems, such as word processors and spreadsheets. Chapter 19 is a catch-all chapter that presents tips and techniques for getting the most from R:BASE System V. An appendix, which summarizes the R:BASE System V vocabulary, can be used as a quick reference to R:BASE commands.

■ HARDWARE REQUIREMENTS

R:BASE System V is a large program that needs a large amount of computer hardware to go with it. The computer hardware requirements for R:BASE System V are listed below:

PC-DOS 2.0 or higher (3.1 or higher for local-area networks)

An IBM PC, XT, AT, or 100%-compatible computer

A hard disk (R:BASE consumes approximately 4 MB, so you may find a 20 MB hard disk preferable to a 10 MB disk)

At least 512K RAM for single-user; 640K RAM for networks

For networking, R:BASE System V supports the IBM PC Network and 100%-compatible networks including 3Com EtherSeries, Novell Advanced Netware, Ungermann-Bass Net/One, and others.

R:BASE System V is not copy protected, and it can be run directly from any hard disk without the use of a key disk in the floppy drive.

■ PURCHASING SOFTWARE ON A DISK

If you would like to try the databases and software systems presented in this book (such as the accounts-receivable system), but don't want to type them in yourself, you can purchase a diskette containing all the appropriate files. See the last page in this book for an order form.

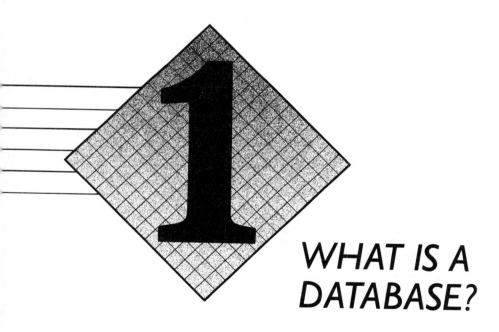

WHAT IS A
DATABASE?

While the term *database management* may sound like just another mysterious computer buzzword, managing a database is as commonplace as storing a Manila folder in a file cabinet. Rolodexes, tickler files, file cabinets, and even shoe boxes full of index cards are all databases. They all hold information (data) in an organized fashion. Each time you use one of these databases to look up information, store new information, create a sorted list, calculate numbers, or make changes, you are *managing* the database.

A computer database management system also allows you to store information in an organized way. However, rather than writing the information on paper and storing it in a file drawer, you store the information on a disk, where it is easily accessible through a computer. Once you've stored information, you can easily retrieve it, sort it, search through it, perform calculations, and make changes and additions.

The greatest advantage to using a computer to manage a database is speed. For example, suppose you had a shoe box full of index cards with names and addresses, stored in alphabetical order by name. If you wanted to print mailing labels for all the California residents, sorted in ZIP-code order (for bulk mailing), you'd have quite a bit of work ahead of you. The process could take hours. If this information were stored on a computer instead, your work would be limited to typing a few commands at the keyboard. The time required to pull out all the California residents and put them into ZIP-code order would be two or three seconds. Then you could go to lunch while the computer printed the mailing labels.

Of course, R:BASE can do much more than print mailing labels, as you'll see throughout the coming chapters.

∎ R:BASE SYSTEM V DATABASES

An R:BASE database can be a collection of many different types of information. Most of this information is stored in *tables,* which consist of neatly organized rows and columns of information. For example, take a look at the table of names and addresses in Figure 1.1. This table consists of six *columns* of information, labeled Last Name, First Name, Address, City, State, and Zip. The table consists of five *rows* of information, sorted into alphabetical order by last name. An R:BASE table could consist of as many as 800 columns and tens of thousands of rows.

Notice how each column in the sample table contains a specific item of information; that is, each last name, first name, address, city, state, and ZIP code occupies a separate column. Generally speaking, when structuring an R:BASE table, you want to break the information into as many separate, meaningful columns as possible because this gives you the greatest flexibility in managing a database. For example, notice how the table in Figure 1.2 combines the city, state, and ZIP code into a single column named CSZ.

This sample table has some distinct disadvantages over the first one. For example, suppose you wanted to sort this table into ZIP-code order or pull out all the California residents? You couldn't do either operation with this table because the state and ZIP code are combined within the CSZ column. As you'll see in the many examples throughout this book, it's always a good idea to place each item of information in its own column.

■ MANAGING A DATABASE

Once you've defined a structure for a table, you need to begin managing it. You may do any of the following tasks:

1. Add new information to the table.

2. Sort the table into a meaningful order.

3. Search the table for types of information.

4. Calculate sums and averages from information in the table.

5. Print the information in an organized fashion.

6. Edit (change) information in the table.

7. Delete superfluous information from the table.

Last Name	First Name	Address	City	State	Zip
Adams	Anthony	123 A St.	Berkeley	CA	94710
Baker	Betty	345 B St.	New York	NY	12345
Carlson	Marianne	P.O. Box 123	Houston	TX	54321
Carrera	Fred	3211 Fox St.	L.A.	CA	92991
Davis	Julie	671 Alpine Way	Newark	NJ	87654

■ *Figure 1.1:*
Sample table in a database.

These tasks are no different from those performed with a shoe-box database. However, with the shoe box, you have to do all the labor; with R:BASE managing the table, you just do the thinking and a little typing. R:BASE does all the work—quickly, efficiently, and without errors.

◼ DATABASE DESIGNS

There are many ways to structure or *design* a database. For example, the table in Figure 1.1 is useful for keeping track of basic mailing information. But a business manager using this table might also want to keep track of appointments or credit charges for each of the individuals in the list. In this case, two tables could be used in a database, as shown in Figure 1.3.

This database design keeps track of a *one-to-many* relationship between individuals in the Customer table and charges recorded in the Charges table. For every one customer in the Customer table, there may be many rows of charges in the Charges table. The two tables are *related* to one another based upon their common Last Name column.

The advantage of the one-to-many design is that it allows you to find basic information quickly, such as the address of Mr. Adams, as well as to find and total the charges that he has incurred during any period of time. By breaking the information into two separate tables, you avoid repeating the address, city, state, and ZIP code with every charge transaction that occurs and thereby avoid wasting a lot of disk space (as well as time).

A one-to-many relationship among tables can be used in other settings too. For example, note the structure of the basic inventory database in Figure 1.4. It consists of three tables: Master Inventory, Sales, and Purchases.

◼ *Figure 1.2: Table with city, state, and ZIP code in one column.*

Last Name	First Name	Address	CSZ
Adams	Anthony	123 A St.	Berkeley, CA 94710
Baker	Betty	345 B St.	New York, NY 12345
Carlson	Marianne	P.O. Box 123	Houston, TX 54321
Carrera	Fred	3211 Fox St.	L.A., CA 92991
Davis	Julie	671 Alpine Way	Newark, NJ 87654

The Master Inventory table contains a single row for each item in the store (or warehouse). The Sales and Purchases tables record individual sales and purchase transactions. The tables are all related to one another through the Item Number column; that is, each table contains a column for recording the item number. These three tables can provide much business information. For example, through a procedure known as *updating,* R:BASE can instantly recalculate the Master Inventory table to determine the current quantity of any item in stock by using the data in the Sales and Purchases tables.

The sample inventory database structure is sometimes called a *master file–transaction file* relationship. The Master Inventory table keeps track of the status quo of each item in stock, while the two transaction tables, Sales and Purchases, maintain a history of every individual sale or purchase.

■ LEARNING THE ROPES

Before we get too carried away with database-design theory here, it's a good idea to learn all of the techniques for managing a single table first. Once you've learned to handle one table, you will easily expand your skills to design and manage databases with multiple tables. Beginning with the next chapter, you'll learn how to create and manage an R:BASE database with a single table. In the process, you'll develop a powerful mailing-list management system.

■ SUMMARY

In this chapter, we've established that

A database is a collection of information, or data.

Most information in a database is stored in tables.

A table consists of orderly rows and columns of information.

A database may consist of several tables.

Multiple tables can be related to one another based upon a common column of information.

Multiple tables in a database allow you to design systems that record and manage one-to-many and master file–transaction file relationships, which are both commonly used in inventory and accounting systems.

CUSTOMER TABLE

Last Name	First Name	Address	City	State	Zip
Adams	Anthony	123 A St.	Berkeley	CA	94710
Baker	Betty	345 B St.	New York	NY	12345
Carlson	Marianne	P.O. Box 123	Houston	TX	54321
Carrera	Fred	3211 Fox St.	L.A.	CA	92991
Davis	Julie	671 Alpine Way	Newark	NJ	87654

CHARGES TABLE

Last Name	Date	Amount
Adams	6/1/86	123.45
Adams	6/8/86	92.00
Adams	7/8/86	456.78
Davis	6/2/86	99.99
Davis	8/1/86	544.00

■ *Figure 1.3:*
Two related tables in a database.

MASTER INVENTORY TABLE

Item Number	Item Name	In Stock	Price	Reorder
10001	Apples	100	.45	50
10002	Bananas	150	.65	40
10003	Cherries	50	.39	55

SALES TABLE

Item Number	Units Sold	Date
10001	5	6/1/86
10003	10	6/1/86
10001	5	6/1/86
10001	17	6/1/86

PURCHASES TABLE

Item Number	Units Bought	Date
10003	10	6/1/86
10002	20	6/1/86

■ *Figure 1.4:*
Sample structure for an inventory database.

2

CREATING A
DATABASE

In this chapter, you'll learn how to create an R:BASE database. If you have R:BASE System V readily available, you may want to try these examples as you read. If you haven't already done so, you'll need to install R:BASE System V on your computer first. If you are using a single-user microcomputer, refer to the *Single-User Installation and Startup Guide* that came with your R:BASE System V package for installation instructions. If you will be using R:BASE System V on a network, refer to the *Multi-User Guide* for installation and start-up instructions.

■ STARTING R:BASE SYSTEM V

The first step in using R:BASE System V is, of course, to start the computer and boot up so that the DOS C> prompt appears on the screen. Then, from the C> prompt, type in the command

■   RBSYSTEM

and press the Enter key. Once the R:BASE system is running, you'll see the Main menu, as shown in Figure 2.1.

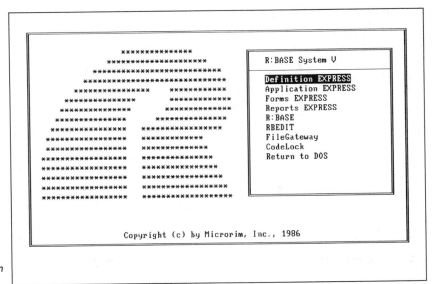

■ *Figure 2.1:*
The R:BASE System V Main menu.

At the right edge of the screen are nine options, eight of which are *modules* in R:BASE System V. You can select a module by moving the highlighter with the up arrow (↑) and down arrow (↓) keys on your keyboard. (If the keys don't work at first, press the Num Lock key once, and then try again.) To select an option, you move the highlighter to that option and then press the Enter (or Return) key, marked with the ←┘ symbol on the IBM keyboard.

■ CREATING A DATABASE

The easiest way to create a database is to use the *Definition Express* module on the RBSystem menu. To enter the Definition Express module, press Enter while the Definition Express option is highlighted on the menu. You'll see the Definition Express Main menu appear on the screen as in Figure 2.2.

To select options from this menu, you can move the highlighter up and down with the arrow keys. (You can also move the highlighter quickly to an option by typing the option number using the number keys at the top of the keyboard.) When the highlighter is on the menu option you want, press Enter.

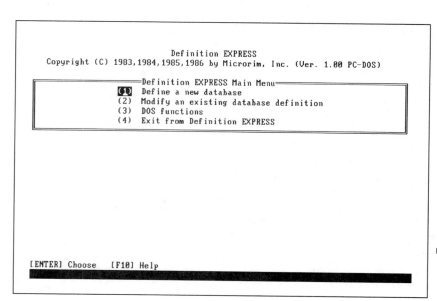

```
                          Definition EXPRESS
        Copyright (C) 1983,1984,1985,1986 by Microrim, Inc. (Ver. 1.00 PC-DOS)

                    ═══Definition EXPRESS Main Menu═══
                    (1)  Define a new database
                    (2)  Modify an existing database definition
                    (3)  DOS functions
                    (4)  Exit from Definition EXPRESS




 [ENTER] Choose    [F10] Help
```

■ *Figure 2.2:*
The Definition Express Main menu.

In this example, we want to create a new database. So with option 1 (Define a New Database) highlighted, press Enter to select that option. R:BASE replies by asking that you

∎   Enter your database name, (1–7 characters)

We'll begin by creating a relatively simple mailing-list database. It's best to use a name that is easy to remember, although you may have to use an abbreviated form since the database name is limited to a maximum of seven characters. For this example, type in the name Mail and press Enter.

After you name the database, a new screen appears, as shown in Figure 2.3.

Notice that the screen is asking for the name of this table. As we discussed earlier, an R:BASE database may consist of several tables, and so each table must have a unique name. A table name may contain a maximum of eight letters. For this example, we'll create a table of names and addresses. Type in Names as the table name. (If you need to make a correction as you type, use the arrow keys or the Backspace key to reposition the cursor and retype the name.) When the correct name is typed in, press the Enter key. The screen will look like Figure 2.4.

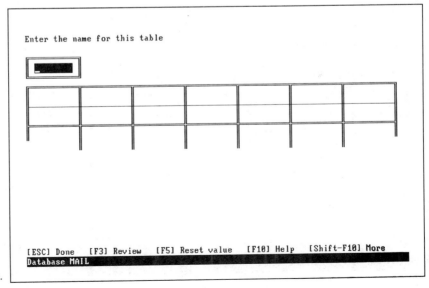

∎ *Figure 2.3:*
Screen for
defining a
database table.

Defining Column Names

For the first table, we'll name the columns L:Name, F:Name, Company, Address, City, State, Zip, and Ent:Date. Notice that we've abbreviated some of the column names and used a colon rather than a space in some of the names (for example, Ent:Date stands for Entry Date). This is because column names are limited to a maximum width of eight characters, and they may not contain blank spaces.

When defining a table structure, you need to fill in more than just the column names. You need to define the *type* of data and the maximum *width* of the data to be stored in the column. The types of data used in R:BASE tables are listed in Figure 2.5.

All of the columns in our first table, except for Ent:Date, will be Text data. Ent:Date will be Date data. Figure 2.6 shows the exact structure that we'll use for the Names table.

Notice that we've assigned the Zip column the Text data type. This may seem odd at first, since we often think of ZIP codes as numbers; however, they have some characteristics that make them unlike actual numbers. For example, some ZIP codes contain hyphens, such as 92038-2802. Some foreign ZIP codes contain letters, such as A123I. Because these examples are not true numbers, R:BASE would not know how to handle these data if they were entered into a numeric column. In order to play it safe, we've defined the Zip column as Text data.

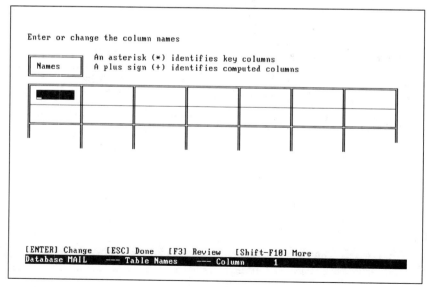

■ *Figure 2.4:*
Table name entered on the screen.

To define the table structure, you simply type in the name of the first column in the first box on the screen, and press Enter. For this example, type in the column name L:Name and press Enter. The column name box now contains the column name, and a menu of data types appears, as shown in Figure 2.7.

To select an option from the menu of data types, use the arrow and Enter keys as with previous menus. In this example, the Text option is already highlighted, so just press the Enter key.

Data Type	Used to Store
Text	Any textual information that has no numeric value, such as names and addresses. Maximum length for a Text column is 1500 characters.
Currency	Dollar amounts, such as the price of an item or an hourly wage.
Integer	Whole numbers that do not have any decimal places. Sometimes used for identification numbers, such as account numbers or part numbers.
Real	Real numbers that may contain decimal places. Used to store numeric quantities such as −123.45 or 6543.2123.
Double	Very large numbers, outside the range $\pm 9 * 10^{\pm 37}$. (Generally only used in scientific and engineering applications.)
Date	Dates usually stored in MM/DD/YY format.
Time	Time, usually displayed in HH:MM:SS format (e.g., 12:31:46), in either a 24-hour clock or an AM/PM 12-hour clock.
Note	Like a Text column, holds nonnumeric textual information. However, maximum length of a Note column is 4050 characters. (You should only use this if you need the extra characters, because it consumes more disk space.)
Computed	A column that receives its value from the computation of other columns. For example, if a table contains two columns named Qty and Unit:Price, a Computed column named Total could contain the results of multiplying Qty times Unit:Price.

■ *Figure 2.5:*
Table of R:BASE
data types.

Next, the screen asks for the maximum width of data in this column and suggests a width of eight characters. Many last names are longer than eight characters, so we'll assign a maximum width of 15 characters

Column Name	Type of Data	Maximum Length
L:Name	Text	15
F:Name	Text	15
Company	Text	20
Address	Text	25
City	Text	15
State	Text	5
Zip	Text	10
Ent:Date	Date	

■ *Figure 2.6:*
Structure for the Names table.

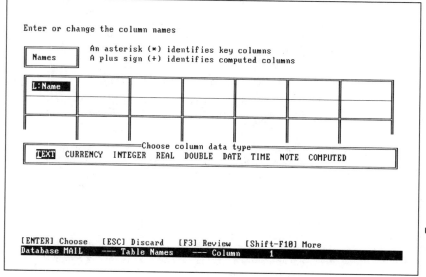

■ *Figure 2.7:*
Column name entered onto the screen.

to this column. Type in the number 15 (using the number keys at the top of the keyboard), and press Enter.

Next R:BASE displays the question

∎   Do you want this column to be a key? Yes No

Key columns are used to speed processing in some operations, but are of no concern to us now. Just press the Enter key to select No. At this point, the contents of the first column are defined, and the highlighting moves to the second column, as shown in Figure 2.8.

You can now define the structure of the second column, or you can use the arrow keys to back up and make corrections to the first column. If you are following along on-line, go ahead and fill in the definitions for the remaining columns using the information in Figure 2.6. The exact steps to follow are summarized below:

1. Type in F:Name, press Enter, select Text, type in 15, press Enter, and select No.

2. Type in Company, press Enter, select Text, type in 20, press Enter, and select No.

3. Type in Address, press Enter, select Text, type in 25, press Enter, and select No.

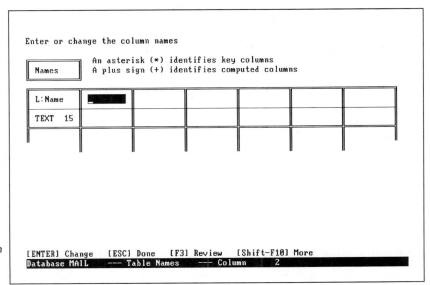

∎ *Figure 2.8:*
The first column
defined in the
Names table.

4. Type in City, press Enter, select Text, type in 15, press Enter, and select No.

5. Type in State, press Enter, select Text, type in 5, press Enter, and select No.

6. Type in Zip, press Enter, select Text, type in 10, press Enter, and select No.

7. Type in Ent:Date, press Enter, select Date, press Enter, and select No.

It is not necessary to define a width for the Ent:Date column because R:BASE uses a predefined width for dates.

Once all of the column names have been entered, the screen will look like Figure 2.9. Notice that the L:Name and F:Name columns have disappeared from the screen. This is because there is not enough room for the columns to be displayed, but rest assured, these columns are still in the table.

Making Changes

You can easily make changes and corrections after entering column names. The keys that you use to help with modifications and their effects are listed in Figure 2.10.

For example, if you accidentally left out the State column name and needed to back up and fill it in, you could use the left arrow key to move character by character or Shift-Tab (hold down the Shift key and press the Tab key) to move by columns to highlight the Zip column. Then you would press F1 to insert a blank column, and you could fill in the new column name and structure as usual. Pressing the End key would return the highlighting to the last column name in the table.

Getting Help

Another one of your options listed on the bottom of the screen is to press the F10 key to get help. Pressing this key will display some helpful advice, here as well as on most R:BASE screens. After reading the help screen, press any key to return to the task at hand.

Saving the Table Structure

Once you've defined your table structure and made any necessary corrections, press the Esc key to save your work. Another menu appears on the screen, as shown in Figure 2.11, which allows you to add more tables to the database or to refine an existing database. We'll discuss these more advanced features in later chapters. For now, select option 7

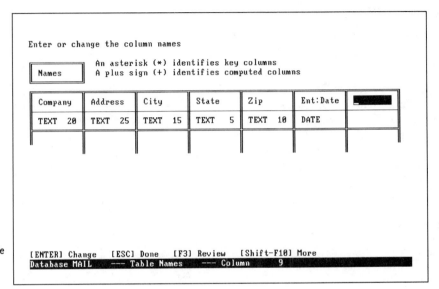

```
Enter or change the column names

┌─────────┐    An asterisk (*) identifies key columns
│ Names   │    A plus sign (+) identifies computed columns
└─────────┘

┌─────────┬─────────┬─────────┬─────────┬─────────┬─────────┬─────────┐
│ Company │ Address │ City    │ State   │ Zip     │ Ent:Date│ ███████ │
├─────────┼─────────┼─────────┼─────────┼─────────┼─────────┼─────────┤
│ TEXT 20 │ TEXT 25 │ TEXT 15 │ TEXT  5 │ TEXT 10 │ DATE    │         │
│         │         │         │         │         │         │         │
└─────────┴─────────┴─────────┴─────────┴─────────┴─────────┴─────────┘

[ENTER] Change   [ESC] Done   [F3] Review   [Shift-F10] More
Database MAIL     --- Table Names     --- Column      9
```

■ *Figure 2.9:*
The Names table defined on the screen.

Key Name	Effect
Home	Moves highlighting to the first column
End	Moves highlighting to the last column
←	Moves the cursor left through the highlighted area, character by character
→	Moves the cursor right through the highlighted area, character by character
Tab	Moves highlighting one column to the right
Shift-Tab	Moves highlighting one column to the left
F1	Inserts a new column at the highlighted position
F2	Deletes the highlighted column
↵	Defines the structure of the highlighted column
F10	Gets help
Break	Abandons the table structure

■ *Figure 2.10:*
Keys used to modify table structure.

(Return to Definition Express Main menu) to save the Names table in the Mail database, and return to the Express menu.

■ MODIFYING AN EXISTING DATABASE DEFINITION

Option 2 from the Definition Express Main menu lets you change any existing database definitions. You can add or delete fields, columns, or tables with this option. You can also modify data types and widths, change column names, and so forth.

Since we don't need to modify the Mail database now, we can skip over this menu option. (Chapters 8 and 9 will discuss these topics in more detail.)

■ USING DOS FUNCTIONS

Option 3 on the Definition Express Main menu lets you use various DOS commands without leaving R:BASE. This is entirely optional

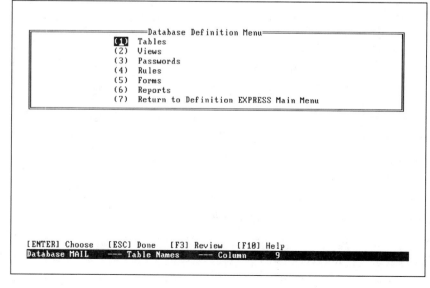

```
                         ═Database Definition Menu═
                    (1)  Tables
                    (2)  Views
                    (3)  Passwords
                    (4)  Rules
                    (5)  Forms
                    (6)  Reports
                    (7)  Return to Definition EXPRESS Main Menu
```

```
  [ENTER] Choose    [ESC] Done    [F3] Review    [F10] Help
  Database MAIL    --- Table Names    --- Column    9
```

■ *Figure 2.11:*
Additional options for defining a database.

and is provided only as a convenience. Selecting this option displays the menu shown in Figure 2.12.

Suppose you wish to view a list of all files that begin with the letters MAIL on the current directory. To do so, you could select option 2 (Directories). From the next menu, select option 2 (Display a Directory). R:BASE will display the prompt

■   Enter a directory path or [ENTER] for current directory

You can enter a directory path and use DOS wildcards to create a filename template as well. In this case, we want to see all the files with the first four letters MAIL on the current directory, so type in the template

■   MAIL＊.＊

and press Enter. The screen shows the files

■   MAIL1.RBF
    MAIL2.RBF
    MAIL3.RBF

These files, together, form the Mail database you just created.

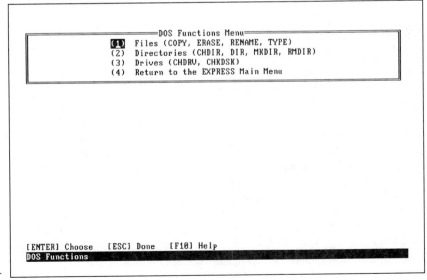

■ *Figure 2.12:*
The DOS
Functions menu.

The prompt "Press any key to continue" appears near the bottom of the screen. Press any key, and select 5 to return to the DOS Functions menu. Then select 4 to return to the Definition Express Main menu.

■ EXITING DEFINITION EXPRESS

When you've finished defining a database structure for the time being, select option 4, Exit from Definition Express, to return to the RBSystem Main menu. (You can do so now if you are following along on-line.)

■ EXITING R:BASE SYSTEM V

To exit R:BASE System V entirely and return to the DOS prompt, select Return to DOS from the R:BASE System V prompt. You will see the DOS C> prompt (or whatever prompt specifies your hard disk) appear on the screen.

You should **always** exit R:BASE System V and return to the DOS C> prompt before turning off your computer. Failure to do so might result in loss of data or corrupted (unusable) files.

■ DATABASE LIMITATIONS

There are a few limitations to the size of an R:BASE database. A single database can have a maximum of 80 tables assigned to it. Each individual table may have a maximum of 80 columns. However, a database also can contain a maximum of 800 columns. Therefore, a database could contain a maximum of 10 tables if each contained 80 columns, or 20 tables if each contained 40 columns. This is a very large maximum, and it is unlikely that you will run out of room in an R:BASE database.

Numbers stored in Dollar columns can take on values in the range $\pm$ \$99,999,999,999,999.99. Integer column numbers can have values in the range $\pm$999,999,999. Real numbers can accept values in the range $\pm 9 \times 10^{\pm 37}$. Double numbers can store values in the range $\pm 9 \times 10^{\pm 307}$.

The maximum number of rows in a table or database is limited only by the amount of disk storage on your computer.

■ SUMMARY

You have now created your first database, and it's ready to start storing information. Before moving on to the next chapter, take a moment to review the techniques that we used to create the Mail database:

To begin creating a database, select the Definition Express option from the R:BASE System V Main menu. Then select option 1 from the next menu.

When prompted, enter the name of the database.

When prompted, fill in a name for the first table in the database.

Type in the name, data type, and maximum width for each column in the table.

For help while working with the database, press the F10 key. Then press any key to remove the help screen.

Press the Esc key after defining all the column names to be used in the table.

Always exit R:BASE System V before turning off your computer. Select *Return to DOS* from the RBSystem Main menu to do so.

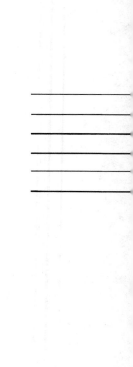

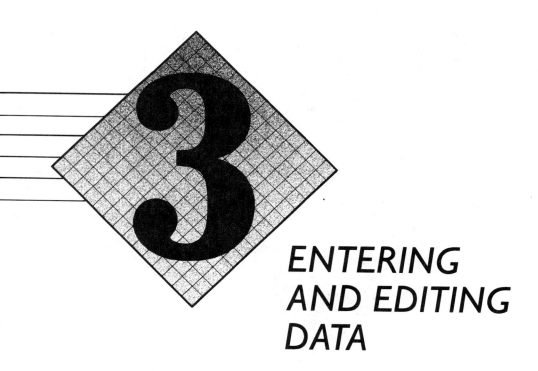

3

ENTERING
AND EDITING
DATA

Now that you've created a database with an empty table in it, you can start storing information. In this chapter, we'll discuss techniques for opening an existing database, adding new data to it, and changing (editing) existing data.

If you exited R:BASE in the last chapter (so that the DOS C> prompt is showing), enter the command

■   RBSYSTEM

and press Enter to bring back the RBSystem Main menu.

■ THE R:BASE COMMAND MODE

To work with your database in an *interactive* fashion (whereby you enter a single command and R:BASE performs it), select R:BASE from the RBSystem Main menu. This brings up instructions for opening a database, as in Figure 3.1.

Before we get into the specifics of opening a database and adding data to it, let's discuss two alternative techniques for working interactively with a database: the *command mode,* which displays only the symbol R>

```
 OPEN ...

 OPEN opens an existing database. You must open a database to work with
 the data stored in it. If you do not want to open a database now,
 press [ESC].
                          ══Choose a database══
 MAIL   TEST
```

■ *Figure 3.1:*
Instructions for opening a database.

on the screen, and the *prompt mode,* which displays instructions for entering commands.

The *command mode* is generally used by individuals who are experienced enough with R:BASE to enter commands without any help. In command mode, you type in a *command* or a *command line,* which gives R:BASE specific instructions on how to perform a task.

The *prompt mode,* which is currently on the screen, helps the less experienced user build command lines with instructions and simpler menu selections. We'll use the prompt mode in this chapter and the next, and then start using the command mode later.

If, at any time, you find that you've inadvertently switched to the command mode (and only the R > prompt appears on your screen), you can switch back to the prompt mode by typing in the command

■   PROMPTS

next to the R > prompt, and pressing Enter.

■ *OPENING A DATABASE*

The first step in using any database is to *open* it so that R:BASE has access to it. The prompt mode on the screen (and in Figure 3.1) is currently showing a prompt to help you open a database. The bottom menu shows the names of all databases currently available on disk. (Figure 3.1 shows the names Mail and Test, although your screen may show more or fewer file names.) To open the Mail database, move the cell pointer to the name Mail, and press Enter. The screen now displays the command

■   OPEN MAIL

that your selection has built at the top of the screen. Your options at the top of the screen are

■   – Execute – Edit – Reset – Help – Quit ─────────

To *execute* the Open Mail command, press Enter to select the Execute option. R:BASE displays

■   Database exists
     Press any key to continue

R:BASE is simply telling you that you've opened an existing database and that you can press any key to continue.

When you press a key to continue, R:BASE displays a menu of options for interacting with your database, as shown in Figure 3.2. You can use the arrow keys to highlight any option and then press Enter to select the option. Before doing so, however, let's quickly try a simple exercise for entering a command without the aid of the prompts.

Opening a Database from the Command Mode

Let's take a moment to try entering the command to open the Mail database without the aid of the prompts. At the top of the Prompt menu, notice the instruction

■   To leave PROMPTS for R:BASE command mode, press [ESC].

If you press the Esc key now, you'll see only the prompt

■   R>

on your screen.

```
                    Prompts are organized under these topics.
              For a list of commands that have prompts, choose All commands.

                    To leave PROMPTS for R:BASE command mode, press [ESC].

  ═Data Manipulation════Database Operations════════Utilities═
  Look at data          Open a database          Application development
  Print data            Exit                     Database maintenance
  Add data              Data Input               R:BASE environment
  Edit data             Data Output              Edit an ASCII file
  Import/export data    Create a database        DOS functions
  Relational operations Modify a database        All commands
```

■ *Figure 3.2:*
The Prompt
menu.

The command you executed to open the Mail database in the prompt mode was Open Mail. To perform this same task in the command mode, type the command

■   OPEN MAIL

next to the R> prompt, and press Enter. Again, R:BASE will display the "Database exists" prompt and then redisplay the R> prompt so that you can enter more commands.

To simplify matters, we'll return to the prompt mode. To do so, type in the command

■   PROMPTS

and press the Enter key. The Prompt menu will appear on the screen.

■ ADDING
DATA TO A
TABLE

Now that you've opened the database, you can enter data into it using any one of a variety of techniques. We'll start with the simplest technique in this chapter.

From the Prompt menu, highlight the Add Data option, and then press Enter. This brings up the instructions and options shown in Figure 3.3.

The Append and Input commands are used when transferring data from one table to another and are irrelevant for our present needs. The Enter command is used only with *custom forms,* which we'll discuss in Chapter 7. For now, highlight the Load command and press Enter. This brings up some new options, as shown in Figure 3.4.

In this example we want to type in new data from the keyboard, so select the Keyboard option from the menu. Next the screen displays the names of all tables in the currently open database. In this example, the database contains only the single table Names. Press Enter to select the Names table.

Next the screen displays the names of all the columns in the Names table and asks which ones you want to enter data into, as shown in Figure 3.5. In this example, just press the Esc key to select all the column names.

The next screen asks if you want to have *prompts* appear when entering data (these prompts show the names and types of columns as you enter data, as you'll see in a moment). When typing in new data, it's a good idea to use the prompts, so press Enter to select Prompts.

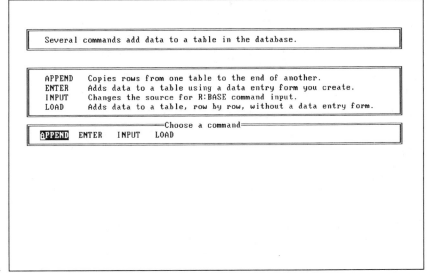

```
┌────────────────────────────────────────────────────────────────────┐
│ Several commands add data to a table in the database.              │
└────────────────────────────────────────────────────────────────────┘

┌────────────────────────────────────────────────────────────────────┐
│ APPEND    Copies rows from one table to the end of another.        │
│ ENTER     Adds data to a table using a data entry form you create. │
│ INPUT     Changes the source for R:BASE command input.             │
│ LOAD      Adds data to a table, row by row, without a data entry form. │
└════════════════════════Choose a command════════════════════════════┐
│ APPEND  ENTER   INPUT   LOAD                                        │
└────────────────────────────────────────────────────────────────────┘
```

■ *Figure 3.3:*
Instructions and options for adding new data.

```
┌────────────────────────────────────────────────────────────────────┐
│ Load data into a table from the keyboard or from a file.          │
└────────────────────────────────────────────────────────────────────┘

┌────────────────────────────────────────────────────────────────────┐
│ LOAD adds data to a table without using a data entry form. You can type │
│ the data at the keyboard or read it from an R:BASE input file created │
│ with the UNLOAD command or by editing an ASCII delimited file.     │
└════════════════════════Choose an input source══════════════════════┐
│ Keyboard  File                                                     │
└────────────────────────────────────────────────────────────────────┘
```

■ *Figure 3.4:*
Instructions for specifying source of incoming data.

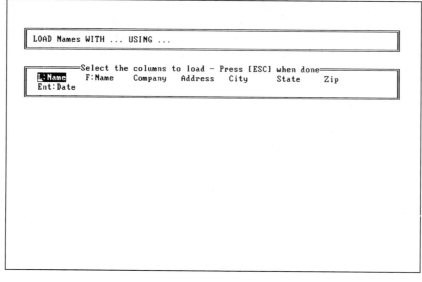

■ *Figure 3.5:*
Screen for selecting columns to load.

Finally, the command line that you've built through your menu selections appears at the top of the screen, as follows:

■   – Execute – Edit – Reset – Help – Quit ───────
     LOAD Names WITH PROMPTS

Select Execute to execute the Load Names with Prompts command. (As you may have guessed, you could have typed this command directly next to the command mode R > prompt, rather than selecting options from prompts, to achieve the same goal.) The screen displays the message

■   Press [ESC] to end, [ENTER] to continue

Press the Enter key to start entering new data. R:BASE will display the name and type of each column. You just type in the data that you wish to store for a single row, pressing Enter after each item. For example, suppose you wish to store the following information in the first row:

     L:Name: Smith
     F:Name: Sandy
     Company: Hi Tech, Inc.

> Address: 456 N. Rainbow Dr.
> City: Berkeley
> State: CA
> Zip: 94711
> Ent:Date: 6/1/86

When R:BASE displays the prompt

∎   L:Name (TEXT):

you type in the name **Smith** and press the Enter key. You can use the Backspace key to make corrections before pressing the Enter key, but don't worry about mistakes yet. They're easy to correct later.

When R:BASE displays the prompt

∎   F:Name (TEXT):

type in the first name, **Sandy,** and press Enter. Continue entering data until you've typed in all the information for the first row. The screen will look like Figure 3.6.

Once you've entered the data for a single row, R:BASE again displays the prompt

∎   Press [ESC] to end, [ENTER] to continue

Press Enter to add another row to the table. If you're following along on-line, try entering the following rows into the table:

> Jones, Mindy, ABC Co., 123 A St., San Diego, CA, 92122, 06/15/86
>
> Miller, Marie, Zeerox Inc., 234 C St., Los Angeles, CA, 91234, 06/01/86
>
> Adams, Bart, DataSpec Inc., P.O. Box 2890, Malibu, CA, 92111, 06/15/86
>
> Miller, Anne, Golden Gate Inc., 2313 Sixth St., Berkeley, CA, 94711, 06/01/86
>
> Baker, Robin, Peach Computers, 2311 Coast Hwy., San Diego, CA, 92112, 06/15/86

Again, don't worry about typographical errors—they will be easy enough to correct later.

After you've entered the rows, press the Esc key when R:BASE displays the prompt

■   Press [ESC] to end, [ENTER] to continue

This will bring back the Prompt menu. At this point, the Names table has six rows in it. When we edit the table, you will be able to see all the rows and make changes as well.

■ EDITING
A TABLE

In computer terminology, the term *edit* means to make a change in the database. For example, if you find that you've misspelled a name or entered the right data in the wrong column, you would need to edit the Names table. Similarly, if some of the people listed in the Names table moved and changed their addresses, you would need to edit the table to change the existing addresses.

There are many commands and techniques that you can use in R:BASE to edit a database. For our first example, we'll use the simplest method.

Before you edit a database, it needs to be open. In this example, we've already opened the Mail database. To move into the *edit mode*

```
LOAD Names WITH PROMPTS
 Begin R:BASE Data Loading

 Press [ESC] to end, [ENTER] to continue
 L:Name    (TEXT    ):Smith
 F:Name    (TEXT    ):Sandy
 Company   (TEXT    ):Hi Tech, Inc.
 Address   (TEXT    ):456 N. Rainbow Dr.
 City      (TEXT    ):Berkeley
 State     (TEXT    ):CA
 Zip       (TEXT    ):94711
 Ent:Date  (DATE    ):6/1/86_
```

■ *Figure 3.6:*
First row typed in
on the screen.

from the Prompt menu, select the Edit Data option from the menu. Doing so will display the instructions and options shown in Figure 3.7.

For general editing, you'll want to select the Edit option (do so now). You'll be given the options for tabular editing or editing with a custom form. Select Tabular Edit. Next you'll be asked to specify the name of the table to edit. Select Names.

The next screen lets you select particular columns to edit. In this example, select (All) so that you have access to all the columns. Next, you'll be given an opportunity to display the data in sorted order. Press the Esc key for now to skip this option.

You'll next be given a chance to limit the number of rows displayed on the screen while editing. To have access to all the rows, press the Esc key. When you are done, the top of the screen will display the command line you've created, along with options for changing the command line, as follows:

■ – Execute – Edit – Reset – Help – Quit ————————
   EDIT ALL FROM Names

The command line tells R:BASE to display all the columns in the Names table on the *edit screen* so that you can make changes. When you select Execute to perform the command, you'll see the data appear as in Figure 3.8. This is an *edit screen*, which allows you to make changes to the data in the table.

Figure 3.9 lists keys that you can use to help edit the table.

```
┌──────────────────────────────────────────────────────────────────────┐
│ ┌──────────────────────────────────────────────────────────────────┐ │
│ │ Several commands change data values in a database.               │ │
│ └──────────────────────────────────────────────────────────────────┘ │
│                                                                        │
│ ┌──────────────────────────────────────────────────────────────────┐ │
│ │ CHANGE    Changes values in a column. The new value can be a constant│
│ │           or the result of an expression.                          │ │
│ │ DELETE    Deletes rows from a table or the key index of a column.  │ │
│ │ EDIT      Displays data either from a table or using a data entry form.│
│ │ REMOVE    Removes a table, form, report, or view from the database or a│
│ │           column from a table.                                     │ │
│ ├─────────────────────────Choose a command────────────────────────┤ │
│ │ CHANGE  DELETE  EDIT    REMOVE                                      │ │
│ └──────────────────────────────────────────────────────────────────┘ │
└──────────────────────────────────────────────────────────────────────┘
```

■ *Figure 3.7:*
Options for editing a database.

```
            Press [ESC] when done, [F2] to delete, [F5] to reset   More→
   L:Name        F:Name         Company              Address            C
   ──────────    ──────────     ──────────────       ──────────────     ─
   Smith         Sandy          Hi Tech, Inc.        456 N. Rainbow Dr.  B
   Jones         Mindy          ABC Co.              123 A St.           S
   Miller        Marie          Zeerox Inc.          234 C St.           L
   Adams         Bart           Dataspec Inc.        P.O. Box 2890       M
   Miller        Anne           Golden Gate Co.      2313 Sixth St.      B
   Baker         Robin          Peach Computers      2311 Coast Hwy.     S
```

■ *Figure 3.8:*
The Names table,
ready for editing.

Key	Function
↑	Moves highlighting up one row
↓	Moves highlighting down one row
Tab	Moves highlighting one column to the right
Shift-Tab	Moves highlighting one column to the left
→	Moves the cursor one character to the right
←	Moves the cursor one character to the left
Ctrl →	Moves highlighting to the last column in the row
Ctrl ←	Moves highlighting to the first column in the row
Home	Moves highlighting to the top of the screen
End	Moves highlighting to the bottom of the screen
PgUp	Shows the previous screenful of data
PgDn	Shows the next screenful of data
Del	Deletes the character over the cursor
Ins	Inserts a space at the cursor position
F2	Deletes the currently highlighted row

■ *Figure 3.9:*
Keys used with
the Edit
command.

Let's try a couple of editing exercises. Suppose you want to change the ZIP code in the first row from 94711 to 94721. First, you need to move the highlighting to the Zip column. You could either press the Tab key six times, or you could jump to the last column by holding down the Ctrl key and pressing the right arrow key, then pressing Shift-Tab (hold down the Shift key and press the Tab key). The Zip column in the first row will be highlighted, as shown in Figure 3.10.

Next, you can move the cursor three spaces to the right by pressing the right arrow key three times. The cursor will appear below the 1 in the ZIP code, as in the following:

■ 9471<u>1</u>

Just type the number **2** (using the numbers at the top of the keyboard) to change the 1 to a 2, so the ZIP code looks like this:

■ 9472<u>1</u>

Now let's change Golden Gate Inc. to Golden Gate Co. First, move down four rows by pressing the down arrow key four times. Then, move left to the Company column by pressing Shift-Tab four times (hold down the Shift key and press the Tab key four times). The Company column will be highlighted, as shown in Figure 3.11.

```
 ┌─────┐         Press [ESC] when done, [F2] to delete, [F5] to reset
 │←More│         Address              City          State   Zip        Ent:Date
 └─────┘         ───────────────────  ────────────  ─────   ────────   ────────
     c.          456 N. Rainbow Dr.   Berkeley      CA      █94711█     06/01/86
                 123 A St.            San Diego     CA      92122       06/15/86
                 234 C St.            Los Angeles   CA      91234       06/01/86
     c.          P.O. Box 2890        Malibu        CA      92111       06/15/86
   Inc.          2313 Sixth St.       Berkeley      CA      94711       06/01/86
   ters          2311 Coast Hwy       San Diego     CA      92122       06/15/86
```

■ *Figure 3.10:*
*The Zip column
highlighted in the
Names table.*

To move the cursor over to the <u>Inc.</u> portion of the Company, press the right arrow key, or just hold it down, until the cursor is under the letter <u>I</u>, as follows:

■   Golden Gate <u>I</u>nc.

Next, type in the the word *Co.* so that the item appears like this:

■   Golden Gate Co<u>.</u>.

We just need to delete the extraneous period now. Do so by pressing the Del key. Now the item reads

■   Golden Gate Co<u>.</u>

Editing data in this fashion is easy, once you get used to the keystrokes used to control the highlighting and the cursor. If there are other errors in your table, try correcting them now. Refer to Figure 3.9 for a list of the keys to use for editing.

If, while editing a single field of data, you find that you've made a mistake, you can "undo" your edit *as long as the highlight is still on the same field.* To restore the original contents to the field being edited, press the F5 key on your keyboard.

```
 ←More          Press [ESC] when done, [F2] to delete, [F5] to reset    More→
 Company                 Address              City           State   Zip
 ---------------         ------------------   -----------    ------  --------
 Hi Tech, Inc.           456 N. Rainbow Dr.   Berkeley       CA      94721
 ABC Co.                 123 A St.            San Diego      CA      92122
 Zeerox Inc.             234 C St.            Los Angeles    CA      91234
 DataSpec Inc.           P.O. Box 2890        Malibu         CA      92111
 Golden Gate Inc.        2313 Sixth St.       Berkeley       CA      94711
 Peach Computers         2311 Coast Hwy       San Diego      CA      92122
```

■ *Figure 3.11:*
The Company
column
highlighted.

■ *DELETING ROWS FROM A TABLE*

You can also delete a row from a table while the edit screen is showing. To do so, use the up and down arrow keys to move the highlighting to the row that you want to delete (don't do so now, however). When that row is highlighted, press the F2 key. R:BASE will double-check before deleting the row, giving you a chance to change your mind. Press Enter to delete the row or press Esc to change your mind.

■ *EXITING THE COMMAND MODE*

You have now added some rows to your database using the Add Data option from the Prompt menu, and you've edited (changed) some items of information using the Edit Data option from the Prompt menu. To make sure that everything is safely stored on disk before turning off the computer, you need to exit R:BASE and get back to the DOS C> prompt.

Move the highlighter to the Exit option on the Prompt menu (the middle column, second option down), and press Enter. The Exit command appears at the top of the screen. Select Execute, and R:BASE will store your new data on disk and return to the RBSystem Main menu. To return to the DOS prompt, select Return to DOS from the RBSystem Main menu. (As you may have guessed, you can type the command Exit right next to the R> prompt to exit R:BASE as well.)

■ *SUMMARY*

In this chapter we've touched on the fundamentals of working *interactively* with a database, focusing on techniques for entering and editing data in a table.

To enter the R:BASE *command mode* or *prompt mode*, select R:BASE from the RBSystem Main menu.

To work interactively with your database, you can use the *prompt mode*, which helps you build command lines through menus, or you can type in commands directly at the *command mode* R> prompt.

Before working with a database, you must open it, either with the Open command or with the appropriate selections from the Prompt menu.

To enter new data into a table, select the Add Data and Load options from the Prompt menu to build the command line

■   LOAD *Names* WITH PROMPTS

where *Names* is the name of the table to edit.

To change data on a table, select the Edit Data option from the Prompt menu to build the command line

■   EDIT ALL FROM *Names*

where *Names* is the name of the table to edit.

The arrow, PgUp, PgDn, Tab, Ins, and Del keys let you manage the cursor and highlighter while editing data on a table.

The F2 key lets you delete a row from a table in edit mode.

The F5 key "undoes" any editing within the highlighter.

To exit the R:BASE interactive mode, select Exit from the Prompt menu, or type in the command Exit at the R> prompt, and press Enter.

SORTING

In this chapter we'll discuss techniques for displaying data in a sorted order. The rows in a database can be sorted into any order you wish, such as alphabetical by name, ZIP-code order for bulk mailing, chronological order, or numerical order. Your sorts can be in ascending order, such as A to Z in alphabetical sorts, smallest to largest in numerical sorts, or earliest to latest in date sorts. Optionally, sorts can be in descending order, for example, Z to A, largest to smallest, or latest to earliest. Furthermore, you can combine sort orders to achieve "sorts within sorts."

We'll begin working more with the R:BASE command mode (indicated by the R> prompt) in this chapter. While the prompt mode is certainly adequate for building command lines in R:BASE, it's a good idea to practice entering commands at the R> prompt. You may eventually want to learn to program in the R:BASE programming language; and even if you don't, the command mode is a bit faster than the prompt mode.

If you've exited R:BASE since the last chapter, enter the command RBSystem at the DOS C> prompt to call up the RBSystem Main menu. Select the R:BASE option, and open the Mail database as discussed in the last chapter. You'll see the Prompt menu on the screen.

■ SORTING FROM THE PROMPT MENU

We saw in the last chapter that the Edit command allows you to select columns to sort the table on (although we skipped over the option then). Actually, several different commands in R:BASE allow you to specify sort orders. In this chapter, we'll discuss sorting with the Edit command and the Select command. Unlike the Edit command, the Select command only displays the data on the screen; it does not allow you to make changes. Nonetheless, the Select command is useful for getting a quick view of your database.

Suppose that you want to see a list of all the rows on your database, sorted into alphabetical order by last name. Begin by selecting the Look at Data option from the Prompt menu, which displays the screen shown in Figure 4.1.

In this example we'll use the Select command to view data. Move the highlighter to the Select option and press Enter. R:BASE will ask for the name of the table to display. Select Names. R:BASE will ask for the columns to display. Select (All).

Now R:BASE displays a screen for selecting columns to sort on, as shown in Figure 4.2. To display the data in alphabetical order by last name, highlight the L:Name option and press Enter. R:BASE will ask if you want the data sorted in Ascending order (A to Z) or Descending

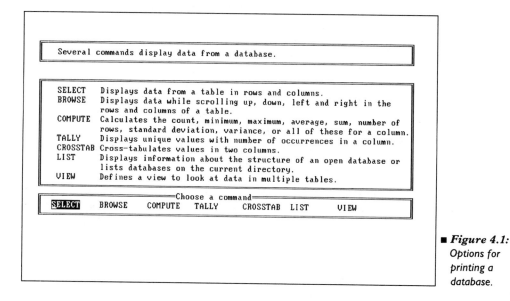

■ *Figure 4.1:* Options for printing a database.

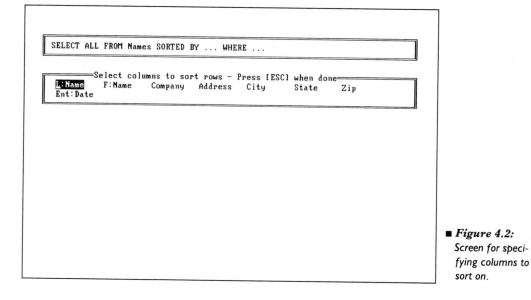

■ *Figure 4.2:* Screen for specifying columns to sort on.

order (Z to A). Select Ascending. R:BASE then gives you the opportunity to select more sort columns. In this case, just press the Esc key.

R:BASE displays a screen for *searching* the database (a topic we'll discuss in the next chapter). Press Esc to bypass this screen.

Now you can see at the top of the screen that you've built the command, as follows:

■ ───── Execute – Edit – Reset – Help – Quit ─────
SELECT ALL FROM Names SORTED BY L:Name

The command tells R:BASE to display all the columns from the Names table, sorted on the L:Name column. Press Enter to select the Execute option. R:BASE displays as many columns as will fit on the screen sorted by last name, as shown in Figure 4.3.

Specifying Columns to Display

The Select command displays only as many columns as will fit on the screen; therefore, you probably will not be able to see all your data. You can, however, specify particular columns to display in a Select command and even specify the order (from left to right) that they will appear on the screen. Let's look at an example and sort the rows into descending order by date along the way. First, press any key to return to the Prompt menu.

```
SELECT ALL FROM Names SORTED BY L:Name
  L:Name           F:Name          Company           Address
  --------------   -------------   ----------------  --------------------
  Adams            Bart            DataSpec Inc.     P.O. Box 2890
  Baker            Robin           Peach Computers   2311 Coast Hwy
  Jones            Mindy           ABC Co.           123 A St.
  Miller           Anne            Golden Gate Co.   2313 Sixth St.
  Miller           Marie           Zeerox Inc.       234 C St.
  Smith            Sandy           Hi Tech, Inc.     456 N. Rainbow Dr.
Press any key to continue_
```

■ *Figure 4.3:*
Names table sorted by last name.

From the Prompt menu, select the Look at Data option. Then choose the Select command and the Names table, as in the last example. R:BASE shows a menu for selecting columns to display, as shown in Figure 4.4.

To display the entry date (Ent:Date column) in the leftmost column, move the highlighter to the Ent:Date column and press Enter. To display the L:Name column next, move the highlighter to L:Name and press Enter. To display the F:Name column, move the highlighter to F:Name and press Enter. The names of the columns you selected appear below the menu on the screen as follows:

■ Ent:Date L:Name F:Name

Press Esc to indicate that you've finished selecting columns to display.

Next, the screen for selecting sort columns appears (as in Figure 4.2). In this example, select Ent:Date, then select Descending, and then press Esc to finish selecting sort columns.

When the screen for entering search criteria appears, press Esc to bypass it. The command line at the top of the screen reads

■ SELECT Ent:Date L:Name F:Name FROM Names SORTED +
    BY Ent:Date = D

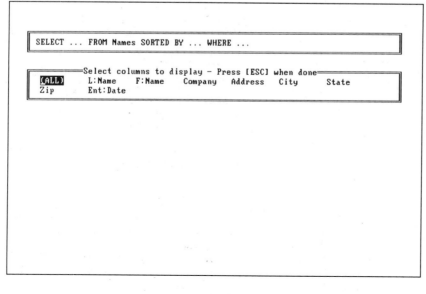

```
┌──────────────────────────────────────────────────────────────┐
│ SELECT ... FROM Names SORTED BY ... WHERE ...                  │
└──────────────────────────────────────────────────────────────┘

┌════Select columns to display - Press [ESC] when done════┐
│ [ALL]     L:Name   F:Name    Company   Address   City      State │
│ Zip       Ent:Date                                               │
└──────────────────────────────────────────────────────────────┘
```

■ *Figure 4.4:*
Screen to select columns to display.

This command tells R:BASE to display the Ent:Date, L:Name, and F:Name columns from the Names table, sorted by Ent:Date in descending (=D) order. Select Execute to execute the command, and the data appear on the screen accordingly, as in Figure 4.5.

Press any key when you are finished viewing the data.

So far, we've only sorted the Names table by a single column. On a very large table, this type of single-column sort would probably not produce the result that you had in mind. For example, suppose you had a table with 10,000 names on it, and you decided to sort them into alphabetical order by last name. You might find that there were 100 Smiths, listed in totally random order by first name, as follows:

Smith,   Norma
Smith,   Alan D.
Smith,   Jake
Smith,   Rudolph
Smith,   Sam
Smith,   Anne
.
.
.

and so on . . .

```
SELECT Ent:Date L:Name F:Name FROM Names SORTED BY Ent:Date=D
Ent:Date L:Name              F:Name
──────── ───────────────     ───────────────
06/15/86 Jones               Mindy
06/15/86 Adams               Bart
06/15/86 Baker               Robin
06/01/86 Smith               Sandy
06/01/86 Miller              Marie
06/01/86 Miller              Anne
Press any key to continue_
```

■ *Figure 4.5:*
*Columns from
the Names table
in descending
date order.*

You probably would want the data sorted by last name, and within common last names, sorted by first name, as in the following:

Smith,   Alan D.
Smith,   Anne
Smith,   Jake
Smith,   Norma
Smith,   Rudolph
Smith,   Sam
.
.
.

and so on . . .

You can easily handle these sorts within sorts by listing multiple column names in the Sorted By clause.

Sorts within Sorts

To perform sorts within sorts, you merely need to select multiple sorting columns, in order from most important to least important. For example, suppose you want to display the Names database sorted by last name, and within common last names, you want the rows sorted by first name. In this case, you need to select L:Name as the first sort order and F:Name as the second sort order. Let's work through an example.

From the Prompt menu, select Look at Data, then the Select command, and then the Names table. Select (All) from the screen for specifying columns to display. From the Sort Options menu, select L:Name and Ascending to specify L:Name as the most important sort order. Then select F:Name and Ascending order. The columns you selected for sorting are displayed below the menu, as follows:

■   L:Name F:Name

Press Esc to finish selecting sort orders, and press Esc again to bypass the search criteria screen. The command you've built reads

■   SELECT ALL FROM Names SORTED BY L:Name F:Name

This command tells R:BASE to display all the columns from the Names table, sorted by last name and by first name within identical last names. When you select Execute from the top menu, R:BASE follows the command.

The Names table is too small to demonstrate the full range of sorts within sorts. Suffice it to say that you can sort on up to ten columns, which gives you tremendous flexibility in defining sort orders even in very large tables. We'll see more examples of sorts within sorts later in the chapter, but first we'll discuss a shortcut for displaying table data in sorted order.

■ SORTING FROM THE R> PROMPT

You've probably noticed that the commands that your menu selections have produced have all had a similar format, or *syntax* in computer argot. That syntax is

■   SELECT <disp-columns> FROM <table-name> SORTED +
   BY <columns>

where <disp-columns> contains the names of the columns to display (or the All command to display all columns); <table-name> is the name of the table containing the columns, and <columns> is the name of the column (or columns) to sort by. You can enter commands directly from the R> prompt using this same syntax.

For example, suppose you want to see the Names table sorted into ZIP-code order, and furthermore, you want to see the Zip, City, L:Name, and F:Name columns on the screen. To type in the appropriate command directly at the R> prompt, first press the Esc key to leave the Prompt menu so that the R> prompt appears on the screen. Next, type in the command

■   SELECT Zip City L:Name F:Name FROM Names SORTED BY +
   Zip

and press Enter. The appropriate columns, in ZIP-code order, appear on the screen as in Figure 4.6.

Suppose you want to display all the columns in alphabetical order by company. To do so, you would type in the command

■   SELECT ALL FROM Names SORTED BY Company

and press Enter. R:BASE displays the table in alphabetical order by Company name, as in Figure 4.7.

When typing in long commands directly at the R> prompt, you continue a command from one line to the next by ending the first line with a space followed by a plus sign (+). (**Note:** Because a computer screen can accommodate more characters per line than a page of this

```
R>SELECT Zip City L:Name F:Name FROM Names SORTED BY Zip
   Zip        City           L:Name         F:Name
   ------     ----------     ---------      ---------
   91234      Los Angeles    Miller         Marie
   92111      Malibu         Adams          Bart
   92122      San Diego      Jones          Mindy
   92122      San Diego      Baker          Robin
   94711      Berkeley       Miller         Anne
   94721      Berkeley       Smith          Sandy
R>_
```

■ *Figure 4.6:* Names table sorted into ZIP-code order.

```
R>SELECT ALL FROM Names SORTED BY Company
   L:Name         F:Name         Company           Address
   ---------      ---------      ---------------   ------------------
   Jones          Mindy          ABC Co.           123 A St.
   Adams          Bart           DataSpec Inc.     P.O. Box 2890
   Miller         Anne           Golden Gate Co.   2313 Sixth St.
   Smith          Sandy          Hi Tech, Inc.     456 N. Rainbow Dr.
   Baker          Robin          Peach Computers   2311 Coast Hwy
   Miller         Marie          Zeerox Inc.       234 C St.
R>_
```

■ *Figure 4.7:* Names table in alphabetical order by Company.

book can, you should be careful in entering sample commands. Your plus sign will often fall in a different place than appears here.) Then press Enter to move the cursor to the next line and continue typing in the line. For example, the single command below tells R:BASE to display the City, L:Name, and F:Name columns from the Names table, sorted by city, by last name within each city, and by first name within each last name (within each city).

■ SELECT City L:Name F:Name FROM Names SORTED BY +
  City L:Name F:Name

The data are displayed in alphabetical order across all three columns, as shown in Figure 4.8.

To display the data in chronological order by entry date, with common dates sorted alphabetically by last and first name, use the command

■ SELECT Ent:Date L:Name F:Name FROM Names SORTED BY +
  Ent:Date L:Name F:Name

This produces the listing shown in Figure 4.9.

Any column in a table can be sorted in descending order by using the =D option with the column name. For example, to sort the Names

```
R>SELECT City L:Name F:Name FROM Names SORTED BY City +
+>L:Name F:Name
City                L:Name              F:Name
----------------    ----------------    ----------------
Berkeley            Miller              Anne
Berkeley            Smith               Sandy
Los Angeles         Miller              Marie
Malibu              Adams               Bart
San Diego           Baker               Robin
San Diego           Jones               Mindy
R>_
```

■ *Figure 4.8:*
Names table
sorted by city and
last and first
name.

table in descending alphabetical order by last name, enter the command

■   SELECT ALL FROM Names SORTED BY L:Name = D

This produces the display shown in Figure 4.10.

```
R>SELECT Ent:Date L:Name F:Name FROM Names SORTED BY +
+>Ent:Date L:Name F:Name
  Ent:Date L:Name          F:Name
  ---------  ------------    ----------------
  06/01/86 Miller          Anne
  06/01/86 Miller          Marie
  06/01/86 Smith           Sandy
  06/15/86 Adams           Bart
  06/15/86 Baker           Robin
  06/15/86 Jones           Mindy
  R>_
```

■ *Figure 4.9:*
Data listed
chronologically
and
alphabetically.

```
R>SELECT ALL FROM Names SORTED BY L:Name=D
  L:Name          F:Name          Company               Address
  ---------       ------------     ---------------------  --------------------
  Smith           Sandy           Hi Tech, Inc.         456 N. Rainbow Dr.
  Miller          Marie           Zeerox Inc.           234 C St.
  Miller          Anne            Golden Gate Co.       2313 Sixth St.
  Jones           Mindy           ABC Co.               123 A St.
  Baker           Robin           Peach Computers       2311 Coast Hwy
  Adams           Bart            DataSpec Inc.         P.O. Box 2890
  R>_
```

■ *Figure 4.10:*
Names displayed
in descending
alphabetical
order.

You can mix and match ascending and descending sorts. For example, the command below displays data in descending chronological order and ascending alphabetical order:

■ SELECT Ent:Date L:Name FROM Names SORTED BY + Ent:Date = D L:Name

This display is shown in Figure 4.11.

Again, our sample table is too small to show the full power of R:BASE sorting. But suppose you had a table listing salespersons' last names, first names, sales amounts, and dates of sales. You could display the data in chronological order by date, and within common dates, alphabetical order by name, and within common names, descending order of sales amounts, using the command

■ SELECT ALL FROM Sales SORTED BY S:Date L:Name + F:Name Amount = D

The result might look like this:

06/01/86	Adams	Andy	$999.99
06/01/86	Adams	Andy	$89.90
06/01/86	Adams	Andy	$1.23
06/01/86	Miller	Mike	$1000.00
06/01/86	Miller	Mike	$987.65
06/01/86	Miller	Nancy	$1234.56
06/01/86	Miller	Nancy	$899.00
06/02/86	Adams	Andy	$1200.00
06/02/86	Adams	Andy	$888.99

.
.
.

and so on . . .

■ SORTING THE EDIT SCREEN

Recall that in the last chapter when you selected the Edit Data and Edit commands from the Prompt menu, R:BASE displayed a screen for selecting sort orders—the same screen, in fact, that the Select command

```
R>SELECT Ent:Date L:Name FROM Names SORTED BY +
+>Ent:Date=D L:Name
 Ent:Date L:Name
 -------- ----------------
 06/15/86 Adams
 06/15/86 Baker
 06/15/86 Jones
 06/01/86 Miller
 06/01/86 Miller
 06/01/86 Smith
 R>_
```

■ *Figure 4.11:*
Names table
sorted in
descending date
and ascending
name order.

displays. You can specify a sort order for the edit screen in the same way that you specify a sort order for the Select command.

You can access the edit screen directly from the R > prompt, using the Edit command and the same syntax as the Select command. For example, to put the Names table into alphabetical order by last name on the edit screen, you could enter the command

■   EDIT ALL FROM Names SORTED BY L:Name F:Name

The edit screen would display all data in alphabetical order by last name, as shown in Figure 4.12.

Presorting the data in an edit screen can make it easier to find specific items in a large table. You can specify columns with the Edit command, along with a sort order. The command below presorts the Names table into descending chronological order and displays the L:Name, F:Name, and Ent:Date columns for editing, as shown in Figure 4.13.

■   EDIT Ent:Date L:Name F:Name FROM Names SORTED BY +
     Ent:Date = D

Needless to say, a Select or Edit command that includes five or ten Sorted By columns can become lengthy. Before you attempt any exceptionally long commands, there are a few things you should know about how to handle them, as well as some common errors that might occur.

```
                  Press [ESC] when done, [F2] to delete, [F5] to reset    More→
    L:Name         F:Name         Company            Address               C
    ─────────────  ─────────────  ─────────────────  ──────────────────────  ─
    Adams          Bart           DataSpec Inc.      P.O. Box 2890         M
    Baker          Robin          Peach Computers    2311 Coast Hwy        S
    Jones          Mindy          ABC Co.            123 A St.             S
    Miller         Anne           Golden Gate Co.    2313 Sixth St.        B
    Miller         Marie          Zeerox Inc.        234 C St.             L
    Smith          Sandy          Hi Tech, Inc.      456 N. Rainbow Dr.    B
```

■ *Figure 4.12:*
Edit screen sorted into alphabetical order.

```
                   Press [ESC] when done, [F2] to delete, [F5] to reset
    Ent:Date  L:Name             F:Name
    ────────  ─────────────────  ───────────────
    06/15/86  Jones              Mindy
    06/15/86  Adams              Bart
    06/15/86  Baker              Robin
    06/01/86  Smith              Sandy
    06/01/86  Miller             Marie
    06/01/86  Miller             Anne
```

■ *Figure 4.13:*
Edit screen sorted and limited to three columns.

■ MODIFYING PROMPT MODE COMMANDS

When building command lines through the Prompt menu selections, you probably will not make errors very often, because the prompt mode "knows" the correct syntax for all the R:BASE commands. However, you may occasionally change your mind about some menu selections you made when you see the final command at the top of the screen, as follows:

■   —— Execute – Edit – Reset – Help – Quit
        SELECT ALL FROM Names SORTED BY F:Name L:Name

As you know, the Execute command will send the command to R:BASE to be processed immediately. The other options from the top menu are summarized here:

Edit   Displays the command line inside a box, and allows you to make changes to it. You can use the left and right arrow keys to position the cursor anywhere in the command line. You can use the Ins key to insert a blank space and the Del key to delete a character. You can also type new text over existing text.

Reset   Jumps back to the first menu selection you made for the command, and allows you to reselect menu items for the command.

Help   Displays helpful instructions and options for using the command.

Quit   Abandons the command line altogether and returns you to the Prompt menu.

More often than not, you'll probably be able to select Execute to process the command line immediately. When entering your own command lines at the R > prompt, however, you will be more likely to make mistakes. (The advantage of entering commands at the R > prompt is that it is faster; the disadvantage is that doing so requires some familiarity with the syntax of the commands.) The most common errors when entering commands at the R > prompt are discussed in the next section.

■ CORRECTING
R> PROMPT
COMMANDS

Some commands that you type in at the R> prompt may extend beyond the 80 characters that most screens allow. When this is the case, you need to break the command into two or more lines using the plus (+) symbol. Preferably, you should break a command line at a place where a space would naturally fall and put the + after the space. Press the Enter key after typing the +, and continue the command on the next line, as shown in the following example:

■ SELECT L:Name F:Name Company Ent:Date Zip FROM +
   Names SORTED BY Zip L:Name F:Name Ent:Date = D

When you break a command at a space, the R> prompt will appear on the second line, so what you'll actually see on the screen is

■ R>SELECT L:Name F:Name Company Ent:Date Zip FROM +
   R>Names SORTED BY Zip L:Name F:Name Ent:Date = D

If you don't break a line at a natural space, the command will still work properly, but you'll see a +> prompt, rather than the R> prompt, on the second line, as follows:

■ R>SELECT L:Name F:Name Company Ent:Date Zip FR +
   +>OM Names SORTED BY Zip L:Name F:Name Ent:Date = D

The problem with this second method is that it is more likely to produce errors. For example, the command

■ R>SELECT L:Name F:Name Company Ent:Date Zip FR +
   +>OM Names SORTED BY Zip L:Name F:Name Ent:Date = D

will produce an error because there is a space inserted in the middle of the word FROM (just before the +). To avoid errors, it's best to break a line at a natural space between words.

Unless you are a truly superb typist, you're likely to get error messages from time to time as you work with R:BASE, particularly with longer commands. No need to worry, you can't do any harm by typing in an invalid command. The worst that will happen is that the computer will beep and display a message. For example, typing in the command

■   SELECT ALL FROM Bananas

causes the computer to beep and R:BASE to display the following message:

■   – ERROR – Bananas is an undefined table

which means that there is no table named Bananas in the open database. Perhaps you've misspelled the table name, or you've forgotten to open the database containing the table. To review the table names, use the List Tables command to display the names of all the tables in the open database.

Another common error is to enter a command such as

■   SELECT ALL FROM Names SORTED BY LastName F:Name

R:BASE displays this message:

■   – ERROR – Column LastName is not in the table Names

indicating that there is no LastName column in the table. The actual column name is L:Name.

Some errors are caused by incorrect syntax. For example, if you typed in the command

■   SELECT FROM Names SORTED BY L:Name F:Name City

R:BASE would display the message

■   – ERROR – Syntax is incorrect for the command

and, as a helping hand, will display a *syntax chart*, as shown in Figure 4.14.

The syntax chart in Figure 4.14 shows that the Select command can be followed either by the word *ALL* (for all columns) or by a list of column names (*collist*). You can use the =S (sum) and =w (width) options (which we'll discuss later) in the column list. The next portion of the command is *FROM tblname*, meaning that the word FROM and the name of the table follow. Optionally, the term SORTED BY and a list of column names (collist) follow. Finally, the *Where* clause can follow, using a list of conditions (*condlist*). (The Where clause is discussed in the next chapter.) Our syntax error occurred because we forgot to include the All option or a list of column names after the Select command.

Fortunately, you don't have to type in an entire command from scratch just because of a simple error. R:BASE remembers your command, even after displaying the error message. You can use the following keys to bring back the command line and correct the errors in it:

Ctrl-right arrow	Recalls the entire line.
Right arrow	Each press brings back one character from the line.
★★	Pressing the asterisk key twice brings back the entire command, even if it is broken onto several lines.
Ins	Inserts a blank space into the line.

For example, suppose you enter the command

■ EDIT ALL FROM Names SORTED BY LName +
    F:Name Ent:Date = D

R:BASE rejects the line because it can't find the LName column. To correct the error (change LName to L:Name), press the right arrow key

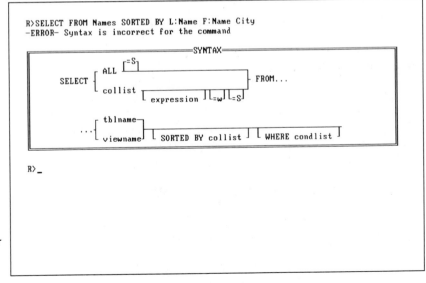

■ *Figure 4.14:*
Syntax chart for the Select command.

repeatedly to bring back all characters up to the error, as below:

■   EDIT ALL FROM Names SORTED BY L_

Next, press the Ins key to insert a space, and then type in the missing colon, so that the line looks like this:

■   EDIT ALL FROM Names SORTED BY L:_

Now you can recall the rest of the line by holding down the Ctrl key and pressing the right arrow. The entire line appears on the screen, as follows:

■   EDIT ALL FROM Names SORTED BY L:Name F:Name +
    Ent:Date = D

Press Enter to enter the command.

Abbreviating Commands

Another way to deal with long commands is to use abbreviations. Most R:BASE commands can be trimmed down to only the first four letters. For example, the command line

■   SELECT ALL FROM Names SORTED BY L:Name F:Name +
    Ent:Date

can be abbreviated to

■   SELE ALL FROM Names SORT BY L:Name F:Name Ent:Date

You can also use column numbers rather than their names in column lists, as long as you include a number sign (#). For example, this rather lengthy command:

■   SELECT Ent:Date L:Name F:Name Address FROM Names +
    SORTED BY Ent:Date = D L:Name F:Name

can be abbreviated to:

■   SELE #8 #1 #2 #4 FROM Names SORT BY #8 = D #1 #2

From the R> prompt, you can use the List command, along with the table name, to see column numbers (for example, LIST Names).

For purposes of clarity, we'll continue to use the longer versions of commands throughout this book.

■ SUMMARY

In this chapter we've discussed numerous commands and techniques for displaying data in a table in sorted order. We've also learned more about entering commands at the R> prompt without the aid of the prompt mode. The techniques we've discussed are summarized below.

When displaying and editing data in the prompt mode, you can specify columns to sort on from a menu that appears as you build your command line.

From the R> prompt, you can use the Sorted By command with the Select or Edit command to specify columns to sort by.

Descending sorts can be achieved by selecting the Descending option in the prompt mode or by using the =D symbol in a command line.

To perform sorts within sorts, specify the columns to sort on in order of most important to least important.

Long commands that exceed the width of the screen must be split by using the plus symbol (+), preferably after a natural space between words.

If you make a mistake while entering a command, you will get an error message. After you see such a message, you can recall a command line and correct it, using the right arrow, Ctrl and right arrow, asterisk, and Ins keys.

Most R:BASE commands can be abbreviated to the first four letters of the command. Column numbers (displayed with the List *table name* command) can be used instead of column names.

Next, we'll discuss techniques for searching, or filtering, a table.

SEARCHING

In this chapter, we'll discuss techniques for searching, or *filtering* or *querying,* a table. When you filter a table, you access only those rows that meet a specific search criterion. For example, from the Names table, you might want to list everyone who has an entry date of June 1, 1986, or perhaps everyone who has an entry date in the first quarter of 1986. Alternatively, you might want to list all the individuals who live in a certain city or work for a certain company.

There is no limit to the ways that you can filter a table. Furthermore, you can mix sorting and searching criteria however you wish. For example, suppose you needed to send a form letter to all the individuals listed in a table who work for ABC Company in the state of California. You could easily pull these individuals out of the table, sorted in ZIP-code order, so that you could get the benefits of bulk mailing.

■ SEARCHING FROM THE PROMPT MODE

When you display or edit data using the Look at Data or Edit Data options from the Prompt menu, the last screen to appear before the final command is displayed allows you to specify criteria for filtering the database. We haven't put this screen to use in previous chapters, so let's work through some exercises now to learn how to use this screen.

Suppose there are 1000 names or more on the Names table, and you wish to edit a row for an individual named Miller. If you do not specify a filtering criteria, you'll need to scroll through many rows on the edit screen to locate the appropriate row to edit. Optionally, you can limit the edit screen to displaying only rows with the last name Miller.

First, make sure the Mail database is open. Then, select Edit Data from the Prompt menu and Edit from the next menu. Select Tabular Edit, and select Names as the table to edit. Select (All) to have access to all columns. From the next screen, you can specify a sort order or press Esc to bypass the option.

The screen that follows lets you specify searching criteria, as shown in Figure 5.1.

In this case we want to limit the display to individuals with the last name Miller. Therefore, select L:Name as the column to search on. The screen displays several operators for performing the search, as follows:

■   EQ NE GT GE LT LE EXISTS FAILS CONTAINS

We'll discuss these options throughout the chapter, but for now select EQ (which stands for "equals"). The screen then instructs you to

■   Enter a comparison value:

R:BASE needs to know what L:Name should equal for the search. In this case, we're looking up Miller, so type in Miller and press the Enter key. Next, the screen displays the prompt

■   Choose an operator to combine conditions
    – Choose (Done) when done.

For now, select Done.

The command you've built appears at the top of the screen, as follows:

■   EDIT ALL FROM Names WHERE L:Name EQ Miller

This command tells R:BASE to display all the columns from the Names table on the edit screen, but only those rows that have Miller in the L:Name column. When you select Execute to execute the command, the Millers appear on the edit screen as in Figure 5.2.
You can make any changes that you wish or press Esc to return to the Prompt menu.

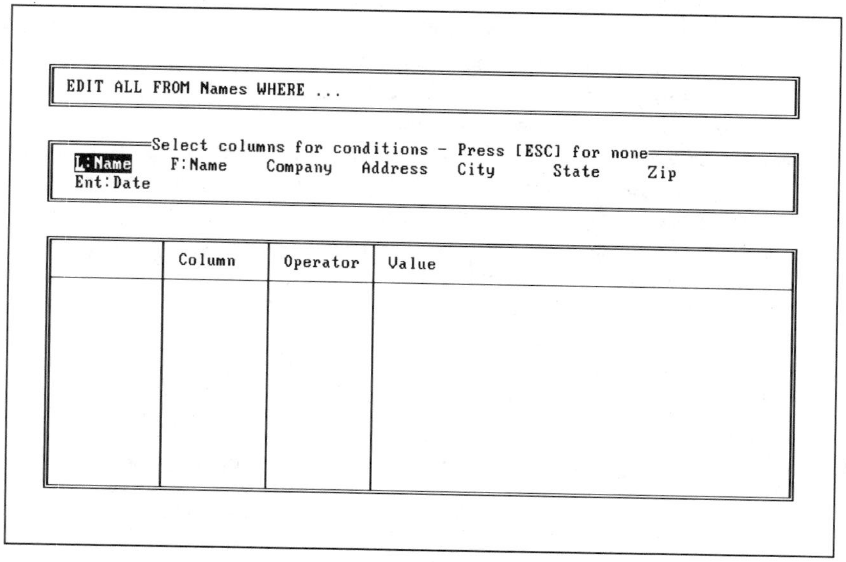

■ *Figure 5.1:*
Screen for specifying search criteria.

Let's look at another example using multiple search criteria. Suppose that this table had 10,000 names on it, and of those about 100 had the last name Miller. If you wanted to look up Anne Miller's address, specifying Miller for the search would still leave you with 100 names to search through. To make this search easier, you could search for rows with the last name Miller and the first name Anne. Let's work though an example.

From the Prompt menu, select Look at Data. Choose the Select option, the Names table, and (All) columns. You can specify a sort column or press Esc to bypass the option. When the search criterion screen appears, select L:Name to search on the Last Name column, select EQ for "equals," and type in Miller (followed by a press on the Enter key) to specify Miller as the comparison value (the last name to look for).

When the prompt

■   Choose an operator to combine conditions
     – Choose (Done) when done.

appears, select the And option. Then select F:Name as the second column to search on and EQ as the operator, and enter Anne as the comparison value (and press Enter). Your screen will look like Figure 5.3.

Select (Done) to finish entering the search criteria. The new command that you've just created will appear on the top of the screen

```
                 Press [ESC] when done, [F2] to delete, [F5] to reset    More→
       L:Name    F:Name       Company          Address                  C
       --------  --------     ----------------  -----------------        --
       Miller    Marie        Zeerox Inc.       234 C St.                L
       Miller    Anne         Golden Gate Co.   2313 Sixth St.           B
```

■ *Figure 5.2:*
Millers ready for editing.

as follows:

■   SELECT ALL FROM Names WHERE L:Name EQ Miller AND +
     F:Name EQ Anne

This command tells R:BASE to display all the columns from the Names
table that have Miller in the L:Name column and Anne in the F:Name
column. When you select Execute to execute the command, R:BASE displays the one row in the table that meets these search criteria, as in Figure
5.4. Press any key when you are finished viewing the data.

■ SEARCHING
FROM THE
R > PROMPT

You've probably noticed that both searches you performed included the
new command Where, followed by the search condition; for example:

■   WHERE L:Name EQ Miller AND F:Name EQ Anne

For the rest of this chapter, we'll discuss numerous searching techniques that you can use with the Where clause.

```
┌─────────────────────────────────────────────────────────────┐
│  ┌────────────────────────────────────────────────────────┐  │
│  │ SELECT ALL FROM Names WHERE ...                         │  │
│  └────────────────────────────────────────────────────────┘  │
│  ┌═Choose an operator to combine conditions - Choose (Done) when done═┐
│  │ AND  OR  AND NOT   OR NOT    (Done)                     │  │
│  └────────────────────────────────────────────────────────┘  │
│  ┌──────┬─────────┬──────────┬──────────────────────────┐    │
│  │      │ Column  │ Operator │ Value                     │    │
│  │      ├─────────┼──────────┼──────────────────────────┤    │
│  │      │ L:Name  │ EQ       │ Miller                    │    │
│  │ AND  │ F:Name  │ EQ       │ Anne                      │    │
│  │      │         │          │                           │    │
│  │      │         │          │                           │    │
│  │      │         │          │                           │    │
│  └──────┴─────────┴──────────┴──────────────────────────┘    │
└─────────────────────────────────────────────────────────────┘
```

■ *Figure 5.3:*
Search for Anne
Miller.

In the interest of brevity, we'll discuss commands as entered at the R> prompt. You can type them in as displayed, or use the prompt mode to build them. (By now, you should be able to figure out how to build a Select or Edit command using the prompt mode.) Press the Esc key to leave the Prompt menu and get to the R> prompt.

All R:BASE searching techniques are handled by the Where clause. The Where clause can be used with both the Select and Edit commands, as well as with several other commands that we'll discuss later. In its simplest form, the Where clause contains a column name, the equal sign (=) or EQ symbol, and the search value.

For example, suppose you wanted to display all the Millers in the Names table. First, be sure that the Mail database is open and that the R> prompt is displayed. From the R> prompt, enter the command

■   SELECT ALL FROM Names WHERE L:Name = Miller

Then press the Enter key. This would display all the Millers on the table, as shown in Figure 5.5.

The function of the EQ symbol is identical to that of the equal sign, so the following command would perform exactly the same task:

■   SELECT ALL FROM Names WHERE L:Name EQ Miller

```
SELECT ALL FROM Names WHERE L:Name EQ Miller AND F:Name EQ Anne
   L:Name            F:Name            Company            Address
   ----------------  ----------------  ---------------    ----------------
   Miller            Anne              Golden Gate Co.    2313 Sixth St.
Press any key to continue_
```

■ *Figure 5.4:*
Anne Miller
displayed on the
screen.

You can, as usual, specify that only certain columns be displayed. For example, to see the dates and names of people whose entry dates are June 1, enter the command

■ SELECT Ent:Date L:Name F:Name FROM Names WHERE +
Ent:Date = 06/01/86

The display will appear as shown in Figure 5.6.

You can still specify sort orders by using the Sorted By clause *before* the Where clause. For example, to display Berkeley residents in alphabetical order by name, you would enter the command

■ SELECT City L:Name F:Name Company FROM Names +
SORTED BY L:Name F:Name WHERE City = Berkeley

The screen will display Berkeley residents in alphabetical order by name, as Figure 5.7 shows.

With the addition of some *logical operators*, your searching capabilities are greatly expanded.

```
R>SELECT ALL FROM Names WHERE L:Name = Miller
  L:Name          F:Name          Company           Address
  ------------    ------------    ---------------   ------------------
  Miller          Marie           Zeerox Inc.       234 C St.
  Miller          Anne            Golden Gate Co.   2313 Sixth St.
R>_
```

■ *Figure 5.5:*
Millers displayed from the Names table.

■ WHERE CLAUSE OPERATORS

Figure 5.8 shows several *operators* that can be used with the Where clause. Note that the *operator* and *symbol* can be used interchangeably. For example, LE is equivalent to < =.

Suppose that you wanted a listing of all the individuals whose last names begin with the letters A through M. You could enter the command

■   SELECT ALL FROM Names WHERE L:Name < N

This would produce the display shown in Figure 5.9.

To display individuals with names beginning with the letters N through Z, you could use the command

■   SELECT ALL FROM Names WHERE L:Name > M

Suppose you wanted to display everyone *except* Berkeley residents on your tables. You could use the not-equal operator, as below:

■   SELECT ALL FROM Names WHERE City < > Berkeley

```
R>SELECT Ent:Date L:Name F:Name FROM Names WHERE Ent:Date = 06/01/86
   Ent:Date L:Name          F:Name
   ———————— ———————————————  ————————————
   06/01/86 Smith            Sandy
   06/01/86 Miller           Marie
   06/01/86 Miller           Anne
   R>_
```

■ *Figure 5.6:*
Names data
displayed for
06/01/86.

To display these same individuals in alphabetical order and show the city on the screen, you could use the command

■   SELECT L:Name F:Name City FROM Names SORTED BY +
     L:Name F:Name WHERE City < > Berkeley

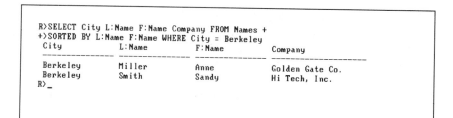

```
R>SELECT City L:Name F:Name Company FROM Names +
+>SORTED BY L:Name F:Name WHERE City = Berkeley
  City             L:Name           F:Name          Company
  ---------------- ---------------- --------------- ----------------
  Berkeley         Miller           Anne            Golden Gate Co.
  Berkeley         Smith            Sandy           Hi Tech, Inc.
R>_
```

■ *Figure 5.7:*
Berkeley residents displayed in alphabetical order.

Operator	Symbol	Definition
EQ	=	Equal
NE	< >	Not equal
GT	>	Greater than
GE	> =	Greater than or equal to
LT	<	Less than
LE	< =	Less than or equal to
CONTAINS		Embedded in text column

■ *Figure 5.8:*
Where clause operators.

This would produce the display shown in Figure 5.10.

The operators (excluding CONTAINS) work with any type of data. For example, to display people whose entry dates are later than June 1,

```
R>SELECT ALL FROM Names WHERE L:Name < N
  L:Name           F:Name          Company           Address
  ---------------  --------------  ----------------  ------------------
  Jones            Mindy           ABC Co.           123 A St.
  Miller           Marie           Zeerox Inc.       234 C St.
  Adams            Bart            DataSpec Inc.     P.O. Box 2890
  Miller           Anne            Golden Gate Co.   2313 Sixth St.
  Baker            Robin           Peach Computers   2311 Coast Hwy
R>_
```

■ *Figure 5.9:*
Individuals with last names beginning with A through M.

```
R>SELECT L:Name F:Name City FROM Names SORTED BY +
+>L:Name F:Name WHERE City <> Berkeley
  L:Name           F:Name          City
  ---------------  --------------  ---------------
  Adams            Bart            Malibu
  Baker            Robin           San Diego
  Jones            Mindy           San Diego
  Miller           Marie           Los Angeles
R>_
```

■ *Figure 5.10:*
Alphabetical listing excluding Berkeley residents.

1986, you could use the command

- SELECT Ent:Date L:Name F:Name FROM Names WHERE +
  Ent:Date > 06/01/86

Suppose you wanted to pull out only those people in the 92111 ZIP-code area. Furthermore, you wanted them displayed alphabetically by last and first names. You could use the command

- SELECT Zip L:Name F:Name City FROM Names +
  WHERE Zip = 92111

If you wanted to send something to all the people in the ZIP-code range 92000 to 99999, you could filter out the appropriate data using this command:

- SELECT ALL FROM Names WHERE Zip > = 92000

Embedded Searches

Here's a tricky one for you. Suppose you want to list everyone in the Names table with an address on Rainbow Drive. If you enter the command

- SELECT ALL FROM Names WHERE Address = Rainbow

R:BASE displays the following message:

- – WARNING – No rows satisfy the WHERE clause

indicating that nobody's address equals "Rainbow." But we know that at least one row contains an address on Rainbow. Even so, R:BASE is correct—the address 456 N. Rainbow Dr. does not *equal* Rainbow. However, that address *contains* the word Rainbow. In this example, we need to use the CONTAINS operator, as follows:

- SELECT ALL FROM Names WHERE +
  Address CONTAINS Rainbow

This command displays the data we want, as shown in Figure 5.11.

The CONTAINS operator can only be used with Text columns, which means that you cannot use a Where clause like

■ WHERE Ent:Date CONTAINS 85

or

■ WHERE Ent:Date CONTAINS 06/

because Ent:Date is a Date data type. However, you can pull out *ranges* of data such as these using the AND and OR operators.

AND and OR Operators

You can specify multiple criteria in a Where clause by using the AND and OR operators. For example, suppose you wanted a listing of Berkeley residents whose entry dates are on June 1. The command below would display them for you:

■ SELECT ALL FROM Names WHERE Ent:Date = 06/01/86 + AND City = Berkeley

You might want a display with these same data listed in alphabetical order by last name, showing only the entry date, name, and address.

```
R>SELECT ALL FROM Names WHERE Address CONTAINS Rainbow
  L:Name          F:Name          Company          Address
  ───────────     ───────────     ───────────      ──────────────
  Smith           Sandy           Hi Tech, Inc.    456 N. Rainbow Dr.
R>_
```

■ *Figure 5.11:*
Rainbow Drive residents displayed on the screen.

You could enter the command

- SELECT Ent:Date L:Name F:Name Address FROM Names +
  SORTED BY L:Name F:Name +
  WHERE Ent:Date = 06/01/86 AND City = Berkeley

When using search criteria with embedded blanks (such as the space between San and Diego), you may have problems if your search values are items that contain blanks. For example, if you typed in

- SELECT ALL FROM Names WHERE City = San Diego AND +
  State = CA

you might get this somewhat confusing error message:

- – ERROR – Conditions must be separated by "AND" or "OR"

This occurred because the blank space in "San Diego" confused R:BASE. You can rectify this situation by enclosing that portion of the search in quotation marks, as follows:

- SELECT ALL FROM Names WHERE City = "San Diego" +
  AND State = CA

R:BASE will understand that the item within the quotation marks is a single value. The quotation marks can't do any harm, so use them whenever you use a value that could be confusing.

Suppose you wanted a listing of everyone whose entry date is in the month of June; in other words, in the range of June 1 to June 30. The command below displays those rows:

- SELECT ALL From Names WHERE Ent:Date > = 06/01/86 +
  AND Ent:Date < = 06/30/86

To put that same display in chronological order and show only date, name, and company, you would use the following command:

- SELECT Ent:Date L:Name F:Name Company FROM Names +
  SORTED BY Ent:Date +
  WHERE Ent:Date > = 06/01/86 AND Ent:Date < = 06/30/86

Now, what if you want to send something to everyone who lives on the 2300 block, or higher, of Sixth Street. Piece of cake, right? The command is

- SELECT ALL FROM Names +
  WHERE Address > = 2300 AND Address CONTAINS Sixth

If you wanted to pull out all the people whose last names begin with the letters J through M, you could use this command:

- SELECT ALL FROM Names WHERE L:Name > = J AND +
  L:Name < N

The AND operator is good for locating specific information to edit. For example, suppose you need to change Marie Miller's address. You could enter the command

- EDIT ALL FROM Names WHERE L:Name = Miller AND +
  F:Name = Marie

This would display Marie's data on the edit screen, as shown in Figure 5.12.

Suppose you wanted to send something to both San Diego and Los Angeles residents. You could use the OR operator to perform both

```
                    Press [ESC] when done, [F2] to delete, [F5] to reset      More→
        L:Name          F:Name        Company           Address                   C
        ──────────────  ───────────   ─────────────────  ──────────────────────── ──
        Miller          Marie         Zeerox Inc.        234 C St.                 L
```

∎ *Figure 5.12:*
Edit screen
limited to Marie
Miller.

searches at once, as in the command below (note that the command includes quotation marks because these search criteria contain blanks):

- SELECT ALL FROM Names WHERE City = "San Diego" OR + City = "Los Angeles"

Sometimes you have to think a little before performing a search. For example, had we used the command

- SELECT ALL FROM Names WHERE City = "San Diego" + AND City = "Los Angeles"

no rows would have been displayed, because it's impossible for a row to have both San Diego and Los Angeles in the City column at the same time.

Reversing the situation, the command

- SELECT ALL FROM Names WHERE City = "San Diego" + AND State = CA

will display all San Diego, California, residents. However, the command

- SELECT ALL FROM Names WHERE City = "San Diego" OR + State = CA

will display *all* California residents, regardless of city, and *all* San Diego residents, regardless of state (which is probably not what you had in mind).

With the OR operator, only one of the searching criteria needs to be true for the command to display the data. Hence, the OR operator generally broadens the result of the search. The AND operator, however, requires that both criteria be met, which generally narrows the result of the search.

The AND operator is most frequently used to search for data that fall within a range. For example, to pull out all individuals in the 92000 to 92999 ZIP-code area, you would use the command

- SELECT ALL FROM Names WHERE Zip > = 92000 AND + Zip < = 92999

If instead you used the following command:

- SELECT ALL FROM Names WHERE Zip > = 92000 OR + Zip < = 92999

you'd get everyone in the table, which again is probably not what you intended. The reason is that even though the ZIP code 12345 is *not* greater than or equal to 92000, it *is* less than 92999, and hence 12345 would be displayed in this OR search. So would any other number, for that matter.

Another common mistake that people make when performing AND and OR searches is attempting to use English syntax rather than R:BASE syntax. For example, a common mistake is to use a command like

■ SELECT ALL FROM Names WHERE Zip > = 92000 AND +
   < = 92999

Reading that in English, it looks like you're trying to pull out all the ZIP codes between 92000 and 92999. However, that's not what it says to R:BASE. In R:BASE syntax, both criteria must be *complete* expressions. Zip > = 92000 is a complete expression, but < = 92999 is not. The computer will wonder what < = 92999 means, and it will display an error message. To avoid problems, be sure to use complete expressions on both sides of the AND and OR operators.

In the last sentence, "*both* sides of the AND and OR operators" doesn't mean that you can only use a single AND or OR. In fact, you can have up to ten conditions in a Where clause. For example, the command

■ SELECT ALL FROM Names WHERE City = "San Diego" AND +
   State = CA AND Ent:Date > = 06/01/86 AND Ent:Date +
   < = 06/30/86 AND L:Name > = G AND L:Name < = P

is perfectly okay. You'll get San Diego, California, residents with entry dates in June whose last names begin with the letters G through P.

Sometimes, combining AND and OR conditions in a single Where clause can produce unexpected results. Generally speaking, R:BASE interprets the conditions in a Where clause from left to right. For example, the command

■ SELECT Zip L:Name F:Name FROM Names WHERE +
   Zip > 92000 AND L:Name > = M OR F:Name > = M

will display everyone with first or last names starting with the letter M or higher, regardless of whether the ZIP code is greater than 92000. In other words, R:BASE has interpreted the Where clause as follows:

[Zip > 92000 AND L:Name > = M] OR [F:Name > = M]

[Either of these is true] or [this is true]

Had you entered this command as

- SELECT Zip L:Name F:Name FROM Names WHERE +
  L:Name > = M OR F:Name > = M AND Zip > 92000

R:BASE would have displayed all the individuals whose first or last names begin with the letter M or greater, and who furthermore live in areas with ZIP codes greater than 92000. In other words, R:BASE interpreted the Where clause as the following:

[L:Name > = M OR F:Name > = M] AND [Zip > 92000]
[either of these is true] and [this is true also]

It may take you a few trial-and-error runs to get these more complex searches down. Be sure to check the results of a search visually if you are in doubt about the accuracy of your Where clause.

Distinction Between Uppercase and Lowercase Letters

R:BASE normally makes no distinction between uppercase and lowercase letters when searching a table. For example, the command

- SELECT ALL FROM Names WHERE L:Name = miller

will produce exactly the same results as the command

- SELECT ALL FROM Names WHERE L:Name = MILLER

If you would rather that R:BASE did not ignore uppercase and lowercase distinctions, you can enter the command

- SET CASE ON

at the R > prompt. With the Case option, the command

- SELECT ALL FROM Names WHERE L:Name = MILLER

would not display any data from the Names table, because all the last names were entered with only the initial letter capitalized.

To return to "normal" searches, in which R:BASE ignores uppercase and lowercase distinctions, enter the command

∎ SET CASE OFF

at the R > prompt.

You can check the current status of the Case option from the R > prompt at any time by entering the command

∎ SHOW

You'll see the current status of many other settings as well, which we'll discuss throughout the book.

∎ COMPARING COLUMNS IN SEARCHES

You can also compare the contents of two columns to perform a search. For example, suppose you had a table that contained Gross Sales and Salary columns for salespeople. You might want to display all those individuals whose salaries are greater than their gross sales.

When comparing two columns in a search, you need to follow the operator with the letter A. Figure 5.13 shows the operators used for comparing columns in a table.

In our hypothetical Sales table, you could find all the individuals whose salaries were less than their gross sales using the command

∎ SELECT ALL FROM Sales WHERE Salary <A G:Sales

∎ *Figure 5.13: Where clause operators for comparing two columns.*

Operator	Symbol	Definition
EQA	= A	Equal
NEA	< >A	Not equal
GTA	>A	Greater than
GEA	> = A	Greater than or equal to
LTA	<A	Less than
LEA	< = A	Less than or equal to

To see how this works, we can compare the contents of the F:Name and L:Name columns in our sample Names table. The command

- SELECT ALL FROM Names WHERE F:Name > = A L:Name

will display all the individuals whose first names are alphabetically greater than or equal to their last names. The command

- SELECT ALL FROM Names WHERE F:Name < = A L:Name

will display those whose first names are alphabetically less than or equal to their last names.

■ MORE SEARCH OPTIONS

You can also search for certain types of data in a table. Figure 5.14 shows additional search operators that can be used in any Where clause.

The EXISTS and FAILS operators can be used to find all the filled rows and all the blank rows, respectively. For example, the command

- SELECT ALL FROM Names WHERE L:Name EXISTS

would display all the rows because all the L:Name columns contain data. For the same reason, the command

- SELECT ALL FROM Names WHERE L:Name FAILS

would not display any rows in this example. However, if there were any blank L:Name rows in the Names table, the FAILS operator would have found them.

Operator	Definition
EXISTS	Column contains some data
FAILS	Column contains no data
COUNT = n	A specific row number
COUNT = LAST	The last row in a table
LIMIT = n	Only n number of rows are displayed

■ *Figure 5.14:*
Additional search operators for the Where clause.

The COUNT operator lets you find data in a specific location. For example, the command

- SELECT ALL FROM Names WHERE COUNT = 5

will display the fifth row in the table. The command

- SELECT ALL FROM Names WHERE COUNT = LAST

will display the last row.

You can use the LIMIT operator to limit the amount of data displayed. The command

- SELECT ALL FROM Names WHERE L:Name = Miller AND +
  LIMIT = 1

will display only the first of the Millers in the Names table.

■ GLOBAL EDITS WITH THE WHERE CLAUSE

We've already learned how to use the Where clause to limit the amount of data displayed on the screen during the edits. The Where clause can also be used with the Change and Delete commands to perform *global edits*.

A global edit is one that is performed throughout the entire table (or database) with a single command. For example, suppose you have 5000 entries in the Names table. Eventually, you learn that in some cases the city Los Angeles is stored as L.A. and in other cases it is spelled out. This little inconsistency is causing you problems because you always need to include two options, such as

- Where City = "Los Angeles" OR City = L.A.

in your Where clauses. The solution to this problem is to make them consistent.

You could go into the edit mode and change each L.A. to Los Angeles by retyping them. Or you could perform a global edit to change all of them to Los Angeles with a single command. Obviously, the latter is more convenient.

The Change command allows you to perform just this sort of global edit. The general syntax for the Change command is

- CHANGE *column name* TO *value* IN *table name* WHERE *condition(s)*

(To access the Change command from the Prompt menu, select the Edit data option, and then select the Change option from the submenu.)

So, in a hypothetical table named MaiList, you could change each L.A. to Los Angeles by entering the command

- CHANGE City TO "Los Angeles" IN MaiList WHERE City = L.A.

You must be careful when using this command, though. It has a high "whoops" factor, which means that by the time you finish saying "whoops," the damage is done. For example, suppose you had entered the wrong command

- CHANGE City TO "Los Angeles" IN MaiList WHERE CITY > = L

The > = operator in this Where clause tells R:BASE to put Los Angeles in the City column of every row in the table that contains a city starting with the letters L through Z. If there were originally 500 cities that met this criterion, there are now 500 Los Angeles cities in their place, whether they were originally Las Vegas, Madrid, or Seattle. The bad news is that you cannot reverse this command. You'd have to re-enter all the cities through the edit mode. Do be careful.

For practice, you can safely try it out on the Names table. From the R> prompt, enter the command

- CHANGE City TO S.D. IN Names WHERE City = "San Diego"

R:BASE will display this message:

- The value for City in NAMES has been changed in 2 row(s)

If you then enter the command

- SELECT City FROM Names

you'll see that all of the San Diego cities have been changed to S.D.

In this case, we can reverse the global edit by simply changing all S.D. data back to San Diego. Do so now by entering the command

■   CHANGE City TO "San Diego" IN Names WHERE City = S.D.

If you view the City column again, you'll see that the name "San Diego" has returned.

You can also globally delete rows from a table, but we won't try this with the Names table—we need those data for future experiments. The general syntax for global deletions is the following:

■   DELETE Rows FROM *table name* WHERE *condition(s)*

(To access the Delete Rows command from the Prompt menu, select the Edit Data option, and then select the Delete and Rows commands from the submenus.)

Referring back to our hypothetical Sales table, which contains salespersons' salaries and gross sales, you could use the command

■   DELETE Rows FROM Sales WHERE Salary >A G:Sales

which would instantly eliminate all those whose salaries were greater than their gross sales. Assuming that five people met this unfortunate criterion (and fate), R:BASE would display the message

■   5 row(s) have been deleted from SALES

If you ever wanted to delete all the rows from the Names table that did not contain either a last name or company value, you could use the command

■   DELETE Rows FROM Names WHERE L:Name FAILS AND +
      Company FAILS

(**Note:** R:BASE actually puts the symbol **-0-** in empty columns, rather than leaving them blank. The **-0-** symbol is referred to as a *null value.*)

■ *SUMMARY*

In this chapter, we've discussed many techniques for specifying search criteria with the Where clause. Because we are working with our small

Names table, we could not experiment with the full range of search options. If we had more columns on our sample. table, we could do more filtering. For example, had we included a Title column (for Mr., Ms., and so forth), we could have searched for all the doctors by using a **Where Title = Dr.** clause. Or had we included a Job Title (J:Title) column, we could have pulled out all the company presidents and vice presidents by using a **Where J:title CONTAINS Pres** clause. In a Phone column, we could use a **Where Phone CONTAINS (415)** clause to pull out everyone in the 415 area code. There seem to be no limitations to the types of searches that you can perform.

In the next chapter, we'll discuss techniques for displaying information from an R:BASE table. First, take a moment to review some of the techniques we've discussed in this chapter.

All searching in R:BASE is performed with the Where clause, which can be used with the Select, Edit, Change, and Delete commands (and others, as we'll discuss later).

R:BASE provides many comparative operators for performing searches, including equal (= or EQ), not equal (<> or NE), less than (< or LT), greater than (> or GT), less than or equal to (<= or LE), and greater than or equal to (>= or GE).

The CONTAINS operator allows you to search for information embedded in Text columns.

The AND and OR operators allow you to specify multiple search criteria, and thereby allow you to broaden or narrow the results of a search.

When searching for data that contain blank spaces (for example, City = San Diego), it's a good idea to use quotation marks (for example, City = "San Diego"), particularly when you are using AND and OR operators.

Searching for data that fall within a range is handled with the AND operator. For example, the clause

■   WHERE Ent:Date >= 01/01/86 AND Ent:Date <= 03/31/86

accesses all rows with dates in the first quarter of 1986.

Where clauses that contain many AND and OR conditions are interpreted from left to right.

You can force R:BASE to take uppercase and lowercase into consideration when performing searches by entering the Set Case On command at the R> prompt. The Set Case Off command returns R:BASE to the normal searching technique, which ignores case during searches. The Show command shows the current status of such settings.

You can perform a search that compares two columns in a table by adding the letter A to the operator (for example, =A, <>A, >A, <A, >=A, and <=A).

You can perform searches for specific types of information by using the EXISTS, FAILS, COUNT = n, COUNT = LAST, and LIMIT = n operators.

The Change command allows you to globally edit a table using a Where clause.

The Delete Rows command allows you to globally delete rows from a table using a Where clause.

PRINTING
REPORTS

In this chapter, we'll discuss various techniques for displaying R:BASE data, including printing out information on a printer and storing it in a separate file. You can print formatted reports, mailing labels, and form letters. R:BASE also lets you control various display characteristics, such as column widths and page lengths.

To try the sample exercises in this chapter, run R:BASE in the usual fashion, and select R:BASE from the RBSystem Main menu. Open the Mail database, and press the Esc key to leave the Prompt menu. The R> prompt should appear on your screen.

■ DIRECTING
THE OUTPUT

So far, we've displayed the results of all Select commands on the screen. The Output command allows you to print out these data on a printer or to display them in a separate file that you can print out later. Options for the Output command are the following:

Output Screen	Data are displayed on the screen.
Output Printer	Data are displayed on the printer.
Output *d:filename.ext*	Data are stored on a file. (*d:filename.ext* stands for any file name. The *d:* stands for a letter specifying a disk drive.)

The With command allows you to combine Output options. For example, the Output Screen with Printer command displays data on both the screen and printer. The command

■ Output C:MyReport.TXT WITH BOTH

stores a copy of the output on a file named MyReport.TXT on drive C, and it also displays the data on both the screen and printer.

Output to the Printer

If you have a printer handy, you can try the Output command from the R> prompt. To direct the display to both the screen and the printer, enter the command

■ OUTPUT SCREEN WITH PRINTER

Next, enter the command

■   SELECT ALL FROM Names SORTED BY L:Name F:Name

A copy of the first four columns (all that will fit) will appear on the screen and printed page. Later on, we'll describe how to format the columns so that they will all fit. For now, display the rest of the columns by entering the command

■   SELECT City State Zip Ent:Date FROM Names SORTED BY +
     L:Name F:Name

The City, State, Zip, and Ent:Date columns are displayed on the screen and printer. To eject the printed page (and clear the screen), enter the command

■   NEWPAGE

The printed report is displayed on the printer, as shown in Figure 6.1.

L:Name	F:Name	Company	Address
Adams	Bart	DataSpec, Inc.	P.O. Box 2890
Baker	Robin	Peach Computers	2311 Coast Hwy.
Jones	Mindy	ABC Co.	123 A St.
Miller	Anne	Golden Gate Co.	2313 Sixth St.
Miller	Marie	Zeerox, Inc.	234 C St.
Smith	Sandy	Hi Tech, Inc.	456 Rainbow Dr.

City	State	Zip	Ent:Date
Malibu	CA	92111	06/15/86
San Diego	CA	92112	06/15/86
San Diego	CA	92122	06/15/86
Berkeley	CA	94711	06/01/86
Los Angeles	CA	91234	06/01/86
Berkeley	CA	94721	06/01/86

■ *Figure 6.1:*
*Names table on
the printed page.*

To disconnect from the printer and return to the normal screen display, enter this command:

■   OUTPUT SCREEN

Output to a File

You can direct displays to disk files rather than to the screen. This allows you to integrate the R:BASE display into an external word processor (such as WordStar) or to use a print spooler (such as the DOS PRINT.COM program), which is a program that allows you to use your computer at the same time a file is being printed. In this example, we'll store the display on a file named MyReport.TXT. If you are using a hard-disk system, enter the command

■   OUTPUT MyReport.TXT WITH SCREEN

Next, enter the command

■   SELECT ALL FROM Names

When the R> prompt reappears, return to the normal screen display by using the command

■   OUTPUT SCREEN

You can verify that the file exists by using the Type command at the R> prompt. Enter the command

■   TYPE MyReport.TXT

You'll see the contents of the MyReport.TXT file on the screen, as shown in Figure 6.2.

When naming these text files with the Output command, you can specify a directory and path name as well. For example, the command

■   OUTPUT C:\WP\MyReport.TXT

stores the MyReport.TXT file in the WP directory on drive C.

To access the Output command from the Prompt menu, select the Print Data option. Then select Output to begin building a command. From the submenu, select Screen or Printer, or press Esc to enter a file name for the output. The prompts will also allow you to enter a second output device, or you can press Esc to use a single output device. As usual, select Execute after constructing the command line.

■ CONTROLLING DISPLAY CHARACTERISTICS

You can control the length and width of screen displays, printed reports, and files using the Set Width and Set Lines commands. You can also control the width of individual columns with the Select command by specifying widths with column names.

Controlling Page Length

When displaying large tables, R:BASE will pause after printing 20 lines of text. You can change this setting using the Set Lines command. For example, the standard 8½-by-11-inch sheet of paper can hold 66 lines of text per page. The command

■   SET LINES 66

```
R>TYPE MyReport.TXT
  L:Name          F:Name          Company             Address
  ------------    ------------    ------------        ------------
  Smith           Sandy           Hi Tech, Inc.       456 N. Rainbow Dr.
  Jones           Mindy           ABC Co.             123 A St.
  Miller          Marie           Zeerox Inc.         234 C St.
  Adams           Bart            DataSpec Inc.       P.O. Box 2890
  Miller          Anne            Golden Gate Co.     2313 Sixth St.
  Baker           Robin           Peach Computers     2311 Coast Hwy
R>_
```

■ *Figure 6.2:*
Contents of the MyReport.TXT file.

will change the page length to 66 lines. To return to the normal page length, enter the command

■   SET LINES 20

To set the page length from the Prompt menu, select the R:BASE Environment option from the menu, and then select the Set option and the Keywords and Characters option from the submenus. Select Execute, and press the down arrow key nine times to highlight the Lines per Page option. Type in the new page length, and press the Enter and Esc keys when you are finished.

Controlling Width

R:BASE normally displays as much data as will fit across 79 characters. You can change this to a maximum of 256 or a minimum of 40 characters using the Set Width command. For example, if your printer uses wide paper, the command

■   SET WIDTH 132

will take advantage of the full paper width. This command will also cause screen displays to wrap around the screen, as in Figure 6.3.

```
R>SET WIDTH 132
R>SELECT ALL FROM Names
  L:Name          F:Name         Company              Address
City            State    Zip      Ent:Date
  --------------- -------- ---------- -------------------- --------------------------

  --------------- -------- ---------- --------
  Smith           Sandy          Hi Tech, Inc.        456 N. Rainbow Dr.
Berkeley        CA       94721      06/01/86
  Jones           Mindy          ABC Co.              123 A St.
San Diego       CA       92122      06/15/86
  Miller          Marie          Zeerox Inc.          234 C St.
Los Angeles     CA       91234      06/01/86
  Adams           Bart           DataSpec Inc.        P.O. Box 2890
Malibu          CA       92111      06/15/86
  Miller          Anne           Golden Gate Co.      2313 Sixth St.
Berkeley        CA       94711      06/01/86
  Baker           Robin          Peach Computers      2311 Coast Hwy
San Diego       CA       92122      06/15/86
R>_
```

■ *Figure 6.3:*
Screen display of
Names table with
132-character
width.

If you print data with compressed print (an option available on most dot matrix printers), the Set Width command will allow you to use more columns on the printed page.

The Set Width command will also affect displays stored on files. When you use the Type command, however, you may not see the columns that extend beyond the right edge of the screen. If you load the file into a word processor, the columns will be there.

To set the page width from the Prompt menu, select the R:BASE Environment option from the menu; then select the Set option and the Keywords and Characters option from the submenus. Select Execute, and press the down arrow key ten times to highlight the Width per Line option. Type in the new page width, and press the Enter and Esc keys when you are finished.

Controlling Column Widths

To specify the widths of individual columns, use the Select command, followed by the column name, an equal sign (=), and the number of spaces that you want in the column. For example, the command

■   SELECT L:Name = 9 F:Name = 9 Company = 10 Address = 12 +
     City = 12 State = 2 Zip = 5 Ent:Date = 8 FROM Names +
     SORTED BY L:Name F:Name

will fit all the columns onto an 80-column screen by using more vertical space, as shown in Figure 6.4.

Color Displays

If you have a color monitor, you can use any combination of colors on the screen that you wish. Just enter the command

■   SET COLOR

at the R > prompt. The screen will display a table of options for both foreground and background colors. Use the arrow keys to move the cursor to the color that you want for the foreground, and then press the Enter key to choose the color. Press the right arrow key to move to the background color options, move the cursor to the color that you want, and press Enter again. Press the Esc key when you're finished making your selections. You'll return to the R > prompt, with the colors that you selected in effect. (See Chapter 19 for more on color display.)

To set the screen colors from the Prompt menu, select the R:BASE Environment option from the menu, and then select the Set and Color options from the submenus. Select Execute, and choose your screen colors as discussed above.

Clearing the Screen

To clear any existing data from the screen, type in the command

■ CLS

or optionally, type the command

■ NEWPAGE

next to the R> prompt, and press Enter. Note that this only erases the screen display and has no effect on information in the database.

Date Displays

R:BASE typically displays the date in MM/DD/YY format. You can alter the format of date displays using the Set Date command and

```
R>SELECT L:Name=9 F:Name=9 Company=10 Address=12 +
+>City=12 State=2 Zip=5 Ent:Date=8 FROM Names +
+>SORTED BY L:Name F:Name
L:Name    F:Name    Company    Address       City         St Zip   Ent:Date
--------  --------  ---------  ------------  -----------  -- -----  --------
Adams     Bart      DataSpec   P.O. Box      Malibu       CA 92111 06/15/86
                    Inc.       2890
Baker     Robin     Peach      2311 Coast    San Diego    CA 92122 06/15/86
                    Computers  Hwy
Jones     Mindy     ABC Co.    123 A St.     San Diego    CA 92122 06/15/86
Miller    Anne      Golden     2313 Sixth    Berkeley     CA 94711 06/01/86
                    Gate Co.   St.
Miller    Marie     Zeerox     234 C St.     Los Angeles  CA 91234 06/01/86
                    Inc.
Smith     Sandy     Hi Tech,   456 N.        Berkeley     CA 94721 06/01/86
                    Inc.       Rainbow Dr.
R>_
```

■ *Figure 6.4:*
Names table displayed with column widths specified.

any of the options below:

MM	Displays the month as a number, 01 through 12
MMM	Displays the month as a three-letter abbreviation, Jan through Dec
MMM +	Displays the month spelled out, January through December
DD	Displays the day as a number, 1 through 31
WWW	Displays the day of the week as a three-letter abbreviation, Sun through Sat
WWW +	Displays the day of the week spelled out, Sunday through Saturday
YY	Displays the year as a two-digit number, 86
YYYY	Displays the year as a four-digit number, 1986
CC	Allows dates for the B.C. range to be entered

You can also use other characters such as commas and colons in dates. When setting a date format, enter the command Set Date followed by the appropriate format in quotation marks. For example, to display dates in "January 30, 1986" format, enter the command

■   SET DATE "MMM + DD, YYYY"

To see the dates in this format, enter the command

■   SELECT Ent:Date FROM Names

Figure 6.5 shows an example of dates listed in the "MMM + DD, YYYY" format. Examples of other formats are listed below:

Format	Example
WWW: MMM DD, YYYY	Sun: Jun 01, 1986
MMM + DD YYYY (WWW +)	June 01 1986 (Sunday)
MM/YY	06/86
YY-MMM-DD	86-Jun-01
MMM + DD	June 01

When entering dates into a database, R:BASE assumes that you mean this century whenever you enter two digits for the year (for example, if you use YY for the year in the Set Date format, and enter 86 as the year, R:BASE assumes that you mean 1986). To enter dates in other centuries, use a four-digit format (YYYY) in the Set Date command and in the entered date as well (for example, Set Date "MM/DD/YYYY" and 06/01/1842).

If you need to use B.C. dates, use CC in the format, as in the following command:

■   SET DATE "MM/DD/YYYY CC"

To enter a B.C. date, add the letters BC to your entry; for example,

■   06/01/3000 BC

To enter an A.D. date into a database field, just enter the date without any letters, as follows:

■   06/01/1986

Note that regardless of the date format that you set to display dates, you can enter the date in any format you wish as long as the sequence of month, day, and year matches the sequence of the date format. For example, in the command

■   SET DATE "WWW + : MMM + DD, YYYY"

```
R>SET DATE "MMM+ DD, YYYY"
R>SELECT Ent:Date L:Name F:Name Company FROM Names SORTED BY Ent:Date
   Ent:Date          L:Name          F:Name          Company
   ------------------ --------------- --------------- --------------------
   June 01, 1986      Smith           Sandy           Hi Tech, Inc.
   June 01, 1986      Miller          Marie           Zeerox Inc.
   June 01, 1986      Miller          Anne            Golden Gate Co.
   June 15, 1986      Jones           Mindy           ABC Co.
   June 15, 1986      Adams           Bart            DataSpec Inc.
   June 15, 1986      Baker           Robin           Peach Computers
R>_
```

■ *Figure 6.5:*
Dates displayed in MMM + DD, YYYY format.

the sequence is weekday, month, day, and year. (Weekday is always calculated automatically from the date, so you never need to type it in yourself.) You can enter dates into a date field using any of the formats below, since each follows the same sequence of month, day, and year.

■ Jun 01 1986
06/01/1986
06-01-1986
June 06, 1986

You can specify a sequence for entering dates that is separate from the sequence in which dates are displayed. To do so, use the command Set Date Seq to define the sequence for entering dates. Use the command Set Date For to define the display format. For example, entering the commands

■ SET DATE SEQ MMDDYY
SET DATE FOR "YY-MMM-DD"

allows you to enter dates in MM/DD/YY sequence, but displays them in "86-Jun-01" format.

Time Formats

Even though we did not include a column with the Time data type in this database, now is a good time to discuss R:BASE time formats, since they follow the same basic style as date formats. The command to define the sequence of hours, minutes, and seconds for entering times into a database is Set Time Seq followed by the sequence of characters. The command for displaying times is Set Time For followed by the time format. The commands below allow you to enter and display times in HH:MM:SS AM/PM format:

■ SET TIME SEQ HHMMSS AP
SET TIME FOR "HH:MM:SS AP"

The symbols you can use in time formats are listed below:

HH   Hours as a two-digit number, 01 through 24
MM   Minutes as a two-digit number, 00 though 60

SS   Seconds as a two-digit number, 00 through 60

AP   A.M. or P.M. displayed

If you do not set your own time format, R:BASE uses the format HH:MM:SS, wherein the time is displayed on a 24-hour clock in the format HH:MM:SS. For example, 2:30 in the afternoon is displayed as 14:30:00. Examples of the time 2:30:15 P.M. displayed in several different formats are listed below:

Format	Example
HH:MM:SS	14:30:15
HH:MM:SS AP	2:30:15 PM
HH:MM AP	2:30 PM
SS Seconds	15 Seconds

To set the date or time format from the Prompt menu, select the R:BASE Environment option from the menu, and then select the Set option and the Keywords and Characters option from the submenus. Select Execute and any one of the options Date Sequence, Date Format, Time Sequence, or Time Format. Type in the new sequence or format, and press the Enter and Esc keys when you are finished.

Viewing Settings

For a quick review of the various settings we've discussed in this chapter (and additional settings we'll discuss later), type in the command

■   SHOW

at the R> prompt, and press Enter.

You can also view the settings from the Prompt menu by selecting R:BASE Environment from the menu and Show from the submenu. Select Execute to view the settings, and press Esc when you are finished.

■ PRINTING FORMATTED REPORTS

R:BASE includes a report generator that allows you to create customized reports with headings, footings, totals, subtotals, and modified column displays. In this section, we'll experiment with reports and develop a Directory report for the Names table, similar to the one shown in Figure 6.6.

Developing a report can be broken down into seven steps:

1. Design the report on paper, marking headings, footings, and detail (the body of the report).

2. Determine variables for the report on paper (information that is to be included in the report but does not come directly from the table).

3. Enter the report generator, name the report, and define the associated table.

4. Define report variables on-line.

5. Enter report headings and footings.

6. Identify the location of report columns and variables.

7. Save the report format.

	Mailing List Directory	
May 31, 1986		Page: 1
Adams, Bart	DataSpec Inc.	Jun 15,1986
P.O. Box 2890	Malibu, CA 92111	
Baker, Robin	Peach Computers	Jun 15,1986
2311 Coast Hwy.	San Diego, CA 92112	
Jones, Mindy	ABC Co.	Jun 15,1986
123 A St.	San Diego, CA 92122	
Miller, Anne	Golden Gate Co.	Jun 1,1986
2313 Sixth St.	Berkeley, CA 94711	
Miller, Marie	Zeerox Inc.	Jun 1,1986
234 C St.	Los Angeles, CA 91234	
Smith, Sandy	Hi Tech, Inc.	Jun 1,1986
456 N. Rainbow Dr.	Berkeley, CA 94721	

■ *Figure 6.6:*
Directory report for the Names table.

Each of these steps is discussed in detail below.

Step 1: Design the Report

The first step in developing a report is to jot down on paper a rough draft of how you want each printed page to look. Note the headings that appear at the top of each page, footings that appear at the bottom of each page, and detail (the main body of the report where rows from the table are displayed). Figure 6.7 shows a sample rough draft.

Step 2: Define Report Variables

Report variables are any type of information that does not come directly from a database table (excluding headings and footings). Page numbers, dates, totals, and subtotals are all variables. Special characters that you want to insert into a column, such as commas, can be defined as variables as well.

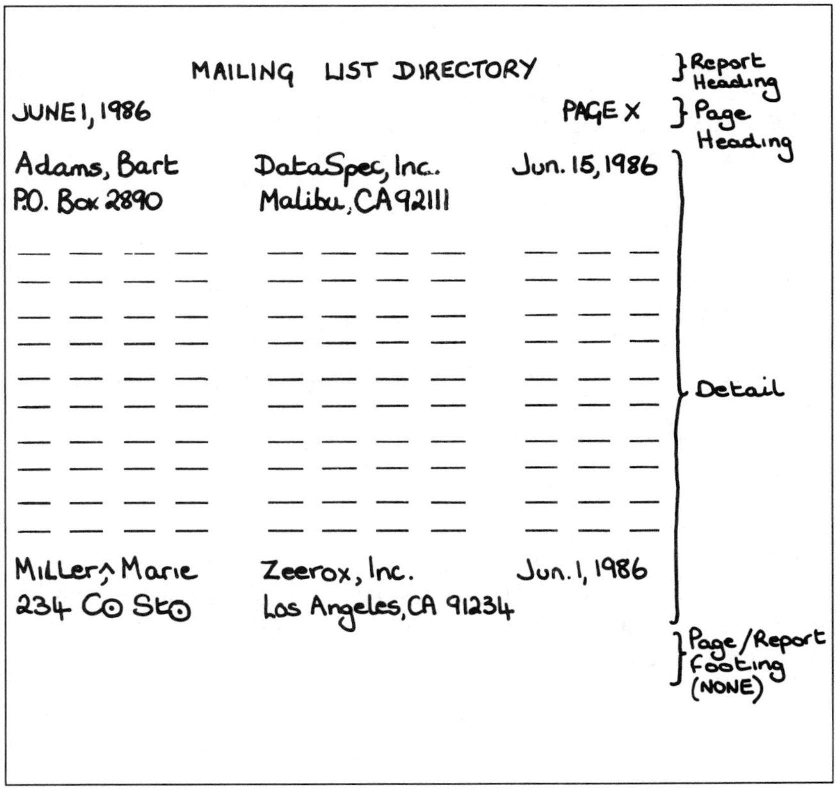

■ *Figure 6.7:*
Rough draft of a
report on paper.

Similarly, in our Directory report, the name is a variable because it is modified to include a comma and has extraneous blanks removed, as in *Miller, Marie*. The City, State, and Zip columns are also modified, as in *San Diego, CA 92122*. Jot down brief names for each of the following variables (but do not use spaces in the variable names):

> PgNo = Page number
> RepDate = Report date
> Comma = ","
> FullName = Last and first names, separated by a comma
> FullCSZ = City, state, and ZIP code with a comma inserted

Once you've jotted down this information, you can go on-line and develop the report format.

Step 3: Enter the Report Generator

There are three different methods that you can use to enter the R:BASE report generator (also called *Reports Express*). From the RBSystem Main menu, select the Reports Express option. From the Prompt menu, select the Data Output and Reports options. From the R:BASE R> prompt, enter the command

■   REPORTS

and press Enter.

If a database is not already open, you'll see the Reports Express Main menu, as shown in Figure 6.8. Select option 1 (Choose a Database) to open a database file. Highlight the appropriate file name and press Enter.

Once a database is open, you'll see the Report Options menu, as shown in Figure 6.9. (Notice that the name of the currently open database also appears in the highlighted *status bar* near the bottom of the screen.)

We'll discuss options 2 to 5 later. For now, you want to create a new report format, so select option 1 (Edit/Create a Report). R:BASE displays the names of any existing reports and the option (New) to create a new report, as follows:

■   ───────────────── Choose a report ─────────────────
    Standard (New)

To create a new report, highlight the (New) option and press Enter.

Next, R:BASE asks that you enter a name for the new report, up to eight characters long, as below:

■ Enter your report name (1-8 characters)

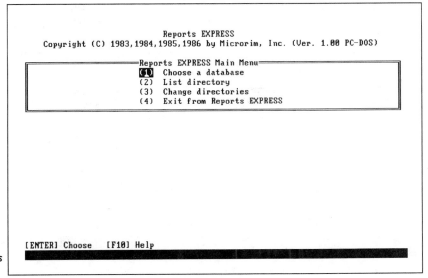

■ *Figure 6.8:*
Reports Express
Main menu.

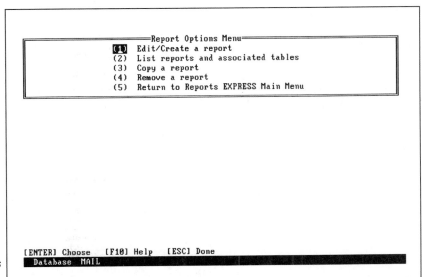

■ *Figure 6.9:*
Report Options
menu.

For this example, enter the name Director (short for Directory), and press Enter.

Next, R:BASE asks for the name of the table containing the data to be printed, as follows:

■ ————————————— Select a table or view ——————————————
  Names
  _____

The Mail database contains only the table named Names, so select Names.

Next, R:BASE displays the *Reports Definition menu* and screen. This is your clean slate for creating your report format. Now, you can begin to design the actual report format.

Step 4: Define Variables On-Line

To define variables to use in a report, select the Expression option from the Reports Definition menu. From the submenu, select Define. Next, R:BASE will ask you to enter an expression. You define a variable by typing in a variable name (from one to eight characters in length with no spaces), followed by a space, an equal sign (=), another space, and an expression or code to define the contents of the variable.

First, define the PgNo (page number) variable by typing in the following:

■ PgNo = .#PAGE

.#PAGE is a code that is always used to display page numbers in reports. After you press the Enter key, you'll see the expression on the screen, as shown in Figure 6.10, and R:BASE will ask for the next expression.

Next, define the RepDate (report date) variable. The code for the date is .#DATE. Type in the expression

■ RepDate = .#DATE

and press Enter. .#DATE uses the system date that you entered when booting DOS or through the DOS Date command. The new expression appears on the screen, as shown in Figure 6.11.

Note that you can also include the time of day on a report using the code .#TIME (but we won't do so in this example). Like .#DATE,

.#TIME uses the system time that you entered when booting DOS or through the Time command from the DOS prompt.

Define the Comma variable next. When you are defining literal characters for use in a report, surround them with quotation marks.

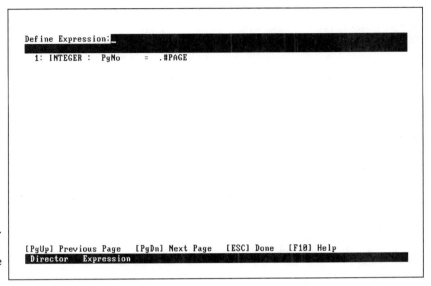

■ *Figure 6.10:*
PgNo variable defined on the screen.

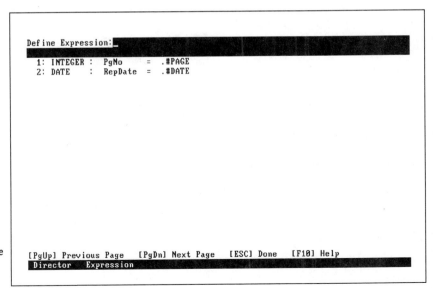

■ *Figure 6.11:*
RepDate variable defined on the screen.

Type in the expression for the Comma variable as

■　Comma = ","

and press Enter.

Next we'll define the FullName variable, which contains the last name, a comma, and the first name.

To join Text data, you can use either of the following two operators:

&　Joins two items of text, placing a blank space between them.

+　Joins two items of text without a blank space.

Since we want to place the comma right next to the last name, with a space after the comma and then the first name, enter the expression

■　FullName = L:Name + Comma & F:Name

This expression will print all the names in the following format:

■　Miller, Anne

When you press the Enter key, you'll see that the FullName variable and its expression are listed with the others. You've also noticed by now that R:BASE automatically places the type of data that the variable contains to the left of each variable name (for example, Date, Integer, and Text). You need not concern yourself with these data types yet.

We want to display the city, state, and ZIP code in the format

■　San Diego, CA 92345

We'll use the variable FullCSZ for this format. Type in the expression

■　FullCSZ = City + Comma & State & Zip

Press Enter after typing in the expression. Then press the Esc key to indicate that you've finished entering expressions. You'll see all the variable names and their expressions listed on the screen as in Figure 6.12.

Making Corrections

If you find that you've made an error in an expression and you wish to change it, select the Define option from the menu. Type in the entire

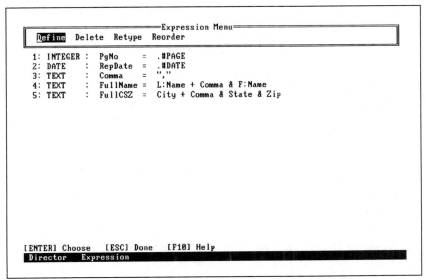

∎ *Figure 6.12:*
Report variables
and expressions
defined.

corrected expression, including the variable name, and press Enter.
R:BASE will inform you that the variable name already exists and ask if
you want to replace the original expression with the new one. Select Yes
to do so.

Now you are ready to design the layout of the report. Press Esc to
return to the Reports Definition menu.

Step 5: Lay Out the Report Headers and Footers

A report can have three types of headers and three types of footers, as
summarized below:

Symbol	Name	Type
RH	Report header	Displayed once at the top of the report
PH	Page header	Displayed at the top of each page
BH	Break header	Appears at the top of each group in a report (used for reports containing subtotals)
BF	Break footer	Appears at the bottom of each group in a report (used for reports containing subtotals)

PF Page footer Displayed at the bottom of each page

RF Report footer Displayed once at the bottom of the report

The symbol for each type of header and footer will appear highlighted in the far-left margin of the screen. Learning to specify, insert, and delete header and footer types can be tricky (although it's easy once you get used to it). Take a moment to review the keys that you can use while designing a report format, as shown in Figure 6.13, before developing the Directory report.

Let's add a report header to the Director report that consists of the words "Mailing List Directory" with a blank line beneath. We'll also add a page header that shows the date the report was printed and the page number. (We'll deal with break headers and footers in a later chapter.)

To move the cursor onto the screen and begin laying out the report format, select Edit from the top menu. Notice that the cursor moves to the right of the RH (report header) symbol. The bottom-right corner of the screen displays the indicator <1: 1, 1>. This shows the current row position of the cursor, the number of rows in the report format, and the current column position of the cursor.

To fill in the heading "Mailing List Directory" centered as the report header, hold down the right arrow key until the cursor reaches column 25 (the indicator will read <1:1, 25>) and type in

■ Mailing List Directory

Now we want to add another RH (report header) line so that there will be a blank line beneath this heading. To do so, make sure the expand mode is on. (Look for the word "Expand" in the highlight near the bottom of the screen. If you do not see it, press the F9 key.) When the expand mode is on, press the Enter key. Notice that this creates a new line with the symbol RH.

On the next line we'll begin the page heading. To create the next section, press the F8 key. Another new line appears, this one with the symbol PH (page header) in it. On this line, press the space bar once and type the word

■ Date:

Hold down the right arrow key until the cursor reaches column 58 (the indicator will read <3:3, 58>). Type in the word

■ Page:

Key	Function
F1	Inserts a blank line above the current line.
F2	Deletes the current line.
F9	Turns the expand mode on and off. The word "Expand" appears near the bottom of the screen when the expand mode is on.
F7	With the expand mode on, moves the cursor to the previous section, or creates a new section if one does not exist. With the expand mode off, moves the cursor to the previous section.
F8	With the expand mode on, moves the cursor to the next section, or creates a new section if one does not exist. With the expand mode off, moves the cursor to the next section.
↑	Moves the cursor up one line. If the expand mode is on, creates a new line in the current section.
↓	Moves the cursor down one line. If the expand mode is on, creates a new line in the current section.
→	Moves the cursor to the right one character.
←	Moves the cursor to the left one character.
Ctrl-→	Moves the cursor to screen column number 255.
Ctrl-←	Moves the cursor to screen column number 1.
Ins	Inserts a space at the cursor position.
Del	Deletes the character at the cursor position.
Tab	Moves the cursor to the next tab setting (10 spaces).
Shift-Tab	Moves the cursor to the previous tab setting (10 spaces).
Home	With the expand mode on, moves to the upper-left corner of the current section. With the expand mode off, moves to the upper-left corner of the report format.
End	With the expand mode on, moves to the bottom-right corner of the current section. With the expand mode off, moves to the bottom-right corner of the report format.
F10	Displays a help screen.
Esc	Exits from editing and redisplays the menu.

◼ *Figure 6.13:*
Keys used when creating reports.

Press the Enter key to create another blank line. This one will also be a PH line and will serve as a blank line in the page header.

Now there are two sections on the screen: RH (report header) and PH (page header), as shown in Figure 6.14. Next we'll begin placing *variable* data (items from the Names table and report variables) on the report.

Step 6: Locate Column and Variable Positions

To *locate* (or place) a table column name or report variable on the report format, you press the F6 key. Generally, it's easier to place the cursor to the far left of the location of the column data or variable first, and then press the F6 key. Let's get started.

To locate the report date (RepDate) variable in the page heading, first use the arrow keys to move the cursor to the right of the Date: text (<3: 4, 8> on the indicator). Next, press F6 to locate the variable. R:BASE displays the prompt

■   Column or variable name:

In this case we want to locate the RepDate variable, so type in the name

■   RepDate

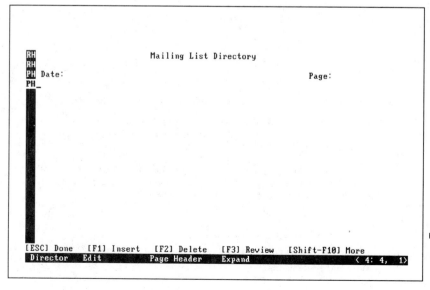

■ *Figure 6.14:*
Report header
and page header
on the screen.

and press Enter. R:BASE asks that you

■   Move cursor to start location and press [S]

Since the cursor is already in the start location, just press the letter S. An S appears on the screen, and R:BASE asks that you

■   Move cursor to end and press [E] or [W]

The cursor automatically moved about 30 spaces to the right (which is the maximum width for Date data). This is a good location for the end of the date, so just type the letter E. The E appears on the screen. Now you can see the starting and ending location where the date will appear in the printed report (between the S and the E, aligned to the left).

Next you can locate the PgNo variable. Move the cursor to column 64 (the indicator will read <3:4, 64>), and press F6. Now suppose you've forgotten the names of the variables and columns available to this report. To quickly review them, press the F3 key. Press Esc after viewing the variable and column names.

Enter PgNo as the variable name, and press Enter. When R:BASE asks for the start location, press S. When R:BASE asks for the end location, move the cursor to column 73 and type E. Now the page heading includes the word Date: followed by a location for the RepDate variable and the word Page: followed by the location of the PgNo variable, as shown below:

■   Date: S   E   Page: S E

Now we need to fill in locations for table data to appear on the screen. But these do not belong in a heading or footing, because headings and footings only appear once on each page or once in the entire report. Instead, we'll locate the table column names in a *detail* section of the report.

The Detail Section of the Report

The detail section displays data repeatedly on a page. In fact, it is generally repeated once for each row in the table. We need to create a detail section for this report now. First, press the down arrow key to move the cursor to the next row down (row 4). Next, make sure that the expand mode is on (press F9 if the word "Expand" does not appear in the status bar at the bottom of the screen). Then press F8 to create the next section. The letter D (for Detail) appears at the far-left edge of the new line.

First let's locate the FullName variable (which, as you'll recall, displays the L:Name and F:Name from the database table). Move the cursor to <5,2> and press F6. Type in FullName as the variable name, and press Enter. Type S to mark the start location. Move the cursor to 5,30, and press E to mark the end location.

Use the right arrow key to move the cursor to <5,35>, press F6, and enter Company as the column name to display. Press S to start the location; then move the cursor to <5,53> and press E.

To locate the Ent:Date column, move the cursor to <5,58> and press F6. Type Ent:Date as the column name and press Enter. Type S to mark the start location. Move the cursor to <5,73> and press E. If most of your report seems to disappear from the screen, press Ctrl-left arrow (hold down the Ctrl key and press the left arrow key) to move the cursor back to column 1.

Assuming that the expand mode is still on, you can just press the down arrow key to create another detail line. To locate the Address variable, move the cursor to <6, 5> and press F6. Enter Address as the column name, press S, move the cursor to <6, 29>, and press E. Move the cursor to <6, 35> and use the F6 key to locate FullCSZ from <6, 35> to <6, 73>.

To insert a blank line between names printed in the directory, press the down arrow key to create another detail line. (You can press Ctrl-left arrow to move the cursor back over to column 1.) You'll see the start and end locations of all the column names and variables on the screen as in Figure 6.15.

Now that the report format is laid out, you only need to save it.

Step 7: Save the Report Format

To save the report format, press the Esc key to bring back the Reports Definition menu. Press the Esc key again to call up the Report Exit Options menu. This menu offers the following options:

■   Save Changes   Discard Changes   Return

Select Save Changes to save the report format. (Selecting Discard Changes "abandons" any new or changed information in the report, while selecting Return returns you to the Reports Definition menu.) You'll see the message "Storing Report" appear on the screen briefly. From the next menu to appear, select option 5 (Return to Reports Express Main menu) and then option 4 (Exit from Reports Express). You'll be returned to the place from which you entered Reports Express (either the R> prompt, the Prompt menu, or the RBSystem Main menu).

Now let's try out the report. If you are not at the R> prompt now, work your way to it before trying the rest of the examples in this chapter. (Select R:BASE from the RBSystem Main menu, or press Esc, or both if the Prompt menu is on the screen.)

■ DISPLAYING AND PRINTING REPORTS

To display the directory report in sorted order, use the Print command, followed by the name of the report and the Sorted By clause. In this example, enter the command

■ PRINT Director SORTED BY L:Name F:Name

The report will appear on the screen, as shown in Figure 6.16.

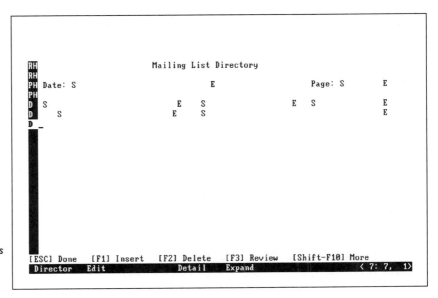

■ *Figure 6.15:*
All column names and variables located on the screen.

```
R>PRINT Director SORTED BY L:Name F:Name
                  Mailing List Directory

   Date: 10/30/86                            Page:        1

   Adams, Bart                Dataspec Inc.           06/15/86
       P.O. Box 2890          Malibu, CA 92111

   Baker, Robin               Peach Computers         06/15/86
       2311 Coast Hwy.        San Diego, CA 92122

   Jones, Andy                ABC Co.                 06/15/86
       123 A St.              San Diego, CA 92122

   Miller, Anne               Golden Gate Co.         06/01/86
       2313 Sixth St.         Berkeley, CA 94711

   Miller, Marie              Zeerox Inc.             06/01/80
       234 C St.              Los Angeles, CA 91234

   Smith, Sandy               Hi Tech, Inc.           06/01/86
       456 N. Rainbow Dr.     Berkeley, CA 94721

   R>_
```

■ *Figure 6.16: Director report displayed on the screen.*

To print out the report on a printer, enter the following commands:

■ OUTPUT PRINTER
PRINT Director SORTED BY L:Name F:Name

After the report is printed, you can enter the command

■ NEWPAGE

to eject the report from the printer. Then enter the command

■ OUTPUT SCREEN

to disconnect from the printer.

You can also send a copy of the report to a disk file using the Output *d:filename.ext* command.

To display the dates in the report in **Jan 1, 1986** format, enter the command

■ SET DATE "MMM DD, YYYY"

and print the report.

To print the report using only certain rows from the Names table, use the Where clause after the Sorted By clause, as below:

■ PRINT Director SORTED BY L:Name F:Name WHERE +
  City = "San Diego"

Printing on Single Sheets

When displaying lengthy reports on the printer, you can use either continuous-form (tractor-fed) paper or single sheets. For continuous form, use the Output Printer option before entering the Print command. For single sheets, use the command

■ OUTPUT PRINTER WITH SCREEN

before entering the Print command.

Compressed and Expanded Print

Most dot-matrix printers allow you to use special printer attributes such as compressed or expanded print. Some printers even allow you to change type sizes and fonts. You can use these settings in your reports if you know the appropriate codes for your printer. For example, the Oki-data MicroLine 83A printer uses ASCII code 29 for compressed print, code 31 for expanded print, and code 30 for regular print. To use the settings in a report, you would need to define three variables (in the same way we defined the PgNo and RepDate variables in the Director report), as below:

■ ComPrint = <29>
  ExpPrint = <31>
  RegPrint = <30>

Next, you would locate these variables in the report, just as you would locate any other variable. For example, to print the heading in expanded print, locate the ExpPrint variable either above or to the left of the heading. To return to normal print for the body of the report, locate the RegPrint variable beneath or to the right of the heading. Be sure to put the variable for normal printing below the last line of the report so that the printer returns to normal printing after printing the reports.

Some printers use multicode sequences to activate special attributes. For example, the Epson printer uses **Esc +** to start and stop underlining. The ASCII code for the Esc key is always 27. The ASCII code for the minus (−) sign is 45. Therefore, you could define a variable to start and stop underlining, as below:

■   PrUnder = <27 45>

Locate the PrUnder variable before and after the text that you want underlined in the report.

Different printers use different codes for special print attributes. Figure 6.17 shows codes for some popular printers. See your printer manual for the codes that your printer uses.

■ EDITING FORMATTED REPORTS

Quite often, you'll find that you want (or need) to make changes to a report format after viewing the report. To do so, just reenter the Reports Express module using any one of the three techniques discussed earlier in this chapter. Select the name of the report that you want to edit from the menu that appears.

Your original report format will appear on the screen. You can use the Edit and Expression options from the menu to add, change, or delete text, variables, and column names on the report format. Use the function keys (F1, F2, F6, F7, F8, and F9) to insert and delete lines and sections.

Relocating Variables and Column Names

To change the location of a column name or variable on the report format, move the cursor inside the existing S and E symbols for the column or variable. Press the F6 key, and R:BASE will allow you to assign new start and end locations for the column or variable.

Deleting Variables and Column Names

To remove a located column name or variable from the report format, move the cursor inside the S and E of the appropriate column or variable, hold down the Shift key, and press F2.

Reordering Variables

Variables must be defined in the order that they are created. For example, the two expressions below are out of order because the

Manufacturer	Printer Model	Normal Print	Compressed Print	Expanded Print-On	Expanded Print-Off
BMC	PB101	<27 78>	<27 79>	<14>	<15>
Brother	HR-1	<27 80>	<27 77>		
C. Itoh	Prowriter	<27 78>	<27 81>	<14>	<15>
	8510 or 1550	<27 78>	<27 81	<14>	<15>
Comrex	CR-1	<27 80>	<27 77>		
Epson	RX or FX	<18>	<15>	<27 87 49>	<27 87 50>
	MX80 or MX100	<18>	<15>	<27 83>	<27 84>
	MX w/ Graftrax	<18>	<15>	<27 83>	<27 84>
	MX w/o Graftrax	<18>	<15>	<14>	<20>*
IBM	PC Printer	<18>	<15>	<14>	<20>*
IDS	Prism 80 and				
	132	<29>	<31>	<01>	<02>
	Microprism	<29>	<31>	<01>	<02>
NEC	PC-8023-A	<27 78>	<27 81>	<14>	<15>
Okidata	82A, 83A, 84	<30>	<29>	<31>	<30>
	92, 93	<30>	<29>	<31>	<30>
Panasonic	1090	<18>	<15>	<27 83>	<27 84>
PMC	DMP85	<27 78>	<27 81>	<14>	<15>
Star Micronics	Gemini, Delta	<18>	<15>		
	Radix	<18>	<15>		
TEC	DMP85	<27 78>	<27 81>	<14>	<15>
Victor	6020	<18>	<15>	<14>	<20>*

*Expanded print automatically stops at the end of the printed line.

■ *Figure 6.17:*
Attribute codes for various printers.

Comma variable is defined *after* it is used in the FullCSZ variable:

- FullCSZ = City + Comma & State & Zip
  Comma = ","

To reorder the variables and expressions, select Expressions and Reorder from the report menus. R:BASE will display the prompt

- Enter expression name: New position:

In this example, you could enter FullCSZ as the expression name and 2 as its new position, to place the Comma variable above the FullCSZ variable.

Deleting Variables

To delete a variable, select Expression and Delete from the report menus. The variable will be deleted from the list of expressions. Furthermore, the variable will be deleted from the report format if it was already in use there.

Changing Variables

To change a variable (expression), select Define from the Expressions menu. Type in the new variable name and expression exactly as you want it to appear in the expressions list. R:BASE will double-check for permission. Select Yes to replace the original variable and expression with the new one.

Saving Changes

Press the Esc key when you are finished editing, and use the same techniques discussed earlier to save the modified report format.

■ MAILING LABELS

Mailing labels are simple to produce with the R:BASE report generator. First, make sure that the Mail database is open and that the R>

prompt appears on the screen. Then, enter the command

■   REPORTS

Select option (1) to Edit/Create a report, select (New), and enter the report name **Labels.** Next, enter **Names** as the associated table.

Select the Expression and Define options from the menus, and enter the following expressions:

■   Comma = ","
FullName = F:Name & L:Name
FullCSZ = City + Comma & State & Zip

After entering all the variables, the screen will look like Figure 6.18. Press Esc after you've defined the variables.

To lay out the report format, select the Edit option from the menu. Turn on the expand mode (press F9 until "Expand" appears on the status line); then press F8 twice so that the RP section changes to D. (Mailing labels consist only of detail lines.)

On the first line, press F6 and enter FullName as the variable to locate. Start the variable at <1,1> and end it at about <1,35>.

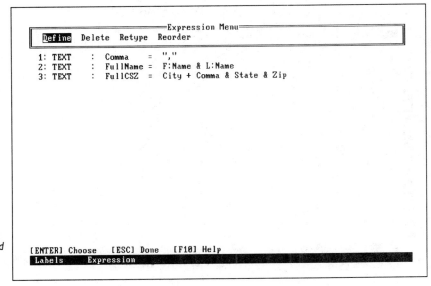

■ *Figure 6.18:*
Variables defined
for mailing
labels.

Press the down arrow to create another detail line. Press F6 and enter Company as the column name. Start the location at <2,1> and end it at about <2,20>. Press the down arrow to create a third detail line, and press F6 to locate the Address variable. Start the location at <3,1> and end it at about <3, 25>. Press the down arrow to create a fourth detail line, and press F6 to locate the FullCSZ variable. Start the location at <4,1> and end it at about <4,35>.

Since most mailing labels are one inch tall and most printers print six lines to the inch, you'll want to be sure that R:BASE prints six lines for each label. Press the down arrow two more times to make a total of six detail lines. Your screen should look like Figure 6.19.

Press Esc after laying out the format. To ensure that R:BASE does not attempt to skip pages while printing labels, select the Configure option from the top menu. Set the number of lines per page to zero by typing the number 0 and pressing Enter. (We'll discuss these configuration settings in more detail later.) Press Esc twice to call up the Exit Options menu.

Select Save Changes to save the report format. Select options (5) and (4) from the next menus to return to the R> prompt.

Before printing labels, you can check the alignment of the labels in the printer. To do so, enter the command

■　OUTPUT PRINTER

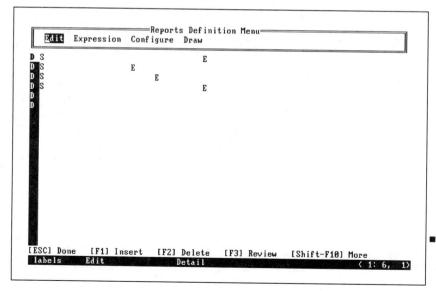

■ *Figure 6.19:*
Mailing label
format laid out
on the screen.

at the R> prompt. Then, to print two mailing labels, enter the command

■   PRINT Labels WHERE LIMIT = 2

If the mailing-label alignment is not correct, adjust the labels in the printer, then press Ctrl-right arrow (hold down the Ctrl key and press the right arrow key) to repeat the Print command. Press Enter. Repeat this process until the labels are properly aligned in the printer.

To print the labels in ZIP-code order (for bulk mailing) use the command

■   PRINT Labels SORTED BY Zip

The labels will appear on the screen. The label format designed here is for single-column, 3½-by-15/16-inch (or 1-inch) continuous-form mailing labels.

When printing labels, you can use the Where clause to specify search criteria, as follows:

■   PRINT Labels SORTED BY Zip WHERE Ent:Date = 06/01/86

After the labels are printed, enter the command Output Screen to detach from the printer.

■ *FORM LETTERS*

The R:BASE Reports command provides a quick and easy way to create form letters from a table. To try one out, first make sure that the Mail database is open and that the R> prompt appears on the screen. Then, enter the command

■   REPORTS

Select option (1) to Edit/Create a report, and select (New). Name the form letter **Letter1**. Select **Names** as the table to use with the report.

Next, select the Expression and Define options to define the following variables:

■   LetDate = .#DATE
    Comma = ","
    FullName = F:Name & L:Name

FullCSZ = City + Comma & State & Zip
Salut = F:Name + ":"

The Salut variable will be used as part of the salutation for the letter. It consists of the first name, with a colon attached. Hence, with the addition of the word **Dear**, the report will print the salutation as **Dear Marie:**.

After entering the variables, the screen should look like Figure 6.20. Press Esc twice after you've defined the variables.

Next you'll want to lay out the form letter. To begin, select Edit from the top menu. Make sure the expand mode is on (press F9 if it isn't); then press F8 to change the RH (report header) symbol to the PH (page header) symbol.

With the cursor in <1,1>, press F6 and enter LetDate as the name of the variable to locate. Make <1,1> the start location and <1,30> the end location. Use the arrow keys and the F6 key to locate the rest of the column names and variables as listed below:

Column/Variable Name	Start	End
FullName	<3,1>	<3,30>
Company	<4,1>	<4,20>
Address	<5,1>	<5,25>
FullCSZ	<6,1>	<6,40>

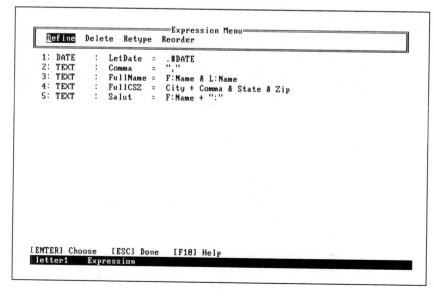

```
                          =Expression Menu=
  Define  Delete  Retype  Reorder

  1: DATE    :  LetDate  =  .#DATE
  2: TEXT    :  Comma    =  ","
  3: TEXT    :  FullName =  F:Name & L:Name
  4: TEXT    :  FullCSZ  =  City + Comma & State & Zip
  5: TEXT    :  Salut    =  F:Name + ":"




  [ENTER] Choose   [ESC] Done   [F10] Help
   letter1    Expression
```

■ *Figure 6.20:*
Variables for the form letter defined.

Move the cursor to row 8, column 1 <8,1> and type in the word
Dear. Press the space bar, press F6, and enter Salut as the variable
name. Start the location at <8,6> and end it at <8,25>. Then move
the cursor to line 10 and type in the letter. Be sure to press the Enter key
before you get to the right edge of the screen when you're typing the letter. (R:BASE does not automatically wrap the text down to the next
line.) Figure 6.21 shows a sample letter typed onto the screen, with
start and end locations for column names and variables. You can use
the arrow keys to move the cursor around, and you can use the Ins and
Del keys to insert spaces and delete characters as necessary. Use the
F1 (or Enter) key to insert new lines and the F2 key to delete lines as
necessary.

You may have noticed that every line in this report is defined as a
page header (PH) in the left column. We do not need any other type of
line in this report, because each letter is to be printed on a separate
page, and page headings always print once on each page. (In a sense,
we've tricked the report generator into printing form letters by giving it
only page headers to print.)

When your letter looks the way you want it to, press the Esc key
twice to work your way to the exit options. Select Save Changes, and
then select options (5) and (4) from the next menus to work your way
back to the R> prompt.

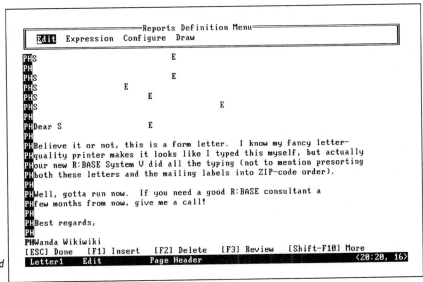

■ *Figure 6.21:*
*Form letter typed
on the screen.*

Printing the Form Letters

To print the form letters, align the paper in the printer so that there is a page perforation (or the start of a new page) just above the print head. (To do so, it's best to turn the printer off, line up the paper, and then turn the printer back on so that R:BASE "knows" where the top of the page is.)

Before printing the letters, you can specify a date format for the date at the top of the letter. For letters, you might want to enter the command

■   SET DATE "MMM + DD, YYYY"

for a more formal date format.

To print letters on continuous-form paper, enter the command

■   OUTPUT PRINTER

at the R > prompt. To print letters one page at a time (on letterhead, for instance) enter the command

■   OUTPUT PRINTER WITH SCREEN

at the R > prompt, and then enter the command

■   PRINT Letter1 SORTED BY Zip

to print letters in ZIP-code order. (Might as well print the letters in the same order as the mailing labels, no?)

As with other types of printing, you can use the Where clause to specify search criteria for printing letters. For example, to print letters for everyone with entry dates of June 1, 1986, enter the command

■   PRINT Letter1 SORTED BY Zip WHERE Ent:Date = 06/01/86

Figure 6.22 shows a form letter created by the Letter1 report format, with the date set to "MMM + DD, YYYY".

■ MANAGING REPORTS

The Mail database now has three report formats associated with it: Director, Labels, and Letter1. To see the names of report formats associated with a database, enter the command

∎   LIST REPORTS

at the R > prompt. The screen will display all report formats, as shown in Figure 6.23.

The Reports Express and Report Options menus offer additional techniques for managing reports. Recall that when you enter the report generator with a database already opened, the Report Options menu presents these options to you:

∎   (1) Edit/Create a report
(2) List Reports
(3) Copy a report
(4) Remove a report
(5) Return to Reports EXPRESS Main Menu

We've used the Edit/Create option with all the reports in this chapter already. The other options from this menu are summarized below:

List Reports	Displays a list of reports associated with the currently open database, and displays the names of their associated tables. (Same as entering the command List Reports at the R > prompt.)
Copy a Report	Copies an existing report in the database to another report in the same database. R:BASE will prompt you for the name of the report to copy and a name for the new, copied report. Useful for creating new reports that resemble existing reports or that use the same expressions.
Remove a Report	Prompts you for the name of the report to remove, and deletes the report format from the database.
Return to Reports Express Main menu	Returns you to the highest-level menu in the report generator, discussed below.

The Reports Express Main menu presents the following options:

∎   (1) Choose a database
(2) List directory
(3) Change directories
(4) Exit from Reports EXPRESS

August 28, 1986

Marie Miller

Zeerox Inc.

234 C St.

Los Angeles, CA 91234

Dear Marie:

Believe it or not, this is a form letter. I know my fancy letter-quality printer makes it looks like I typed this myself, but actually our new R:BASE System V did all the typing (not to mention presorting both these letters and the mailing labels into ZIP-code order).

Well, gotta run now. If you need a good R:BASE consultant a few months from now, give me a call!

Best regards,

Wanda Wikiwiki

■ *Figure 6.22:*
Form letter printed by the Letter I report.

```
                          Any key to continue,[ESC] to return_

  Report     Table
  --------   --------

  director   Names
  labels     Names
  letter1    Names
```

■ *Figure 6.23:*
Reports in the Mail database.

These options are summarized below:

Choose a Database	Lets you open a new database from which to create a report format.
List Directory	For users who often store data on many different directories on a hard disk, this option displays the prompt

■ **Enter a directory path or [ENTER] for current directory**

Pressing Enter displays the names of all files on the current directory. Optionally, you can enter a path and directory name, and DOS file name wildcard characters. For example, entering

■ **\DB*.DBF**

displays the names of all files on the directory name DB that have the extension .DBF.

Change Directories	For more advanced users who use many directories on their hard disk, this option prompts you to enter the name of a new drive and directory, and it changes the default directory to the one you specified.
Exit from Reports Express	Returns you to the place where you initiated Reports Express, either the R> prompt, the Prompt menu, or the RBSystem Main menu.

■ SUMMARY

In this chapter, we've discussed many techniques for managing R:BASE displays. In later chapters, we'll discuss more advanced techniques for formatting reports, including totals and subtotals. Take a moment to review some of the techniques that we've discussed in this chapter.

The Output command is used to direct the output of R:BASE displays. Options are Screen, Printer, *d:filename.ext,* or any combination using the With and Both options.

The Set Width, Set Lines, Set Color, Set Date, and Set Time commands define various display characteristics of the screen and printer.

The $=w$ option allows you to define column widths with the Select command (for example, SELECT L:Name = 10, F:Name = 10).

The Reports command allows you to design report formats. The general steps for developing a report format are as follows:

1. Design the report on paper.

2. Determine the variables to be used in the report.

3. Name the report and associated table using the report generator.

4. Define the report variables on-line with the Expression and Define options.

5. Fill in headings and footings on the report with the Edit option.

6. Locate column and variable positions on the report with the F6 key.

7. Save the report by quitting the menu and selecting Save Changes.

Use the Print <*report name*> command to print reports. Optionally, use the Sorted By and Where clauses to sort and filter reports.

To take advantage of special print attributes, enter codes as report variables and locate those codes in the report as you would any other variable or column name.

To edit report formats, enter the Reports command and the name of the report; then select options similar to those used when creating the report format.

Use the List Reports command to view the report formats associated with a database.

In the next chapter, we'll learn techniques for customizing displays and editing forms on the screen.

7

TAILORING
SCREEN
DISPLAYS

In this chapter, we'll discuss techniques for creating custom forms for entering and editing table rows. The techniques used to create custom forms are similar to those that we used to create custom reports.

If you are following along on-line, make sure that the Mail database is open and that the R > prompt is displayed.

∎ CREATING CUSTOM FORMS

There are two primary reasons for creating custom forms: 1) they generally look better than the standard displays, and 2) you can add helpful advice to your screens to simplify the process of entering and editing data.

Let's look at an example. Figure 7.1 shows the standard display used for entering rows with the Load *table* with Prompts command. Figure 7.2 shows a custom form. Notice how the column names are spelled out (for example, Entry Date rather than Ent:Date) and that the instructions for managing the highlighting and cursor appear at the bottom of the screen.

To create custom forms in R:BASE, use Forms Express to "draw" a facsimile of the form on the screen, in much the same way that you used Reports Express to draw a facsimile of printed reports in the last chapter.

```
R>LOAD Names WITH PROMPTS
  Begin R:BASE Data Loading

  Press [ESC] to end, [ENTER] to continue
  L:Name    (TEXT    ):Janda
  F:Name    (TEXT    ):Creah
  Company   (TEXT    ):UCLA Medical Center
  Address   (TEXT    ):345 Westwood Blvd.
  City      (TEXT    ):Los Angeles
  State     (TEXT    ):CA
  Zip       (TEXT    ):92112
  Ent:Date  (DATE    ):12/01/86_
```

∎ *Figure 7.1:*
The Load with Prompts display.

As with Reports Express, you can enter Forms Express using any of three different techniques. From the RBSystem Main menu, select the Forms Express option. From the Prompt menu, select Data Input and Forms, and then Execute. From the R> prompt, type in the command

■   FORMS

and press Enter.

If, upon entering Forms Express, there is no database open, you'll be given the opportunity to Choose a Database. When a database is open, Forms Express displays the menu options below:

■   (1) Edit/Create a form
    (2) List forms
    (3) Copy a form
    (4) Remove a form
    (5) Return to Forms EXPRESS Main Menu

To create a new form or change an existing one, select option (1). R:BASE asks that you choose a form or select (New) to create a new form. For this exercise, select (New). R:BASE asks that you

■   Enter the form name:

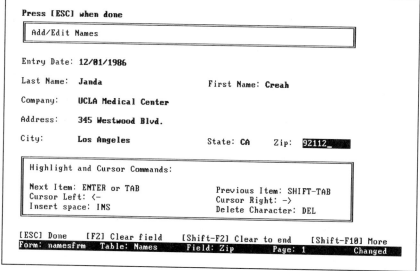

■ *Figure 7.2:*
Custom form for entering and editing data.

For our first sample form, type in NamesFrm and press Enter. Next, the screen will ask

■   Do you want to customize form characteristics? Yes No

You can customize the form later, so just select No for now. The screen then displays the names of tables in the open database and asks that you select a table for the form. For this example, select Names.

Next the screen asks

■   Do you want to customize table characteristics? Yes No

There is no need for this yet, so select No for the time being. Next the Form Definition menu appears (which resembles the Report Definition menu), presenting the following options:

■   Edit   Expression   Customize   Draw

The Edit option allows you to "draw" your form on the screen and locate column names in much the same way that you would on a report format screen. The keys used for creating forms are listed in Figure 7.3. (Additional keys can be used when creating more complicated forms, which we'll discuss in Chapter 11.)

Key	Purpose
F1	Insert a blank line above the cursor
F2	Delete the current line
F3	Display column and variable names
F4	Repeat a character
F6	Locate or relocate a column name or variable
F10	Display a help screen
Shift-F10	Display more function keys at the bottom of the screen
Ins	Insert a space at the cursor
Del	Delete the character at the cursor
↑	Move the cursor up one line
↓	Move the cursor down one line

■ *Figure 7.3:*
Keys used to create and edit forms.

Key	Purpose
→	Move the cursor right one character
←	Move the cursor left one character
Ctrl-→	Move the cursor to the right of the screen
Ctrl-←	Move the cursor to the left of the screen
Tab	Move the cursor ten spaces to the right
Shift-Tab	Move the cursor ten spaces to the left
Home	Move the cursor to the top left of the screen (or page)
End	Move the cursor to the bottom right of the screen (or page)
Enter	(◄─┘) Move the cursor down a line
Esc	Finish the current task and bring back the previous menu

■ *Figure 7.3:*
Keys used to create and edit forms.
(continued)

Select Edit from the menu so that the menu disappears and the cursor is on the screen ready to lay out the form format. To begin creating the form we displayed earlier, use the arrow keys to move the cursor to row 2, column 3 (as indicated by the symbol <2,3> at the bottom-right corner of the screen), and type in the title

■   Add/Edit Names

Given your experience in drawing report formats in the last chapter, you should be able to move the cursor easily to any location you wish using the arrow keys. (In fact, forms are much easier to draw because there is no need for headings, detail lines, footings, and so forth.) The starting locations for the various prompts on the NamesFrm form are listed below. Position the cursor to the coordinates listed in the left column, and type in the prompts listed in the right column. Figure 7.4 shows how your screen should look after typing in all the prompts.

Location	Prompt
<2,3>	Add/Edit Names
<5,1>	Entry Date:
<7,1>	Last Name:
<7,40>	First Name:
<9,1>	Company:
<11,1>	Address:
<13,1>	City:
<13,40>	State:
<13,54>	Zip:

<16,3>	Highlight and Cursor Commands:
<18,3>	Next Item: ENTER or TAB
<18,42>	Previous Item: SHIFT-TAB
<19,3>	Cursor Left: ←
<19,42>	Cursor Right: →
<20,3>	Insert Space: INS
<20,42>	Delete Character: DEL

Locating Column Names

After all the prompts are on the screen, locate the column names on the screen using the same techniques we used to locate columns and variables on the report format. For example, to locate the Ent:Date field next to the Entry Date prompt, move the cursor to row 5, column 13 <5,13>, and press the F6 key. R:BASE will ask that you

∎ Enter column or variable name:
   (Press [ENTER] for menu selection)

(If at some point you cannot remember the name of a column or variable, you can press the Enter key to select the appropriate column name from a menu.) For this example, type in **Ent:Date** and press Enter.
   R:BASE asks the following:

∎ Do you want to define an expression for Ent:Date? Yes No

```
   Add/Edit Names


   Entry Date:

   Last Name:                     First Name:

   Company:

   Address:

   City:                          State:      Zip:


   Highlight and Cursor Commands:

   Next Item: ENTER or TAB        Previous Item: SHIFT-TAB
   Cursor Left: <-                Cursor Right: ->
   Insert space: INS              Delete Character: DEL_


   [ESC] Return  [F1] Insert  [F2] Delete  [F3] Review  [Shift-F10] More
   Form: NamesFrm   Edit        Table: Names              Page 1  <20,61>
```

∎ *Figure 7.4:*
Prompts typed
into the form.

Since Ent:Date is a column name, we don't need to define an expression for it, so select No. R:BASE then asks

■ Do you want to customize field characteristics? Yes No

We can customize the form later for a fancier display, so for now just select No.

Next R:BASE asks that you

■ Move cursor to start location and press [S]

With the cursor on <5,13>, press the letter S on your keyboard. The S appears on the screen and the cursor jumps to <5,42>. The screen displays

■ Move cursor to end and press [E]

With the cursor on <5,42>, type the letter E. That completes the job of locating the Ent:Date column name on the form. You'll see the S and the E for the Ent:Date column name next to the Entry Date prompt, as in Figure 7.5.

Use the same technique of positioning the cursor, pressing F6, and typing S and E to place the rest of the column names on the form. You

```
    Add/Edit Names

   Entry Date: S                    E_

   Last Name:                 First Name:

   Company:

   Address:

   City:                      State:     Zip:


   Highlight and Cursor Commands:

   Next Item: ENTER or TAB         Previous Item: SHIFT-TAB
   Cursor Left: <-                 Cursor Right: ->
   Insert space: INS               Delete Character: DEL


 [ESC] Return  [F1] Insert  [F2] Delete  [F3] Review  [Shift-F10] More
 Form: namesfrm   Edit            Table: Names            Page 1  < 5,43>
```

■ *Figure 7.5:*
Start and end locations for the Ent:Date column.

can answer No to the two "Yes No" questions that appear on the screen for each of these column names. The column names, start locations, and end locations to use on this form are listed below:

Column Name	Start	End
L:Name	<7,13>	<7,23>
F:Name	<7,52>	<7,66>
Company	<9,13>	<9,32>
Address	<11,13>	<11,37>
City	<13,13>	<13,27>
State	<13,47>	<13,51>
Zip	<13,60>	<13,69>

After you're finished locating all of the column names, press Esc. Your screen should look like Figure 7.6.

Drawing Boxes on the Screen

For a fancier display, you can add double- or single-bar boxes. To do so, select Draw from the top menu. The submenu displays the options

∎   Single line   Double line   Erase

Select **Double line** to draw a double-line box.

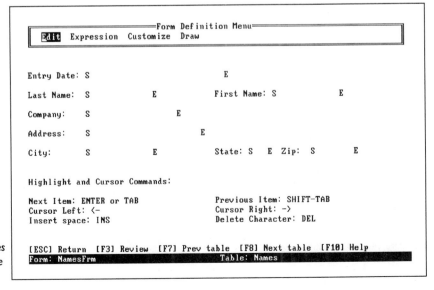

∎ *Figure 7.6:*
Column names
located on the
screen.

Notice that in the upper-right corner the screen displays Pen Up. This indicates that you can freely move the cursor without drawing anything on the screen. Let's draw a box around the screen title at the top of the screen.

With the Pen Up indicator still on, move the cursor to <1,3>. To put the pen down, press the F4 key (the upper-right corner now reads Pen Down). Hold down or repeatedly press the right arrow key until the cursor gets to <1,70>. You'll notice that with Pen Down, the cursor draws the double line as it moves. Press the down arrow key twice to move the cursor to <3,70>. Hold down the left arrow key until the cursor reaches <3,1>. Press the up arrow key twice to move the cursor to <1,1>. Now press the right arrow key to move the cursor to <1,4>. That completes the box drawn around the title.

Note that it is easier to draw boxes if you do not start on a corner, which is why we began this box at <1,3> rather than <1,1>.

To draw a box around the instructions at the bottom of the screen, first press F4 to lift the pen (Pen Up). Move the cursor to <15,3>. Press F4 to put the pen back down; then press the right arrow until the cursor reaches <15,70>. Press the down arrow repeatedly to move the cursor to <21,70>. Press the left arrow until the cursor reaches <21,1>. Press the up arrow to move the cursor to <15,1>; then press the right arrow to move the cursor to <15,4>. Press F4 to lift the pen. Figure 7.7 shows the form with the boxes added.

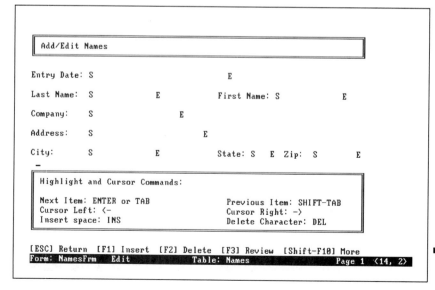

■ *Figure 7.7:*
Boxes drawn on the custom form.

When you are finished, press the Esc key. The top menu for drawing boxes appears on the screen again. The Single Line option works in the same fashion as the Double Line option we just used, but it draws only a single thin line. The Erase option erases either single or double lines as you move the cursor over the lines with the pen down.

Press Esc to leave the Draw menu and return to the Form Definition menu. For now, we're done drawing our form, so press Esc again to view the exit options, as listed below:

∎   Save Changes   Discard Changes   Return

As with Reports Express, selecting Save Changes saves you work and brings you to a higher-level menu. Select options (5) and (4) from the next menus that appear to work your way back to where you started (either the RBSystem Main menu, the Prompt menu, or the R> prompt).

∎ USING A FORM FOR DATA ENTRY

To enter new data using the new form, type in the Enter command, followed by the name of the form. For this example, type in the command

∎   ENTER NamesFrm

and press the Enter key. The form appears on the screen, as shown in Figure 7.8.

Type data into the highlighted area, and then press Enter to move the highlighting to the next prompt. You can move from item to item using the Tab key. You can move the cursor within the highlighted area by using the arrow keys. Use the Ins and Del keys to insert and delete characters inside the highlighted area. Figure 7.9 shows the NamesFrm screen with data for a new row. If you're following along on-line, type these data into the screen.

After you've entered all the data on the screen, a menu will appear at the top of the screen, as follows:

∎

| Add | Duplicate | Edit again | Discard | Quit |

These options are summarized below:

Add
: Adds the data on the screen to the table in the database, thereby saving it. The screen is then cleared so that you can enter another record (row).

Duplicate
: Adds the data on the screen to the database, but does not clear the entry from the screen. Useful for entering records that are similar; for example, many individuals who work for the same company and therefore have the same company name and address.

Edit Again
: Does not save the information on the screen, but instead lets you make further changes before saving the data.

Discard
: Removes the data from the screen and from the database as well if already saved. (Asks for permission first.)

Quit
: Leaves the data-entry mode after saving the current data, and returns to the R > prompt or the Prompt menu.

This menu appears each time you fill in all the prompts on the form. You can also call this menu up at any time while using the form by

```
Press [ESC] when done
┌──────────────────────────────────────────────────────┐
│ Add/Edit Names                                         │
└──────────────────────────────────────────────────────┘

Entry Date: ▐
Last Name:                    First Name:
Company:
Address:
City:                         State:     Zip:

┌──────────────────────────────────────────────────────┐
│ Highlight and Cursor Commands:                         │
│                                                        │
│ Next Item: ENTER or TAB          Previous Item: SHIFT-TAB │
│ Cursor Left: <-                  Cursor Right: ->        │
│ Insert space: INS                Delete Character: DEL   │
└──────────────────────────────────────────────────────┘

[ESC] Done    [F2] Clear field    [Shift-F2] Clear to end    [Shift-F10] More
Form: namesfrm    Table: Names      Field: Ent:Date    Page: 1        Changed
```

■ *Figure 7.8:*
The NamesFrm form on the screen.

pressing the Esc key. Now select the Add option to add the data to the Names table.

The form remains on the screen, but the data are erased. Go ahead and fill out the screen once again, so that it looks like Figure 7.10.

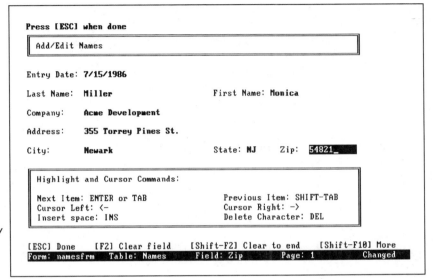

■ *Figure 7.9:*
Data for one new row typed in the NamesFrm screen.

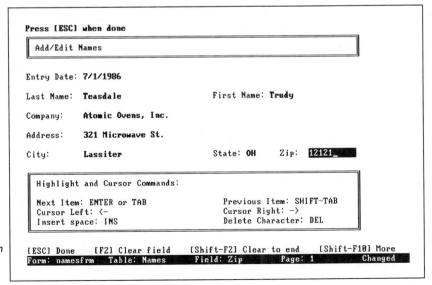

■ *Figure 7.10:*
Entry form with another row typed in.

Suppose that you were about to add another row of data for a person who works at this same company. You could save yourself some typing by selecting the Duplicate option rather than the Add option. The Duplicate option will store these data in the Names table and also keep them on the screen for the next row. Now, just change the Last Name field to **Martin** and the First Name field to **Mary,** so the screen looks like Figure 7.11.

To save these data, press the Esc key and select the Add option. When you're finished entering data, select the Quit option.

From the R> prompt, you can verify that the new data have been added to the table by entering the command

■   SELECT ALL FROM Names

You'll see the new rows at the bottom of the table, as shown in Figure 7.12.

The same form that you created to enter data can also be used to edit data, as we'll discuss next.

■ EDITING DATA WITH CUSTOM FORMS

To edit data using a custom form, use the Edit Using command, followed by the name of the form. For this example, at the R> prompt, enter the command

■   EDIT USING NamesFrm

The first row from the table appears on the screen, along with a menu of editing options, as shown in Figure 7.13.

You can move the highlighting with the Tab and Shift-Tab keys, and you can make changes within the highlighted area using the arrow, Ins, and Del keys. After making the necessary changes, press the Esc key and bring back the menu. You can then select any of the options from the menu, as listed below:

Option	Function
Edit	Move the cursor into the form to make changes
Save	Save current changes on the screen

Add New   Enter modified data into the database as a new row, and leave the original row in the database unchanged

Delete   Delete the row from the table

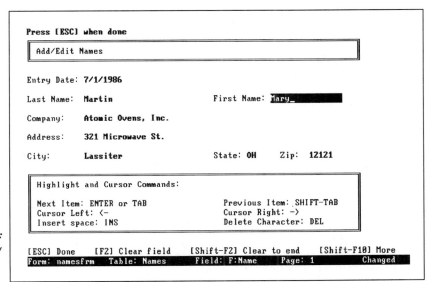

```
Press [ESC] when done
┌─────────────────────────────────────────────────────────────────┐
│ Add/Edit Names                                                    │
└─────────────────────────────────────────────────────────────────┘

Entry Date: 7/1/1986

Last Name:  Martin                First Name: Mary_

Company:    Atomic Ovens, Inc.

Address:    321 Microwave St.

City:       Lassiter              State: OH    Zip:  12121

┌─────────────────────────────────────────────────────────────────┐
│ Highlight and Cursor Commands:                                    │
│                                                                   │
│ Next Item: ENTER or TAB              Previous Item: SHIFT-TAB      │
│ Cursor Left: <-                      Cursor Right: ->             │
│ Insert space: INS                    Delete Character: DEL         │
└─────────────────────────────────────────────────────────────────┘

[ESC] Done    [F2] Clear field   [Shift-F2] Clear to end    [Shift-F10] More
Form: namesfrm   Table: Names        Field: F:Name     Page: 1        Changed
```

∎ **Figure 7.11:**
Third new row added to the Names table.

```
R>SELECT ALL FROM Names
L:Name           F:Name        Company             Address
───────────────  ───────────   ──────────────────  ──────────────────
Smith            Sandy         Hi Tech, Inc.       456 N. Rainbow Dr.
Jones            Mindy         ABC Co.             123 A St.
Miller           Marie         Zeerox Inc.         234 C St.
Adams            Bart          DataSpec Inc.       P.O. Box 2890
Miller           Anne          Golden Gate Co.     2313 Sixth St.
Baker            Robin         Peach Computers     2311 Coast Hwy
Miller           Monica        Acme Development    355 Torrey Pines St.
Teasdale         Trudy         Atomic Ovens, Inc.  321 Microwave St.
Martin           Mary          Atomic Ovens, Inc.  321 Microwave St.
R>_
```

∎ **Figure 7.12:**
New rows added to the Names table.

Reset	Undo the latest edits (assuming they have not already been saved on the database)
Previous	Save any changes made to the current row; then skip to the previous row in the table (when only one table is being edited)
Next	Save any changes in the current row; then skip to the next row in the table (when only one table is being edited)
Quit	Return to the R> prompt or the Prompt menu

The general procedure for editing records in a table is to pinpoint the row to edit using the Next and Previous options from the menu. Once the row to edit is on the screen, select the Edit option and make the necessary changes using the arrow, Tab, Ins, Del, and other keys to move the highlight and the cursor. While the cursor is inside the form for editing, you can also use the following keys (as indicated at the bottom of the screen):

F2	Empty the entire currently highlighted field
Shift-F2	Delete the contents of the currently highlighted field to the right of the cursor
F5	Bring back the unedited contents of the currently highlighted field
F7	Skip back to the previous row in the table
F8	Skip to the next row in the table
F10	Display help
Shift-F10	Show more function keys at the bottom of the screen
Esc	Return to the top menu

When you've finished editing the row, press Esc to bring back the top menu. Selecting Save, Add New, Previous, Next, or Quit will save all the changes you've made. Selecting Reset (before selecting any of the other commands) will undo all the changes you've just made. You may want to practice on your own to get used to editing with the form.

The process of looking for the rows that you want to edit can be sped up considerably by using the Sorted By and Where clauses. For example, if you want to edit the data for somebody with the last name of Miller, from the R> prompt you can enter the command

■   EDIT USING NamesFrm WHERE L:Name = Miller

Each time you select the Next option from the top menu, another Miller will be displayed. After the last Miller is displayed, R:BASE will beep to indicate that there are no more Millers left.

To skip through the Millers in alphabetical order by first name while editing, you can enter the command

■   EDIT USING NamesFrm SORTED BY F:Name WHERE +
     L:Name = Miller

If you specifically want to edit data for Marie Miller, you can enter the command

■   EDIT USING NamesFrm WHERE L:Name = Miller AND +
     F:Name = Marie

This single row will be displayed for editing. Select the Edit option and make your changes.

You can also use the edit mode to add new data. Suppose you want to add the name of someone who works at a company already listed in the table (ABC Co., for example). Enter the command

■   EDIT USING NamesFrm WHERE Company = "ABC Co."

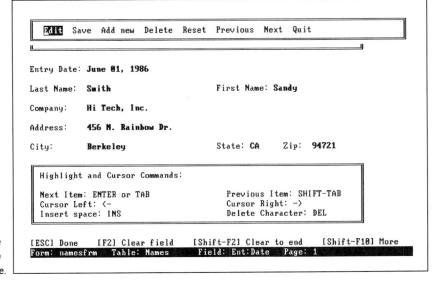

■ *Figure 7.13:*
Data from the first row of the Names table in edit using mode.

The form will appear containing all the data for the first row that contains ABC Co. Select the Edit option, and change whatever is necessary for the new row—probably the L:Name, F:Name, and Ent:Date columns. Then, press Esc and select Add New. The new row will be added to the table, and the original row will be left unchanged.

■ EDITING EXISTING FORMS

To modify an existing form, enter Forms Express again (by entering the command Forms at the R > prompt). From the first menu to appear, select (1) (Edit/Create a Form), and then select the name of the form to edit when R:BASE displays the next menu.

You can use the Edit option from the top menu to change and enter prompts. You can use the Draw option to enter and change boxes. Use the Ins, Del, F1, and F2 keys on the screen to make changes.

To change a location of a field on the form, move the cursor anywhere between the S and E for the field. Press the F6 key as though entering the field for the first time. The screen will ask if you want to customize the characteristics for the field. Select No (we'll discuss *field characteristics* later). R:BASE will ask if you want to relocate the field. Select Yes. R:BASE will eliminate the current location for the field and allow you to reenter the start and end locations for the field.

To delete a field from the screen, move the cursor to any position between the S and the E, and type Shift-F2.

Other ways in which you can customize forms are discussed in the following sections.

■ CUSTOMIZING FORM CHARACTERISTICS

You can customize several overall features of a form, such as its color and top-menu display. To do so, select Customize from the top menu and Form from the submenu. You'll see a screen, as in Figure 7.14, displaying all your options for customizing the overall form. (This same form will appear if you answer Yes to the opening question about customizing form characteristics when you are creating a new form.)

You can use the up and down arrow keys to move the highlight from question to question. Typing Y changes a No answer to Yes, and vice versa. Questions followed by an N/A are not applicable to the form being customized.

The first question on the form reads

■ Assign passwords for this form? .... [N/A]
Read-only password: _____ Modify password: _____

On tables that use password protection (a topic we'll discuss later), you can change this option to Yes, and then assign passwords for Read-only access and Modify access. If you assign a password for Read-only access, only users who know the password will be able to view data through this form. If you assign a Modify password, any user will be able to view data on the form, but only those who know the password will be able to change data on the form.

The second two questions on the screen are

■ Clear the screen before form use? .... [Yes]
Clear the screen after form use? .... [Yes]

Usually you'll want to leave these as Yes so that the form appears on a clear screen and erases itself from the screen when no longer in use.

The next question on the form:

■ Display a status line during form use? .... [Yes]

■ *Figure 7.14:*
Form
Customization
menu.

```
Press [ESC] when done
                        Form Characteristics
Assign passwords for this form? .......................................... [N/A]
      Read-only password: _____      Modify password: _____
Clear the screen before form use? ....................................... [Yes]
Clear the screen after form use? ........................................ [Yes]
Display a status line during form use? .................................. [Yes]
Do you want custom colors for the form? ................................. [No ]
      Foreground color: _____   Background color: _____
      (Press [ENTER] for a color palette)

Do you plan to use the form with the ENTER command? ..................... [Yes]
      Do you want to change the menu? ................................... [No ]
  ┌─────────────────────────────────────────────────────────────────────┐
  │ Add   Duplicate  Edit again  Discard  Quit                          │
  └─────────────────────────────────────────────────────────────────────┘
Do you plan to use the form with the EDIT command? ...................... [Yes]
      Do you want to change the menu? ................................... [No ]
  ┌─────────────────────────────────────────────────────────────────────┐
  │ Edit   Save  Add new  Delete  Reset  Previous  Next  Quit           │
  └─────────────────────────────────────────────────────────────────────┘
[ESC] Done  [F5] Reset  [F10] Help  [↑] Up  [↓] Down
Form: namesfrm   Customize              Table: Names
```

lets you decide whether to leave the status bar on the bottom of the screen while the form is in use [Yes] or to hide it while the form is in use [No].

The next question, shown below, refers to color monitors:

■   Do you want custom colors for the form? .... [No]
    Foreground color: _____ Background color: _____
    (Press [ENTER] for a color palette)

If you change this answer to Yes, you can then press the Enter key twice for a palette of colors to select from. Select the colors for the form in the same fashion as you would using the Set Color command, and then press Esc.

The next question asks whether the form will be used with the Enter command (for entering new data into the table). Usually, you will want to leave this as a Yes answer:

■   Do you plan to use the form with the ENTER command? ...... [Yes]

If you do want to use the Enter command, you can change the menu that automatically appears at the top of the form when you use the Enter command, as the next question in the form indicates:

■   Do you want to change the menu? .... [No]

    Add   Duplicate   Edit again   Discard   Quit

If you select Yes (by typing Y and pressing Enter), R:BASE will ask if you wish to enter a title, which will appear above the menu. Type in the title and press Enter.

Next R:BASE will display all the menu options that the menu can contain. You can select (All) the options or just the ones that you want to appear in the menu. You can also determine the order of the options in the menu by selecting them in the order in which you want them to appear (left to right).

The next question is

■   Do you plan to use the form with the EDIT command? .... [Yes]
    Do you want to change the menu? .... [No]

    Edit   Save   Add new   Delete   Reset   Previous   Next   Quit

As in the previous question, this one allows you to determine whether the form can be used with the Edit command, and it allows you to add a title and modify the top menu.

When you've finished selecting form characteristics, press the Esc key.

■ CUSTOMIZING TABLE CHARACTERISTICS

You can also customize several characteristics of the table associated with the form. Select Customize from the top menu, and then select Table and Characteristics from the submenus to do so. This brings up the Table Characteristics menu. (Also, when you create a new form, the Table Characteristics menu will appear if you select Yes to the opening prompt about customizing table characteristics.) Figure 7.15 shows the Table Characteristics menu on the screen.

The questions on the form are summarized below:

■ Do you want to add new rows to the table? .... [Yes]

```
Press [ESC] when done
                        Table Characteristics
Do you want to add new rows to the table? ............................. [Yes]

Do you want to replace existing rows in the table? ..................... [Yes]
     Is the replace automatic when the user leaves the row? ............ [Yes]

Do you want to delete rows from the table? ............................ [Yes]
     Restrict the delete to the current table? ........................ [Yes]

Is this table on the MANY side of a ONE-to-MANY relationship? ......... [N/A]

Do you want to define a region? ...................................... [No ]
     Do you want a border around the region? .......................... [N/A]
     How many lines in the border - enter 1 or 2: _
     Do you want custom colors for the region? ........................ [N/A]
     Foreground color: _____   Background color: _____
     (Press [ENTER] for a color palette)



[ESC] Done  [F5] Reset  [F10] Help  [↑] Up  [↓] Down
Form: namesfrm    Customize table         Table: Names
```

■ *Figure 7.15:* Table Characteristics menu on the screen.

Unless you do not ever want to add new rows to a table, this answer should be left as Yes. Similarly, the following three answers should be left as Yes unless the data on the table are never to be edited or deleted:

- Do you want to replace existing rows in the table? .... [Yes]
  Is the replace automatic when the user leaves the row? ....[Yes]
  Do you want to delete rows from the table? .... [Yes]
  Restrict the delete to the current table? .... [Yes]

The remaining questions on the menu are for more advanced applications. We'll discuss these in Chapter 11.

■ CUSTOMIZING FIELD CHARACTERISTICS

Whenever you locate, or relocate, a field on the form using the F6 key, the screen will ask if you want to customize the field characteristics. If you answer Yes to this question, the Field Characteristics menu appears on the screen, as in Figure 7.16.

Options on this menu affect only the individual field being located or relocated, not the overall form or table. The first questions

```
Press [ESC] when done
                   Field Characteristics
Will new data be entered in the field? ................................. [Yes]

Can the user change the data displayed in the field? ................... [Yes]
       Restrict changes to the current table? ........................... [Yes]

Do you want to display a default value in the field? ................... [No ]
       Enter the default value OR #DUP to use the previous row value
--------------------------------------------

Do you want custom colors for the field? .............................. [No ]
       Foreground color: _____  Background color: _____
       (Press [ENTER] for a color palette)




[ESC] Done  [F5] Reset  [F10] Help  [↑] Up  [↓] Down
Form: namesfrm   Column    Field: Ent:Date   Type: DATE     Table: Names
```

■ *Figure 7.16:*
Field Characteristics menu.

- Will new data be entered in the field? .... [Yes]
  Can the user change the data displayed in the field? .... [Yes]
  Restrict changes to the current table? .... [Yes]

should all be left with Yes answers, except in more advanced applications involving multiple tables. (Again, this is a topic we'll discuss in Chapter 11.)

The next question about default values will be discussed in detail in the next section.

The last question on the menu, shown below, lets you select color for the single field:

- Do you want custom colors for the field? .... [No]
  Foreground color: _____ Background color: _____
  (Press [ENTER] for a color palette)

Changing the answer to Yes and pressing the Enter key twice will allow you to define colors for the individual field from the color palette.

When you finish defining the field characteristics, press the Esc key to return to the process of locating or relocating the field.

■ DEFINING DEFAULT VALUES

Default values (also called *suggested responses*) are a valuable asset to forms, particularly in forms where information might have to be typed in repeatedly otherwise. For example, NamesFrm contains the column Ent:Date, which is the date that the row was entered into the database. On any given day, this is likely to be the same for every row entered into the database. Therefore, you could make the current date the *default value* for the field. When entering new rows into the database, the current date will automatically appear in the Ent:Date field. You (or whoever is entering the data) can just press the Enter key to accept the default date, or you can type in a new date.

Another example is the State column in the Names table. If 90% of the individuals in the table were from the state of California, you could make CA the default value for the field. That way, when entering data, you need only press Enter to skip over the State field and use the "suggested" value, CA, or you could type a different state into the field.

If you wanted to enter these default values into NamesFrm, you would call up Forms Express and the NamesFrm form. Select Edit to move the cursor to the screen, and place the cursor between the S and the E for the Ent:Date column name. Press F6, and the screen asks if you want to customize the field characteristic. Select Yes, and then change the answer to the question about default values to Yes and press Enter. Type in #DATE (which stands for the current date) as the default value. Press Esc and answer No to the prompt about relocating the field.

To make CA (or another state) the default value for the State field, move the cursor between the S and the E for the State field, and press F6. Select Yes to change the field characteristics and Yes to enter the default field. Type in CA (or whatever abbreviation you wish) as the default value, and press Enter. Answer No to the prompt about relocating the field.

The #DUP function is a special type of default value that repeats whatever was entered into the last row as the default value. An example where this would be useful would be when you are entering data for individuals from several states, but entering them grouped by states. If you entered AK residents first, AK would be the default value for all the records, until you typed in a new state on the form. The new state would be the default value in later records, until you typed in another new state.

When you are finished entering the default values for the fields, use the Esc key to work your way back to the exit options, and select Save Changes. From the R> prompt, enter the command

■   ENTER NamesFrm

to call up the form and enter new data. The form will appear with the default values already in their fields, as shown in Figure 7.17. Pressing Enter while the default value is highlighted accepts the suggested value as the entered data. Optionally, you can type over the suggested value (or use F2 to delete it) to enter a different value into the column.

■ CHANGING THE ORDER OF ENTRY TO FIELDS

When you create a form, the order in which you locate column names on the form determines the order in which R:BASE cycles through them when entering or editing data through the form. You can change the order in which R:BASE cycles the highlighter through the prompts by selecting Customize and Field Order from the top menu in Forms Express. When you select Field Order, you'll be given the following options:

∎   Reorder   Cycle

To change the order, select Reorder. R:BASE displays the current order in which it moves the highlighter through the form and allows you to define a new order. Simply type in the number of the item to reorder and its new position, as instructed on the screen. Press Esc when you are finished.

To test the new order, select the Cycle option from the menu. Press the Enter key repeatedly to see the order in which R:BASE will move the highlighter through the prompts. Press Esc when you are finished.

When you've determined the appropriate order for your form, press the Esc key a few times to get back to the Exit Options menu, and select Save Changes to save the new order.

∎ MANAGING FORMS

You can manage forms in the same way that you manage reports. The Forms Express Main menu lets you manage and view directories, as does the Reports Express Main menu.

```
Press [ESC] when done

┌────────────────────────────────────────────────────────────────┐
│ Add/Edit Names                                                   │
└────────────────────────────────────────────────────────────────┘

Entry Date: September 02, 1986

Last Name:                              First Name:

Company:

Address:

City:                                   State: CA    Zip:

┌─────────────────────────────────────────────────────────────┐
│ Highlight and Cursor Commands:                               │
│                                                              │
│ Next Item: ENTER or TAB            Previous Item: SHIFT-TAB   │
│ Cursor Left: <-                    Cursor Right: ->           │
│ Insert space: INS                  Delete Character: DEL      │
└─────────────────────────────────────────────────────────────┘

[ESC] Done    [F2] Clear field    [Shift-F2] Clear to end    [Shift-F10] More
Form: namesfrm   Table: Names      Field: Ent:Date   Page: 1
```

∎ *Figure 7.17:*
Default values in the Ent:Date and State fields.

The Form Options menu, shown below, allows you to edit, create, list the names of, copy, and remove forms.

■   (1) Edit/Create a form
      (2) List forms
      (3) Copy a form
      (4) Remove a form
      (5) Return to Forms EXPRESS Main Menu

These options work the same as they do under Reports Express.

■ SUMMARY

In this chapter we've discussed Forms Express and various techniques for creating and using custom forms. The important techniques we've discussed in the chapter are summarized below:

To create a custom form, enter Forms Express from the RBSystem Main menu or from the prompt mode, or enter the Forms command at the R> prompt.

The keys used to move the cursor while "drawing" a form on the screen, and used for locating column names, are similar to the keys used in Reports Express.

To draw boxes on the screen, select Draw from the top menu. Use the F4 key to lift and lower the "pen" while drawing boxes.

To use a custom form to enter new data, use the Enter command at the R> prompt, followed by the name of the form.

While entering data into a table through a custom form, press the Esc key to bring up the top menu of options.

To edit data using a custom form, use the command Edit Using followed by the name of the form at the R> prompt.

When creating or editing a custom form in Forms Express, the Customize option on the top menu allows you to further customize form, table, and individual field characteristics.

Default values (or suggested responses) can simplify data entry by suggesting a likely entry into a field. Use Field Customization to enter default values into a field.

The Forms Express Main menu and the Form Options menu provide options for managing forms.

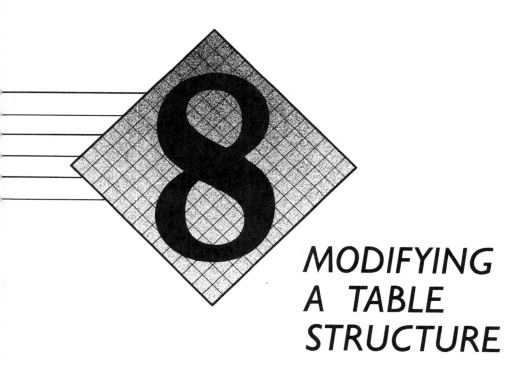

MODIFYING
A TABLE
STRUCTURE

Murphy's law dictates that after carefully planning a database structure and adding some data to it, you'll want to make some changes. For example, you might find that the assigned width of 20 characters is not enough for the Company column in the Names table. You might also decide that you want to add columns to the Names table for telephone numbers and customer numbers.

Once you've made the appropriate modifications to the basic structure of the table, you'll probably want to modify reports and forms accordingly. This chapter explains how to make these modifications.

If you are following along on-line, be sure that the Mail database is open and that the R > prompt is on the screen before you try out these examples.

■ CHANGING A COLUMN DEFINITION

The simplest type of table modification is changing the definition of a column. For example, let's change the width of the Company column from 20 to 25 characters. You use the Change Column command with the following syntax:

■ CHANGE COLUMN *column name* IN *table name*
  TO <*data type*> <*width*>

For our example, at the R > prompt enter the command

■ CHANGE COLUMN Company IN Names TO TEXT 25

The TEXT part of the command assigns the Text data type, and the 25 specifies the new width. (**Note:** Only the Text data type requires that you enter a width.)

That's all there is to it. If you give the command

■ SELECT ALL FROM Names

you'll notice that the column is, indeed, five characters wider. Later in the chapter, we'll change the reports and forms associated with the Names table to take advantage of the new width.

■ ADDING COLUMNS TO A TABLE

There are several ways to add new columns to a table, the easiest being to return to Definition Express (which we used to create the Mail database) and to insert the new columns directly into the table.

Like Forms and Reports Express, you can enter Definition Express in any of three ways. From the R> prompt, simply type in the command

■   RBDEFINE

and press Enter. From the Prompt menu, select Modify a Database and RBDefine from the submenu. From the RBSystem Main menu, you can select the Definition Express option.

The Definition Express Main menu, which appears when you first enter Definition Express, displays the following options:

■   (1) Define a new database
     (2) Modify an existing database definition
     (3) DOS functions
     (4) Exit from Definition EXPRESS

To modify an existing database, select option (2). When you do so, the Database Definition menu will appear and present the options below:

■   (1) Tables
     (2) Views
     (3) Passwords
     (4) Rules
     (5) Forms
     (6) Reports
     (7) Return to Definition EXPRESS Main Menu

In this case, we want to add some columns to the Names table, so select option (1). The Tables menu displays the following options:

■   (1) Add a new table to the database
     (2) Change an existing table
     (3) Remove a table from the database
     (4) Return to the Database Definition Menu

You want to change an existing table structure, so select option (2). The screen will ask for the name of the table to change. Select Names. The table structure appears on the screen as in Figure 8.1.

You can change the table name or any of the column names simply by positioning the cursor with the arrow keys or the Tab key and typing in the new name. You can use the F1 key to insert a column and the F2 key to delete a column. Let's try it out.

First, press the down arrow key to move the highlighter to the L:Name column name. Press F1 to insert a new column. All other column names shift one space to the right. Type in the new column name

■ CustNo

and press Enter. Select Integer as the column type. When the screen asks

■ Do you want this to be a key column?

select No.

Figure 8.2 shows how the screen looks after adding the CustNo (Customer Number) column, as the Integer data type, into the Names table.

Now suppose you also want to add a column for storing phone numbers. First, what data type should a phone number be? Granted, a phone number consists mostly of numbers, but of course it also consists

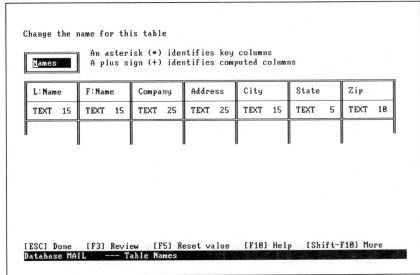

■ *Figure 8.1:*
Names table structure on the screen.

of some nonnumeric characters such as parentheses and a hyphen (for example, (818)555-1212). Therefore, since phone numbers are not truly numbers, they should be treated as Text data. A length of 13 characters should be adequate for storing phone numbers.

To add a column named Phone to the Names table, first press the End key to move the highlighter to the right side of the column names. Type in the column name

■ Phone

and press the Enter key. Select Text as the column type, and enter 13 as the column width when requested. When the screen asks if this should be a key column, select No. Figure 8.3 shows the Names column with the new Phone column added.

Note that you cannot change definitions of existing columns while in Definition Express (when you press the down arrow to change the type definition in an existing column, R:BASE just beeps at you). Use the Change Column command at the R > prompt, which we discussed in the last section, to change column data types and widths.

When you have finished making changes to the table structure, press the Esc key. You can exit Definition Express by working your way back through the menus (select options (4), (7), and (4)).

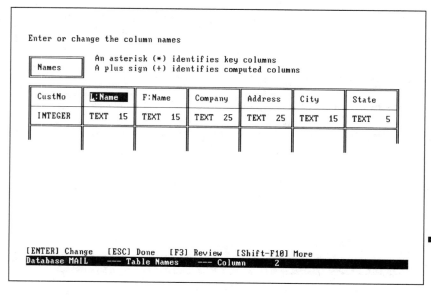

■ Figure 8.2:
CustNo column added to the Names table.

To fill in data for the new columns, make sure you are at the R> prompt and the Mail database is open. Then enter the command

∎ EDIT CustNo L:Name F:Name Phone FROM Names

The screen should look like Figure 8.4.

Notice that the new columns contain null characters (-0-), since there are no data in them. Go ahead and type the data shown in Figure 8.5 in these columns. Press the Esc key after you've filled in the new data.

∎ *MODIFYING REPORTS*

The addition of the CustNo and Phone columns will not affect the Labels or Letter1 reports we developed earlier, but the Director report should be modified to display these new columns. (Alternatively, you could create a fourth report format to display these new data.) In this section, we'll revise the Director report so that it appears as shown in Figure 8.6.

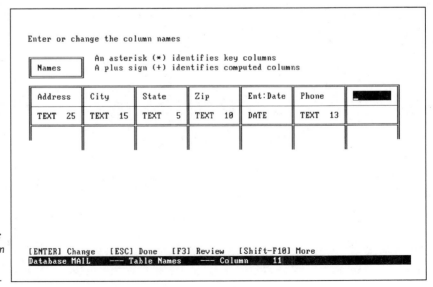

∎ *Figure 8.3:*
Phone column added to the Names table.

The first step in modifying the report is to enter the Reports Express by typing

■ REPORTS

```
                   Press [ESC] when done, [F2] to delete, [F5] to reset
   CustNo    L:Name           F:Name           Phone
   ---------- ---------------- ---------------- ----------------
   -0-        Smith            Sandy            -0-
   -0-        Jones            Mindy            -0-
   -0-        Miller           Marie            -0-
   -0-        Adams            Bart             -0-
   -0-        Miller           Anne             -0-
   -0-        Baker            Robin            -0-
   -0-        Miller           Monica           -0-
   -0-        Teasdale         Trudy            -0-
   -0-        Martin           Mary             -0-
```

■ *Figure 8.4:*
Names table with new columns displayed.

```
                   Press [ESC] when done, [F2] to delete, [F5] to reset
   CustNo    L:Name           F:Name           Phone
   ---------- ---------------- ---------------- ----------------
       1001  Smith            Sandy            (123)555-1212
       1002  Jones            Mindy            (123)555-1010
       1003  Miller           Marie            (123)555-2222
       1004  Adams            Bart             (213)123-4567
       1005  Miller           Anne             (213)234-5678
       1006  Baker            Robin            (345)678-9012
       1007  Miller           Monica           (345)678-1111
       1008  Teasdale         Trudy            (619)455-7442
       1010  Martin           Mary             (619)555-1010
```

■ *Figure 8.5:*
Names table with data in the new columns.

at the R> prompt. Select (1) from the first menu, and select the report name, Director, when requested. From the Reports menu, select the Edit option.

For our modified report, we'll indent the FullName and Address columns a bit and add the CustNo to the left column next to FullName. Then, we'll put the Phone column data under the Ent:Date column.

One way to reposition a column name or variable on the report format is to move the cursor between the S and the E for the appropriate column name or variable and then press F6. (If you are not sure which S and E the cursor is positioned on at a particular moment, press the F3 key. The column or variable name appears at the top of the screen.)

Mailing List Directory

06/05/86		Page: 1
1001 Smith, Sandy	Hi Tech, Inc.	06/01/86
456 N. Rainbow Dr.	Berkeley, CA 94721	(123)555-1212
1002 Jones, Andy	ABC Co.	06/15/86
123 A St.	San Diego, CA 92122	(123)555-1010
1003 Miller, Marie	Zeerox Inc.	06/01/86
234 C St.	Los Angeles, CA 91234	(123)555-2222
1004 Adams, Bart	DataSpec Inc.	06/15/86
P.O. Box 2890	Malibu, CA 92111	(213)123-4567
1005 Miller, Anne	Golden Gate Co.	06/01/86
2313 Sixth St.	Berkeley, CA 94711	(213)234-5678
1006 Baker, Robin	Peach Computers	06/15/86
2311 Coast Hwy.	San Diego, CA 92112	(345)678-9012
1007 Miller, Monica	Acme Development	07/15/86
355 Torrey Pines St.	Newark, NJ 54321	(345)678-1111
1008 Teasdale, Trudy	Atomic Ovens, Inc.	07/01/86
321 Microwave St.	Lassiter, OH 12121	(619)455-7442
1009 Martin, Mary	Atomic Ovens, Inc.	07/01/86
321 Microwave St.	Lassiter, OH 12121	(619)555-1310

∎ *Figure 8.6:*
New format for the Director report.

You can also move column or variable names by inserting spaces with the Ins key. For this report, try doing so now. First, move the cursor to row 5, column 1 (so that the indicator reads <5:7,1>). Press the Ins key five times to shift everything to the right five spaces. Place the CustNo field name in this new space by pressing F6 and typing in the column name CustNo. Make <5:7,1> the start location; then move the cursor to <5:7,5> and type E to mark the end location.

To realign the Company column with the column beneath, move the cursor between the S and the E for the Company. (Remember, if you are not sure which S and E the cursor is between, press the F3 key and look at the top of the screen.) Press F6 and relocate the Company column so that it starts at <5:7,37> and ends at <5:7,37>.

To realign the Address column under the FullName variable, press the down arrow and Ctrl-left arrow so the cursor moves to <6:7,1>. Press the Ins key twice to insert a couple of blank spaces. You'll need to shorten the FullCSZ field to make room for the phone number. Move the cursor to <6:7,37> and press F6. Make <6:7,36> the start location, and move the cursor to <6:7,61> and mark that as the end location.

To place the phone number, move the cursor to <6:7,63>. Press F6 and type in the column name Phone (and press Enter). Start the Phone number at <6:7,63> and end it at <6:7,65>. Figure 8.7 shows the modified Director report format on the screen.

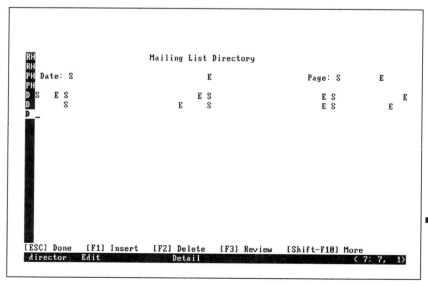

■ *Figure 8.7:*
Director report format with CustNo and Phone added.

You can add columns to a table and delete columns from a table using the F1 and F2 keys in Definition Express.

After changing a table structure, you can use Reports Express and Forms Express to modify existing reports and forms to match the new table structure.

9

MANAGING
MULTIPLE
TABLES

In this chapter, we'll add a new table to the Mail database and explore techniques for setting up a relationship between two tables. We'll also discuss techniques for defining *rules,* which help catch errors before they are stored in a table.

■ DESIGNING RELATIONSHIPS INTO TABLES

Let's start expanding the Mail database so that it can serve as a sales-register system. To do so, we need to add another table to record individual charge transactions. For each charge, we want to record the amount of the charge, the date, and the items purchased.

Since it is likely that each customer will charge many purchases, it makes no sense to record the name and address along with every charge transaction. Instead, we need a *code* that relates numerous charge transactions to an individual in the Names table. We don't want to use last name as this code because it is not accurate enough. For example, if we recorded a charge made by "Smith," we'd have problems sending the bill to the correct individual if there were 20 Smiths listed in the Names table. We could use both first and last name to improve the accuracy, but even this is risky.

A better approach is to use the unique *customer number* that we assigned to each person in the Names table (we did this in the last chapter). Then, the table for charge transactions needs to record only the customer number to set up a link that will eliminate any confusion in billing.

This approach of dividing the data into two separate tables within the database is known as creating a *one-to-many* relationship among the tables. This relationship is so named because for every *one* row on one table, there may be *many* related rows on another table. In this example, for every one individual in the Names table, there may be many individual sales-transaction records stored in the Charges table.

■ ADDING A NEW TABLE TO A DATABASE

Take a moment to look at the structure for the Charges table, described below:

Name	Type	Length	Description
CustNo	Integer		Customer number
ProdNo	Text	8	Product number

Qty	Integer	Quantity purchased
U:Price	Currency	Unit price (as sold)
Tax?	Integer	Is item taxable?
Total	Currency	Calculated total
P:Date	Date	Date of purchase

The customer number (CustNo) will be the key field to relate data from the Charges table to individuals in the Names table. As in the Names table, its data type is Integer. The ProdNo column will store the product number of the item purchased. We could later add an Inventory table listing items in stock to our Mail database and use the ProdNo column to link the Charges table with items in the Inventory table. Each transaction would then reduce the quantity of the product shown to be in inventory. The ProdNo column is Text data with a length of eight characters. Using the Text data type will allow you to enter hyphenated numbers, such as A-111.

The Qty column is for recording the quantity of items purchased. The U:Price column is for the unit price of items purchased. Its data type is Currency, which will cause numbers to be displayed with a leading dollar sign and two decimal places.

The Tax? column will contain a 1 for taxable items or a 0 for nontaxable items. The Total column will contain the total of the row—either the quantity times the unit price for nontaxable items or the quantity times the unit price plus 6% sales tax for taxable items. R:BASE will calculate the total automatically, so you don't need to fill in this column when you're entering data. The P:Date column will store the date of the purchase.

The easiest way to add this new table to a database is through Definition Express. Recall that you can enter Definition Express by entering the command RBDefine at the R> prompt. From the Definition Express Main menu, select option (2), Modify an Existing Database Definition. From the Database Definition menu, select option (1), Tables. From the Tables menu, select option (1), Add a New Table to the Database.

You've already entered column names and data types through Definition Express in earlier chapters, so you should have no trouble creating the Charges table now, although there are a few new twists that deserve some explanation.

Enter the table name Charges in the top box. When entering the column names discussed below, select No each time the screen asks if the column should be a key column. Enter CustNo as the first column name. R:BASE will automatically assign Integer as the data type since the CustNo column name was previously defined in the Names table. Enter ProdNo as the second column name, and select Text as the data type and a length of eight characters. Enter Qty as the third column name, and select Integer as the data type. Enter U:Price as the fourth column name, and select Currency as the data type. Enter Tax? as the fifth column name, and select Integer as the data type.

For the sixth column, enter Total as the column name. Select Computed as the data type. R:BASE will ask that you

■   Enter expression value:

What R:BASE needs to know is how to compute the data in this column. If there were not a Tax? column in this table, the expression could simply be *(Qty★U:Price),* which means the Qty field times the U:Price field. However, we need to find a way to tell R:BASE that if the item is not taxable, then the total for the row is indeed (Qty★U:Price). However, if the item is taxable, then the total is ((Qty★U:Price)★1.06), assuming 6% sales tax. (If the sales tax were 6.5%, the expression would be (Qty★U:Price)★1.065.)

We can use an R:BASE *function* to help solve this problem. First, we need to know how to determine whether an item is taxable, so let's make up a rule. If the Tax? column contains the number 0, the item is not taxable. If the Tax? column contains the number 1, the item is taxable.

Given this knowledge, we can use the IFEQ function to calculate the total for the transaction. The IFEQ function uses this syntax:

■   IFEQ(<this item>,<=this item>,<then this>,<else this>)

The exact expression for you to enter onto the screen is

■   (IFEQ(Tax?,0,Qty★U:Price,(Qty★U:Price)★1.06))

In English, this expression means, "If the Tax? column equals 0, calculate the quantity times the unit price; otherwise calculate the quantity times the unit price times the tax rate."

IFEQ is just one of many functions that R:BASE offers. We'll discuss other functions in Chapter 14. After you've entered the expression correctly, R:BASE asks that you select a data type for the computed result. Select Currency.

Finally, enter P:Date as the last column name, and select Date as its data type. When you are finished defining the table structure, your screen will look like Figure 9.1. Press the Esc key; then select the last item from each of the following submenus to work your way back to the R> prompt.

■ A FORM FOR MULTIPLE TABLES

Now that we've added a second table to the Mail database, let's create a form for entering information into the new Charges table. Rather than just creating a simple form, however, we'll discuss some more advanced techniques that you can use when creating forms with multiple tables and computed columns.

Use Forms Express to create a new form. Make sure that the Mail database is open, and enter the command

■   FORMS

at the R> prompt. Select option (1) to create a new form. Then select (New) when asked to specify a form. Type in **ChrgFrm** as the name of the new form and press Enter. When asked about customizing the form characteristics, select No. Next, R:BASE will ask you to specify the

```
 Enter or change the column names

            An asterisk (*) identifies key columns
 ┌─────────┐ A plus sign (+) identifies computed columns
 │ Charges │
 └─────────┘

 ┌──────────┬─────────┬─────────┬──────────┬─────────┬──────────┬────────┐
 │ CustNo   │ ProdNo  │ Qty     │ U:Price  │ Tax?    │ Total    │ P:Date │
 ├──────────┼─────────┼─────────┼──────────┼─────────┼──────────┼────────┤
 │ INTEGER  │ TEXT  8 │ INTEGER │ CURRENCY │ INTEGER │+CURRENCY │ DATE   │
 │          │         │         │          │         │          │        │
 └──────────┴─────────┴─────────┴──────────┴─────────┴──────────┴────────┘


 [ENTER] Change   [ESC] Done   [F3] Review   [Shift-F10] More
 Database MAIL    --- Table Charges --- Column      7
```

■ *Figure 9.1:*
Charges table defined on the screen.

associated table. Select Charges, and then select No when asked about customizing the table characteristics.

To enter the form layout, select Edit from the top menu. Type in each of the prompts listed below beginning at the row and column position listed in the left column:

Position	Prompt
<2,3>	Enter/Edit Transactions
<5,1>	Customer Number:
<5,30>	Customer Name:
<6,36>	Company:
<8,1>	Product Number:
<8,30>	Taxable? (1 = Yes, 0 = No):
<10,1>	Qty:
<10,19>	Unit Price:
<10,47>	Total:
<12,1>	Date of Sale:
<15,3>	Highlighter and Cursor Movement
<17,5>	Next Item: ENTER or TAB
<17,40>	Previous Item: SHIFT-TAB
<18,5>	Cursor Right: →
<18,40>	Cursor Left: ←
<19,5>	Insert Space: INS
<19,40>	Delete Character: DEL

After typing in the prompts, you can draw some double-line boxes as in Figure 9.2. Remember, select Draw and Double Line from the top menu, and use the F4 key to raise and lower the "pen."

Using Variables in Forms

Like reports, you can use variables (or expressions) to place information on the form that is not readily available from the table in use. We can use form variables in several ways in this form. First, when entering or editing data in the Charges table, you need to enter a customer number. It would be helpful to display the associated person's name and company from the Names table on the form as verification that you've entered the correct customer number.

Second, even though R:BASE automatically calculates the total for the transaction on the database, this does not guarantee that this total will appear on the screen. Therefore, we'll create an expression to calculate and display the total directly on the form.

To begin entering expressions onto the ChrgFrm form, select Expression from the top menu and Define from the submenu. Enter the first expression exactly as shown below:

■   Name1 = F:Name IN Names WHERE CustNo = CustNo

This is a *lookup expression,* which states that the variable Name1 will store the contents of the F:Name column table in the Names table, where the customer number entered onto the form equals the customer number in the Names table. (Hence, if you enter 1001 onto the ChrgFrm, the variable Name1 will contain that person's first name.) It is called a lookup expression because it must look up the appropriate customer number in the Names table to find the correct name.

Press Enter after typing in the first expression, and then type in the second expression exactly as shown below:

■   Name2 = L:Name IN Names WHERE CustNo = CustNo

As you may have guessed, Name2 will contain the last name (L:Name) of the appropriate customer on the Names table. We need to create a

```
┌─────────────────────────────────────────────────────────────┐
│ ╔═══════════════════════════════════════════════════════╗   │
│ ║ Enter/Edit Transactions                               ║   │
│ ╚═══════════════════════════════════════════════════════╝   │
│                                                              │
│  Customer Number:        Customer Name:                      │
│                              Company:                        │
│                                                              │
│  Product Number:         Taxable? (1=Yes, 0=No):             │
│                                                              │
│  Qty:          Unit Price:          Total:                   │
│                                                              │
│  Date of Sale:                                               │
│                                                              │
│ ╔═══════════════════════════════════════════════════════╗   │
│ ║ Highlighter and Cursor Movement                       ║   │
│ ║                                                        ║   │
│ ║   Next Item: ENTER or TAB      Previous Item: SHIFT TAB║   │
│ ║   Cursor Right: ->             Cursor Left: <-        ║   │
│ ║   Insert Space: INS            Delete Character: DEL  ║   │
│ ╚═══════════════════════════════════════════════════════╝   │
│ ▬                                                            │
│  [ESC] Return  [F1] Insert  [F2] Delete  [F3] Review  [Shift-F10] More │
│  Form: chrgfrm    Edit          Table: Charges      Page 1  <20, 1> │
└─────────────────────────────────────────────────────────────┘
```

■ *Figure 9.2:* ChrgFrm with prompts and boxes.

third variable that contains both the first and last name with a space between. Enter the third expression exactly as it appears below:

■ CName = Name1 & Name2

CName is the actual variable that will eventually be displayed on the form.

The fourth expression to enter will store the company of the appropriate person in a variable named CCompany. Enter the fourth expression as

■ CCompany = Company IN Names WHERE CustNo = CustNo

Notice that this formula uses the same basic syntax as the other lookup expressions, as follows:

■ <variable> = <column name> IN <table> WHERE <column name> = <column name>

The fifth expression does not perform a lookup. Instead, it calculates the total sale using the same formula as the computed column, but it stores this result in a variable named ShowTot. Enter the fifth expression as shown below:

■ ShowTot = IFEQ(Tax?,0,Qty*U:Price,(Qty*U:Price)*1.06)

After you've entered all five expressions, press the Esc key. Your screen should look like Figure 9.3.

Locating Variables and Column Names

You've already had experience using the F6 key to locate column and variable names in reports and forms, so you should be able to do so now given only the start and end (S and E) coordinates for each location. Press Esc to bring back the top menu, and select Edit to move the cursor onto the form. Place each of the column and variable names listed in the left column below at the start and end locations listed in the right columns. For now, select No to answer the various questions about defining expressions and customizing field characteristics that appear while you are locating information on the screen.

Column/Variable Name	Start	End
CustNo	<5,18>	<5,21>
CName	<5,45>	<5,75>

CCompany	<6,45>	<6,75>
ProdNo	<8,18>	<8,24>
Tax?	<8,54>	<8,55>
Qty	<10,6>	<10,15>
U:Price	<10,31>	<10,43>
ShowTot	<10,54>	<10,64>
P:Date	<12,15>	<12,44>

Figure 9.4 shows the completed ChrgFrm form on the screen. For added convenience, you can place a default value into the Tax? field. To do so, move the cursor to the S and E coordinates on the Taxable? prompt <8,55> and press F6. Then select Yes in response to the question about customizing field characteristics. Move the highlight to the fourth question (...default value for this field?), type in Y, and press Return to change the No to a Yes. Type in 1 as the default value, and press Enter. Press Esc to leave the Field Customization menu, and select No in response to the question about changing the field's location.

You can put in the current date as the default date for the P:Date column as well. Move the cursor between the S and E for the P:Date column <12,16>, and press F6. Change the answer to the fourth question on the Field Characteristics menu to Yes, and enter #DATE (current date) as the default value for the P:Date column. Press Esc and select No in response to the second question.

When you are done, press Esc to work your way back to the exit options, and select Save Changes. Then keep exiting the other menus to return to the R> prompt.

Testing the Form

To test the form, enter the command

■   ENTER ChrgFrm

at the R> prompt. The form appears on the screen with only the default Taxable? and Date of Sale prompts filled in. Entering any valid customer number (for example, 1001..1009 at this point) immediately displays the customer's name and company on the form. You can press the up arrow key and change the customer number at any time, and the name and company will change accordingly.

To complete the transaction, fill in a product number, a taxable status (1 for Yes, 0 for No), a quantity, and a unit price. The total for the transaction appears on the screen immediately, and the cursor moves to the Date of Sale prompt. You can press the up arrow key to move back to previous prompts and make corrections (the total will be corrected as soon as you make the changes). Optionally, you can press Enter to

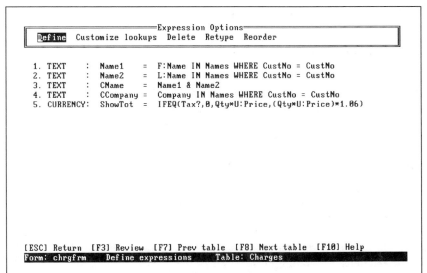

■ *Figure 9.3:*
Expressions
defined for the
ChrgFrm form.

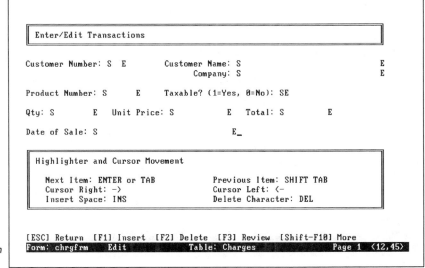

■ *Figure 9.4:*
Completed
ChrgFrm form on
the screen.

accept the default date, or you can type in a new date and press Enter.

Figure 9.5 shows a complete transaction on the screen. When you are finished entering transactions, press Esc (if the top menu is not already on the screen), and select Quit.

You can also use the form for editing transactions by entering the command

■   EDIT USING ChrgFrm

at the R> prompt. As usual, select Quit from the top menu when you have finished editing.

While the ChrgFrm in its current state is useful, there are a few weaknesses that can be corrected. For one, if you enter an invalid customer number (such as 9999), the form will accept your entry and store whatever you save on the Charges table with little or no warning. Later, when billing time comes, nobody will be billed for the transaction because there is no customer number 9999.

Also, if you accidentally enter an invalid tax code (such as 9), the form will accept it and consider the transaction to be for a nontaxable item. We can ensure that errors such as these do not occur when entering transactions by defining *rules* for the form.

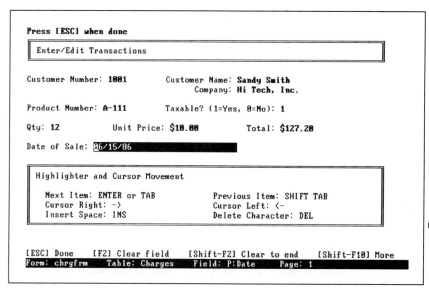

■ *Figure 9.5:*
Completed transaction on the ChrgFrm form.

∎ *DEFINING RULES*

To define rules for a database, use Definition Express. As you may recall, the quickest way to reach Definition Express is to enter the command

∎   RBDEFINE

at the R> prompt. To define rules for an existing database, select option (2), Modify an Existing Database Definition. From the next submenu, select Rules. This brings up the Rules menu, which presents these self-explanatory options:

∎   (1) Add a new rule
    (2) Change an existing rule
    (3) Remove a rule
    (4) Return to the Database Definition Menu

Rule to Reject Invalid Customer Numbers

Our first rule will state that any transaction entered into the Charges table must contain a customer number that exists in the Names table. Otherwise, the transaction will be rejected and the error message "No such customer number!" will appear.

To create the rule, select option (1) from the Rules menu. The screen asks that you

∎   Enter the error message for this rule:

This is the message that you want to appear on the screen when the rule is violated. In this example, type in the message

∎   No such customer number!

and press Enter.

Next the screen asks that you

∎   Choose a table:

Since this rule is based on entries into the Charges table, select Charges. Next the screen asks that you

■ Choose a column to validate:

We want to make sure a valid customer number is entered, so select CustNo as the column to validate.
Next the screen asks that you

■ Choose an operator

and displays the following options. A brief description of each operator is also provided below:

Operator	Meaning
EQ	Equal to a value
NE	Not equal to a value
GT	Greater than a value
GE	Greater than or equal to a value
LT	Less than a value
LE	Less than or equal to a value
CONTAINS	Embedded in text
EXISTS	Contains any value
FAILS	Contains no value
EQA	Equals any value in a column
NEA	Does not equal any value in a column
GTA	Greater than any value in a column
GEA	Greater than or equal to any value in a column
LTA	Less than any value in a column
LEA	Less than or equal to any value in a column

In our example, the rule is that the customer number entered into the Charges table must *equal any* customer number in the Names table, so you want to select EQA (EQual Any) for this rule.

The screen asks that you choose the table to be used for comparison. We want to check the Names table for valid customer numbers, so select Names. The screen asks that you

■ Choose the column to compare:

We're comparing customer numbers in this rule, so select CustNo. Now the rule is defined, and your screen should look like Figure 9.6. In English this screen says, "Display the error message 'No such customer number!' unless the customer number entered into the Charges table equals any customer number in the Names table."

The screen asks that you

∎   Choose a logical operator:

and presents the following options:

∎   AND OR   AND NOT   OR NOT   (Done)

We don't need any additional ANDs, ORs, or NOTs to further define this rule, so select Done. The Rules menu appears on the screen. Before testing this rule, let's define a few more rules.

Rule to Reject Invalid Tax Codes

Suppose we want a rule that displays the error message "Tax must be 1 or 0!" unless the Tax? column in the Charges table contains a one or a zero.

Rule message: No such customer number!

	Column	Table	Operator	Value/Column	Table
	CustNo	Charges	EQA	CustNo	Names

═══Choose a logical operator═══
AND   OR   AND NOT   OR NOT   (Done)

[ESC] Done   [F3] Review   [F5] Reset value   [F10] Help   [Shift-F10] More
Database MAIL   --- Table Charges --- Rule   1

∎ *Figure 9.6:*
Rule to reject
invalid customer
numbers.

Let's define such a rule now. Select option (1) to add a new rule.

As the error message for the rule, enter this sentence:

■   Tax must be 1 or 0!

When asked to choose a table, select Charges, since the Tax? column is part of the Charges table. When asked to choose the column to validate, select Tax?, since this is the column of interest in this rule. When asked to choose an operator, select EQ. We don't want EQA here because we're not searching an entire column for a valid Tax? entry; we just want to compare to a couple of predefined values (either 1 or 0). When asked to enter a value to be used for comparison, enter **1** and press Enter.

So far, the rule states that the Tax? column must equal one to be valid. Actually, either a one or a zero is a valid entry in the Tax? column. Therefore, we need to work on the rule some more.

The screen asks that you

■   Choose a logical operator

In this case, the Tax? column must equal one *or* zero, so select OR. The screen asks for the column to validate, and you select the Tax? column. The screen asks that you select an operator for this part of the expression. Select EQ. The screen asks that you enter a value to be used for comparison, so you enter **0**. Now the rule is defined, as shown in Figure 9.7.

In English, the screen says, "Display the error message 'Tax must be 1 or 0!' unless the Tax? column contains 1 or the Tax? column contains 0." Since you are finished with this rule, select (Done) from the bottom menu.

Rule to Reject Duplicate Customer Numbers

We created the CustNo column in both the Names and the Charges tables so that we could tell which customer each charge transaction referred to. This will only work if every customer in the Names table has a unique customer number. (Obviously, if two people in the Names table have the customer number 1001, then any transactions referring to customer number 1001 in the Charges table are going to create problems. You'd have to flip a coin to decide which customer number 1001 gets stuck with the bill for the charges.)

To ensure that every customer in the Names table has a unique customer number, we can define a rule that rejects duplicate customer numbers before they are added to the Names table.

To create such a rule, select (1) to add a new rule. Enter the sentence

■   Duplicate customer number!

as the error message, and press Enter.

When the screen asks that you choose a table, select Names (because it is the customer numbers on the Names table that we are concerned about). When the screen asks that you choose a column to validate, select CustNo. When you are asked to choose an operator, select NEA (Not Equal Any), because in order to be valid, a new customer number must not equal any existing customer numbers.

When asked to choose the table for comparison, select Names, because the new customer number must not equal any existing customer numbers in the Names table. When asked to choose the column for comparison, select CustNo again, obviously. The completed rule appears on the screen as in Figure 9.8.

In English the screen says, "Display the error message 'Duplicate customer number!' unless the new customer number does not equal any existing customer numbers in the CustNo column of the Names table."

Since you are finished with this rule, select (Done) from the bottom menu.

You can exit Definition Express now and return to the R > prompt. To do so, select options (4), (7), and (4) to leave the higher-level menus.

■ *Figure 9.7:*
Rule to validate
Tax? entry.

```
Rule message:  Tax must be 1 or 0!

       |  Column  | Table    | Operator |  Value/Column   | Table
       |  Tax?    | Charges  | EQ       |  1              |
  OR   |  Tax?    | Charges  | EQ       |  0              |




                       ══Choose a logical operator══
   AND   OR   AND NOT   OR NOT   (Done)


[ESC] Done   [F3] Review   [F5] Reset value   [F10] Help   [Shift-F10] More
Database MAIL    --- Table Charges  --- Rule      2
```

Testing the Rules

To test the rules for the Charges table, enter the command

■   ENTER ChrgFRM

at the R> prompt. When the form appears on the screen, fill out the form with an invalid customer number (such as 5555) and an invalid Tax? code (such as 3). After filling in the form and pressing Esc to bring up the top menu, select Add to add the new data to the Charges table. You'll hear a beep and see your error message at the top of the screen:

■   "No such customer number!"

Enter a new customer number (such as 1001) into the CustNo field, and press Enter. Press Esc and select Add again, and notice that you get the new error message

■   Tax must be 1 or 0!

You'll need to change the Tax? entry to either a one or a zero. Press Esc and select Add once again. Since no rules are violated by the new data, R:BASE accepts the row and asks for the next one. There's no need to keep testing the rules, so just press Esc and select Quit.

	Column	Table	Operator	Value/Column	Table
	CustNo	Names	NEA	CustNo	Names

Rule message: Duplicate customer number!

═══Choose a logical operator═══
AND OR AND NOT OR NOT (Done)

[ESC] Done   [F3] Review   [F5] Reset value   [F10] Help   [Shift-F10] More
Database MAIL   --- Table Names   --- Rule   3

■ *Figure 9.8:*
Rule for rejecting duplicate customer numbers.

To test the rule for the Names table, enter the command

■   ENTER NamesFrm

at the R > prompt. Enter an existing customer number (such as 1001), and fill in any data you like for the rest of the form. When you select Add from the top menu, R:BASE displays the following error message:

■   Duplicate customer number!

You must fill in a new customer number (such as 1010), press Enter, then press Esc and select Add again to add the customer to the Names table.
    When you are finished experimenting, select Quit from the top menu.

■ AUTOSKIP
ON FORMS

R:BASE includes an Autoskip feature, which can help speed data entry. With the Autoskip feature off, you need to press the Enter key after filling in a highlighted item on the screen. With the Autoskip feature on, the highlighting automatically moves to the next item on the screen when the highlighted area is filled.
    To use the Autoskip feature, from the R > prompt use the command

■   SET AUTOSKIP ON

Entering the command Set Autoskip Off will disable Autoskip. The Show command displays the current status of the feature. Next we'll add new rows to the Charges table. Leave Autoskip on to see how it works.

■ ADDING
DATA TO THE
CHARGES
TABLE

We'll add data to the Charges table using the same procedure as we did for adding data to the Names table. Since we've already created a form for this table, simply enter the command

■   ENTER ChrgFrm

Enter the following data into the Charges table using the ChrgFrm form. We'll use these new data in the next chapter.

CustNo	ProdNo	Qty	U:Price	Tax?	P:Date
1001	A-111	12	10.00	Y	06/15/86
1001	B-222	5	12.50	Y	06/15/86
1001	C-434	2	100.00	Y	06/15/86
1004	A-111	5	10.00	Y	06/15/86
1004	Z-128	10	12.80	N	06/15/86
1007	A-111	10	10.00	Y	06/15/86
1007	Z-128	10	12.80	N	06/15/86
1002	B-222	12	12.50	Y	07/01/86
1002	A-111	10	10.00	Y	07/01/86

After you've entered the new data, press Esc and select the Quit option from the menu. To verify your entries, enter the command

- SELECT ALL FROM Charges

at the R > prompt. If necessary, you can enter

- EDIT ALL FROM Charges

and make changes.

■ SUMMARY

In this chapter, we've added a new table and form to the Mail database. We've also created some rules to minimize the likelihood of erroneous data being entered into the database. In summary, we've learned that

When dividing data into separate tables, you need a common field in each of the tables to identify the relationships between the rows.

When there are many rows on one table for every one row on another table, the relationship between the two tables is called a *one-to-many* relationship.

Tables may contain *computed* columns, which derive their value from other columns already in the row.

Forms Express lets you define variables (expressions) to display data from other tables and perform calculations on custom forms.

Definition Express allows you to define rules for rejecting invalid data before they are stored on a table.

The Set Autoskip command lets you determine whether the Enter key must be pressed after each field on a custom form is filled in.

In the next chapter, you'll learn some techniques for managing numbers in a table.

10

MANAGING NUMBERS IN A TABLE

In this chapter, we'll explore a variety of techniques for managing numbers in a database. We'll work with the Compute, Tally, and Change commands and also discuss techniques for performing calculations "on-the-fly."

■ MATH AND STATISTICS

You can use the Compute command to perform various calculations on numeric data in a table. The general syntax for the Compute command is

■ COMPUTE <command> <column name> FROM <table name> WHERE <conditions>

Commands that you can use with the Compute command are listed in Figure 10.1.

Let's look at some examples. If you want to find the total sales in the Charges table, enter the command

■ COMPUTE SUM Total FROM Charges

R:BASE displays the sum, as follows:

■ Total Sum = $1,085.45

Command	Function
Ave	Computes the average of a numeric column
Count	Counts the number of entries in a column
Max	Selects the highest number, alphabetically highest text string, or latest date from a column
Min	Selects the smallest number, alphabetically lowest text string, or earliest date from a column
Rows	Determines how many rows are in a table
Sum	Computes the sum of numeric data in a column
All	Computes all of the above
Stdev	Computes the standard deviation of a numeric column
Variance	Computes the variance of a numeric column

■ *Figure 10.1:*
Commands used with the Compute command.

(Your results will depend on the data in your Charges table.)

If you want to calculate the average of the Total column, enter the command

■   COMPUTE AVE Total FROM Charges

R:BASE displays the average, as follows:

■   Total Average = $120.61

Suppose that you wanted to know how many items of product number A-111 were sold. You would need to sum the Qty column for all the rows that contain that product number. The command to do so is

■   COMPUTE SUM Qty FROM Charges WHERE ProdNo = A-111

R:BASE displays the sum

■   Qty Sum = 37

If you wanted to know how much money customer number 1001 has spent, you would enter the command

■   COMPUTE SUM Total FROM Charges WHERE CustNo = 1001

R:BASE shows the following:

■   Total Sum = $405.45

To see the total amount of sales in the month of June, you would enter the command

■   COMPUTE SUM Total FROM Charges WHERE P:Date > = +
     06/01/86 AND P:Date < = 06/30/86

R:BASE displays

■   Total Sum = $693.25

If you wanted to know how many individual rows contained the product number A-111, you would use the Count command with the appropriate Where clause, as follows:

■ COMPUTE COUNT ProdNo FROM Charges WHERE +
  ProdNo = A-111

R:BASE responds with

■ ProdNo Count = 4

To calculate the largest single sale in the Total column, you would enter the following command:

■ COMPUTE MAX Total FROM Charges

R:BASE displays

■ Total Maximum = $212.00

To calculate the smallest value in the Total column, enter this command:

■ COMPUTE MIN Total FROM Charges

R:BASE shows

■ Total Minimum = $53.00

To compute the standard deviation of all the values in the Total column, enter this command:

■ COMPUTE STDEV Total FROM Charges

R:BASE displays the following result:

■ Total Std Dev = $44.64

To compute the variance of the Total column, enter the command

■ COMPUTE VARIANCE Total FROM Charges

R:BASE displays this result:

■ Total Variance = $1,992.40

To see the overall statistics of the Total column, use the All command, as follows:

■   COMPUTE ALL Total FROM Charges

R:BASE displays all eight calculations, as below:

Total Count =   9
Rows =   9
Minimum = $53.00
Maximum = $212.00
Sum = $1,085.45
Average = $120.61
Std Dev = $44.64
Variance = $1,992.40

The Max and Min commands work with nonnumeric data, and they are useful for finding ranges. For example, to view the earliest date in the P:Date column of the Charges table, enter the command

■   COMPUTE MIN P:Date FROM Charges

R:BASE displays the following:

■   P:Date Minimum = 06/15/86

To view the latest date, enter the command

■   COMPUTE MAX P:Date FROM Charges

and you'll see

■   P:Date Maximum = 07/01/86

To find the alphabetically lowest last name in the Names table, enter the command

■   COMPUTE MIN L:Name FROM Names

R:BASE displays

■   L:Name Minimum = Adams

To see the alphabetically highest last name, enter this command:

■   COMPUTE MAX L:Name FROM Names

R:BASE shows

■   L:Name Maximum = Teasdale

You can use the Tally command to display a *frequency distribution* of unique items in a table. For example, to see how many rows contain each of the product numbers in the Charges table, enter the command

■   TALLY ProdNo FROM Charges

The tally statistics will appear on the screen as follows:

ProdNo	Number of Occurrences
A-111	4
B-222	2
C-434	1
Z-128	2

The Tally command is also useful for working with the Names table. For example, to see all the different ZIP codes and how many people are in each ZIP-code area, enter the command

■   TALLY Zip FROM Names

R:BASE shows the statistics, as below:

Zip	Number of Occurrences
12121	2
54321	1
91234	1
92111	1
92112	1
92122	1
94711	1
94721	1

To access the Compute or Tally command from the prompt mode, select Look at Data or Print Data from the Prompt menu.

■ USING THE CHANGE COMMAND

In previous examples we calculated numerous statistical and arithmetic results on existing data in a table. You can also perform mathematical operations on data in tables and store the results of the calculation in the table. To do so, use the Change command with the general syntax

■   CHANGE *<column name>* TO *<expression>* IN *<table name>*
     WHERE *<conditions>*

For example, suppose you wanted to increase the unit price of part number A-111 in all rows in the Charges table. First, you could use the Select command to view the existing values, as below:

■   R>SELECT ProdNo U:Price FROM Charges

R:BASE displays the existing data as follows:

ProdNo	U:Price
A-111	$10.00
B-222	$12.50
C-434	$100.00
A-111	$10.00
Z-128	$12.80
A-111	$10.00
Z-128	$12.80
B-222	$12.50
A-111	$10.00

To increase the unit price for part number A-111 by 10%, enter this command:

■   CHANGE U:Price TO U:Price * 1.10 IN Charges +
     WHERE ProdNo = A-111

R:BASE displays the message

■   The value for U:Price has been changed in 4 row(s) in Charges

To see the results of the calculation, once again enter the Select command, as follows:

■   R>SELECT ProdNo U:Price FROM Charges

You'll see the results of the calculation (all part numbers A-111 now are $11.00 instead of $10.00) as below:

ProdNo	U:Price
A-111	$11.00
B-222	$12.50
C-434	$100.00
A-111	$11.00
Z-128	$12.80
A-111	$11.00
Z-128	$12.80
B-222	$12.50
A-111	$11.00

You can use the Change command to place a fixed number into a field as well. For example, to change all the part number A-111 unit prices back to $10.00, you can enter the following command:

■   CHANGE U:Price TO 10.00 IN Charges WHERE +
    ProdNo = A-111

R:BASE once again displays the message

■   The value for U:Price has been changed in 4 row(s) in Charges

Using the Select command to view the data shows that the unit price for part number A-111 is back to $10.00.

■   SELECT ProdNo U:Price FROM Charges

ProdNo	U:Price
A-111	$10.00
B-222	$12.50
C-434	$100.00
A-111	$10.00
Z-128	$12.80
A-111	$10.00
Z-128	$12.80
B-222	$12.50
A-111	$10.00

You need to be careful when using the Change command, because once it makes its changes, there is no easy way to undo them. For example, if you had entered the command (and don't do so)

■   CHANGE U:Price TO 10.00 IN Charges WHERE U:Price > 0

then *every* row in the Charges table would have $10.00 in the U:Price column, regardless of what was in there before. Furthermore, there would be no way to go back and undo the damage in a single command. You would need to replace the original data, record by record in the edit mode. (Assuming that you had the original data still available to you on a printout.) Be careful with the Change command.

The Change command can also be used in lieu of a computed column. For example, suppose the Total column in the Charges table were a Currency column, and you wanted to fill in the total for each transaction. (Since Total is a computed column, this will not work, but just suppose Total is not a computed column.) To assign the quantity times the unit price to the Total column in each row of the Charges table, you would enter the command

■   CHANGE Total TO Qty * U:Price IN Charges WHERE Qty > 0

Then, to add 6% tax to each of the rows that have the number 1 in the Tax? column, you could enter the command

■   CHANGE Total TO Total * 1.06 IN Charges WHERE Tax? = 1

Of course, this method is not as easy as creating a computed field, but it is available to you as an option.

∎ PERFORMING CALCULATIONS "ON-THE-FLY"

Another method for performing calculations in table columns is to place the appropriate expression in the Select command or to place it in a report format. Rather than storing the results of calculations in the database, you can simply store the "raw data" (such as Qty, U:Price, and Tax? in the Charges table) and view the results of calculations only when you need them. This technique has the slight advantage of eliminating computed columns (which saves some disk space), but it is also useful for performing ad hoc calculations on columns "on-the-fly."

Let's just suppose that we had not included the Total column in the Charges database. How could you see the results of the quantity times the unit price? You could simply specify Qty*U:Price as a field to view in the Select command, as follows:

∎   SELECT ProdNo Qty U:Price Qty * U:Price FROM Charges

The results of this command are shown below:

ProdNo	Qty	U:Price	Computed
A-111	12	$10.00	$120.00
B-222	5	$12.50	$62.50
C-434	2	$100.00	$200.00
A-111	5	$10.00	$50.00
Z-128	10	$12.80	$128.00
A-111	10	$10.00	$100.00
Z-128	10	$12.80	$128.00
B-222	12	$12.50	$150.00
A-111	10	$10.00	$100.00

There is one slight problem with this display: It does not take into account the tax on taxable items. If you wanted to add 6% tax only to those items where the Tax? column was not 0, then you could use the command

∎   SELECT ProdNo Qty U:Price Tax? +
    IFEQ(Tax?,0,Qty * U:Price,(Qty * U:Price) * 1.06) +
    FROM Charges

The results of this Select command are shown below:

ProdNo	Qty	U:Price	Tax?	Computed
A-111	12	$10.00	1	$127.20
B-222	5	$12.50	1	$66.25
C-434	2	$100.00	1	$212.00
A-111	5	$10.00	1	$53.00
Z-128	10	$12.80	0	$128.00
A-111	11	$10.00	1	$106.00
Z-128	10	$12.80	0	$128.00
B-222	12	$12.50	1	$159.00
A-111	10	$10.00	1	$106.00

Needless to say, this technique is not as convenient as using the computed Total column, but it could come in handy in certain situations. For example, suppose you had a table with 30 or 40 numeric columns in it, and you wanted the freedom to perform calculations on any number of columns to try out various "what-if" analyses occasionally. Rather than having another 30 or 40 computed columns, you could just use expressions in the Select command to try out various calculations as the need arose.

■ R:BASE OPERATORS

In this chapter we've been using multiplication, with the * operator, in all our calculations. Of course, R:BASE also provides operators for addition, subtraction, division, and percentages. These are shown in Figure 10.2 in their order of *precedence*. Precedence refers to the order in which the calculations take place. For example, the formula 10 + 5 * 2 results in 20, because the multiplication takes precedence over (occurs before) the addition. You can use parentheses to change the order of precedence. For example, the formula (10 + 5) * 2 results in 30, because the operation inside the parentheses takes precedence. We'll discuss the arithmetic operators in more detail in Chapter 14.

R:BASE also offers many *functions* for performing advanced trigonometric and financial calculations. These too are discussed in Chapter 14.

Operator	Function	Example
–	Unary minus	– 10 + 5 = –5
**	Exponentiation	3 * *2 = 9 (3 squared) 27 * *(1/3) = 3
*	Multiplication	3 * 5 = 15
/	Division	100 / 10 = 10
%	Percentage	50 % 100 = 50
+	Addition	2 + 2 = 4
–	Subtraction	10 – 5 = 5
+	Concatenation	"ABC" + "DEF" = "ABCDEF"
&	Concatenation (with space)	"ABC" & "DEF" = "ABC DEF"

■ *Figure 10.2:*
R:BASE
mathematical
operators.

■ SUMMARY

In this chapter we've described the following commands for performing calculations with a table:

The Compute command allows you to calculate sums and averages, as well as to determine the highest item, the lowest item, and number of specific items in a table. The Where clause allows you to specify criteria for the calculations.

The Tally command displays the unique items and the number of occurrences of each item in a table column.

The Change command allows you to perform calculations on data in a table and store the results in the table and to place a fixed number into a field. It can also be used in lieu of a computed column.

You can perform calculations "on-the-fly" by using expressions in the Select command.

In the next chapter, we'll look at techniques for printing totals and subtotals in reports.

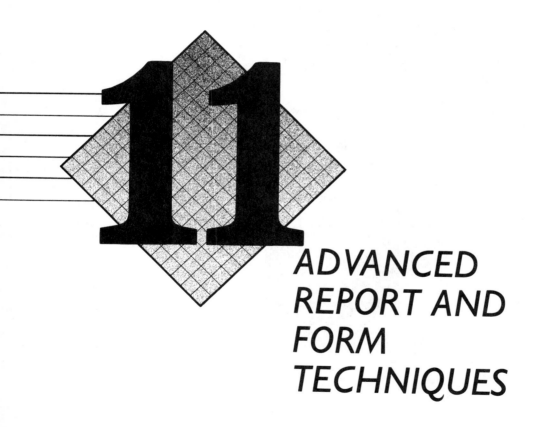

11

ADVANCED REPORT AND FORM TECHNIQUES

In this chapter, we'll describe some advanced reporting techniques, such as displaying totals and subtotals, as well as techniques for using data from multiple tables. We'll develop a report named Sales that shows charge transactions, subtotals for each individual, and a grand total at the end of the report. Figure 11.1 shows a sample of the report.

■ ADVANCED DESIGN TECHNIQUES

When designing more sophisticated reports, it is important to mark the heading, footing, and detail lines on a rough draft of the report, as shown in Figure 11.2.

Notice that there are several headings and footings specified, as described below:

Report heading	Appears on the first page of the report only.
Page heading	Appears once at the top of each page in the report.
Break heading	Appears at the top of each subtotal break.
Detail	Data printed once for each row within a subtotal section.
Break footing	Displayed at the bottom of each subtotal break.
Report footing	Displayed once at the end of the entire report.

Although we haven't included one here, a report can also contain a page footing, which is printed once at the bottom of each page.

■ ADVANCED USE OF REPORT VARIABLES

The next step in designing a report is to determine what variables you will need. We'll need the usual .#DATE and .#PAGE for the report date and page number. We'll also need variables for the totals and subtotals. In English, we can define these variables as follows:

SubTotal	Sum of the Total column for each individual
GrandTot	Sum of the Total column in all rows

```
                        Charge Transactions
        Date: 09/11/86                              Page: 1

        Customer

            Prod #     Qty    Unit Price     Total        Date

        1001 Sandy Smith: Hi Tech, Inc.

            A-111       12      $10.00       $127.20     06/15/86

            B-222        5      $12.50        $66.25     06/15/86

            C-434        2     $100.00       $212.00     06/15/86
                                            ─────────
        Subtotal:                            $405.45

        1002 Mindy Jones: ABC Co.

            A-111       10      $10.00       $106.00     07/01/86

            B-222       12      $12.50       $159.00     07/01/86
                                            ─────────
        Subtotal:                            $265.00

        1004 Bart Adams: Dataspec Inc.

            A-111        5      $10.00        $53.00     06/15/86

            Z-128       10      $12.80       $128.00     06/15/86
                                            ─────────
        Subtotal:                            $181.00

        1007 Monica Miller: Acme Development

            A-111       10      $10.00       $106.00     06/15/86

            Z-128       10      $12.80       $128.00     06/15/86
                                            ─────────
        Subtotal:                            $234.00
                                            ─────────
        Grand Total:                        $1085.45
```

■ *Figure 11.1:*
Sample of the
Sales report.

In this example, most of the data will be from the Charges table, but we'll need to get the name and company for each individual from the Names table. In simple English, we can define the necessary variables as follows:

FullName   First and last names from the Names table

NameCo   Full name plus company from the Names table

After you've sketched a rough draft of the final report on paper, you can begin using Reports Express to lay out the report format. Recall that you can enter Reports Express by entering the command

∎   REPORTS

at the R > prompt. Select option (1) from the Report Options menu to Edit/Create a report. Select (New) and enter

∎   Sales

as the report name. When asked to select the associated table, select Charges.

	Charge Transactions				
Report Heading	Date: 06/10/86			Page: 1	
Page Heading	Customer				
	Prod #	**Qty**	**Unit Price**	**Total**	**Date**
Break Heading	1001 Sandy Smith—Hi Tech, Inc.				
Detail Lines	A-111	12	$10.00	$127.20	06/15/86
	B-222	5	$12.50	$66.25	06/15/86
	C-434	2	$100.00	$212.00	06/15/86
				_____	
Break Footing	SubTotal:			$405.45	
Report Footing	Total:			$1085.45	

∎ *Figure 11.2:*
Rough draft of
the Sales report.

We'll begin by defining the variables to be used in the report. Select Expression from the top menu and Define from the submenu. The report date and page number variables are simple to define. Type in the first expression

■   RepDate = .#DATE

and press Enter. Enter the page number variable by typing in the expression

■   PgNo = .#PAGE

GrandTot and SubTotal Variables

The GrandTot and SubTotal variables are entered using the Sum Of command in the expression. Since the SubTotal variable for each customer is the sum of the Total column from the relevant rows in the Charges table, enter the command as

■   SubTotal = SUM OF Total

The GrandTot variable is also the sum of the Total column, so enter the expression

■   GrandTot = SUM OF Total

It may seem odd that both of these variables use the same expression, but the difference between them will be determined by configuration settings later. The SubTotal variable will be automatically reset to zero after each subtotal block.

You can define report variables by using any of the operators shown in Figure 11.3.

Variables from Other Tables

Next we need to enter some variables that will insert some of the data from the Names table into the Sales report. The general syntax for defining columns from other tables is

■   *variable* = *column name* IN *table name* WHERE *expression*

The technique is similar to the lookup in the form in the last chapter. Define a variable called Name1, which is the first name from the Names table. The expression to enter is

- Name1 = F:Name IN Names WHERE CustNo = CustNo

The Where clause expression CustNo = CustNo tells R:BASE which name to get from the Names table. In English, the formula reads, "The Name1 variable is the first name from the Names table, where the customer number in the Names table equals the customer number in the Charges table."

We also need the last name from the Names table. Enter the expression as follows:

- Name2 = L:Name IN Names WHERE CustNo = CustNo

Now we need the company data from the Names file. The expression is

- CompName = Company IN Names WHERE CustNo = CustNo

Finally, we'll store the name and company combined in a variable called NameCo by entering the following expression:

- NameCo = Name1 & Name2 + ":" & CompName

After you've defined all the variables, they should look like Figure 11.4. Press the Esc key twice to return to the Reports menu.

Operator	Function
+	Sum of columns or variables (or links two text strings)
−	Difference of columns or variables
*	Product of columns or variables
/	Quotient of columns or variables
%	Percent of columns or variables
&	Links two text strings with a space inserted
SUM OF	Computes the sum of a column

∎ *Figure 11.3: Operators used when defining report variables.*

■ CONFIGURING BREAKPOINTS

The next step is to define the *breakpoints* for the report. Breakpoints indicate where one group or subtotal of data ends and another begins. From the top menu, select Configure, which brings up the screen shown in Figure 11.5.

The first four options on the configuration screen are not relevant at the moment; however, the columns under the Breakpoints heading are. You can move the cursor to this section of the screen using the arrow keys.

In our sample report, we want to print a subtotal for each customer in the Charges table. Therefore, CustNo is the break column in the table. To supply the configuration screen with this information, move the highlighter to the default [None] prompt just to the right of the Break1 prompt. Type in CustNo as the name of the column, and then press the Tab key to move to the Variable Reset column.

When using subtotals in a report, the variable must be reset to zero at the end of each section so that it can start accumulating the next subtotal from zero. Therefore, you should type in Y to change the default [NO] to [YES]. The screen will ask which variable(s) to reset within this breakpoint. You want to reset the SubTotal variable, so select SubTotal. The screen will ask if you want to reset other variables. Just press Esc.

At this point you've made CustNo the break variable and specified SubTotal as the variable to reset to zero after each customer subtotal is

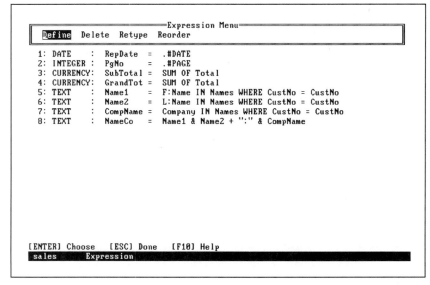

■ *Figure 11.4:*
Variables defined for the Sales report.

displayed. The section of the screen that defines the Break1 break column should look like this:

■ Break1   CustNo   [YES]

Now that you've told R:BASE that there will be subtotals based on the CustNo column, you can begin laying out the report format. Press Esc to bring back the top menu.

■ LAYING OUT THE FORMAT

To begin laying out the report format, select Edit from the top menu. The blank screen will appear with a report heading (RH) symbol on the first line.

Report Heading

To fill in the report heading, move the cursor to <1,30> and type in

■ Charge Transactions

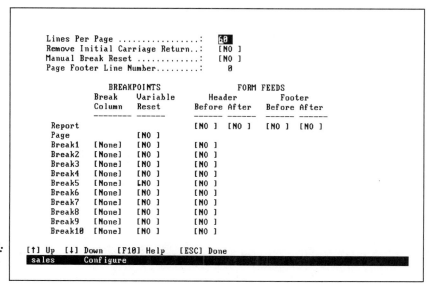

```
Lines Per Page .................:    60
Remove Initial Carriage Return..:   [NO ]
Manual Break Reset .............:   [NO ]
Page Footer Line Number.........:    0

                 BREAKPOINTS              FORM FEEDS
             Break    Variable      Header        Footer
             Column   Reset      Before After  Before After
             -------- -------    ------ ------  ------ ------
Report                          [NO ] [NO ]   [NO ] [NO ]
Page                 [NO ]
Break1   [None]      [NO ]      [NO ]
Break2   [None]      [NO ]      [NO ]
Break3   [None]      [NO ]      [NO ]
Break4   [None]      [NO ]      [NO ]
Break5   [None]      [NO ]      [NO ]
Break6   [None]      [NO ]      [NO ]
Break7   [None]      [NO ]      [NO ]
Break8   [None]      [NO ]      [NO ]
Break9   [None]      [NO ]      [NO ]
Break10  [None]      [NO ]      [NO ]

[↑] Up  [↓] Down   [F10] Help   [ESC] Done
sales       Configure
```

■ *Figure 11.5:*
Configuration screen.

Press Enter to begin the second RH line. At <2,1> type in

■   Date:

With the cursor on <2,7> press F6, enter **RepDate** as the variable name, and mark <2,7> as the start location and <2,36> as the end location.

Move the cursor to <2,60> and enter the heading

■   Page:

Move the cursor to <2,66> and press F6. Enter PgNo as the variable name, <2,66> as the start location, and <2,70> as the end location. Press Enter to create another blank RH line. (This line will appear as a blank line on the printed report.)

Page Heading

To begin the page heading, press F8 so that the PH symbol appears. At <4,1> type in

■   Customer

and press Enter. The start locations for the remaining column titles for the page heading are listed below. Move the cursor to the position in the left column, and type in the text in the right column.

Location	Text
<5,5>	Prod #
<5,15>	Qty
<5,23>	Unit Price
<5,42>	Total
<5,55>	Date

Press Enter after typing in all the column headings.

Break Heading

Press F8 to start the next section, H1 in this case. To place the customer number, name, and company in the break heading, move the cursor to <7,1>. Press F6 and enter CustNo as the column name.

Start the location at <7,1> and end it at <7,5>. Move the cursor to <7,7>, press F6, enter NameCo as the variable name, and press Enter. Mark <7,7> as the start location and <7,50> as the end location. Press Enter to put in a blank break heading (H1) line.

This H1 heading will appear at the top of each subtotal group (each customer in this example) when the report is printed.

Detail Lines

You'll only need one detail line for this report. Press F8 to begin the next section. A detail (D) line will appear.

When locating currency data on the report format, the screen will ask

■ Print in check format? Yes No

If you answer Yes, the currency data in the printed report will be displayed with leading asterisks as below:

■ * * * * * * * *$123.45

Since this is unnecessary on this report, you can always answer No to this prompt while placing column names on the Sales report format. Locate column names at the start and end locations listed below, using the F6, arrow, S, and E keys.

Column Name	Start	End	Check Format?
ProdNo	<9,5>	<9,12>	
Qty	<9,14>	<9,17>	
U:Price	<9,20>	<9,32>	No
Total	<9,35>	<9,47>	No
P:Date	<9,55>	<9,70>	

After placing all the column names, you can press Ctrl-left arrow to bring the cursor back to column 1.

Break Footing

A break footing appears once at the end of each subtotal group. When using subtotals, the break footing should include the variable name that controls the subtotal. You can also add text and underlines, as we'll do in this example.

First, press F8 to start the first break footing. The F1 symbol appears in the left margin. Move the cursor to <10,35> and type in 13 hyphens. Press Enter, and move the cursor to <11,5>. Type in the word

■   Subtotal:

Move the cursor to <11,35>, press F6, and enter SubTotal as the variable name. Start the SubTotal variable at <11,35> and end it at <11,47>. (Again, you can select No in response to printing the subtotal in check format.) Press Enter to create a blank line in the break footing.

Report Footing

All we need now is the grand total to appear at the bottom of the report. Since this needs to appear only once at the end of the report, this will be a report footing. Press F8 twice to start an RF section. Move the cursor to <13,35> and type in 13 hyphens. Press Enter, and move the cursor to <14,1>. Type in the words

■   Grand Total:

Move the cell pointer to <14,35>, press F6, and enter

■   GrandTot

as the variable name. Start the variable at <14,35> and end it at <14,47>. Again, answer No to the prompt about printing in check format.

When you are finished, your screen should look like Figure 11.6. You can press Esc twice to work your way back to the Save options, and select Save Changes. Exit all the next menus to return to the R> prompt.

Printing the Report

Now you can print the report using the Print command. For example, enter the command

■   PRINT Sales

The report will resemble Figure 11.1 at the beginning of this chapter.

You can use the Sorted By and Where clauses to sort and filter the report. Use the Output command to direct the report to the printer or a file.

∎ CLEARING REPORT VARIABLES

When printing different reports that use identical variable names, or when printing multiple copies of a report, your subtotals and totals may be inaccurate if the existing variables are not cleared first. For a quick view of the current status of variables, you can enter the command

∎   SHOW VARIABLES

at the R> prompt.

To clear the variables (to ensure that the report is starting with new variable values), enter the command

∎   CLEAR ALL VARIABLES

at the R> prompt.

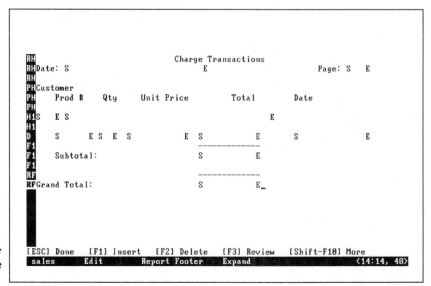

∎ *Figure 11.6:*
Format for the
Sales report.

As a general safety precaution, it's a good idea to make a point of entering the Clear All Variables command at the R> prompt just before using the Print command to print a report with totals or subtotals. That way, you'll always be sure the totals and subtotals in the report are accurate. Chapter 14 discusses R:BASE variables in more detail.

■ *NESTED SUBTOTALS*

In the sample Sales report, we used only a single breakpoint column: Customer Number. R:BASE will let you define up to ten breakpoints for a single report. For example, you could create a report format that presents subtotals for each customer, and within each customer, subtotals by product code. The sample Charges table is too small to demonstrate this, but the hypothetical report in Figure 11.7 shows how such a format might appear. Notice that a subtotal appears for each customer. Furthermore, a subtotal for each product purchased appears within each customer listing. Notice also that the various report sections are written onto the sample report.

To create such a report, you would need to define two subtotaling variables using the Expression and Define options in Reports Express. You'd probably still want a GrandTot variable for the grand total, as below:

■   SubTot1   SUM OF Total
    SubTot2   SUM OF Total
    GrandTot SUM OF Total

Using the Configure options from Reports Express, you would want CustNo to be the Break 1 column and ProdNo to be the Break 2 column. Each of these columns must reset the appropriate subtotaling variable. In this example, Break 1 is based on the CustNo column and resets the SubTot1 variable. Break 2 is based on the ProdNo column and resets the SubTot2 variable. Figure 11.8 shows the configuration screen with two breakpoints defined.

When laying out the report format, Reports Express will give you the opportunity to define two break headings (H1 and H2) and two break footings (F1 and F2). These multiple break headings and footings should surround the detail lines and be nested within one another as shown below:

■   RH   Report Header
    PH   Page Header

Charge Transactions

Date: 09/11/86   Page: 1

Customer

Prod. #	Qty	Unit Price	Total	Date

1004 Bart Adams: Dataspec Inc.

A-111	5	$10.00	$ 53.00	06/15/86

Subtotal for product A-111 $ 53.00

| Z-128 | 10 | $12.80 | $128.00 | 06/15/86 |
| Z-128 | 1 | $12.80 | $ 12.80 | 07/01/86 |

Subtotal for product Z-128 $140.80

Total for customer 1004 $193.80

1007 Monica Miller: Acme Development

| A-111 | 10 | $10.00 | $106.00 | 06/15/86 |
| A-111 | 10 | $10.00 | $106.00 | 07/15/86 |

Subtotal for product A-111 $212.00

| Z-128 | 10 | $12.80 | $128.00 | 06/15/86 |
| Z-128 | 10 | $12.80 | $128.00 | 07/01/86 |

Subtotal for product Z-128 $256.00

Total for customer 1007 $468.00

Grand total of all customers: $661.80

■ *Figure 11.7:*
A report with
two subtotal
breakpoints.

H1	Break Header 1 (customer number)
H2	Break Header 2 (part numbers)
D	Detail Lines
F2	Break Footer 2 (with SubTot2 variable to show subtotal)
F1	Break Footer 1 (with SubTot1 variable to show subtotal)
PF	Page Footing
RF	Report Footing (including the GrandTot variable if any)

Figure 11.9 shows the report format used to print the sample report in Figure 11.7 above. Variable and column names are shown between the appropriate S and E locations (though these, of course, do not appear on your screen).

The same basic structure can be used with any number of headings. For example, if a report contained five levels of subtotaling, then you would need to define five subtotaling variables. Each of these would need to be reset at each breakpoint.

When laying out the report format, you'd still want to nest the various break headings and footings within one another, as follows:

■
RH	Report Header
PH	Page Header
H1	Break Header 1
H2	Break Header 2
H3	Break Header 3

■ *Figure 11.8:*
Two breakpoints defined for a report.

```
H4        Break Header 4
H5          Break Header 5
 D   Detail Lines
F5          Break Footer 5 (and subtotaling variable)
F4        Break Footer 4 (and subtotaling variable)
F3      Break Footer 3 (and subtotaling variable)
F2    Break Footer 2 (and subtotaling variable)
F1  Break Footer 1 (and subtotaling variable)
PF   Page Footing
RF   Report Footing (and grand total variable if any)
```

Any section in the report, be it a heading, a detail line, or a break header or footer, can consist of any number of lines and any number of variables or table columns. If you wish to display a cumulative total along with (or in place of) a subtotal, don't reset the variable. (In other words, leave the Variable Reset column of the configuration sheet at the default [NO] setting for the appropriate breakpoint and variable.)

```
RH                          Charge Transactions
RH  Date:   S   RepDate          E                    Page: S PgNo E
RH
PH  Customer
PH      Prod. #        Qty   Unit Price         Total      Date
PH
H1  S CustNo E S NameCo E
H2
 D      S  ProdNo  ES Qty E S U:Price E S   Total   E    S P:Date E
F2                                         ___________
F2      Subtotal for product S ProdNo E  S  SubTot1  E
F1                                         ===========
F1      Total for customer S CustNo E     S  SubTot2  E
F1
RF                                         ___________
RF      Grand Total of all customers:     S  GrandTot E
```

■ ***Figure 11.9:*** *Report layout for a report with two breakpoints.*

A breakpoint doesn't need a subtotal variable. For example, you might want to put breakpoints for State and City in a report format for the Names table. Doing so will display the names grouped by state and grouped by city within each state. The grouping, in this case, is only for organization and therefore you need not define subtotal variables.

■ BOXES AND LINES ON REPORTS

Like Forms Express, you can draw boxes and lines on reports with the Draw option from the top menu. The lines and boxes will appear on the screen when you print the report, but may not appear on the printed report (it depends on your particular printer). Your best bet is to draw a simple box on a report format with the Draw options from the menu, save the report, and then print a copy of the report with the Output Printer and Print commands.

If the box does not appear on the printed report, you can erase it using the Erase option on the Draw menu in Reports Express. Even if the boxes do not appear on your printed report, you can still use hyphens and the underscore character on your keyboard to draw underlines on your report. (These will show up on any printer's output.)

■ CREATING A FORM THAT SERVES TWO TABLES

One of the most powerful features of R:BASE System V is its ability to display data from multiple tables on a single form and to allow data to be entered and edited on both tables simultaneously. With the use of *master table lookups* you can even create a form that allows instant display of existing data for editing, or instant entry of new data should the initial entry not exist yet. We'll discuss this aspect of forms later in the chapter.

Rather than create an entirely new form to demonstrate this capability, we'll modify a copy of the NamesFrm form created earlier. To make the copy, make sure the Mail database is open, and enter the command

■   FORMS

at the R> prompt to enter Forms Express.

From the opening Forms Express menu, select option (3) to copy a form. The screen asks that you

∎ Enter name of the form to copy:

Type in NamesFrm and press Enter. The screen asks that you

∎ Enter the new form name:

Type in Both and press Enter. Now there are two identical forms in the Mail database, named NamesFrm and Both.

To begin changing the Both form to serve two tables, select (1) to Edit/Create a form. When requested, select Both as the name of the form to edit, and then select Edit to move the cursor onto the form.

We'll place a *region* for displaying data from the Charges table near the bottom of the screen. Use the down arrow key to move the cursor down to the bottom box (at <16,1>), and press F2 seven times to erase the box and its contents. The bottom portion of the screen is now empty, giving you room to create a region.

Creating the Region

Notice that the words **Table: Names** appear in the middle of the status bar at the bottom of the screen. This indicates that the form is currently "attached to" the Names table. To create a region on the form for the Charges table, you first need to attach the form to the Charges table. To do so, press the F8 key. The screen asks for the name of the new table to attach to. Select Charges from the menu. (Note that the status bar at the bottom of the screen indicates that the form is now attached to the Charges table.)

The first question to appear on the screen is the following:

∎ Do you want to customize table characteristics?

Select Yes and take a look at the Table Characteristics menu. Notice the question

∎ Do you want to define a region?

Move the highlighter to this question, and change the answer to Yes (by typing the letter Y and pressing Enter).

The form will reappear on the screen, along with the request to

■ Move the cursor to locate a corner of the region—press [ENTER]

Now you can "draw" the region where you want rows from the Charges table to appear. Move the cell pointer to <16,1> and press Enter. The screen now asks that you

■ Move the cursor to paint the region's area—press [ENTER] when done.

Press the down arrow key six times to move the highlighter to <22,1>; then press the right arrow key to stretch the highlighter all the way to the right, to <22,80>. Your screen should look like Figure 11.10.

Press Enter after highlighting the region area. The screen displays the message

■ Region created. Press any key to continue

When you press any key, the Table Characteristics menu reappears on the screen.

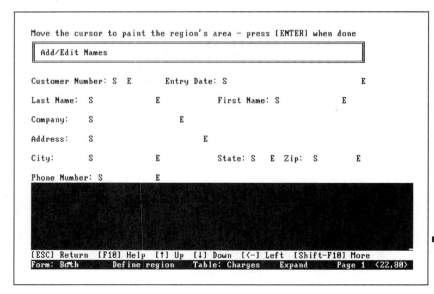

■ *Figure 11.10:*
Region area highlighted on the form.

A couple of questions on the menu refer to the appearance of the region on the form. The first question

■   Do you want a border around the region?

lets you draw a border around the region so that it stands out on the form. The choice is yours, but generally the form will look better with the border, so Yes is the preferred answer. The second question

■   How many lines in the border: Enter 1 or 2

lets you determine whether the border is displayed with a single line or a double line. For this example, 2 is preferred because it will match the existing box near the top of the screen. (Again, however, this is purely an aesthetic decision.)

If you have a color monitor, you can also define colors for the region by answering the appropriate questions on the Table Characteristics menu. When you are finished, press Esc to see the form on the screen.

Locating Text and Prompts in the Region

Now you can place text and column names from the Charges table inside the region. The procedure for doing so is the same as for any form. For typing in text, position the cursor with the arrow keys and type in the text. For this example, place the cursor at each of the start locations in the left column below, and type in the text listed in the right column:

Start Location	Text
<17,2>	Cust #
<17,10>	Prod #
<17,19>	Tax?
<17,25>	Qty
<17,32>	Unit Price
<17,51>	Total
<17,63>	Date of Sale

You can locate column names with the F6 key and arrow keys. When locating columns, the screen will ask the usual questions, such as

■   Do you want to define an expression for *<column name>*?

For the current form, you can select No each time this question appears. The screen will also ask

■   Do you want to customize field characteristics?

Generally, you can just answer No to each of these questions. However, you might want to put the default value of 1 in the Tax? column and the default #DATE in the P:Date column, as we've done before.

Using the F6 key and the arrow keys, place the column names listed below at the start and end locations listed to the right of each column name:

Column Name	Start	End
CustNo	<18,2>	<18,5>
ProdNo	<18,10>	<18,17>
Tax?	<18,20>	<18,21>
Qty	<18,24>	<18,27>
U:Price	<18,30>	<18,41>
Total	<18,43>	<18,55>
P:Date	<18,58>	<18,79>

When you are finished, your screen should look like Figure 11.11.

Since there may be many rows in the Charges table associated with a single row in the Names table, you'll want to duplicate the column locations in the region. That way, when a particular customer is displayed on the screen, you'll be able to scroll through and edit any of the transactions.

Copying Column Names into Tiers

When a form, or a region on a form, displays several rows from a table simultaneously, you can copy the column names into tiers (multiple rows of the same column names). The process for doing so is simple. First, press Shift-F4 (hold down the Shift key and press F4). The screen asks that you

- Move cursor to locate a corner of the area to be duplicated—press [ENTER]

Using the arrow keys, move the cursor to the left column of the area to copy (<18,2> in this example), and press Enter. Next the screen asks that you

- Move cursor to paint the area to be duplicated—press [ENTER]

Using the right arrow key, extend the highlighter to <18,79> to "paint over" all the column name locations. Press Enter when you are finished. Automatically, the entire region will be filled with the column name locations, as in Figure 11.12.

At this point you've finished creating the screen portion of the new form named Both. Before testing it, however, we can add another feature called a *master table lookup*. Press Esc to get to the top menu.

Defining a Master Lookup Expression

A master lookup expression is used in forms that serve multiple tables to define a relationship between the multiple tables. Generally,

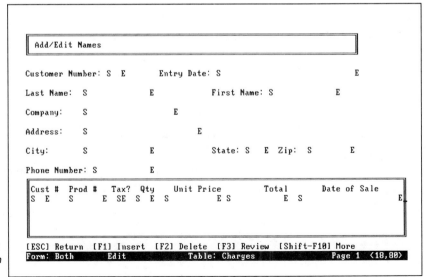

■ Figure 11.11: *Text and column names located in the region.*

the expression takes the form

■   <column> = <column> IN <table> WHERE <id> = <id>

The <column> portion is the name of any column in the named
<table>. The <id> portion is the name of the matching columns in
the two tables. In this example, you want to select Expression from the
top menu and Define from the submenu, and enter the master lookup
expression

■   L:Name = L:Name IN Names WHERE CustNo = CustNo

When the screen asks if you want to customize lookup characteristics,
select No.

When using the form later, R:BASE will automatically assume that
the last CustNo in the expression is the customer number just entered
onto the form. It will use that expression to match up the customer
number entered onto the form to customer numbers in the Names and
Charges tables. L:Name in this case is simply an arbitrary column
selected for convenience. The purpose of the expression is not to look
up a particular L:Name. Actually, the overall purpose is to attempt to
find out if the customer number entered onto the form already exists.

```
 ┌──────────────────────────────────────────────────────────────┐
 │  ┌─────────────────────────────────────────────────────────┐  │
 │  │ Add/Edit Names                                          │  │
 │  └─────────────────────────────────────────────────────────┘  │
 │                                                                │
 │  Customer Number: S   E      Entry Date: S               E     │
 │                                                                │
 │  Last Name:  S            E          First Name: S       E     │
 │                                                                │
 │  Company:    S                 E                               │
 │                                                                │
 │  Address:    S                    E                            │
 │                                                                │
 │  City:       S            E          State: S   E Zip:  S    E  │
 │                                                                │
 │  Phone Number: S          E                                    │
 │  ┌──────────────────────────────────────────────────────────┐ │
 │  │Cust #  Prod #   Tax?  Qty   Unit Price      Total    Date of Sale│
 │  │S   E   S     E SE  S  E  S      E S       E  S              E│ │
 │  │S   E   S     E SE  S  E  S      E S       E  S              E│ │
 │  │S   E   S     E SE  S  E  S      E S       E  S              E│ │
 │  │S   E   S     E SE  S  E  S      E S       E  S              E│ │
 │  └──────────────────────────────────────────────────────────┘ │
 │  [ESC] Return  [F1] Insert  [F2] Delete  [F3] Review  [Shift-F10] More│
 │  Form: Both        Edit          Table: Charges      Page 1  <18,79>│
 └──────────────────────────────────────────────────────────────┘
```

■ *Figure 11.12:*
Column names
copied in the
Charges region.

(The syntax of expressions in R:BASE, however, requires that a column name be included.)

We'll see the effects of this master lookup expression in a moment, and this will, perhaps, shed more light on this expression.

For the time being, we're finished creating the form. Press the Esc key until the exit options appear on the screen, and select Save Changes. Then exit all the higher-level menus to work your way back to the R > prompt.

Conflicting Rules

There is one slight catch to using multiple tables on a single form. Any rule that attempts to check the validity of data entered onto the Charges region of the form may break the rule when new data have just been entered onto the form, because of the way in which R:BASE treats data entered onto the form.

There is a simple way to avoid any conflicts with rules, however. Before using the form that serves multiple tables, enter the command

■ SET RULES OFF

next to the R > prompt. This will cause R:BASE to ignore all previously created rules when using the form that serves multiple tables. Later, after using the form, you can enter the command

■ SET RULES ON

to reinstate the rules.

■ USING THE FORM THAT SERVES TWO TABLES

You can use the new form with either the Edit or the Enter command. To try out the new form in the edit mode, enter the command

■ EDIT USING Both

at the R > prompt.

You'll notice right away that the form displays both the first row in the Names database and all the charges associated with that name, as in Figure 11.13.

You can select Next or Previous to scroll through the names in the Names table and watch how the form displays data.

To edit data in either table, select Edit from the top menu as usual. Once the cursor is inside the form, you can use the following keys in addition to the Enter, arrow, and Tab keys:

F9   Switch from one region (or table) to the next

F7   Skip back one row

F8   Skip forward one row

For example, if you press F9 while the cursor is still in the Names region of the screen, the cursor will jump down to the Charges region. Once inside the Charges region, you can press F8 and F7 to scroll up and down through the rows (that contain data) in the Charges region. Pressing F9 again brings the cursor back up to the Names portion of the form.

Of course, you can change any data on the form that you wish. When you are finished editing, press Esc and select Quit from the top menu.

To enter new data through the form, enter the command

■   ENTER Both

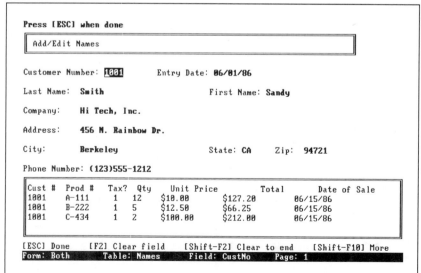

Figure 11.13: Data displayed from both the Names and Charges tables.

at the R > prompt. The form appears with no data in it, ready to accept new data.

Here is where the master lookup expression comes in. Normally, when entering data into a database, R:BASE will accept any entry you type in, or it will check the rules (if any) to see if a violation took place. But with the master lookup expression defined, R:BASE will simply display existing data if you enter an existing customer number.

For example, if you enter customer number 1003 onto the form and press Enter, the screen will display all existing data for customer number 1003. You can simply press F9 to move to the Charges region of the form and then type in new charges for this customer. After entering the new charges, press Esc and select Add.

If, for your next data entry, you enter a new customer number (such as 9999) and press Enter, the top portion of the screen will display the message

■ Master lookup row not found—Press [ENTER] to add, [ESC] to continue

R:BASE is telling you that the customer number you entered does not exist yet in the Names table, and it gives you two options. If you press Enter, a row for the new customer number will be created on the Names table, and you can fill in the remaining data (including data on the Charges table) for this new customer. If you press Esc, R:BASE will reject the new customer number and let you enter another one.

As usual, press Esc and select Quit when you are finished entering new data.

With some experience entering and editing data through a form that serves multiple tables, you'll soon find this method convenient for managing multiple tables.

■ TIPS AND TECHNIQUES FOR MULTITABLE FORMS

Before concluding this chapter, there are a few more tips and techniques that you should know about forms and regions.

Changing a Region

You can change the size, location, or appearance of a region using Forms Express. When the appropriate form is on the screen, you can insert lines above or beneath the region using the F1 key (assuming that there is room on the form to insert new lines). You can also delete lines above or beneath the region using the F2 key. (The F2 key will only delete lines that do not have column names or variables located. If necessary, use Shift-F2 to delete column and variable names, and then use F2 to delete the line.)

To make changes to the actual region, such as changing column locations, text, or the region's size, you'll first need to remove the duplicated tiers. Make sure the name of the table that the duplicated tiers serve (Charges in this example) appears in the status bar. Then press Shift-F4. The screen will ask for permission before removing the duplicated tiers.

Once the duplicated tiers are removed, you can freely change text and column name locations inside the region using the arrow, F6, Ins, and Del keys.

To change the size of a region, first make sure that the table the region serves is attached. When the name of the table associated with the region appears in the status bar, press F9. The cursor moves to the upper-left corner of the region, and the entire region is highlighted. You can then alter the size of the region with the arrow keys.

After you've made your changes to the column locations and text inside the region, you can use the Shift-F4 key again to copy the column names.

Preventing Changes to the Customer Number

When using the form with multiple tables and the Enter command, the user can enter any customer number. If the customer number exists, the data are displayed on the screen. At this point, the user could change the customer number, but the results of doing so could cause problems, because the corresponding charges on the Charges table will not automatically be updated to reflect the new customer number.

To prevent changes to the CustNo column, you can enter Forms Express and edit the form named Both. Make sure the Names table is attached (press F7 if Charges is attached). Move the cell pointer anywhere between the S and E for the CustNo column for the Names table (in this example, <5,18>) and press F6. When the screen asks if you want to customize field characteristics, select Yes. On the Field Characteristics menu you'll see the question

■ Can the user change the data displayed in the field?

If you change the answer to this question to No, the user will not be allowed to change the number of an existing customer.

Reordering Table Names

If in the future you create a form that serves more than two tables, you might want to change the order in which the F9 key cycles through the tables in the form. To do so, select Customize from the top menu in Forms Express. From the submenus select Table and Reorder. The screen will display instructions for changing the order of the tables in the database. (The technique is virtually identical to that used for changing the order of expressions.)

■ SUMMARY

In this chapter we've used some more advanced features from the Reports menu. In the next chapter, we'll look at some *relational* commands for combining and summarizing multiple tables.

The techniques we've used in this chapter are summarized below:

The report heading and footing each appear once, at the top and bottom of the entire report.

Page headings and footings appear at the top and bottom of each page in the report.

Breakpoint headings and footings appear each time there is a subtotal or subheading break in the report. Breakpoints are determined by a change in the contents column that you specify. For example, we used CustNo as the breakpoint column in this example, so subtotals were calculated for each unique customer number.

Variables for totals and subtotals are defined using the Sum Of command when defining report variables.

Column names from other tables are defined using the syntax

■ *variable name = column name* IN *table name* WHERE *conditions*

To print a report with totals and subtotals, first enter the Clear All Variables command; then enter the Print command followed by the name of the report.

To create a region on a form to serve as a separate table, use the F8 key first to attach the separate table. Answer Yes to the prompt about customizing table characteristics and Yes to the question about defining a region.

To place text and locate column names in a region, use the arrow keys and the F6 key to mark the start and end locations for each column name.

To duplicate a series of column names (called *tiers*) in a region, use Shift-F4.

To allow simultaneous editing and entering of data in a form that serves multiple tables, create a master lookup expression with the syntax

■ <column> = <column> IN <table> WHERE <id> = <id>

Before using a form that serves multiple tables, enter the command Set Rules Off at the R> prompt.

You can access a form that serves multiple tables by using either the Enter or the Edit Using command followed by the name of the form.

12

COMBINING
AND COPYING
TABLES

R:BASE offers six commands for combining and copying tables in a database: Project, Append, Union, Intersect, Subtract, and Join. Like all commands, these can be entered directly at the R> prompt. Alternatively, you can build from these commands by selecting Relational Operations from the Prompt menu.

You can also view data from up to five tables simultaneously by using *views*. Views are created in Definition Express and are discussed later in this chapter.

Before trying the sample operations in this chapter, make sure that the Mail database is open and the R> prompt is on the screen. Keep in mind that your results may differ if your Names or Charges table contains data other than those used in the sample operations.

■ COPYING TABLES WITH PROJECT

The Project command makes a copy of all or part of a table, creating a new table in the process. It is useful for making backup copies of tables, creating summary tables, and reordering columns and rows in a table. The basic syntax for the project command is

■   PROJECT *new table name* FROM *existing table name* USING +
      column names SORTED BY *column names* WHERE *conditions*

The Sorted By and Where clauses are optional with this command, and All can be used in place of individual column names.

Let's suppose that you want to create a list of names, telephone numbers, and entry dates for everyone in the Names table whose entry dates are between June 1 and June 15, 1986. Furthermore, you want to store the list in order by telephone number. To create a new table named PhoneLst for these data, enter the command

■   PROJECT PhoneLst FROM Names USING Phone +
      L:Name F:Name Ent:Date SORTED BY Phone WHERE +
      Ent:Date > 5/31/86 AND Ent:Date < = 6/15/86

After performing the requested task, R:BASE responds with this message:

■   Successful project operation   6 rows generated

To see the contents of the new PhoneLst table, use the Select command, as follows:

■　SELECT ALL FROM PhoneLst

R:BASE displays the new PhoneLst table, as below:

Phone	L:Name	F:Name	Ent:Date
(123)555-1010	Jones	Mindy	06/15/86
(123)555-1212	Smith	Sandy	06/01/86
(123)555-2222	Miller	Marie	06/01/86
(213)123-4567	Adams	Bart	06/15/86
(213)234-5678	Miller	Anne	06/01/86
(345)678-9012	Baker	Robin	06/15/86

Using the Project Command to Rearrange Columns

Let's take a look at how you can use the Project command to rearrange columns in a table (don't, however, try this out on-line—let's retain the column arrangement we already have). Suppose that you want to rearrange the columns in the Names table so that Ent:Date is the column farthest left and CustNo is the column farthest right. First, you would need to copy the Names table to a temporary table (named Temp in this example), specifying all the column names in the order that you want them, as below:

■　PROJECT Temp FROM Names USING Ent:Date L:Name +
　　F:Name Company Address City State Zip Phone CustNo

When you leave out the Sorted By and Where clauses, you retain the original sort order and ensure that all the rows from the Names table are copied to the Temp table. To ensure that the Project command was correctly executed, you could look at the Temp table by entering

■　SELECT ALL FROM Temp

Next, you would need to remove the original Names table using the Remove command, as below:

■　REMOVE Names

Finally, you would change the name of the Temp table to Names, using the Rename command, as follows:

■ RENAME TABLE Temp TO Names

R:BASE will respond with

■ Table Temp renamed to Names

If you then look at the Names table by entering

■ SELECT ALL FROM Names

you'll see that the Ent:Date column is indeed in the position farthest left, as shown in Figure 12.1. Using the List command with the table name will display the new column order, as shown in Figure 12.2.

Using the Project Command to Rearrange Rows

Although the Sorted By clause allows you to arrange rows in any order that you wish, you might want to use a quicker method when

```
R>SELECT ALL FROM Names
 Ent:Date L:Name          F:Name          Company
 _____ _____    _____    _____
 06/01/86 Smith           Sandy           Hi Tech, Inc.
 06/15/86 Jones           Mindy           ABC Co.
 06/01/80 Miller          Marie           Zeerox Inc.
 06/15/86 Adams           Bart            Dataspec Inc.
 06/01/86 Miller          Anne            Golden Gate Co.
 06/15/86 Baker           Robin           Peach Computers
 07/15/86 Miller          Monica          Acme Development
 07/01/86 Teasdale        Trudy           Atomic Ovens, Inc.
 07/01/86 Martin          Mary            Atomic Ovens, Inc.
R>_
```

■ *Figure 12.1:*
Columns rearranged in the Names table.

you're working with a large table. If this is the case, you can use the Project command to rearrange all the rows in a table.

For example, suppose you regularly send letters in ZIP-code order to the individuals listed in the Names table. You can create a sorted version of the Names table by first using the Project command to make a copy of the Names table sorted by ZIP code, as in the command below (again, don't try this on-line now):

- PROJECT Temp FROM Names USING ALL SORTED BY Zip

At this point, the table named Temp has the same information as the Names table; however, the Temp table data are sorted into ZIP-code order. You can verify this with the command

- SELECT Zip L:Name F:Name FROM Temp

Next, you can remove the Names table using the command

- REMOVE Names

Then change the name of the Temp table to Names, using the command

- RENAME TABLE Temp TO Names

```
R)LIST Names

    Table: Names          No lock(s)
    Read Password: No
    Modify Password: No

    Column definitions
    # Name      Type     Length        Key   Expression
    1 Ent:Date DATE
    2 L:Name    TEXT      15 characters
    3 F:Name    TEXT      15 characters
    4 Company   TEXT      30 characters
    5 Address   TEXT      25 characters
    6 City      TEXT      15 characters
    7 State     TEXT       5 characters
    8 Zip       TEXT      10 characters
    9 Phone     TEXT      13 characters
   10 CustNo    INTEGER

    Current number of rows:      9

R)_
```

■ *Figure 12.2:*
New column arrangement for the Names table.

Now you could use the Select command without a Sorted By clause, and the rows in the Names table would be displayed in ZIP-code order, as Figure 12.3 shows.

Using the Project Command to Make a Backup Copy

To make a backup copy of a table within the same database, use the Project command with the Using All option, as below:

■   PROJECT Backup FROM Names USING ALL

In summary, the Project command makes a copy of all or part of a table, creating an entirely new table.

■ ADDING ROWS WITH APPEND

The Append command copies rows from one table onto the bottom of another table. Only the columns that have identical names, types, and widths in the two tables are copied.

```
R>SELECT Zip CustNo L:Name F:Name Company FROM Names
Zip        CustNo      L:Name          F:Name         Company
---------- ---------- --------------- --------------- --------------------
12121         1009 Martin          Mary           Atomic Ovens, Inc.
12121         1008 Teasdale        Trudy          Atomic Ovens, Inc.
54821         1007 Miller          Monica         Acme Development
91234         1003 Miller          Marie          Zeerox Inc.
92111         1004 Adams           Bart           Dataspec Inc.
92122         1002 Jones           Mindy          ABC Co.
92122         1006 Baker           Robin          Peach Computers
94711         1005 Miller          Anne           Golden Gate Co.
94721         1001 Smith           Sandy          Hi Tech, Inc.
R>_
```

■ *Figure 12.3:*
New Names table
in ZIP-code order.

The Append command is often used for managing *transaction* tables and *history* tables, particularly in inventory and accounting systems. For example, the Charges table in the Mail database could grow indefinitely throughout the course of the year. However, most businesses bill monthly, so there is no need to keep all the transactions of the year on the Charges table.

Instead, after the customers have been billed at the end of the month, you could move all of that month's transactions to a history table for later reference, emptying the Charges table to make room for the following month's transactions.

Let's try using the Append command with the Charges table. Figure 12.4 shows the current contents of that table.

Now we'll create a table named History for storing transactions, and we'll give it the same structure as the Charges table. You can easily copy the *structure* of the Charges table with the Project command, as below:

■ PROJECT History FROM Charges USING ALL WHERE CustNo
 FAILS

R:BASE responds with the message

■ –WARNING– No rows satisfy the WHERE clause
 Successful project operation   0 rows generated

```
R>SELECT CustNo=5 ProdNo Qty=4 U:Price=8 Tax?=3 Total=8 P:Date FROM Charges
   CustN ProdNo   Qty  U:Price  Tax Total      P:Date
   _____ _____   ____ _____  ___ _____   _____
   1001  A-111    12    $10.00   1   $127.20  06/15/86
   1001  B-222     5    $12.50   1    $66.25  06/15/86
   1001  C-434     2   $100.00   1   $212.00  06/15/86
   1004  A-111     5    $10.00   1    $53.00  06/15/86
   1004  Z-128    10    $12.80   0   $128.00  06/15/86
   1007  A-111    10    $10.00   1   $106.00  06/15/86
   1007  Z-128    10    $12.80   0   $128.00  06/15/86
   1002  B-222    12    $12.50   1   $159.00  07/01/86
   1002  A-111    10    $10.00   1   $106.00  07/01/86
R>_
```

■ *Figure 12.4:*
*Current contents
of the Charges
table.*

Even though no rows were copied, a History table now exists with the same structure as the Charges table. If you use the Select All command to view the History table, you'll see this:

■ SELECT ALL FROM History
–WARNING– No data exists for this table

At the end of June, to move June transactions to the History table, enter the following:

■ APPEND Charges TO History WHERE P:Date > = 6/1/86 +
AND P:Date < = 6/30/86

R:BASE responds with this message:

■ Successful append operation   7 rows added

Using the Select command to view the contents of the History table verifies that it now contains June transactions, as Figure 12.5 shows.

With these transactions listed in the History table, you can use the Delete Rows command with a Where clause to delete them from the Charges table, as follows:

■ DELETE ROWS FROM Charges WHERE P:Date > = 6/1/86 +
AND P:Date < = 6/30/86

R:BASE replies

■ 7 row(s) have been deleted from Charges

If you use the Select command to view the contents of the Charges table, you'll see that only the July transactions remain, as shown in Figure 12.6.

When the end of July rolls around, you can append the July transactions to the History table using this command:

■ APPEND Charges TO History WHERE P:Date > = 7/1/86 +
AND P:Date < = 7/31/86

R:BASE displays the following message:

■ Successful append operation   2 rows added

If you use the Select command to view the contents of the History table now, you'll see that it contains both the June and July transactions, as shown in Figure 12.7.

```
R>SELECT CustNO=5 ProdNo Qty U:Price=8 Tax?=3 Total=8 P:Date FROM History
  CustN ProdNo    Qty       U:Price  Tax Total     P:Date
  ----- --------  --------- -------- --- --------- --------
   1001 A-111        12     $10.00    1  $127.20 06/15/86
   1001 B-222         5     $12.50    1   $66.25 06/15/86
   1001 C-434         2    $100.00    1  $212.00 06/15/86
   1004 A-111         5     $10.00    1   $53.00 06/15/86
   1004 Z-128        10     $12.80    0  $128.00 06/15/86
   1007 A-111        10     $10.00    1  $106.00 06/15/86
   1007 Z-128        10     $12.80    0  $128.00 06/15/86
  R>_
```

■ *Figure 12.5:*
June transactions in the History table.

```
R>SELECT CustNo=5 ProdNo Qty=4 U:Price=8 Tax?=3 Total=8 P:Date FROM Charges
  CustN ProdNo    Qty U:Price  Tax Total     P:Date
  ----- --------  --- -------- --- --------- --------
   1002 B-222       12  $12.50   1  $159.00 07/01/86
   1002 A-111       10  $10.00   1  $106.00 07/01/86
  R>_
```

■ *Figure 12.6:*
July transactions in the Charges table.

To clear the transactions from the Charges table, use the command

- DELETE ROWS FROM Charges WHERE P:Date > = 7/1/86 +
  AND P:Date < = 7/31/86

If you attempt to view the Charges table with the Select command, you'll see that it is empty, as below:

- SELECT ALL FROM Charges
  –WARNING– No data exists for this table

Now the Charges table is clear for adding new transactions for August, and the History table has a record of all June and July transactions.

If you've followed along on-line through these exercises, let's delete the History table and put the Charges table back into its original condition. First, remove the now empty Charges table with the command

- REMOVE Charges

Then, change the name of the History table to Charges with the following command:

- RENAME TABLE History TO Charges

```
R>SELECT CustNo=5 ProdNo Qty=4 U:Price=8 Tax?=3 Total=8 P:Date FROM History
  CustN ProdNo   Qty  U:Price  Tax Total      P:Date
  _____ _____ ____ _____ ___ _____   _____
  1001 A-111     12   $10.00    1  $127.20 06/15/86
  1001 B-222      5   $12.50    1   $66.25 06/15/86
  1001 C-434      2  $100.00    1  $212.00 06/15/86
  1004 A-111      5   $10.00    1   $53.00 06/15/86
  1004 Z-128     10   $12.80    0  $128.00 06/15/86
  1007 A-111     10   $10.00    1  $106.00 06/15/86
  1007 Z-128     10   $12.80    0  $128.00 06/15/86
  1002 B-222     12   $12.50    1  $159.00 07/01/86
  1002 A-111     10   $10.00    1  $106.00 07/01/86
R>_
```

■ *Figure 12.7:*
June and July
transactions in
the History table.

Everything should now be as it was before we started these exercises.

■ COMBINING TWO TABLES WITH UNION

The Union command allows you to combine all or part of two existing tables into a new third table. The Union command requires that the two tables have at least one common column (a key field). Common columns are those that have identical names, data types, and widths.

The basic syntax for the Union command is the following:

■ UNION *table 1* WITH *table 2* FORMING *table 3* USING *column + names*

The Union command will combine common columns into a single column on the new table. If you specify All in the Using portion of the command, the new table will include all the columns from the two original tables. If you specify only certain column names in the Using portion, the new table will contain the named columns in the order that you specified.

Suppose that you want a listing of the product numbers, customer numbers, names, quantities, and unit prices from the Charges and Names tables. You could create a new table (named Temp in this example) with the appropriate information using the command below:

■ UNION Charges WITH Names FORMING Temp USING +
ProdNo CustNo L:Name F:Name Qty U:Price

R:BASE responds as follows:

■ Successful union operation   14 rows generated

If you then enter the command

■ SELECT ProdNo = 6 CustNo = 5 L:Name = 10 F:Name = 7 +
Qty = 4 U:Price = 8 FROM Temp

R:BASE displays the contents of the new Temp table, as shown in Figure 12.8.

Notice that several rows have a null character in the ProdNo column. These null characters indicate that those individuals were not listed in the Charges table (because they didn't make any purchases). When one table has rows that do not match the second table, the Union command will copy those rows to the new table and add null characters to the columns in nonmatching rows.

Let's use the Union command to combine the Names and Charges tables in another way. Suppose that you want a listing of all customer numbers and company names, followed by a list of items purchased. Although we could just create a new table, for this example we'll remove the existing Temp table with the command

■   REMOVE Temp

Then, we'll create a new Temp table using the Union command, with the Names table entered first and with the appropriate column names listed in the Using portion, as below:

■   UNION Names WITH Charges FORMING Temp +
    USING CustNo Company ProdNo Qty U:Price

R:BASE responds with the following:

■   Successful union operation   14 rows generated

```
R>SELECT ProdNo=6 CustNo=5 L:Name=10 F:Name=7 Qty=4 +
+>U:Price=8 FROM Temp
 ProdNo CustN L:Name     F:Name  Qty  U:Price
 ------ ----- ---------- ------  ---  ---------
 A-111  1001  Smith      Sandy    12  $10.00
 B-222  1001  Smith      Sandy     5  $12.50
 C-434  1001  Smith      Sandy     2  $100.00
 A-111  1004  Adams      Bart      5  $10.00
 Z-128  1004  Adams      Bart     10  $12.80
 A-111  1007  Miller     Monica   10  $10.00
 Z-128  1007  Miller     Monica   10  $12.80
 B-222  1002  Jones      Andy     12  $12.50
 A-111  1002  Jones      Andy     10  $10.00
 -0-    1003  Miller     Marie    -0-  -0-
 -0-    1005  Miller     Anne     -0-  -0-
 -0-    1006  Baker      Robin    -0-  -0-
 -0-    1008  Teasdale   Trudy    -0-  -0-
 -0-    1009  Martin     Mary     -0-  -0-
R>_
```

■ *Figure 12.8:*
Results of the
Union command.

To view the contents of the new Temp table, enter this command:

■   SELECT ALL FROM Temp

You should see the display shown in Figure 12.9.

Again, notice how the Union command handled nonmatching rows. Since the Charges table showed no transactions for customers 1003, 1005, 1006, 1008, and 1009, these rows were displayed in the Temp table with null values in the ProdNo, Qty, and U:Price columns. As you'll see, the Intersect command handles this situation differently.

Go ahead and enter the command

■   REMOVE Temp

to delete the Temp table, and we'll experiment with the Intersect command.

■ COMBINING TABLES WITH THE INTERSECT COMMAND

The Intersect command is similar to the Union command, except that it does not generate rows with null values. For example, when combining the Charges and Names tables with the Union command, rows from the Names table that were not listed in the Charges table appear in the Temp table with null values. With the Intersect command, nonmatching rows are not added to the new table.

Like the Union command, the Intersect command requires that the two tables have at least one common column (with identical names, data types, and widths). The general syntax for the Intersect command is identical to the syntax for the Union command, as shown below:

■   INTERSECT *table 1* WITH *table 2* FORMING *table 3* USING +
     column names

If you combine the Names and Charges tables with the Intersect command, as below:

■   INTERSECT Charges WITH Names FORMING Temp USING +
     ProdNo CustNo L:Name F:Name Qty U:Price

R:BASE will respond with this message:

■   Successful intersect operation   9 rows generated

If you then enter the command

■   SELECT ProdNo CustNo L:Name = 10 F:Name = 10 Qty = 4 +
     U:Price = 8 FROM Temp

you'll see the contents of the Temp table, as shown in Figure 12.10. As
the figure shows, only the customers that appear in both the Names and
Charges tables are included in the new table.
    Let's try another example. First, enter

■   REMOVE Temp

to eliminate the Temp table. Now we'll create a table with customer
numbers and company names, followed by product numbers,
quantities, and unit prices. Enter the command

■   INTERSECT Names WITH Charges FORMING Temp USING +
     CustNo Company ProdNo Qty U:Price

```
R>SELECT ALL FROM Temp
  CustNo      Company                          ProdNo    Qty        U:Price
  ----------  -------------------------------  --------  ---------  -----------------
        1001  Hi Tech, Inc.                    A-111          12           $10.00
        1001  Hi Tech, Inc.                    B-222           5           $12.50
        1001  Hi Tech, Inc.                    C-434           2          $100.00
        1002  ABC Co.                          B-222          12           $12.50
        1002  ABC Co.                          A-111          10           $10.00
        1003  Zeerox Inc.                      -0-           -0-          -0-
        1004  Dataspec Inc.                    A-111           5           $10.00
        1004  Dataspec Inc.                    Z-128          10           $12.80
        1005  Golden Gate Co.                  -0-           -0-          -0-
        1006  Peach Computers                  -0-           -0-          -0-
        1007  Acme Development                 A-111          10           $10.00
        1007  Acme Development                 Z-128          10           $12.80
        1008  Atomic Ovens, Inc.               -0-           -0-          -0-
        1009  Atomic Ovens, Inc.               -0-           -0-          -0-
R>_
```

■ *Figure 12.9:*
Results of the
second Union
command.

If you use the Select command to view the results of the Intersect command, as below:

■   SELECT ALL FROM Temp

you'll see that only the customers listed in both the Names and Charges tables made it to the Temp table, as Figure 12.11 shows.

We've seen that the Union command transferred all the rows from both the Names and Charges table to the new table, including those that did not have common customer numbers. The result was that we could see the purchases made by various customers, as well as see the customers who made no purchases. The Intersect command, however, copied only those rows that had common values in both the Names and Charges tables. Therefore, we saw a listing of purchases made by various customers, without seeing the customers who didn't make purchases.

Suppose you wanted to see a listing of only those customers who didn't make any purchases (the opposite of what the Intersect command provided). In this case, you could use the Subtract command. Again, remove the Temp table so that we can use it for the next exercise by entering

■   REMOVE Temp

```
R>SELECT ProdNo CustNo L:Name=10 F:Name=10 Qty=4 U:Price=8 FROM Temp
  ProdNo    CustNo      L:Name     F:Name    Qty  U:Price
  --------  ----------  ---------  --------  ----  --------
  A-111          1001   Smith      Sandy       12   $10.00
  B-222          1001   Smith      Sandy        5   $12.50
  C-434          1001   Smith      Sandy        2  $100.00
  A-111          1004   Adams      Bart         5   $10.00
  Z-128          1004   Adams      Bart        10   $12.80
  A-111          1007   Miller     Monica      10   $10.00
  Z-128          1007   Miller     Monica      10   $12.80
  B-222          1002   Jones      Mindy       12   $12.50
  A-111          1002   Jones      Mindy       10   $10.00
R>_
```

■ *Figure 12.10:*
Results of the
first Intersect
command.

```
R>SELECT ALL FROM Temp
  CustNo      Company                              ProdNo    Qty         U:Price
  ----------  ----------------------------------   --------  ----------  -----------------
        1001  Hi Tech, Inc.                        A-111           12          $10.00
        1001  Hi Tech, Inc.                        B-222            5          $12.50
        1001  Hi Tech, Inc.                        C-434            2         $100.00
        1002  ABC Co.                              B-222           12          $12.50
        1002  ABC Co.                              A-111           10          $10.00
        1004  Dataspec Inc.                        A-111            5          $10.00
        1004  Dataspec Inc.                        Z-128           10          $12.80
        1007  Acme Development                     A-111           10          $10.00
        1007  Acme Development                     Z-128           10          $12.80
  R>_
```

■ *Figure 12.11:*
Results of the
second Intersect
command.

■ VIEWING DIFFERENCES WITH SUBTRACT

The Subtract command forms a new table of rows that do not match on two existing tables. The general syntax for the command is

■   SUBTRACT *small table* FROM *large table* FORMING +
    new table USING *column names*

The *small table* is not necessarily physically smaller than the *large table,* but instead it might be a subset of the other table. For example, even if the Charges table contained 1000 rows, it would be the smaller table in this example because it might not contain every customer number. The Names table is the *large table* because it does contain every customer number.

To find out which customers in the Names table did not make purchases (that is, the ones that do not appear on the Charges table), subtract the Charges table from the Names table using the command

-   SUBTRACT Charges FROM Names FORMING Temp

R:BASE responds with the following:

-   Successful subtract operation   5 rows generated

When you enter the command

-   SELECT ALL FROM Temp

you'll see the five customers who are not included in the Charges table, as shown in Figure 12.12.

    Note that if you do attempt to subtract a large table from a smaller one, you'll end up with no rows on the new table, as below (note the message "0 rows generated"):

-   SUBTRACT Names FROM Charges FORMING Temp
    Successful subtract operation   0 rows generated

```
R>SELECT ALL FROM Temp
CustNo    L:Name           F:Name        Company
----------  -----------------  ----------------  -----------------------------
     1003 Miller           Marie         Zeerox Inc.
     1005 Miller           Anne          Golden Gate Co.
     1006 Baker            Robin         Peach Computers
     1008 Teasdale         Trudy         Atomic Ovens
     1009 Martin           Mary          Atomic Ovens
R>_
```

■ *Figure 12.12:*
Results of the
Subtract
command.

■ COMBINING TABLES WITH JOIN

The Join command works in much the same way as the Union command, except for two important differences:

The Join command allows you to compare column data from two tables using any of the various operators, such as equal, not equal, greater than, and less than.

The columns used for comparing the two tables may have different names; however, the two columns must be of the same data type and length.

The general syntax for the Join command is

■ JOIN *table 1* USING *column name* WITH *table 2* USING +
column name FORMING *table 3* WHERE *operator*

The operator used with the Where clause may be any of the following:

Operator	Meaning
EQ	Equal
NE	Not equal
GT	Greater than
GE	Greater than or equal to
LT	Less than
LE	Less than or equal to

Since the Names and Charges tables both have a column named CustNo, we'll demonstrate this command with a hypothetical database.

Suppose that you have a database with two tables: one named Sales and the other named Commiss. The Sales table contains salespersons' names and sales amounts, as below:

Name	Sales
Andrews	$12,500.00
Baker	$17,000.00
Carlson	$10,000.00
Edwards	$ 5,000.00
Davis	$45,000.00

The Commiss table contains commission rates and cutoff values, starting with a base rate of 15% for a $10,000 sale and adding another 2% for each $5000 in sales, as below:

SalesAmt	Rate
$10,000.00	0.15
$15,000.00	0.02
$20,000.00	0.02
$25,000.00	0.02

We want to use the Join command to combine the Sales table, using the Sales column for comparison, with the Commiss table, using the SalesAmt column for comparison, to form a new table named Rates, and we want to use the greater than or equal to operator for the comparison.

To do this, we use the command

■   JOIN Sales USING Sales WITH Commiss USING SalesAmt +
     FORMING Rates WHERE ge

The resulting Rates table is listed below:

Name	Sales	SalesAmt	Rate
Andrews	$12,500.00	$10,000.00	0.15
Baker	$17,000.00	$10,000.00	0.15
Baker	$17,000.00	$15,000.00	0.02
Carlson	$10,000.00	$10,000.00	0.15
Davis	$45,000.00	$10,000.00	0.15
Davis	$45,000.00	$15,000.00	0.02
Davis	$45,000.00	$20,000.00	0.02
Davis	$45,000.00	$25,000.00	0.02

Notice that Mr. Andrews receives a 15% commission for his $12,500 sale; Mr. Baker receives 15%, plus another 2%, for his $17,000 sale; and Mr. Davis receives 15%, plus another 6% (2% three times) for his $45,000 sale. Displaying this table without the SalesAmt column makes the table clearer, as shown in Figure 12.13.

Notice also that the Join command creates a row for each comparison that satisfies the Where operator. Davis is listed four times because his $45,000 sale is greater than or equal to all of the SalesAmt figures in the Commiss table. However, Edwards's $5000 sale was not included in the Rates table, because it was not greater than or equal to any of the SalesAmt cutoff values in the Commiss table.

∎ CONSTRUCTING VIEWS

A *view* is a *pseudo-table* that, rather than containing data of its own, displays data from up to five related tables. The tables in a view must have at least one key column (with the same column name, width, and data type) in common. Once you have created a view, you can view data through it as you would any other table. For example, you can use the view with the Select command and the Sorted By and Where clauses. You can also use the view as a table for creating report formats in Reports Express.

There are limitations on views, however. Since a view only displays data from existing tables, you cannot enter data directly into it. Nor should you edit data through the view. (For that matter, you cannot create forms for a view at all.) Instead, you'll want to enter and edit data through the actual tables from which the view gets its data. Nonetheless, a view is a convenient tool for viewing data from multiple tables quickly and easily.

```
R>SELECT Name Sales C:Rate FROM Rates
Name                     Sales            C:Rate
-----------------------  ---------------  --------
Andrews                  $12,500.00       0.15
Baker                    $17,000.00       0.15
Baker                    $17,000.00       0.02
Carlson                  $10,000.00       0.15
Davis                    $45,000.00       0.15
Davis                    $45,000.00       0.02
Davis                    $45,000.00       0.02
Davis                    $45,000.00       0.02
R>_
```

∎ *Figure 12.13:*
Rows from the
Rates table.

For this exercise, we'll create a view that displays the customer number, product number, quantity, tax status, unit price, transaction total, and date of sale from the Charges table, along with the appropriate last name, first name, and company from the Names table. To further demonstrate the power of views, we'll limit the view to customers in the state of California (although R:BASE does not require that you place such limits on views). We'll name the view CaTrans (for California Transactions).

Defining a View

To define a view, enter Definition Express by entering the command

■ RBDEFINE

at the R> prompt. From the Definition Express Main menu, select option (2) to modify an existing database definition. From the options submenu, select option (2), Views. You'll see the Views menu with the options below:

■ (1) Add a new view to the database
(2) Change an existing view
(3) Remove a view from the database
(4) Return to the database definition menu

To create a new view, select option (1). You'll see a screen that resembles the one in which you create a new table. The screen asks that you

■ Enter the name for this view:

Like tables, a view can have a name with up to eight letters. (It must begin with a letter and include no spaces or punctuation.) For this example, type in the name

■ CaTrans

and press Enter.

The screen asks for the name of the first table to be used in the view. In this example, we're primarily interested in rows from the Charges table (that is, we want to view every transaction in the Charges table). Therefore, select Charges from the list of table names.

Next, the screen asks which column from Charges you want to include in the view. For this example, select (ALL), though you could select only certain column names. All the column names fill in on the main part of the screen, as shown in Figure 12.14. (The CustNo column is off the left edge of the screen.)

Next, press the Enter key to select the next table for the view. From the menu of table names that appears, select Names. The column names for the Names table appear on a menu at the bottom of the screen.

From the Names table, we'll want the L:Name, F:Name, Company, and State columns. To select a column name, move the highlighter to the appropriate name and press Enter. (We need the State column in this example because we're going to place a Where clause in the view that limits the view to California residents. You can select any other column names that you wish for the view.)

After you select the column names, they appear in the table portion of the screen, as in Figure 12.15. (Most of the column names from the Charges table have been pushed off the left edge of the screen.)

Press Esc to continue constructing the view.

Building Conditions for the View

After selecting the columns for the view, you'll see a screen for placing a Where clause in the view. You can leave this blank

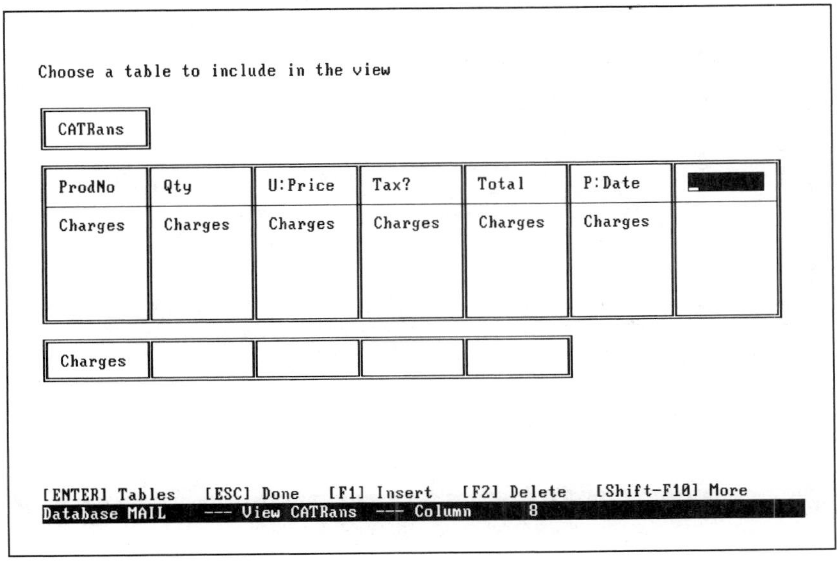

■ *Figure 12.14:*
Column names
from Charges
selected for the
view.

(thereby not limiting the view to any particular rows) by pressing the Esc key. In this example, however, we'll limit the view to California residents.

The screen asks that you

■   Choose column to validate:

Select State, since this is the column of interest. The screen then asks that you select an operator and presents the following (now familiar) operators:

■   EQ   NE   GT   GE   LT   LE   CONTAINS   EXISTS   FAILS

For this example, select EQ (for equals). The screen asks that you

■   Enter value to be used for comparison:

Since we want this view to be limited to California residents, type in CA and press Enter. The completed Where clause definition appears on the screen, along with options for extending the clause, as in Figure 12.16.

You can select a logical operator (such as AND or OR) to add conditions to the Where clause. However, for this example, just select (Done). That completes the view definition. Now select options (4), (7), and (4) from the higher-level menus to leave Definition Express and return to the R > prompt.

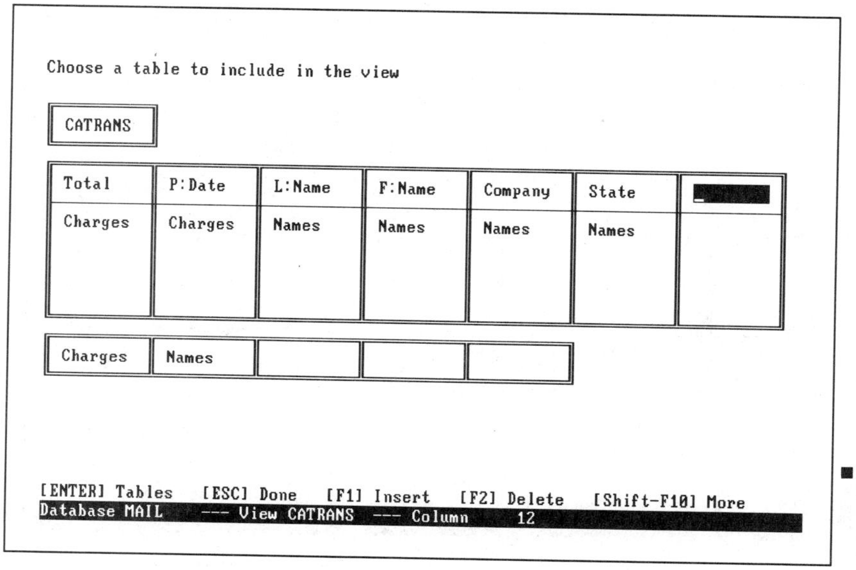

■ *Figure 12.15:*
Column names
from the Names
table in the view.

Using the View

You can use the Select command in the usual way with the view, using the name of the view (that is, CaTrans) in place of a particular table name. For example, suppose you want to see all the transactions for California residents, with name, company, and state for each transaction, sorted into ascending product number order and descending total order. Entering the command below will show the information you want:

■ SELECT ProdNo = 6 Qty = 4 U:Price = 8 Total = 8 +
   CustNo = 6 L:Name = 7 F:Name = 7 Company = 15 State = 2 +
   FROM CaTrans SORTED BY ProdNo Qty = D

The results of this Select command are shown in Figure 12.17.

To see a list of customer numbers and company names with product numbers, quantity purchased, and date of sales, enter the command

■ SELECT CustNo Company = 15 ProdNo Qty Total P:Date +
   FROM CaTrans

The results will appear on your screen as in Figure 12.18.

To use the view as the basis for a report, enter Reports Express in the usual fashion. When asked to supply the name of the table that the report is to display data from, select CaTrans, as though it were a table.

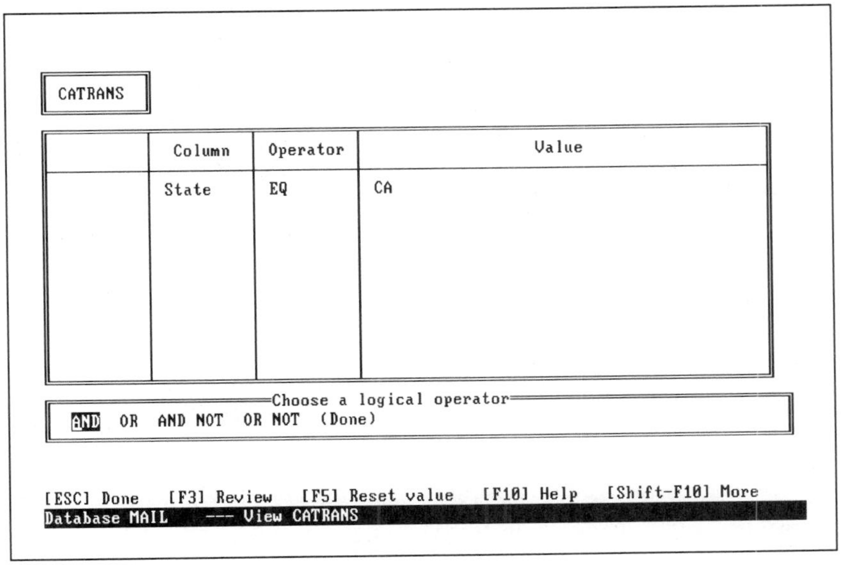

■ *Figure 12.16:*
View limited to California residents.

Again, you cannot create forms for views, but as we saw in the previous chapter, there are other ways to create forms that serve more than one table.

```
R>SELECT ProdNo=6 Qty=4 U:Price=8 Total=8 +
+>CustNo=6 L:Name=7 F:Name=7 Company=15 State=2 +
+>FROM CaTrans SORTED BY ProdNo Qty=D
  ProdNo Qty  U:Price   Total    CustNo L:Name  F:Name  Company             St
  ------ ----  --------  --------  ------ ------  ------  ---------------     --
  A-111   12   $10.00   $127.20    1001 Smith   Sandy   Hi Tech, Inc.       CA
  A-111   10   $10.00   $106.00    1002 Jones   Mindy   ABC Co.             CA
  A-111    5   $10.00    $53.00    1004 Adams   Bart    Dataspec Inc.       CA
  B-222   12   $12.50   $159.00    1002 Jones   Mindy   ABC Co.             CA
  B-222    5   $12.50    $66.25    1001 Smith   Sandy   Hi Tech, Inc.       CA
  C-434    2  $100.00   $212.00    1001 Smith   Sandy   Hi Tech, Inc.       CA
  Z-128   10   $12.80   $128.00    1004 Adams   Bart    Dataspec Inc.       CA
R>_
```

■ *Figure 12.17:*
Display from the CaTrans view.

```
R>SELECT CustNo Company=15 ProdNo Qty Total P:Date FROM CaTrans
  CustNo    Company         ProdNo  Qty     Total        P:Date
  -------   ------------    ------  ------  -----------   --------
     1001 Hi Tech, Inc.     A-111     12      $127.20 06/15/86
     1001 Hi Tech, Inc.     B-222      5       $66.25 06/15/86
     1001 Hi Tech, Inc.     C-434      2      $212.00 06/15/86
     1004 Dataspec Inc.     A-111      5       $53.00 06/15/86
     1004 Dataspec Inc.     Z-128     10      $128.00 06/15/86
     1002 ABC Co.           B-222     12      $159.00 07/01/86
     1002 ABC Co.           A-111     10      $106.00 07/01/86
R>_
```

■ *Figure 12.18:*
Another display from the CaTrans view.

■ *MANAGING VIEWS*

Recall that when you first selected Views from the Definition Express submenu, two menu options were displayed for changing existing views and deleting views, as shown below:

- ■ (2) Change an existing view
  (3) Remove a view from the database

Option (2) allows you to change an existing view in a manner similar to changing the structure of an existing table. (The F1 key lets you insert columns, F2 deletes them.) Option (3) allows you to remove a view from a database altogether.

■ *SUMMARY*

The R:BASE relational commands allow you to copy and combine data from existing tables into new tables. The six relational commands are summarized below:

The Project command allows you to copy a table, or a portion of a table, to a new table. By specifying column names, you can rearrange the order of columns or reduce the number of columns in the copied table. The Where clause allows you to limit the number of rows passed to the copied table, and the Sorted By clause allows you to specify a sort order for the copied table. Figure 12.19 shows an example.

The Append command copies all or some rows from a table and appends them to the bottom of another table. Figure 12.20 shows an example.

The Union command creates a third table, composed of all or some of the columns from two other tables. The existing tables must have a common column (one with identical names, data types, and widths). Common columns are merged into a single column, and all rows are copied from both tables. Figure 12.21 shows an example.

Table1

Item	Qty
Apples	10
Bananas	20
Cherries	30

PROJECT Table3 FROM Table1 USING ALL

Table3

Item	Qty
Apples	10
Bananas	20
Cherries	30

■ *Figure 12.19:*
Example of the
Project command.

The Intersect command creates a third table from all or part of two existing tables. Like the Union command, the Intersect command requires that the tables have at least one common column. Common columns are merged into a single column. Only common rows are copied to the new table. Figure 12.22 shows an example.

The Subtract command creates a third table from two existing tables, composed of rows that do not match on the two tables. Figure 12.23 shows an example.

The Join command can merge two tables that do not have a column with the same name. The use of a Where clause allows you to specify a comparison parameter for performing the search. The columns used for comparison must have the same data type and length. If you use the Join command to combine two tables that have a common column, the column is displayed twice in the new table, and R:BASE displays the following warning:

∎ **–WARNING–** *Column name* is a duplicate column name. You should rename one of them before using.

Figures 12.24 and 12.25 show two examples.

To view data from multiple tables simultaneously, without creating a report format to do so, you can create a *view* that can contain columns from up to five different tables. The tables in the view must have at least one column in common. Use Definition Express to create views.

∎ *Figure 12.20: Example of the Append command.*

Table2		**Table3**	
Item	**Price**	**Item**	**Qty**
Apples	0.25	Apples	10
Bananas	0.50	Bananas	20
Cherries	0.75	Cherries	30
Rutabaga	1.00		

APPEND Table2 TO Table3

Table3	
Item	**Qty**
Apples	10
Bananas	20
Cherries	30
Apples	-0-
Bananas	-0-
Cherries	-0-
Rutabaga	-0-

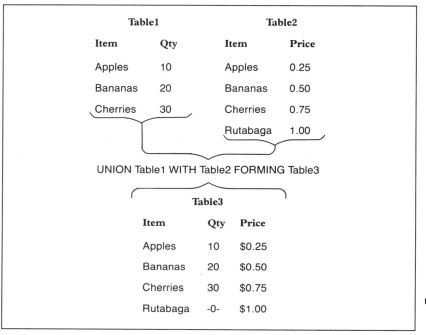

Table1

Item	Qty
Apples	10
Bananas	20
Cherries	30

Table2

Item	Price
Apples	0.25
Bananas	0.50
Cherries	0.75
Rutabaga	1.00

UNION Table1 WITH Table2 FORMING Table3

Table3

Item	Qty	Price
Apples	10	$0.25
Bananas	20	$0.50
Cherries	30	$0.75
Rutabaga	-0-	$1.00

■ *Figure 12.21:*
Example of the Union command.

Table1

Item	Qty
Apples	10
Bananas	20
Cherries	30

Table2

Item	Price
Apples	.25
Bananas	.50
Cherries	.75
Rutabaga	1.00

INTERSECT Table1 WITH Table2 FORMING Table3

Table3

Item	Qty	Price
Apples	10	$0.25
Bananas	20	$0.50
Cherries	30	$0.75

■ *Figure 12.22:*
Example of the Intersect command.

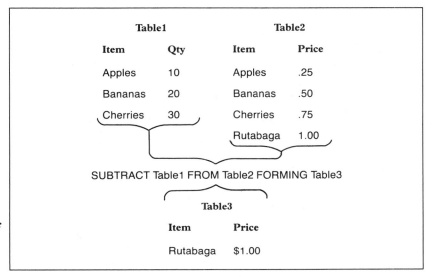

■ *Figure 12.23:*
Example of the
Subtract
command.

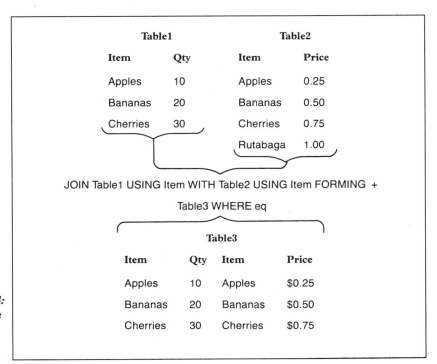

■ *Figure 12.24:*
Example of the
Join command
with the EQ
operator.

	Table1			Table2	
Item	**Qty**		**Item**	**Price**	
Apples	10		Apples	0.25	
Bananas	20		Bananas	0.50	
Cherries	30		Cherries	0.75	
			Rutabaga	1.00	

JOIN Table1 USING Item WITH Table2 USING Item FORMING +

Table3 WHERE ne

Table3

Item	**Qty**	**Item**	**Price**
Apples	10	Bananas	$0.50
Apples	10	Cherries	$0.75
Apples	10	Rutabaga	$1.00
Bananas	20	Apples	$0.25
Bananas	20	Cherries	$0.75
Bananas	20	Rutabaga	$1.00
Cherries	30	Apples	$0.25
Cherries	30	Bananas	$0.50
Cherries	30	Rutabaga	$1.00

■ *Figure 12.25:*
Example of the Join command with the NE operator.

13
DEVELOPING APPLICATIONS

Starting with this chapter, we'll learn techniques for organizing all the tables, forms, and reports in a database into a unified *application*. While R:BASE is a general database-management system, an application is a system of menus that manages all aspects of a specific database for a particular task. For example, an application may manage a mailing, accounts-receivable, general-ledger, or inventory system.

The real advantage of an application is that it allows even a novice user to manage a database by using a series of menus, rather than by typing commands. As we'll learn in this chapter, R:BASE applications are easy to develop. In fact, you can create applications more quickly and efficiently with R:BASE than you can with most database-management systems.

The best way to understand the concept of an application is to develop one and use it. In this chapter, we'll develop a sample application using the familiar Mail database.

∎ DESIGNING AN APPLICATION

Once you've designed and developed the tables, forms, and reports that you want to use in a database, designing the application simply involves defining a hierarchical structure of menus. Figure 13.1 shows the menu structure that we'll use to manage the Names and Charges tables in the Mail database.

The Main menu in the figure presents three options: (1) Manage Customer List (meaning the Names table), (2) Manage Charges List (meaning the Charges table), and (3) Exit (meaning that you want to return to the R> prompt). If the user selects menu option (1), Sub-Menu 1 is displayed on the screen. From this menu, the user can select from several options to add new data to the Names table, edit the table, print any of three different reports, or return to the Main menu. Similarly, if the user selects option (2), a submenu for managing the Charges table is displayed on the screen.

You can design your menu system in any way that you wish. For example, you could include an option on the Main menu for printing reports, and group all the various report options under a separate menu. Also, you can create sub-submenus below submenus. Finally, and perhaps most importantly, you can always change your mind and redesign your application at any time. You can add new menus, change menu items, and even insert new options into existing menus. This is important because application development is usually an iterative process, and perfecting an application usually involves a series of increasing enhancements and refinements.

■ DEVELOPING AN APPLICATION

Once you've mapped out on paper a basic menu structure for your application, you can use Application Express to start building the application. As with Forms and Reports Express, you can enter Application Express from any of three methods. Type in the command Express at the R> prompt, and press Enter; or select Application Development from the Prompt menu; or select Application Express from the RBSystem Main menu.

The Application Express Main menu appears on the screen as in Figure 13.2. Options (1) and (2) let you create or modify an application.

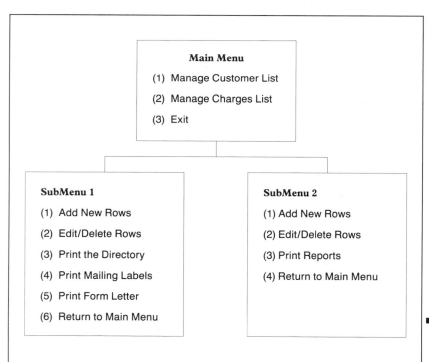

■ *Figure 13.1:*
Menu structure for an application.

Option (3) presents options for managing directories on a hard disk, and option (4) exits Application Express back to wherever you started from.

To create a new application now, select option (1). If there is no database currently open, the screen will ask you to choose a database and present the names of existing databases. If necessary, select Mail as the database name for this application. (**Note:** If at any time you feel lost and want to exit Application Express without saving your work, press the Break key. On most IBM keyboards, you hold down the Ctrl key and press Scroll Lock to break.)

Next, R:BASE asks for a name for the application. The name cannot be longer than eight characters or contain any blank spaces or punctuation marks. For this example, enter the name **MailSys** and press Enter. R:BASE then asks for a name for the Main menu. Again, the name needs to be limited to eight characters. R:BASE suggests the name Main, which is a good suggestion, so press the Enter key.

Now the screen displays options for displaying the menu vertically or horizontally. A vertical menu provides more flexibility, so select the Vertical option by pressing the Enter key.

Next, R:BASE asks for a title for the Main menu. Unlike the menu name, which R:BASE uses to store the program information, the menu title is displayed on the screen and can be of any length with spaces and punctuation marks. Type in the title **Main Menu,** and press Enter. R:BASE automatically centers the title. Then it asks for the text

```
                          Application EXPRESS
        Copyright (C) 1983,1984,1985,1986 by Microrim, Inc. (Ver. 1.00 PC-DOS)

                         ═Application EXPRESS Main Menu═
                          (1)  Define a new application
                          (2)  Modify an existing application
                          (3)  DOS functions
                          (4)  Exit from Application EXPRESS




      [ENTER] Choose    [F10] Help
```

■ *Figure 13.2:*
The Application
Express Main
menu.

for the first menu option. Type in the phrase

■ Manage Customer List

and press Enter. R:BASE then asks for the text for menu option (2). Type in

■ Manage Charges List

and press Enter. R:BASE asks for the text for the third option. Type in the word

■ Exit

You've just developed the first menu as it will appear on the screen later when you use the application. Your screen should look like Figure 13.3. Press the Esc key to continue developing the MailSys application.

Next, R:BASE wants to know if the Esc key should be used to exit the menu. Select the Yes option by pressing the Enter key. (Although option (3) on the Main menu provides for exiting, there is certainly no harm in allowing the Esc key to be used to exit the menu as well.)

R:BASE then asks if you want to develop a custom help screen for this menu. We can add that later, so for now select the No option.

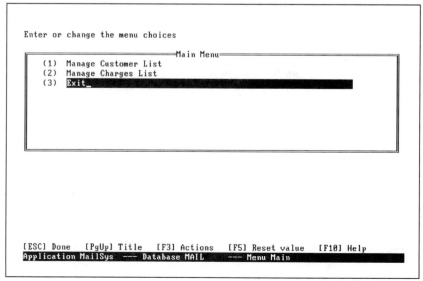

■ *Figure 13.3:*
First menu designed for the MailSys application.

R:BASE needs to know what actions should be associated with the first menu option. Several options are displayed on the screen, as shown in Figure 13.4. The actions that you can associate with a menu option are listed below:

Option	Action
Load	Enter new data into a table.
Edit	Edit and delete data using a predefined form.
Delete	Globally delete rows from a table.
Modify	Edit and delete rows using an edit screen.
Select	Look up specific information in a table.
Print	Print a report.
Custom	Develop a custom action for this menu choice.
Macro	Use a predefined custom action.
Template	Access a custom procedure.
Menu	Build a submenu for this menu option.
Password	Initiate a password.
Exit	Exit this menu.

Some of the more advanced options displayed, such as *Custom, Template, Macro,* and *Password* will be more meaningful to you after we

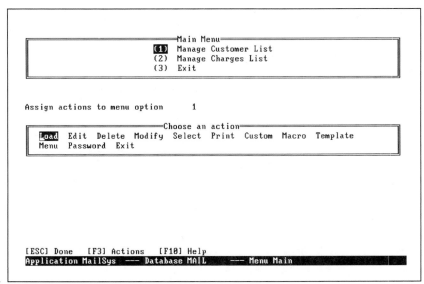

■ *Figure 13.4:*
Screen for selecting actions for menu options.

discuss the R:BASE programming language and R:BASE variables. For now, however, the other options are sufficient for developing the MailSys application.

In this example, you want menu option (1) to branch to a submenu for managing the Names table. Press the down arrow to move the highlighting to the Menu choice and press Enter. When R:BASE asks for a name for the submenu, type in the name **SubMenu1** and press Enter. Select the Vertical option.

R:BASE needs to know what this submenu should look like. The screen will ask that you fill in a title for this submenu. Type in the title

■   Manage Customer List

and press Enter. Next, type in the menu text in the order shown below. Press Enter after typing in each option.

> Add New Customers
> Edit/Delete Customers
> Print the Directory
> Print Mailing Labels
> Print Form Letter
> Return to Main Menu

When you're finished, your screen should look like Figure 13.5. Press Esc after you've filled in the menu options. R:BASE returns you to the Main menu and displays the prompt

■   Do you want another action for the current menu option? Yes No

If you select Yes, you can add additional actions to this menu item. For this example, select No.

Next, R:BASE allows you to define actions for option (2) of the Main menu. Since we want this option to branch to another menu, select the Menu choice, and name the new submenu **SubMenu2**. Select the Vertical option, and fill in the menu title **Manage Charges List**. Then type in the options in the order listed below. When you're finished, your screen should look like Figure 13.6.

> Add New Charges
> Edit/Delete Charges
> Print Charges
> Return to Main Menu

Press Esc after entering the four menu options. R:BASE will ask if you want to define another option for the new submenu. Select the No option.

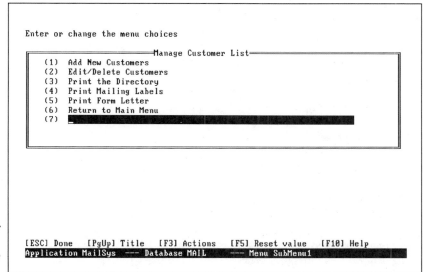

∎ *Figure 13.5:*
SubMenu1
defined on the
screen.

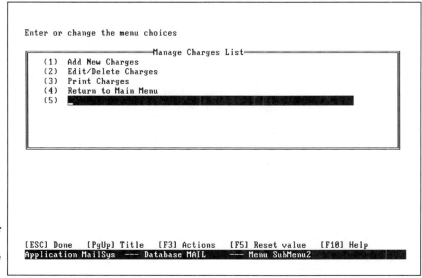

∎ *Figure 13.6:*
SubMenu2
defined on the
screen.

Next, R:BASE asks if you want to assign actions to option (3) of the Main menu. Since this option simply allows the user of the application to exit, select Exit from the choices on the screen.

Managing the Names Table

Now R:BASE is ready to find out what actions you want to assign to the first submenu's options. You'll see the entire menu on the screen, along with the prompt

■　Do you want [ESC] to exit this menu? Yes No

Select Yes. Then R:BASE asks

■　Do you want to create a help screen for this menu?

Select No for now. R:BASE is then ready to assign an action to submenu option (1). Since this option allows the user to add new rows to the Names table, select Load from the choices on the screen. R:BASE asks which table to load, and it displays the names of the various tables in the database. Highlight the Names option and press Enter.

Next, R:BASE asks for the name of the form to use when adding new rows. Select the NamesFrm option, since this is the form we developed earlier for adding and editing data in the Names table. If you had not already defined a form for the Names table, or if you wanted to develop a new form, you could select the New option and develop a form on the spot with Forms Express. Since you've selected an existing form in this case, R:BASE asks

■　Do you want to edit the form?

There is no need to edit the form here, so you can select No. (Optionally, you could select Yes to move straight to Forms Express with the NamesFrm form on the screen ready for editing.) R:BASE asks if you want to assign any more actions to this first submenu choice. Select No.

Now it's time to define actions for submenu option (2). Since this option allows the user to edit and delete data from the Names table, select Edit from the choices on the screen. Select the Names table from the choices presented and the NamesFrm as the form to be used for editing. Again, the screen asks if you want to edit the form. There is no need to do so now, so select No. R:BASE asks how you want the data to be sorted while editing. For this example, select L:Name and Ascending, and then press Esc.

Now you will be given an opportunity to construct a Where clause that can be used to locate a particular record to edit when the application is put to use. Let's suppose that we want this option to ask the user for the last name of the customer to edit prior to displaying the list of customers on the edit screen. Select the L:Name option. R:BASE asks for the operator to be used when filtering the table (equal, not equal, less than, and so on). Select the EQ (equal) option.

The next prompt you'll see is the following:

∎ Do you want the user to enter a comparison value? Yes No

This means "Do you know what rows to filter right now, or should we find out when we actually use the application later?" Select the Yes option. R:BASE asks for the text for the prompt message. Type in the line below:

∎ Enter last name of customer to edit:

and press Enter. Later, we'll see how this option actually works. As with any Where clause, you can add a logical operator (such as AND or OR) to add more conditions. In this example, the single condition is sufficient, so just select (Done).

Since we don't need to define any more actions for this menu option, select No when you see the next prompt.

For submenu option (3), we want the application to print the directory. Select the Print option from the choices on the screen; then select the Names table from the next list of choices displayed. We'll use the Director report we created earlier, so highlight Director and press Enter. The screen asks

∎ Do you want to edit the report?

Answering Yes to this question will move you directly to Reports Express where you can change the format of the report immediately. To use the report format as it stands, select No.

For sort order, select the L:Name option and Ascending, select the F:Name option and Ascending, and then press Esc. (This will sort the customers into last- and first-name order.) To print all customers, press Esc rather than selecting columns to filter rows. Finally, select No when you're asked if you want to add more actions.

Assign actions to the fourth submenu option using the same procedure described above. Select the Print option and the Names table. Select the Labels option as the report format to use and No to the question about editing the report format. Select Zip as the sort order and Ascending. Press Esc twice when you're done. Select No when prompted for additional actions.

For form letters, select the Print option and the Names table once again. Select the Letter1 report format and No to the question about editing the report format. Then select Zip and Ascending as the sort order. Press Esc twice and select No when you're asked about adding more actions.

Of course, you could have selected filtering criteria for the directory, form letters, and mailing labels, just as we did while developing the action for the Edit option. You may want to add some filtering criteria later. We'll discuss techniques for modifying an application later in this chapter.

For the last submenu option, select the Exit choice from the screen. When this option is selected from the submenu, R:BASE will display the SubMenu2 menu.

Managing the Charges Table

Now R:BASE is ready to assign actions to the second submenu. You'll see this submenu appear on the screen. Select Yes when you see the prompt about using the Esc key to exit. Select No to the prompt about defining help screens.

For the first submenu option, select the Load choice, the Charges table, and the ChrgFrm form. Again, the screen will ask if you want to edit the form using Forms Express. There is no need to do so now, so select No. Select No when you're asked about defining more actions for this submenu option.

For submenu option (2), select Modify. This will display an edit screen when the application is put to use. Select the Charges table and the All option to allow editing of all columns. Select CustNo as the sorting column and Ascending as the sorting direction. We don't need to filter the table for editing the Charges table, so press the Esc key twice rather than defining searching columns. Answer No to the prompt about adding more actions.

For submenu option (3), select Print from the choices on the screen. Select the Charges table name. Select the Sales option, since this is the report we developed to display data from the Charges table. You can modify the current report format by selecting Yes to the next prompt about editing the report. In this case, just select No. Select CustNo as the column to sort by and Ascending as the direction; then press Esc twice to bypass the questions about searching. Select No when asked about adding more actions.

For submenu option (4), select Exit from the choices on the screen and No when asked about more actions. At this point, all of the menus are developed, and actions have been assigned to all menu options. The screen asks if you want to change the Express default settings. For the time being, you can just select No. You'll see the message

- Writing application files, please wait

appear on the screen.

R:BASE will then write a long *program* based on the answers you've provided throughout this exercise. It may take a few minutes, but when you see the program you'll probably be glad that R:BASE wrote it for you. (Most database-management systems require that you write these programs yourself, which is why R:BASE is easier and faster for developing application systems.)

The last prompt to appear on the screen will be

- Do you want to create an initial command file? ([F10] for help)

If you answer Yes to this question, the MailSys application will be run automatically when you start R:BASE. Select No for now, since we'll soon be developing new applications.

When all the basic tasks of creating the application are completed, the Application Express Main menu will reappear on the screen. Select option (4) to exit Application Express. Before using the application, you'll need to get back to the R > prompt. (If the R > prompt is not on your screen, select R:BASE from the RBSystem Main menu, or press Esc to exit the Prompt menu.)

∎ RUNNING
THE
APPLICATION

To use an application, you must enter the Run command at the R > prompt using the general syntax

- RUN *application name* IN *application name.*APX

For this example, at the R > prompt, enter the command

- RUN MailSys IN MailSys.APX

The Main menu for the MailSys application will appear on the screen, as shown in Figure 13.7. The rest is easy. To manage the Names table, select option (1). The submenu we created will appear, as shown in Figure 13.8.

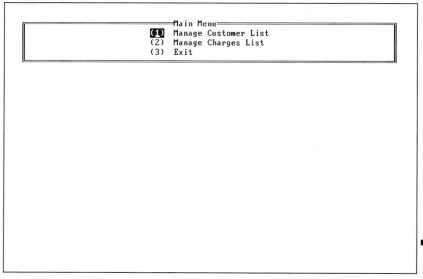

```
                          ┌Main Menu┐
                          (1)  Manage Customer List
                          (2)  Manage Charges List
                          (3)  Exit
```

■ *Figure 13.7:*
The MailSys
Main menu.

```
                        ┌Manage Customer List┐
                          (1)  Add New Customers
                          (2)  Edit/Delete Customers
                          (3)  Print the Directory
                          (4)  Print Mailing Labels
                          (5)  Print Form Letter
                          (6)  Return to Main Menu
```

■ *Figure 13.8:*
Menu for
managing the
Names table.

To add new customers, select option (1). You'll see the custom NamesFrm screen for adding rows. As usual, press Esc and select Quit after you've added new names. You'll be returned to the submenu. To edit the list of customers, select option (2). You'll see the prompt

■ Enter last name of customer to edit:

Type in a last name (**Smith**, for example) and press Enter. You'll see the data for Smith on the screen, ready for editing, as shown in Figure 13.9. When you're finished with the edit screen, select the Quit option to return to the submenu.

When you select menu items that print reports, the screen will display the options

■ Screen   Printer   Both

Highlight the option you want and press Enter. The report will be displayed accordingly, and then you'll be returned to the submenu.

To exit the submenu, select option (6) or press the Esc key. The Main menu will reappear on the screen.

If you select option (2) from the Main menu, you'll see the submenu for managing the Charges table, as shown in Figure 13.10. Notice that when you select option (2), all the data appear on the screen, ready for editing, as shown in Figure 13.11.

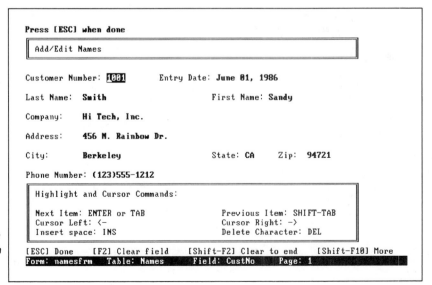

■ *Figure 13.9:*
Data for Smith
ready to be
edited.

A full edit screen appeared because we selected the Modify choice, rather than Edit, when we defined the submenu's options. Press Esc when you're finished editing. To return to the Main menu, select option (4) from the Charges submenu.

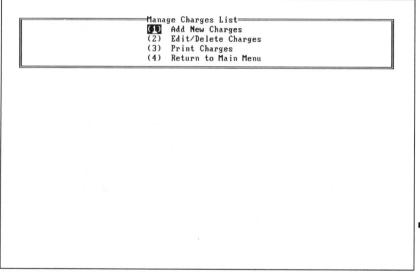

```
                    ┌Manage Charges List══════════════════════╗
                    ║(1)  Add New Charges                      ║
                    ║(2)  Edit/Delete Charges                  ║
                    ║(3)  Print Charges                        ║
                    ║(4)  Return to Main Menu                  ║
                    ╚══════════════════════════════════════════╝
```

■ *Figure 13.10:*
The submenu for managing the Charges table.

```
             Press [ESC] when done, [F2] to delete, [F5] to reset    More→
  CustNo   ProdNo  Qty      U:Price          Tax?      Total         P:Date
  ────────── ──────── ──── ──────────── ──────────── ──────────────── ─────────
  1001     A-111        12       $10.00        1       $127.20 June 1
    1001 B-222          5        $12.50        1        $66.25 June 1
    1001 C-434          2       $100.00        1       $212.00 June 1
    1002 B-222          12       $12.50        1       $159.00 July 8
    1002 A-111          10       $10.00        1       $106.00 July 8
    1004 A-111          5        $10.00        1        $53.00 June 1
    1004 Z-128          10       $12.80        0       $128.00 June 1
    1007 A-111          10       $10.00        1       $106.00 June 1
    1007 Z-128          10       $12.80        0       $128.00 June 1
```

■ *Figure 13.11:*
Edit screen for the Charges table.

To exit the entire MailSys application, select the Exit option from the Main menu. You'll be returned to the R > prompt. From there, you can use the R:BASE command mode commands to manage the data. To run the application again, enter the command

■   RUN MailSys IN MailSys.APX

Take a moment to review all the steps we've used to create the MailSys application and the end result that we've just tested. Remember that we created a Main menu and two submenus, and the application presented these menus in a vertical format.

Each of the submenus included an option for adding new rows to a table. On SubMenu1 we placed the option Add New Customers. On SubMenu2 we placed the option Add New Charges. When assigning actions in Application Express, we chose Load as the action to associate with each of the menu options. Now, when we actually use the application (by entering the Run command at the R > prompt), these two menu options for entering data appear on the MailSys application's submenus. Selecting either option from the MailSys application lets you add new rows to either the Names or the Charges table.

We also defined two submenu items: Edit/Delete Customers and Edit/Delete Charges. While developing the application, we chose Edit as the action for SubMenu1 and Modify as the action for SubMenu2. Later, when we actually used the MailSys application, selecting either of these options allowed us to make changes to either the Names or the Charges table.

Similarly, we created the menu options Print the Directory, Print Mailing Labels, Print Form Letter, and Print Charges. We assigned Print as the action to each of these menu options and specified particular reports to print for each. Later, when using the application, we could print any of these reports simply by selecting the appropriate menu option from the application's menus.

Of course, we also included options to exit each of the menus, and assigned Exit as the action to each of these options. Furthermore, we opted to allow the user to exit any menu by pressing the Esc key. Therefore, when using the MailSys application, you can either select Exit or press Esc to leave the menu that is currently displayed on the screen.

You may want to experiment with the MailSys application for a while. Chances are, you'll come up with some ideas for changes and improvements. We'll discuss techniques for modifying an application in the next section.

■ *MODIFYING THE APPLICATION*

To modify an existing application, enter the Application Express menu in the usual manner and select option (2), to change an existing application. From there, you can perform any of the following tasks:

Change the name of the application.

Remove a menu from the application.

Change a menu title.

Change the text in any menu.

Delete a menu option.

Add a new menu option to any menu.

Insert a menu option between existing options.

Change the method of exiting a menu.

Add or modify help screens.

Change the actions associated with a menu option.

Add actions to any menu option, either before or after existing actions.

When you first select option (2) from the Application Express menu, the screen will display the names of all the existing applications. Select the application that you want to modify by highlighting it and pressing Enter. In this example, select MailSys. R:BASE then displays the prompt

■ Do you want to change the application name? Yes No

Select No to use the same name or Yes to change the name. If you select Yes, R:BASE will prompt you for the new name. You'll then see a new menu, which we'll refer to as the Application menu, as shown in Figure 13.12.

The first option on the Application menu allows you to make changes, and the second option allows you to remove entire menus from the application. The third option allows you to change some of the application environmental settings, such as screen colors and beeping. We'll discuss these options later in the chapter. We'll work through a few changes to the MailSys application just for the practice. But since the general procedure for making changes does not vary much, we'll just describe most of the options briefly.

Changing Menu Options and Actions

To change menu options and actions, select option (1) from the Application menu. The screen will display a list of menus, as follows:

■ MAIN   SubMenu1   SubMenu2

Highlight the name of the menu that you want to change and press Enter. In a little while, we'll make some changes to the menu for managing the Names table, so highlight SubMenu1 and press Enter. The menu is displayed on the screen, ready for editing.

To change the title, type in the new title and press Enter. To retain the original title, just press Enter.

To change the text in a menu option, move the highlighting to the option and type in the new text.

You can also add and insert new menu items. You add a new menu option by pressing the End key. The highlighting will move to the bottom of the menu. Then, you just type in the text for the new menu option and press Enter. To insert a new menu option between existing options, move the highlighting to the option that you want the new

```
┌─────────────────────────Application Menu───────────────────────┐
│         (1)  Change menu text and actions                      │
│         (2)  Remove a menu from the menu tree                  │
│         (3)  Change application environment settings           │
│         (4)  Return to the EXPRESS main menu                   │
└────────────────────────────────────────────────────────────────┘




[ENTER] Choose    [ESC] Previous menu    [F3] Actions    [F10] Help
Application MAILSYS  ─── Database MAIL
```

■ *Figure 13.12:*
Options for
modifying an
existing
application.

item to appear before, and press the F1 key. All the menu options below the highlighting will move down one row. Type in the text for the new menu option and press Enter. To delete a menu option, move the highlighting to the appropriate option and press F2.

When you finish making changes to the menu text, press the Esc key. R:BASE will display the following prompt:

■   Do you want to change ESC or HELP action: Yes No

Select Yes if you want to change the Esc key option for exiting the menus or if you wish to add or modify help screens. If you are following along on-line, select Yes, and we'll add some help screens.

Changing the Escape Action

When you select Yes to the prompt above, R:BASE first asks

■   Do you want [ESC] to exit this menu: Yes No

Select Yes to retain the Esc key method of exiting. You can select No to disable the Esc key if you wish, but generally it is a good idea to keep the Esc key as a way to exit from menus.

Changing Help Actions

After you answer the prompt about the Esc key, R:BASE displays the message

■   Do you want to create a help screen for this menu? Yes No

Since we're going to add a help screen to the MailSys application, select the Yes option. R:BASE asks that you enter a name for the new help screen. As usual, the name cannot be more than eight characters long and cannot contain any spaces or punctuation marks. For this example, enter the name **SubHelp1**.

You'll see a blank screen for entering the help screen text. You can use the arrow keys to move the cursor, just as you did when creating custom forms and reports. Figure 13.13 shows a help screen, which you can type in now if you are following along on-line. Press Esc after you've filled in the help screen text.

Later, when you run the application, you can press the F10 key to view the help screen. Keep in mind that when you develop help screens for an application, each screen must be assigned a unique name.

Changing Menu Actions

Next, you'll be given the opportunity to change the actions that you originally assigned to the menu options in your application. The screen asks

■ Do you want to change the actions associated with this menu?

If you answer No, you'll be given an opportunity to change another menu or to return to the Application Express Main menu. If you answer Yes, the screen will ask

■ Do you want to review all the actions?

Answering Yes takes you step-by-step through each of the menu options and the actions assigned to them. If you answer No, the screen will display the current application menu (SubMenu1 in this example) and the prompt

■ Choose a menu option to change

```
                                            ⟨ 20,  1⟩  [ESC] to exit
                           Manage the Customer List
        Menu options are:

        (1)  Add new customers to the customer list

        (2)  Edit/Delete customers.  When prompted, type in the last name of the
             customer to edit, then press Enter.  Select Edit from the top menu
             to make changes.  Select Next from the top menu to view customers
             with similar last names.  Press F2 to delete a customer.  Press
             Press Escape at any time to bring back the top menu.

        (3)  Print the Customer Directory in alphabetical order

        (4)  Print Mailing Labels in zip code order

        (5)  Edit and print form letters

        (6)  Return to the Main Menu
             _
```

■ *Figure 13.13:*
Help screen for
the MailSys
application.

You can move the highlighter to any option on your custom menu and press Enter to change the action associated with that menu option. For example, if you highlight option (2), Edit/Delete Customers, the screen will show you that the current action assigned to this option is to edit data, using the NamesFrm form, as shown below:

■   ACTION—Edit using form: NamesFrm
    Do you want to insert an action before the current action:

You can insert another action above this action (which means that the newly inserted action will take place first), by selecting Yes in response to the question on the screen. If you select No, the screen asks what you want to do with the current action, as below:

■   Choose an option for this action
    Keep   Replace   Delete

Selecting Keep leaves the menu action as it stands. Selecting Replace allows you to enter a new action in place of the currently defined action. Selecting Delete deletes the currently defined action (but not the associated menu option).

Once you've opted to Keep, Replace, or Delete the current action, the screen asks

■   Do you want another action for the current menu option?

If you answer Yes to this question, you'll be given the opportunity to add another action, which will take place immediately after the existing action(s). If you answer No, you'll see the question

■   Do you want to change another menu action?

If you answer Yes, you'll see all the options for the current application menu (SubMenu1 still, in this example), and you can select another menu option to change. Doing so will repeat the process just described for the newly selected menu option. If you answer No to the question about changing another menu action, the screen will ask

■   Do you want to change another menu?

If you wanted to change something on the Main menu or Sub-Menu2 menu, you could select Yes. Again, you'd be asked which menu to change and which items on that menu to change. When you do not opt to change another menu, the screen displays the following message:

■   Changes to application MAILSYS are complete
    Press [ENTER] to save changes—Press [ESC] to discard them

You can either press the Enter key to save any changes you made to the application or press the Esc key to discard them. In this case, press Enter to save the custom help screen. You'll see the new version of the application whiz by on the screen as R:BASE rewrites the entire application. When done, the screen asks

■   Do you want to create an initial command file?
    ([F10] for help)

For now, just select No. This will bring back the Application Express Main menu, from which you can select option (4) to return to the R > prompt.
    Return to the R > prompt, and we'll test the help screen we added in this exercise. Enter the command

■   RUN MailSys IN MailSys.APX

Select option (1) from the Main menu to manage the customer list. When the submenu appears, press F10 to view the custom help screen (shown in Figure 13.14). Press any key after you're finished viewing the help screen.

■ *APPLICATION ENVIRONMENT SETTINGS*

Whenever you create or modify an application, the Application menu includes the opportunity to

■   (3) Change application environment settings

If you select this option, you'll see the Settings menu below:

■   (1) Set messages
    (2) Set error messages

(3) Set colors
(4) Set bell

If you select option (1), the screen will ask

■   **Do you want to display R:BASE messages?**

If you change this option to Yes, your application will display various R:BASE messages, such as "Successful PROJECT operation", as appropriate. If you select the default No option, these messages will not be displayed while the application is running.

Option (2) presents the prompt

■   **Do you want to display R:BASE error messages?**

R:BASE normally displays messages on the screen when an error occurs. If you select Yes for this option, your application will display these messages. If you select No, your application will not display these R:BASE error messages.

Option (3) allows you to select foreground and background colors for the application. Background colors include

■   **Black   Blue   Green   Cyan   Red   Magenta   Brown   Gray**

```
                                          < 20,  1>  [ESC] to exit
                        Manage the Customer List
Menu options are:

(1) Add new customers to the customer list

(2) Edit/Delete customers.  When prompted, type in the last name of the
    customer to edit, then press Enter.  Select Edit from the top menu
    to make changes.  Select Next from the top menu to view customers
    with similar last names.  Press F2 to delete a customer.  Press
    Press Escape at any time to bring back the top menu.

(3) Print the Customer Directory in alphabetical order

(4) Print mailing labels in Zip-code order

(5) Edit and print form letters

(6) Return to the Main Menu
    _
```

■ *Figure 13.14:*
Custom help
screen for
SubMenu l.

After selecting a background color, you can select a foreground color from the following:

- Blue   Green   Cyan   Red   Magenta   Brown   Gray
  Light Black   Light Blue   Light Green   Light Cyan
  Light Red   Light Magenta   Yellow   White

Selecting option (4) displays the prompt

- Do you want your application to beep at errors?

Selecting Yes will ensure that any errors that occur while your application is in use will be accompanied by an audible beep. Selecting No suppresses this beep.

Deleting Menus and Applications

Although we won't work through a specific example, you can delete a menu using the following procedure. From the Application menu, select option (2) to remove a menu from the menu tree. Highlight the name of the submenu that you wish to delete and press Enter. You cannot remove the Main menu, because R:BASE needs it to get to the submenus.

To delete an entire application, use the Erase command from either the R> prompt or the DOS C> prompt. Applications are stored in three files with the extensions .APP, .APX, and .API. If you wanted to remove the entire MailSys application, you would enter the following commands separately:

- ERASE MailSys.APP
  ERASE MailSys.APX
  ERASE MailSys.API

If you are sure that only these three files have the file name MailSys, you can erase all three simultaneously by entering

- ERASE MailSys.AP?

Don't do so now, however, unless you want to rebuild the entire application.

■ SUMMARY

In this chapter, we've developed our first application. In the remaining chapters, we'll discuss techniques for building more complex applications. For now, take a moment to review some of the basic concepts we've discussed in this chapter:

An application is a set of tables, forms, and reports that are linked together through a series of menus to manage a specific database for a particular task. For example, you could develop applications for managing mailing-list, management, book-keeping, and inventory systems.

To design an application, you typically develop all the tables, forms, and reports for managing a database, and then design a hierarchical system of menus to link everything together through menu choices.

To develop an application, enter the Application Express module.

To run an application, exit from the Application Express Main menu, and return to the R > prompt. Enter the Run command using the syntax

■ RUN *application name* IN *application name*.APX.

To modify an application, select option (2), Modify an Existing Application, from the Application Express Main menu. Answer the prompts and enter information appropriate for the changes that you want to make.

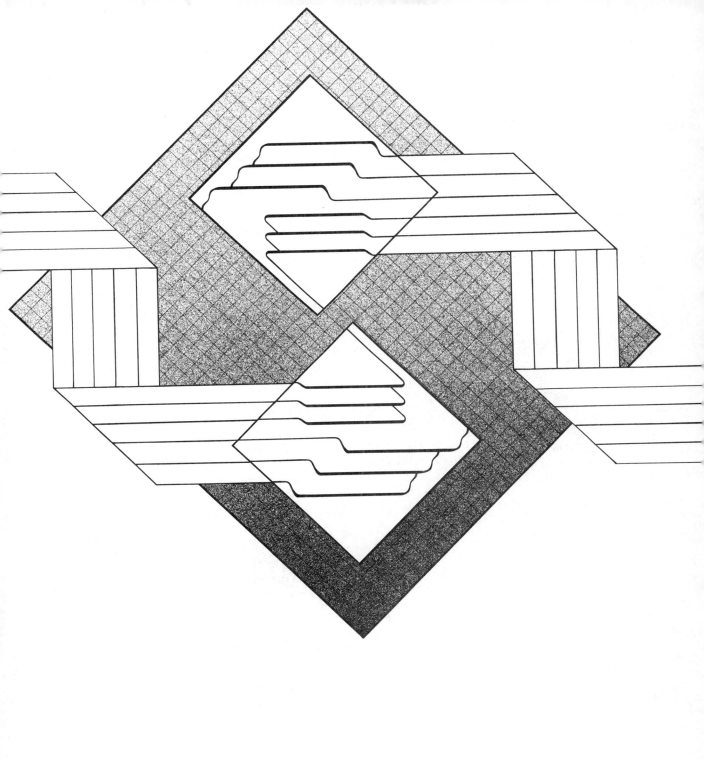

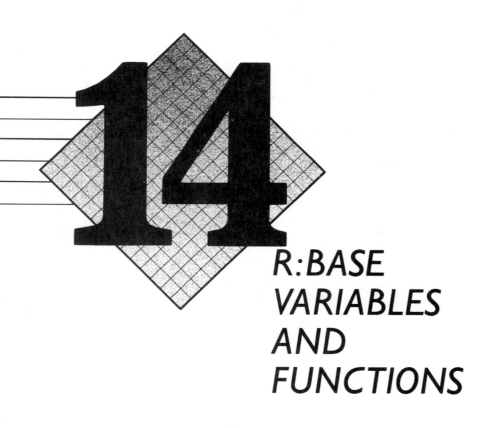

14

R:BASE
VARIABLES
AND
FUNCTIONS

The first step in building complex applications is learning to create and manage R:BASE *variables,* which are also referred to as *global variables.* The adjective refers to the fact that data in variables can be passed from one database to another, and hence are accessible, or "global," to all databases. Unlike information stored in databases and tables, variables are stored in the computer's random access memory (RAM), and they are normally used as temporary, or "scratch pad," data.

A variable is a character or word that holds a value that is subject to change. This definition is identical to the use of variables in basic mathematics. For example, if we state that X equals 10 and Y equals 15, then X plus Y equals 25, and Y minus X equals 5.

In this chapter, we'll explore techniques for creating and manipulating R:BASE variables. We'll discuss the practical applications of variables in the following chapters.

∎ CREATING VARIABLES

In R:BASE, you use the Set Variable command (abbreviated to Set Var or Set V) to store and manipulate variables. The Show Variables command (abbreviated to Show Var or Show V) displays the current value of all the variables. You can also use the Show Variable command to display a single variable. You enter these commands at the R> prompt, and it does not matter whether a database is open.

Here are some examples that you may want to try. First, from the R> prompt, enter the command

∎   SHOW VARIABLES

You'll see three variables, #DATE, #TIME, and #PI displayed on the screen, as below:

Variable	=	Value	Type
#DATE	=	06/19/86	DATE
#TIME	=	5:59:18	TIME
#PI	=	3.14159265358979	DOUBLE

These variables are always available in R:BASE. We used the #DATE variable earlier when we printed dates on our database reports.

Now, enter the command

∎   SET VARIABLE X TO 10

and then enter this command:

- SET VARIABLE Y TO 15

If you now enter the command

- SHOW VARIABLES

you'll see these two new variables added to the table of existing variables, as below:

Variable	=	Value	Type
#DATE	=	06/19/86	DATE
#TIME	=	5:59:41	TIME
#PI	=	3.14159265358979	DOUBLE
X	=	10	INTEGER
Y	=	15	INTEGER

Notice that the new variables have the Integer data type. R:BASE assigned this data type based on the nature of the values being stored (10 and 15).

Now, enter the command

- SET VARIABLE A TO Hello

and then enter this command:

- SET VARIABLE B TO There

If you now enter the command

- SHOW VARIABLES

you'll see the new A and B variables added to the list, as below:

Variable	=	Value	Type
#DATE	=	06/19/86	DATE
#TIME	=	6:00:19	TIME
#PI	=	3.14159265358979	DOUBLE
X	=	10	INTEGER

Y	=	15	INTEGER
A	=	Hello	TEXT
B	=	There	TEXT

R:BASE assigned the Text data type to these new variables, again because it made an assumption based on the nature of the values being stored.

Next, enter each of the commands below, individually, at the R> prompt:

∎ SET VARIABLE Today TO 6/20/86
SET VARIABLE Now TO 12:30:00
SET VARIABLE Salary TO 12345.67
SET VARIABLE DecNumb TO 1.0

Then enter the command

∎ SHOW VARIABLES

You'll see that R:BASE made valid assumptions about the data types of each variable, as shown below:

Variable	=	Value	Type
#DATE	=	06/19/86	DATE
#TIME	=	7:19:15	TIME
#PI	=	3.14159265358979	DOUBLE
X	=	10	INTEGER
Y	=	5	INTEGER
A	=	Hello	TEXT
B	=	There	TEXT
Today	=	06/20/86	DATE
Now	=	12:30:00	TIME
Salary	=	12,345.67	DOUBLE
DecNumb	=	1	DOUBLE

Note that each variable name (A, B, Today, Now, and so on) is purely arbitrary. You can use whatever variable names you like, as long as the name is no more than eight characters in length and does not contain spaces or punctuation marks. The number of variables that you can create is limited only by the amount of computer memory available.

You should be able to use at least 40 variables, and the maximum is about 1000 variables.

Now let's take a look at ways to manipulate variables.

■ *MANIPULATING VARIABLES*

We've already discussed the R:BASE operators that you can use for addition, subtraction, and other operations. You can use all of these operators to create and manipulate variables. For example, to find the cube root of 27, you could enter the command below:

■   SET VAR Cube TO 27 ★ ★ (1/3)

(Recall that ★★ is the exponent sign, and the parentheses ensure that the division (1/3) will take place before the exponentiation.) When you enter the Show Variables command at the R> prompt, you'll see the answer 3 stored in the variable named Cube.

The expression above contains only *constants;* that is, 27 is a constant and (1/3) is a constant because they are numbers. Similarly, the expression below contains two constants, the text string "So" and the text string "Long":

■   SET VARIABLE ByeBye TO "So" & "Long"

After entering this command at the R> prompt, the variable ByeBye will contain the text "So long". (Use Show Variables to see the results.)

Expressions can contain *variables* as well as constants. When using variable names in expressions, however, you should always precede the variable name with a period, in order to avoid confusing variables and constants. For example, recall that we created a variable named A, which contains the word "Hello". We also created a variable named B, which contains the word "there". To use these two variable names in an expression, precede each variable name with a period (or dot), as follows:

■   SET VAR Howdy TO .A & .B

If you enter the Show Variables command after entering this command, you'll see that the variable Howdy now contains the Text string

■   Hello there

You can use the predefined (or *system*) variables in expressions (such as #DATE, #TIME, and #PI), although you should make a habit of preceding these variable names with periods as well. For example, you may recall from geometry that the area of a circle can be found with the formula pi times the radius squared. Assuming that you know the radius is 5, the expression below can calculate the area of the circle and store the result in a variable named Area (note that the #PI variable is preceded with a dot):

■ SET VAR Area TO .#PI * 5 * * 2

The Show Variables command displays the following result:

■ Area = 78.5398163397448 DOUBLE

You can manipulate dates in expressions just as you can manipulate text and numbers. For example, recall that we created a variable named Today a short time ago, and we assigned 6/26/86 to the date. To find out what the date will be 90 days past the Today variable, you could enter the command

■ SET VARIABLE Ninety TO .Today + 90

and then enter the command

■ SHOW VARIABLE Ninety

You'll see the date 90 days beyond Today, as below:

■ 09/18/86

When you mix data types, the results can be confusing. For example, if you add the X variable (which is an Integer data type) to the DecNumb variable (which is a Double number data type), as below:

■ SET VARIABLE Mix TO .X + .DecNumb

when you enter the command

■ SHOW VARIABLES

you'll see that the new variable Mix is the Double data type, as below:

Variable	=	Value	Type
Mix	=	11.0000	DOUBLE

Generally, when you mix an Integer data type with a Double or Currency data type amount, the result will be the data type with the most decimal places. However, you can control the data type of a variable before performing a calculation through a process known as *explicit data typing.*

■ EXPLICIT DATA TYPING

You can define a variable's type by using the Set Variable command without the To option, followed by a data type. For example, the command

■   SET VARIABLE JJ CURRENCY

creates an "empty" variable named JJ with the Currency data type. The command

■   SET VARIABLE Later DATE

creates an empty variable named Later with the Date data type. The data types for variables are the same as those for columns: Integer, Double, Currency, Text, Date, and Time. We'll see the value of explicit data typing in later chapters when we develop command files.

■ PASSING TABLE DATA TO VARIABLES

Variables can also be assigned values directly from a table in a database. To do so, you need to open the appropriate database first. Then you use a version of the Set Variable command with the following syntax:

■   SET VARIABLE *variable name* TO *column name* IN *table name* +
      WHERE *condition*

We can try this one using the Names table in the Mail database. First, open the database from the R> prompt by entering the command

■ OPEN Mail

Now, if you enter the following command:

■ SET VARIABLE Name1 TO F:Name IN Names WHERE +
  CustNo = 1003

the Name1 variable will contain the first name of customer number 1003. If you then enter the command

■ SET VARIABLE Name2 TO L:Name IN Names WHERE +
  CustNo = 1003

the Name2 variable will contain the last name of customer number 1003. If you then enter this command:

■ SET VARIABLE Name TO .Name1 & .Name2

the Name variable will contain the first and last name separated by a space. When you enter the command

■ SHOW VARIABLES

you'll see, among the existing variables, the new Name1, Name2, and Name variables, as below:

Variable	=	Value	Type
.	.	.	.
.	.	.	.
.	.	.	.
Name1	=	Marie	TEXT
Name2	=	Miller	TEXT
Name	=	Marie Miller	TEXT

This technique is especially useful when developing sophisticated applications, as we'll see in the coming chapters.

■ COMPUTED VARIABLES

Variables can also be used to store the results of computations performed on a table. The general syntax for using the Compute command with variables is

■ COMPUTE *variable name* AS *<command> <column name>* +
 FROM *table name* WHERE *conditions*

The Where clause is optional. The commands that can be used with Compute are shown in Figure 10.1.

Suppose, for example, that you want to compute the sum of the Total column in the Charges table and store the result in a variable named GrandTot. Enter the following command:

■ COMPUTE GrandTot AS SUM Total FROM Charges

When you enter the command

■ SHOW VARIABLE GrandTot

you'll see the total, as below:

■ $1,085.45

To compute the average unit price from the Charges table and store the result in a variable named AvgPrice, enter the command

■ COMPUTE AvgPrice AS AVE U:Price FROM Charges

To see the result, enter this command:

■ SHOW VARIABLE AvgPrice

R:BASE will display the average unit price of $21.18.

You can count the number of rows in a table and store this number in a variable using the Rows option with the Compute command, as below:

■ COMPUTE RowCount AS ROWS FROM Names

Enter the command

■ SHOW VARIABLE RowCount

to see that there are nine rows in the table, as the screen now shows.

The optional Where clause allows you to be more specific. For example, to compute the total sales from the Charges table for product number A-111 and store this value in a variable named ATot, enter the command

∎ COMPUTE ATot AS SUM Qty FROM Charges WHERE +
ProdNo = A-111

Enter the command

∎ SHOW VARIABLE ATot

to see the result, 37.

You can verify this calculation by entering the command

∎ SELECT ALL FROM Charges WHERE ProdNo = A-111

which displays all product number A-111 transactions from the Charges table, as shown in Figure 14.1.

```
R>SELECT ALL FROM Charges WHERE ProdNo = A-111
  CustNo    ProdNo   Qty         U:Price        Tax?       Total
  --------  -------- --------    ---------      -----      --------
      1001 A-111          12      $10.00          1        $127.20
      1004 A-111           5      $10.00          1         $53.00
      1007 A-111          10      $10.00          1        $106.00
      1002 A-111          10      $10.00          1        $106.00
R>_
```

∎ *Figure 14.1:*
Product number
A-111
transactions
listed on the
Charges table.

To determine the largest single transaction amount for product number A-111, enter the command

■   COMPUTE HiSale AS MAX Total FROM +
    Charges WHERE ProdNo = A-111

To determine the lowest sale for product number A-111, enter this command:

■   COMPUTE LowSale AS MIN Total FROM Charges WHERE +
    ProdNo = A-111

To count the number of rows in a table that meet a specific criterion, use the Compute command with the Count option rather than with the Rows option. For example, the command

■   COMPUTE RowCount AS COUNT ProdNo IN Charges +
    WHERE ProdNo = A-111

counts the number of rows from the Charges table that have A-111 in the ProdNo column and then stores the result in a variable named RowCount. If you now enter the command

■   SHOW VARIABLES

you'll see, among the other variables we've created in this chapter, those listed below:

Variable	=	Value	Type
GrandTot	=	$1,085.45	CURRENCY
AvgPrice	=	$21.18	CURRENCY
ATot	=	37	INTEGER
HiSale	=	$127.20	CURRENCY
LowSale	=	$53.00	CURRENCY
RowCount	=	4	INTEGER

Note that the data types for the variables have been assigned the same data types as the columns that were computed. Again, R:BASE has made reasonable assumptions about the data types based on the type of data being computed.

■ CLEARING VARIABLES

When you exit R:BASE, all variables (except #DATE, #TIME, and #PI) are immediately erased, and they cannot be recalled other than to recreate them using the Set Variable command. Prior to exiting, however, the variables are available in memory even as you open and close databases.

You also can eliminate variables using the Clear command. For example, the command

■ CLEAR Salary

erases the Salary variable. You can clear all variables (except #DATE, #TIME, and #PI) using the command

■ CLEAR ALL VARIABLES

■ MACRO SUBSTITUTION

You can also use variables as a portion of R:BASE commands using a technique often called *macro substitution.* An example will best demonstrate this technique. First, assume you create a Text variable named ColNames using the Set Variable command, as below:

■ SET VARIABLE ColNames TO "CustNo L:Name F:Name +
   Company"

Assuming that the Mail database is open, you could then use the ColNames variable as part of a command, as long as you precede the variable name with an ampersand (&) character. For example, entering the command

■ SELECT &ColNames FROM Names

displays the CustNo, L:Name, F:Name, and Company columns from the Names table, because R:BASE automatically substitutes the text stored in the variable ColNames into the command. In other words, R:BASE changes the command to

■ SELECT CustNo L:Name F:Name Company FROM Charges

by substituting the contents of the ColNames variable before executing the command. (The substitution takes place "behind the scenes," so you see only the final result and not the actual substitution.)

Macro substitution is an advanced, though often useful, technique used primarily in programming with the R:BASE programming language.

■ LIMITATIONS

An expression in a Set Variable command can be up to 160 characters long. Any expression can contain up to 50 operators and operands. Operands are the data that the operators act upon. For example, the expression below contains three operators: two multiplication signs ($\star$) and one minus sign ($-$). The expression also contains four operands (.A, .X, .Y, and .Z).

■   (.A $\star$ .X) $-$ (.Y $\star$ .Z)

■ R:BASE FUNCTIONS

Most pocket calculators that you can purchase for more than 99 cents have a least a few *function* keys on them. The function keys are included to perform calculations that extend beyond simple arithmetic, such as square roots and logarithms.

R:BASE System V also offers *functions*. In fact, R:BASE offers about 70 functions that you can use to perform sophisticated calculations with variables. These functions can also be used for defining expressions for computed columns in a database and for variables in reports and forms. (In earlier chapters, we've already seen how the IFEQ function can be used to calculate a total sale based on the status of the Tax? column in the Charges table.)

Functions can also be used in command lines, including Sorted By and Where clauses. Furthermore, functions can also be used freely within the R:BASE programming language, a topic we'll discuss in the next chapter.

All functions require at least one *argument*, which is the information that the function operates on. For example, the SQRT function calculates the square root of a number and requires one argument. In the expression below:

■   SET VARIABLE Root TO SQRT(9)

the number 9 is the argument to the function. The result of the calculation is stored in the variable named Root.

The argument can be another variable. For example, the expression below stores the number 9 in a variable named StartNum:

■ SET VARIABLE StartNum TO 9

The next command calculates the square root of the value stored in the StartNum variable and stores the result in a new variable named Root:

■ SET VARIABLE Root TO SQRT(.StartNum)

In most cases, the argument to a function can also be a column name.

When using functions, you must be careful to use the correct data type in the argument. For example, the command

■ SET VARIABLE Root TO SQRT("Smith")

makes no sense, because you cannot possibly calculate the square root of a person's last name. If you try, R:BASE will respond with an error message.

Function arguments can also be expressions in themselves. For example, the command

■ SET VARIABLE Root TO SQRT(80 + 20)

stores the square root of 100 in the variable named Root. (One exception to this rule is text functions, which do not allow expressions in text string arguments.)

Functions may be nested within an expression, as long as there is an equal number of opening and closing parentheses in the expression. For example, the ABS function converts a negative number to a positive number, but leaves a positive number as positive. The square root function accepts only positive numbers. Therefore, you could use the ABS function inside the SQRT function to ensure that the argument to the SQRT function is positive.

In the example below, the negative number − 49 is stored in a variable named NegNumb:

■ SET VARIABLE NegNumb TO − 49

In the next expression, the square root of the absolute value of

NegNumb is stored in the variable named Root. Notice that the parentheses are *balanced* (there are two opening parentheses and two closing parentheses):

■   SET VARIABLE Root TO SQRT(ABS(NegNumb))

Since the ABS function is nested inside the SQRT function, R:BASE first calculates the absolute value of the NegNumb variable, and then calculates the square root of that result. The resulting number, 7, is stored in the variable named Root.

The remainder of this chapter lists the R:BASE functions categorized by the types of calculations they perform. Each function is shown with the correct placement and data types of the argument(s) that the function operates on. The types of arguments include the following:

Number	A real, double-precision, or integer number
Real	Either a real or double-precision number
Date	The Date data type
Time	The Time data type
Integer	The Integer data type
Text	The Text data type
Angle	An angle measurement expressed in radians
List	A list of column names, variables, constants, or expressions

A few other examples of arguments are also included in the summary that follows. These are explained in more detail when they are used.

An example of each function is also included. To verify that the function performs as expected, or to experiment with new values, use the Set Variable and Show Variable commands at the R> prompt on your own computer. For instance, the example shown in the SQRT function is

■   SQRT(81) is 9.

To try this, enter the command

■   SET VARIABLE Test TO SQRT(81)

(Of course, Test is just a sample variable name; you can use any variable name you like.) To see the result, enter the command

■   SHOW VARIABLE Test

or enter this command:

- SHOW VARIABLES

and you'll see that the variable named Test does indeed contain the number 9.

The examples all assume that the variable name used has not already been assigned a data type, either through explicit data typing or through previous use. If you use the same variable name repeatedly, your results may be inconsistent with the examples given. To rectify any discrepancies caused by existing data types, use the Clear All Variables or Clear Variable <*variable name*> command before entering the Set Variable command.

Several additional examples of using R:BASE functions are included at the end of this chapter.

Arithmetic and Mathematical Functions

The arithmetic and mathematical functions that follow perform common calculations on numbers and are used in both scientific and business applications.

- ABS(*Number*)

    Absolute Value—Converts a negative number to a positive number, or leaves a positive number as positive. Examples: ABS(-2) is 2. ABS(2) is 2.

- DIM(*Number,Number*)

    Positive Difference—Subtracts the second *Number* from the first. The result is either a positive number or zero. Examples: DIM(12,10) is 2. DIM(10,12) is 0.

- EXP(*Number*)

    Inverse of Logarithm—Raises the constant *e* (2.71828) to the power of *Number*. Example: EXP(1) is 2.71828.

- LOG(*Number*)

Natural Logarithm—Computes the logarithm base *e* of *Number*, where *Number* is positive. Example: LOG(2.71828182845905) is 1.

- LOG10(*Number*)

  Logarithm Base 10—Returns the logarithm base 10 of *Number*, where *Number* is positive. Example: LOG10(100) is 2.

- SQRT(*Number*)

  Square Root—Returns the square root of *Number*, where *Number* is positive. Example: SQRT(81) is 9.

- AVE(*List*)

  Average—Computes the average of the numbers in *List*. Example: AVE(9,3,4.5,11,15) is 8.5.

- MAX(*List*)

  Highest Value—Finds the largest number in the specified *List* of values. Example: MAX(2, − 3,87,99,16) is 99.

- MIN(*List*)

  Lowest Value—Finds the smallest number in the specified *List* of values. Example: MIN(2, − 3,87,99,16) is − 3.

- MOD(*Number,Number*)

  Modulus—Returns the remainder after dividing the first *Number* by the second *Number*. Examples: MOD(6,4) is 2. MOD(10,5) is 0, because 10 is evenly divisible by 5.

- SIGN(*Number,Number*)

  Sign Transfer—Transfers the sign of the second *Number* to the first *Number*. Example: SIGN(12, − 7) is − 12.

Trigonometric Functions

The trigonometric functions are used primarily in scientific and engineering applications. If your work generally does not require the use of these functions, you can probably skip these. Note that all trigonometric angle measurements are in radians, not degrees. Also, R:BASE will typically display the results of trigonometric functions with 14 decimal places of accuracy, although we'll show only five decimal places in these examples.

■ ACOS(*Number*)

Arccosine—Computes the arccosine of *Number*, where *Number* is a value in the range − 1 to 1. The result is an angle, in radians, between zero and pi. Example: ACOS(− 0.5) is 2.09439.

■ ASIN(*Number*)

Arcsine—Computes the arcsine of *Number*, where *Number* is in the range − 1 to 1. The result is an angle expressed in radians. Example: ASIN(− 0.75) is − 0.84806.

■ ATAN(*Number*)

Arctangent—Computes the arctangent of *Number*, with the result being an angle expressed in radians. Example: ATAN(1) returns 0.78540.

■ ATAN2(*Number*)

Arctangent of Coordinate Angle—Computes the arctangent of *Number*, where *Number* is a coordinate angle expressed in radians. Example: ATAN2(1,1) returns 0.78540.

■ COS(*Angle*)

Cosine—Computes the cosine of *Angle*, where *Angle* is expressed in radians. Example: COS(0.78) is 0.71091.

■ SIN(*Angle*)

Sine—Computes the sine of *Angle,* where *Angle* is expressed in radians. Example: SIN(0.78) returns 0.70328.

■ TAN(*Angle*)

Tangent—Computes the tangent of *Angle,* expressed in radians. Example: TAN(0.78) is 0.98926.

■ COSH(*Angle*)

Hyperbolic Cosine—Computes the hyperbolic cosine of *Angle.* Example: COSH(1.047) results in 1.60004.

■ SINH(*Angle*)

Hyperbolic Sine—Computes the hyperbolic sine of *Angle.* Example: SINH(1.047) returns 1.24905.

■ TANH(*Angle*)

Hyperbolic Tangent—Computes the hyperbolic tangent of *Angle.* Example: TANH(0.785) returns 0.65556.

Conversion Functions

The conversion functions modify the data types of variables and are generally used only in programming. The R:BASE data types were described in Chapter 2 of this book.

■ AINT(*Real*)

Truncates Real Number—Truncates the decimal portion of a real (or double-precision) number, returning only the integer portion in the Real data type. Example: AINT(1.8888) returns 1., where 1. is a real number.

■ ANINT(*Real*)

Rounds Real Number—Rounds the *Real* number to a real

argument. Example: ANINT(1.888) results in 2., where 2. is a real number.

■ INT(*Real*)

Converts Real to Integer Number—Converts a *Real* number to the Integer data type by truncating the decimal portion of the number. Example: INT(9.999) returns 9, where 9 is an integer.

■ NINT(*Real*)

Rounds Real to Integer Number—Converts a *Real* number to an integer by rounding the decimal portion to the nearest whole number. Example: NINT(9.999) returns 10 as an integer.

■ FLOAT(*Integer*)

Converts Integer to Real Number—Converts an integer to the Real data type. Example: FLOAT(9) returns 9 as a real number.

■ CTXT(*Number*)

Converts Number to Text String—Converts *Number* to a text string. Example: CTXT(1.2345) returns "1.2345" as the Text data type.

■ ICHAR(*Text*)

ASCII Code for Character—Returns the ASCII code for a character of *Text*. Example: ICHAR("A") returns 65 as an integer (the ASCII code for the uppercase letter A).

■ CHAR(*Integer*)

Character for ASCII Code—Returns the character associated with the Integer code. Example: SET VAR Beep TO CHAR(7). After assigning this variable, the Show Var Beep command causes the computer to beep. (ASCII character 7 is commonly used to make a terminal or computer beep.)

String-Manipulation Functions

The string-manipulation functions operate on Text data. They allow you to manipulate (and change) uppercase and lowercase, pad text with blank spaces, trim blank spaces from the text, and move sections of text. Many of these functions are used for "tricky" programming techniques. Even though they seem uninteresting or meaningless to beginners and nonprogrammers, they are worth skimming over because you may find them useful occasionally.

■   SFIL(*Text,Number*)

> **Fill Character String**—Creates a text variable consisting of *Text* characters, *Number* characters long. Example: SFIL("-",80) creates a text variable consisting of 80 hyphens.

■   SGET(*Text,Number,Location*)

> **Get from Text**—Selects *Number* characters from a *Text* string starting at *Location*. Example: SGET("CatDogFish",3,4) results in Dog because Dog is three letters long, and it begins at the fourth character in the "CatDogFish" character string.

■   SLEN(*Text*)

> **Length of String**—Returns the length of a *Text* string. Example: SLEN("Snowball") returns 8.

■   SLOC(*Text,Smaller*)

> **Location of Text**—Searches the *Text* string for the *Smaller* string and returns to the starting location of the smaller string within the larger string. If the smaller string is not found inside the larger string, the result is zero. Example: SLOC("CatDogFish", "Dog") returns 4, because the word Dog starts at the fourth character in "CatDogFish". SLOC("CatDogFish","MooMoo") returns 0, because there is no MooMoo inside CatDogFish.

■   SMOVE(*Text,Position 1, Number, String, Position 2*)

> **Moves Text into String**—Moves the characters in *Text*, starting at numeric *Position 1*, for a length of *Number* characters into

String, starting at numeric *Position 2.* Example: SMOVE ("ddogg",2,3,"ABCDE",2) returns "AdogE".

∎ SPUT(*Text,String,Location*)

Puts Text into String—Moves a *String* of characters in *Text* starting at *Location.* Example: SPUT("ABCDE","mm",3) returns "ABmmE".

∎ STRIM(*Text*)

Trims Trailing Blanks—Removes any trailing blank spaces from the *Text* variable. Example: If a variable named Test contains the characters "This is a test   " (notice the *trailing blanks* in front of the closing quotation mark), then STRIM(Test) produces "This is a test" (with the trailing blanks removed).

∎ ULC(*Text*)

Converts Uppercase to Lowercase—Converts all uppercase letters in *Text* to lowercase. Example: ULC("Hi There") returns "hi there".

∎ LUC(*Text*)

Converts Lowercase to Uppercase—Converts all lowercase letters in *Text* to uppercase. Example: LUC("Give me a break") returns "GIVE ME A BREAK".

∎ ICAP1(*Text*)

Uppercases First Letter Only—Converts *Text* to a text string with a capital letter on the first character of the first word only. Example: ICAP1("this Is It") produces "This is it".

∎ ICAP2(*Text*)

Uppercases All First Letters—Converts *Text* to a text string with a capital letter on the first character of each word. Example:

ICAP2("ADAM P. JONES, JR.") produces "Adam P. Jones, Jr.". ICAP2("this is a test") produces "This Is A Test".

■   CTR(*Text,Width*)

Centers Text—Centers *Text* within the specified *Width*. Example: CTR("Best",10) produces " Best ".

■   LJS(*Text,Width*)

Left-Justifies Text—Left-justifies *Text* within the specified *Width*. Example: LJS("Best",10) produces "Best   ".

■   RJS(*Text,Width*)

Right-Justifies Text—Right-justifies *Text* within the specified *Width*. Example: RJS("Best",10) produces "   Best".

Date and Time Functions

The Date and Time functions operate on data stored as the Date or Time data type. These functions can convert Text data to Date and Time data and can isolate portions of dates and times. These can be particularly useful in Where clauses. For example, the TDWK function isolates the day of the week as text. Therefore, the command

■   SELECT ALL FROM Charges WHERE TDWK(P:Date) = + "Tuesday"

displays all columns from the Charges table in which the date falls on a Tuesday.

Note that when operating on dates that are not already stored in columns or variables defined as Date data, the *Date* argument in the function must be enclosed in double quotation marks as shown in the examples below:

■   RDATE(*Mon,Day,Year*)

Converts to Date Data Type—Where *Mon* is an integer from 1 to 12, *Day* is an integer from 1 to 31, and *Year* is an integer representing a year, creates a variable of the Date data type. Example: RDATE(12,31,1986) creates a Date data type containing the date 12/31/1986.

∎ RTIME(*Hrs,Min,Sec*)

Converts to Time Data Type—Where *Hrs* is an integer from 1 to 24, *Min* is an integer from 1 to 60, and *Sec* is an integer representing seconds, creates a variable of the Time data type. Example: RTIME(12,59,30) creates a Time data type containing the time 12:59:30.

∎ JDATE(*Date*)

Julian Date—Converts *Date* to a Julian date in the range of 1 (for 01/01/1900) to 99365 (for 12/31/1999). Example: JDATE("01/01/1900") produces 1.

∎ IDAY(*Date*)

Day of the Month—Returns the day of the month (1–31) of *Date* as an integer. Example: IDAY("12/31/86") produces 31.

∎ IDWK(*Date*)

Integer Day of the Week—Returns the day of the week (1–7) of *Date* as an integer, where Monday is 1. Example: IDWK("12/31/1986") produces 3 (Wednesday).

∎ TDWK(*Date*)

Text Day of the Week—Returns the day of the week of *Date* as text. Example: TDWK("12/31/1986") produces "Wednesday".

∎ IMON(*Date*)

Integer Month—Returns the month (1–12) of *Date* as an integer, where January is 1. Example: IMON("12/31/1986") produces 12.

■ TMON(*Date*)

Text Month—Returns the month of *Date* as text. Example: TMON("12/31/1986") produces "December".

■ IYR(*Date*)

Integer Year—Returns the year of *Date* as an integer. Example: IYR("12/11/86") returns 86.

■ IHR(*Time*)

Integer Hour—Isolates the hour from *Time* data as an integer. Example: IHR(11:59:00) produces 11.

■ IMIN(*Time*)

Integer Minute—Isolates the minute from *Time* data as an integer. Example: IHR(11:59:00) produces 59.

■ ISEC(*Time*)

Integer Second—Isolates the second from *Time* data as an integer. Example: IHR(11:59:22) produces 22.

Financial Functions

The financial functions perform numerous financial calculations that can be used in a variety of business settings. The main trick to using the financial functions is making certain that you do not confuse yearly and monthly data. For example, to find the *monthly* payment for a $150,000 loan, given a term of 20 *years*, and a 9.37% *annual* interest rate, you must first convert the years to months (multiplying by 12) and then convert the annual interest rate to a monthly interest rate (by dividing by 12). You can do so within the function argument. The formula below calculates the *monthly* payment on the loan described above:

■ SET VARIABLE MonPay TO Pmt1(.0937/12,20 * 12,150000)

Note that the interest rate (the first argument) is divided by 12 and the term (second argument) is multiplied by 12.

When calculating values in which interest is compounded daily, you can divide the annual interest rate by 365 and multiply the term by 365. The examples below will demonstrate these conversions.

■   FV1(*Pmt,Int,Per*)

> **Future Value of Payments**—Computes the future value of a series of regular equal payments of the amount specified in *Pmt* and the per-period interest rate specified in *Int* for the number of periods given in *Per.* Example: If you deposit $250 monthly into an account that pays 8% annual interest, how much money will be in the account after ten years? The expression FV1(250,.08/12,10★12) returns the answer, $45,736.51.

■   FV2(*Dep,Int,Per*)

> **Future Value of Deposit**—Computes the future value of a single deposit in the amount specified in *Dep* and the per-period interest rate specified in *Int* for the number of periods given in *Per.* Example: Suppose you deposit $10,000 in an account that pays 8% interest (compounded monthly) for ten years. How much money will be in the account after ten years? The answer is given by the expression FV2(10000,.08/12,10★12), which computes the result $22,196.40.

■   PV1(*Pmt,Int,Per*)

> **Present Value of Cash Flow**—Computes the present value of a series of equal payments of the amount specified in *Pmt* at the periodic interest rate specified in *Int* for the number of periods specified in *Per.* Example: You purchase an annuity into which you pay $200 a month, at an annual interest rate of 10%, for ten years. What is the present value of the annuity? The answer is given by the expression PV1(200,.10/12,10★12), which returns $15,134.23.

■   PV2(*Fv,Int,Per*)

Present Value—Computes the present value based on the future value given in *Fv* at the periodic interest rate specified in *Int* for the number of periods specified in *Per*. Example: You want to have $10,000 in a savings account at the end of ten years. The interest rate, compounded daily, is 8%. How much money must you invest now to ensure $10,000 in the future? The answer is given with the expression PV2(10000,.08/365,10*365), which returns $4493.68.

■   PMT1(*Int,Per,Prin*)

Payment on Loan—Calculates the payment required to pay off a loan with the principal specified in *Prin* at the per-period interest rate given in *Int* for the number of payment periods specified in *Per*. Example: You wish to borrow $5000 dollars for three years at 2.9% interest to buy a car. What will the monthly payment on the loan be? The answer is given by the expression PMT1(.029/12,3*12,5000), which displays the monthly payment $145.19.

■   PMT2(*Int,Per,Fv*)

Payments to Reach Future Value—Calculates the regular payment required to accumulate the future value given in *Fv* at the per-period interest rate given in *Int* for the number of periods given in *Per*. Example: You want to accumulate $10,000 in ten years in an account that pays 7% interest compounded monthly. How much must you pay each month to reach your goal? The answer is given by the expression PMT2(.07/12,10*12,10000), which returns $57.78.

■   RATE1(*Fv,Pv,Per*)

Required Interest Rate—Calculates the interest rate required for the sum of money given in *Pv* to reach the future value given in *Fv* in the term given in *Per*. Example: You have $5000 to invest for ten years. What interest rate will you need to double your money within that time? The answer is given with the expression RATE1(10000,5000,12*10) 0.0058 (monthly interest rate), or when multiplied by 12, 0.0695, or a little under 7% annual interest rate.

- **RATE2(*Fv,Pmt,Per*)**

    Required Interest Rate—Calculates the interest rate required for a series of regular payments given in *Pmt* to reach the future value given in *Fv* in the number of payment periods given in *Per*. Example: You wish to deposit $250 per month into an account for five years. What interest rate is required to accrue $20,000 at the end of the five years? The expression RATE2(20000,250,5★12) returns the answer, 0.00936 monthly interest, or about 11% annual interest.

- **RATE3(*Pv,Pmt,Per*)**

    Required Interest Rate—Calculates the periodic interest rate required for an annuity with the value given in *Pv* to return a series of future cash flows given in *Pmt* for the number of periods given in *Per*. Example: You want to purchase a $100,000 annuity that will pay $1500 monthly for a period of ten years. What interest rate is required to reach your goal? The answer is given in the expression RATE3(100000,1500,10★12), which yields 0.011 monthly interest, or about 12% annual interest.

- **TERM1(*Pv,Int,Fv*)**

    Required Term—Computes the term required for the present value specified in *Pv* to reach the future value given in *Fv* given the periodic interest rate in *Int*. Example: You want to invest $5000 in an account that pays 10% annual interest. How long will it take to double your money? The expression TERM1(5000,.10/12,10000) gives the answer 84 months (or 7 years).

- **TERM2(*Pmt,Int,Fv*)**

    Required Term—Calculates the number of compounding periods for a number of equal payments given in *Pmt* at the periodic interest rate given in *Int* to reach the future value given in *Fv*. Example: You want to deposit $250 a month at 10% annual interest. How long will it take until you accumulate $10,000? The expression TERM2(250,.10/12,10000) gives the answer, 35 months.

- **TERM3(*Pmt,Int,Pv*)**

Computed Term—Calculates the number of periods that an annuity will last, given the payment you wish to receive in each term (*Pmt*), the periodic interest rate for the annuity (*Int*), and the present value of the annuity (*Pv*). Example: You wish to purchase a $20,000 annuity that pays 8% annual interest. How long will the annuity last (before reaching 0) if you receive $250 monthly payments from the annuity? The expression TERM3(250,.08/12,20000) gives the answer, 115 months (or about 9½ years).

Logical Functions

The logical functions make decisions based on two alternatives. We've seen several examples of the IFEQ function in earlier chapters, with the expression

■   IFEQ(Tax?,0,Qty*U_Price,(Qty*U:Price)*1.06)

This expression calculated the total of a transaction, excluding tax if the column named Tax? contained a zero. Otherwise, the total is calculated as the quantity times the unit price times 1.06 (to add 6% sales tax).

In the logical functions, all arguments are assumed to be numeric. For example, the following expression is not allowed:

■   IFEQ(L:Name,"Smith","Yes","No")

because L:Name is not a numeric column, and "Smith", "Yes", and "No" are all Text data.

■   IFEQ(*N1,N2,Yes,No*)

> **If Equal**—Returns the value, or the result of the expression, given in the argument *Yes*, if *N1* equals *N2*. If *N1* does not equal *N2*, then the value or result of the expression specified in the argument *No* is returned. Example: IFEQ(10,10,0,100) returns 0, because 10 is equal to 10. The expression IFEQ(10,9,0,100) returns 100, because 10 does not equal 9.

■   IFLT(*N1,N2,Yes,No*)

> **If Less Than**—Returns the value, or the result of the expression, given in the argument *Yes*, if *N1* is less than *N2*. If *N1* is

greater than or equal to *N2*, then the value or result of the expression specified in the argument *No* is returned. Example: IFLT($-1,0,0,100$) returns 0, because -1 is less than 0. The expression IFLT(10,9,0,100) returns 100, because 10 is not less than 9.

■ IFGT(*N1,N2,Yes,No*)

If Greater Than—Returns the value, or the result of the expression, given in the argument *Yes*, if *N1* is greater than *N2*. If *N1* is less than or equal to *N2*, then the value or result of the expression specified in the argument *No* is returned. Example: IFGT(99,50,0,100) returns 0, because 99 is greater than 50. The expression IFGT(2,99,0,100) returns 100, because 2 is not greater than 99.

■ EXPERIMENTS WITH FUNCTIONS

The easiest way to experiment with functions is to try a few in conjunction with the Select command. For example, if the Mail database is open and the R> prompt is on the screen, you can enter the command

■ SELECT Company = 15 LUC(Company) = 15 + ULC(Company) = 15 ICAP1(Company) = 15 + ICAP2(Company) = 15 FROM Names

to view the Company column from the Names table in its current state, and after treatment with the LUC, ULC, ICAP1, and ICAP2 functions. (For a good fit on the screen, the width is set to 15 characters in each column.) The Company column from each record will be displayed, although the listing below shows only a single row:

ABC Co.   ABC CO.   abc co.   Abc co.   Abc Co.

The commands below set the date format to "MM/DD/YY", and then display the P:Date column, the day of the week (TDWK), the month (TMON), and the Julian date (JDATE) of the date from the Charges table:

■ SET DATE "MM/DD/YY"

SELECT P:Date TDWK(P:Date) TMON(P:Date) JDATE(P:Date) +
FROM Charges

A portion of the resulting display is shown below:

P:Date	COMPUTED	COMPUTED	COMPUTED
06/15/86	Sunday	June	86166
07/01/86	Tuesday	July	86182

Functions in Computed Columns

You can use functions in computed columns. For example, Figure 14.2 shows a table named Loans that consists of the columns named Princ, APR, Years, MoPmt, and TotBack.

MoPmt is a computed field with the expression

■   PMT1(((APR/100)/12),(Years * 12),Princ)

The first argument inside the PMT1 function, ((APR/100)/12), divides the annual interest rate by 100 (so that when the APR is entered as 9.375, it is correctly converted to the decimal 0.09375), and then divides the annual interest rate by 12 for the monthly interest rate. The

```
Enter or change the column names

  ┌────────┐   An asterisk (*) identifies key columns
  │ Loans  │   A plus sign (+) identifies computed columns
  └────────┘

  ┌──────────┬────────┬─────────┬──────────┬──────────┬──────┐
  │ Princ    │ APR    │ Years   │ MoPmt    │ TotBack  │      │
  ├──────────┼────────┼─────────┼──────────┼──────────┼──────┤
  │ CURRENCY │ REAL   │ INTEGER │ +CURRENCY│ +CURRENCY│      │
  ├──────────┼────────┼─────────┼──────────┼──────────┼──────┤
  │          │        │         │          │          │      │
  └──────────┴────────┴─────────┴──────────┴──────────┴──────┘

            ════════════════Choose column data type════════════
   TEXT   CURRENCY   INTEGER   REAL   DOUBLE   COMPUTED

Enter expression value:
PMT1(((APR/100)/12),(Years*12),Princ)_


[ESC] Discard   [F3] Review   [F5] Reset value   [F10] Help   [Shift-F10] More
Database FINANCE --- Table Loans    --- Column    4
```

■ *Figure 14.2:*
Table definition for the Loans table.

second argument, (Years★12), multiplies the years in the loan by 12 to calculate the months. The third argument is the principal of the loan. Hence, for each row entered into the table, R:BASE automatically calculates the monthly payment.

You may notice that immediately after entering the formula, R:BASE changes it to the following:

■   PMT1((('APR'/100)/12),('Years' * 12),'Princ')

R:BASE automatically places single quotation marks around the existing column names when you enter computed field expressions.

The TotBack column is also a computed column, and it calculates the entire payback on the loan using the expression

■   (12 * Years) * MoPmt

which is the term of the loan in months (for example, the number of years times 12) times the monthly payment (already calculated in the MoPmt column). Again, R:BASE automatically adds single quotation marks around column and variable names as below:

■   (12 * 'Years') * 'MoPmt'

As with any table with computed fields, each time you enter or edit data on the Loans table, R:BASE will automatically calculate the payment on the loan and the total payback on the loan.

Functions in Forms

If you want to create a form that allows you to enter data into the Loans table and also display the monthly payment and total payback immediately, you can use Forms Express to create the form.

Once in Forms Express, use the Expression and Define options from the top menu to create the three expressions listed below:

■   MoPymt = PMT1(((APR/100)/12),(Years * 12),Princ)
     TotBack = ((12 * Years) * MoPymt)
     Hold   = Use arrow keys to change, or press Enter

Then use the Edit option to place text, column names, and variable names onto the form using the usual arrow and F6 keys. The Hold variable should be located near the bottom of the screen below all column

names and other variable names. When given the opportunity to customize field characteristics for the Hold variable, select Yes, and change
the answer to the first questions to Yes, as below:

■ Will new data be entered in the field? .... [Yes]
  Can the user change the data displayed in the field? .... [Yes]

Changing these answers to Yes ensures that the highlight cursor will
move into the Hold variable and wait for an entry, thereby giving you
time to view the results of the calculations and to modify the data on the
screen. (Be sure to place the S and E locations wide enough apart to
accommodate the entire message stored in the Hold variable.)

Figure 14.3 shows a Loans form in use. The principal, interest, and
term have already been typed onto the screen, and the monthly payment and total payback have been calculated automatically. The highlight is currently on the Hold variable, waiting for the next keystroke.

Functions in Reports

Functions can be used in reports in the same fashion that they are
used in forms. For example, suppose the Loans table consisted of only
the Princ, APR, and Years columns, without computed columns for the
monthly payment and total payback.

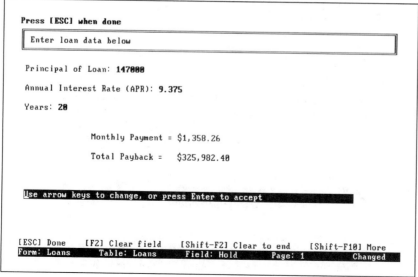

■ *Figure 14.3:*
The Loans form
in use.

You could easily create a report using Reports Express to calculate and display the payment and payback. Once in Reports Express, use the Expression and Define options from the top menus to create the appropriate expressions, as below:

■   MoPmt = PMT1(((APR/100)/12),(Years*12),Princ)
      TotBack = (12*Years)*MoPmt

When locating column and variable names on the report format, include the MoPmt and TotBack variables in the detail lines of the report. (Of course, you can use functions in break footings as well, if you like.)

Using Functions with the Change Command

You can use functions with the Change command to modify existing data in a database. For example, suppose you had initially entered all the names in the Names table with the Caps Lock key on so that all of the last names were in uppercase, as below:

■   SMITH
      JONES
      MILLER
      ADAMS
      MILLER
      BAKER
      MILLER
      TEASDALE
      MARTIN

To convert those names to initial capital letters, use the ICAP1 function in the Change command. (**Note:** When using functions in the Change command, particularly with a Text column, enclose the entire expression in parentheses so that the expression is not taken as the actual text to place into the column):

■   CHANGE L:Name TO (ICAP1(L:Name)) IN Names +
      WHERE L:Name EXISTS

When you use the command

■   SELECT L:Name FROM Names

to view the last name column after entering the Change command, you'll see that the last names have been converted to initial capital letters, as below:

- L:Name
  Smith
  Jones
  Miller
  Adams
  Miller
  Baker
  Miller
  Teasdale
  Martin

As mentioned earlier, the Change command makes many permanent changes to a table immediately. When using functions to change data in columns, it would probably be a good idea to use the Project command to make a copy of the table first, and then practice and experiment with the copied table.

As an alternative to changing the data in the column, you can always use the appropriate function in a report format to modify the data in the printed report only.

■ SUMMARY

Now that you have a basic knowledge of R:BASE memory variables and functions, we can move to the next step in building complex applications: creating *command files*. The commands and techniques we've discussed in this chapter are summarized below:

Enter **SET VARIABLE** *variable name* **TO** *value* to store data in variables.

The Show Variables command displays all currently active variables. Enter **SHOW VARIABLE** *variable name* to display the value of a single variable.

Variables can be calculated using the syntax **SET VARIABLE** *variable name* **TO** *expression*. The expression may contain arithmetic operators and functions.

R:BASE automatically assigns variable data types based on the nature of the data being stored. You can predefine a variable's data type explicitly by entering **SET VARIABLE** *<variable name> <data type>*.

The syntax **SET VARIABLE** *variable name* **TO** *column name* **IN** *table name* **WHERE** *condition* allows you to pass data from tables in an open database to variables.

The syntax **COMPUTE** *variable name* **AS** *<command> <column name>* **FROM** *table name* **WHERE** *conditions* allows you to store the results of table calculations in variables.

Entering **CLEAR** *variable name* erases a single active variable. The Clear All Variables command erases all active variables except #DATE, #TIME, and #PI.

R:BASE offers 70 functions that can be used with variables, in computed columns, in expressions for forms and reports, and in R:BASE commands.

15

THE R:BASE PROGRAMMING LANGUAGE

The Application Express feature provides a quick and easy way to develop applications, but there are limits to its flexibility. As an enhancement, you can write your own R:BASE programs to use in conjunction with those generated by the Application Express feature, or even use your programs as entirely separate tools.

An R:BASE program is called a *command file* because it is a file stored on disk (like a table or database) that contains a series of commands to be carried out. This means that you can store an entire group of commands in a file and process them all with a single command, rather than typing in each command individually at the R> prompt.

For example, suppose you regularly print the Director and Sales reports from the Mail database. Each time you do so, you have to type in the following six commands individually at the R> prompt:

■ OPEN Mail
OUTPUT PRINTER WITH SCREEN
PRINT Director SORTED BY L:Name F:Name
NEWPAGE
PRINT Sales SORTED BY CustNo
OUTPUT SCREEN

You could instead create a command file that contained all these commands in order and have R:BASE automatically perform all six tasks using a single Run command.

But there is much more to creating and using command files than simply storing commands. Command files allow you to perform tasks that are otherwise not possible within R:BASE. In this chapter, we'll discuss some of the basic constructs used in creating command files.

(**Note:** Throughout this chapter, we'll use the terms *command file* and *program* interchangeably.)

■ RECORDING KEYSTROKES

Before we get into the nitty-gritty of creating and running command files, we'll discuss a technique whereby you can create simple *Exec* files by recording keystrokes as you type them. The Exec files you can create through recorded keystrokes are not as powerful as the command files we'll develop later in the chapter. Nonetheless, the technique of recording and playing back keystrokes can save you from repeatedly typing in all the commands necessary to perform a task that you perform often.

To begin recording keystrokes, press Shift-F7 (hold down the Shift key and press the F7 key). The screen asks for the

■   Name of file to record to:

Type in a valid DOS file name (remember, eight characters without spaces or punctuation). You can add a three-letter extension preceded by a period after the file name. For this example, type in the file name

■   Labels.EXC

and press Enter.

Now, type in each of the commands below, pressing the Enter key after each one:

■   CLS
     OPEN Mail
     OUTPUT SCREEN
     PRINT LABELS SORTED BY ZIP
     CLOSE

After typing in the last command, Close, and pressing Enter, press Shift-F7 to stop recording the keystrokes.

To play back the recorded keystrokes, press the Shift-F8 key. The screen asks for the

■   Name of file to play back:

Type in the name of the Exec file (Labels.EXC in this example), and press Enter. You'll see all the commands that you recorded played back on the screen, and R:BASE will execute all of the commands as they are played back.

To view the Labels.EXC file, you can enter the command

■   TYPE Labels.EXC

at the R> prompt. It will contain all the commands you typed in, followed by a Z. (The Z is actually a Ctrl-Z, which marks the end of the recorded keystrokes.)

Again, you can use this technique to create simple Exec files that act much like the command files we'll be discussing in this chapter. However, you cannot include the programming commands such as While, If, Fillin, and others that we'll discuss in this chapter in an Exec file.

■ CREATING COMMAND FILES WITH RBEDIT

You can create command files, or write a program, using the R:BASE RBEdit editor. (You can also use external word processors such as WordStar or Word, as long as you use a nondocument mode or save the program in an unformatted file.) You can access RBEdit from the first menu by selecting the RBEdit option, or you can type in the command

■   RBEDIT

at the R> prompt.

Let's try a simple exercise to practice creating and running command files. From the R> prompt, type in the command

■   RBEDIT

and press Enter. You'll see the short menu of options below:

■   – Old File – New File – Quit————————R:base screen editor

The New File option allows you to create a new command file, the Old File option allows you to modify an existing command file, and Quit returns you to the R> prompt. Select the New File option.

You'll see a blank screen for composing your command file. At the upper-right corner of the screen you'll see

■   <1,1> [ESC] to exit

The <1,1> indicates the row and column position of the cursor, and the [ESC] message reminds you that you can press the Esc key to quit RBEdit. Figure 15.1 lists the keys that you can use while creating and editing command files.

Creating Your First Command File

Type in the command file (or program) shown in Figure 15.2. Press the Enter key after typing in each line. Remember, you can use the arrow keys to move the cursor and correct errors as you type. Use the Ins and Del keys to insert and delete characters and the F1 and F2 keys to insert and delete lines if you need to while making any corrections.

Saving the Command File

Once you've typed in the entire command file, press the Esc key. You'll see the menu

■   – Edit again – Save file – Next File – Quit——————————————

Select the Save File option to store a copy of the command file on disk. R:BASE will display the prompt

■   Name of new file to save:

You can use any valid file name that you wish. A valid file name is no more than eight characters long, without spaces, followed by a period

Key	Function
Enter	Finish the current line and move down one line
↓	Move down one line
↑	Move up one line
→	Move right one character
←	Move left one character
Tab	Move right ten characters
Shift-Tab	Move left ten characters
Ctrl →	Move to the end of the line
Ctrl ←	Move to the beginning of the line
F1	Insert a line above the current line
F2	Delete the current line
F4	Enter and exit repeat mode
Ins	Insert a blank space
Del	Delete a character
Home	Display the first page of text
End	Display the last page of text
PgUp	Move up one page
PgDn	Move down one page

■ *Figure 15.1:*
Keys used with RBEdit.

and a three-letter extension. Typically, command files are stored with the extension .CMD, so type in the file name

■   Sample1.CMD

and press Enter.

Now select the Quit option, and you will be returned to the R> prompt.

Running the Command File

Once you've saved the command file, use the Run command with the name of the file to run the program. In this example, enter the command

■   RUN Sample1.CMD

and press Enter. You'll see the message "Database exists" briefly as the program opens the Mail database. Then the screen will clear, and after a brief pause, you'll see the Director report displayed in alphabetical order by last and first names. Then the screen will clear again (because of the Newpage command), and you'll see the Sales report printed in order by customer number. When the command file is finished, you'll see the message

■   Switching input back to keyboard

which means that R:BASE will be expecting the next command to come from the keyboard, rather than from the command file.

Editing a Command File

To edit an existing command file, use the RBEdit editor. As a short-cut, you can enter the name of the command file along with the RBEdit command, as below:

■   RBEDIT Sample1.CMD

Let's add a couple of commands to clear the screen and then print mailing labels. Move the cursor to the bottom of the command file, just under the C in CLOSE, like so:

■   <u>C</u>LOSE

Press the F1 key twice to insert two blank lines, so the command file looks like Figure 15.3.

Next, type in the command

■   NEWPAGE

Press Enter and type in the command

■   PRINT Labels SORTED BY Zip

When you are finished, your command file should look like Figure 15.4.

Press Esc after making the changes. Again, select the Save File option. R:BASE will display the prompt

■   Name of new file to save [Sample1.CMD]:

To use the Sample1.CMD file name again, press the Enter key. You'll be returned to the R> prompt.

To run the modified command file, once again enter the command

■   RUN Sample1.CMD

```
                                         < 8,  1>  [ESC] to exit
   OPEN Mail
   NEWPAGE
   PRINT Director SORTED BY L:Name F:Name
   NEWPAGE
   CLEAR ALL VARIABLES
   PRINT Sales SORTED BY CustNo
   CLOSE
   _
```

■ *Figure 15.2:*
Sample command file typed in with RBEdit.

You'll see the Director, Sales, and Labels reports printed on the screen, and then you'll see the message

■   Switching input back to keyboard

which means that you are once again back to the normal R:BASE command mode.

As you can see, creating a command file is as easy as calling up the RBEdit editor, typing in the commands that you want to process, saving the command file, and then running it with the Run command. With RBEdit, you can create command files with up to 800 command lines (depending on available memory).

With the addition of input/output, looping, decision making, and a few other tricks of the trade, you can build command files that go far beyond a simple list of commands and perform more sophisticated tasks. We'll discuss these techniques in the remainder of this chapter.

■ INPUT/OUTPUT COMMANDS

The input/output commands allow you to display messages, pause for a response, and assign values to variables from within a command file.

```
                                        < 7,  1>  [ESC] to exit
OPEN Mail .
NEWPAGE
PRINT Director SORTED BY L:Name F:Name
NEWPAGE
CLEAR ALL VARIABLES
PRINT Sales SORTED BY CustNo

-

CLOSE
```

■ *Figure 15.3:*
Blank lines added to the Sample1.CMD command file.

The three primary input/output commands for R:BASE are Write, Pause, and Fillin.

Displaying Messages with the Write Command

The Write command uses the general syntax

■   WRITE *"message"* AT *<row>* *<column>*

The At portion is optional. Most screens contain 24 rows and 80 columns; the upper-left corner is row 1, column 1, and the lower-right corner is row 24, column 80.

To try the command, create a simple command file named IO1.CMD by entering

■   RBEDIT IO1.CMD

at the R> prompt. Fill in the lines

■   NEWPAGE
     WRITE "This is the first message . . . "

```
                                          < 8, 27>  [ESC] to exit
   OPEN Mail
   NEWPAGE
   PRINT Director SORTED BY L:Name F:Name
   NEWPAGE
   CLEAR ALL VARIABLES
   PRINT Sales SORTED BY CustNo
   NEWPAGE
   PRINT Labels SORTED BY Zip_
   CLOSE
```

■ *Figure 15.4:*
Edited
Sample1.CMD
command file.

Press Esc when you're done writing the command file, and select the Save File option. Press Enter to use the file name IO1.CMD. When the R> prompt reappears, the command file will clear the screen and display the message

■   This is the first message . . .

before returning to the R> prompt.

You can use the optional At command with the Write command to specify the exact row and column position for displaying information on the screen. To test this, try using RBEdit to create a command file named IO2.CMD. Enter the two command lines below into the command file:

■   CLS
     WRITE "This is the middle" AT 12,31

Press Esc and select Save File to save the file with the file name IO2.CMD. Then, from the R> prompt, enter the command

■   RUN IO2.CMD

and press Enter to test the command file.

Combining Text and Numbers

Sometimes, you may want to display a message from within a command file that contains both text and numeric data, such as the following message:

■   You just won $100,000.00!

You cannot directly combine textual and numeric data in a variable for display. However, by using the CTXT function to convert the numeric data to textual data, you can indeed combine the two types of data. Here is an example.

Use RBEdit to create a command file named IO3.CMD. Enter the following lines into the command file:

■   CLEAR ALL VARIABLES
     SET VARIABLE Prize CURRENCY
     SET VARIABLE Prize TO 100000.00

```
SET VARIABLE Msg TO "You just won" & CTXT(Prize) + "!"
WRITE .Msg AT 20,1
```

Save the command file by pressing Esc and selecting Save File from the menu. When the R> prompt reappears, enter the command Run IO3.CMD and press Enter. You'll see the message "You just won $100,000.00!" appear at row 20, column 1 on the screen, and then the R> prompt will reappear. Let's discuss why.

The first line in the command file, Clear All Variables, simply erases any existing variables. Then the command

■   SET VARIABLE Prize CURRENCY

creates an empty variable named Prize, which is predefined as the Currency data type.

The next line

■   SET VARIABLE Prize TO 100000.00

stores the number 100,000 in the variable named Prize. The next line

■   SET VARIABLE Msg TO "You just won" & CTXT(Prize) + "!"

concatenates (joins) the numeric Prize variable to the textual string "You just won", and then concatenates the character "!" to the numeric Prize variable.

Normally, these items could not be strung together because the Prize variable is numeric and the characters in quotation marks are text. However, the CTXT function converts the Prize variable to Text data within the Set Variable command, so R:BASE accepts the concatenation.

The last line in the command file

■   WRITE .Msg AT 20,1

displays the entire .Msg variable at row 20, column 1 on the screen.

Pausing Execution with the Pause Command

The Pause command temporarily causes R:BASE to stop processing the commands in a command file until the user presses a key. The Pause command is usually used with a message displayed with the Write command. For example, use RBEdit to create a command file named IO4.CMD, and type in the commands below:

■ NEWPAGE
  WRITE "Press any key to continue " AT 12,30
  PAUSE
  WRITE "Thank you" AT 23,5

Save the command file, and then run it by entering

■ RUN IO4.CMD

The screen will clear, and you will see the following:

■ Press any key to continue

After you press a key, R:BASE will continue processing commands, and you'll see the message

■ Thank you

near the bottom of the screen.

Filling in Variables with the Fillin Command

The Fillin command pauses program execution and waits for some data to be entered by the user. Whatever the user types in on the screen is stored in a variable. Generally, it is a good idea to define the data type for the variable explicitly before using the Fillin command.

The general syntax for the Fillin command is as follows:

■ FILLIN *variable name* USING *"message"* AT <*row*> <*column*>

To try the command, use RBEdit to create a command file named IO5.CMD. Type in the lines shown below:

■ NEWPAGE
  SET VARIABLE YourName TEXT
  FILLIN YourName USING "Enter your name: " AT 12,5
  NEWPAGE
  SET VARIABLE Reply TO "Hello " & .YourName
  WRITE .Reply AT 12,30

Note that the command file first clears the screen (NEWPAGE) and creates an empty variable named YourName of the Text data type. The Fillin command displays the message "Enter your Name: " at row 12, column 5 and waits for a value to be entered from the keyboard. Then the command file clears the screen and creates a variable named Reply that consists of the word "Hello", followed by the YourName variable. The last line of the program displays the Reply variable at row 12, column 30.

When you run the command file, it will first ask for your name. Type in your name and press Enter. You'll then see the message "Hello", followed by your name, as below:

■   Hello Joe

■ PROGRAMMER COMMENTS

You can add comments to your programs (command files) that are never displayed and that do not affect the program in any way. Generally, the purpose of these comments is to write helpful notes to yourself within a program. If you ever need to go back and modify a program many weeks or months later, the comments can help you translate the commands into English.

Comments in R:BASE programs must begin with an asterisk and an opening parenthesis and end with a closing parenthesis *(. . . .). For example, the line below is a valid program comment:

■   *(This is a program comment)

To make comments more visible in a program, programmers often add extra asterisks or hyphens, as in the two examples below:

■   *(* Program to display menus)
      *(– – – – – – – – – – – – – – – – – – Update the master file)

You must remember to add the closing parenthesis to a comment; otherwise R:BASE might think that the entire program is a comment and ignore all commands. When that happens, you'll be returned to the command mode with the + > prompt showing. To correct the problem, type in a closing parenthesis next to the + > prompt and press Enter. Then use RBEdit to find the faulty comment and rectify it.

Figure 15.5 shows the IO5.CMD command file with some programmer comments added. Note that the first two comments provide the name of the command file, as well as a brief description of what the program does. Additional comments describe individual routines within the command file.

We'll use comments throughout the remaining sample programs in this book to help clarify various commands and routines.

∎ LOOPING WITH WHILE AND ENDWHILE

One of the most common techniques used in programming is the *loop*. A loop allows a command file to repeat a single command, or several commands, as long as some condition exists. The general syntax for the While and Endwhile commands is

∎ WHILE *condition* THEN
　　do *this command*
　　and *this command*
　　ENDWHILE

Keep in mind that every While command in a program *must* have an Endwhile command associated with it.

Figure 15.6 shows a sample program with a While loop in it.

Let's look at the logic of the program, line by line. The first two lines are simply programmer comments. The Newpage command then

∎ *Figure 15.5:*
Command file
with comments.

```
*(****************************** IO5.CMD)
*(--------------- Test the FILLIN command)
*(Clear the screen and initialize YourName variable)
NEWPAGE
SET VARIABLE YourName TEXT
*(-- Ask for user's name, and store in YourName variable)
FILLIN YourName USING "Enter your name: " AT 12,5
NEWPAGE
*(-- Create variable named Reply, and display it)
SET VARIABLE Reply TO "Hello" & YourName
WRITE .Reply AT 12,30
```

clears the screen, as follows:

■   *(* Loop1.CMD)
     *(– – – – – – – – – – – – – – Program to test a WHILE Loop)
     NEWPAGE

Next, the program creates a variable named Counter and assigns it
the value 1, as follows:

■   *(– – – – – – – – – – – – – Create a variable named Counter)
     SET VARIABLE Counter TO 1

The next line starts a loop that will repeat all commands between the
While and Endwhile commands, as long as the Counter variable is less
than or equal to 10:

■   *(– – – – – – – – – – – – – – – – – – Repeat loop 10 times)
     WHILE Counter < = 10 THEN

Within the While loop, these lines create a variable named Progress,
which contains the text "Loop Number" and the current value of the
Counter variable converted to text. The Write command then displays
this prompt on the screen:

■   *(– – – – – – – – – – – – – Create a prompt and display it)
     SET VARIABLE Progress TO "Loop Number" & CTXT(.Counter)
     WRITE .Progress

```
*(******************************** Loopl.CMD)
*(--------------- Program to test the WHILE loop)
NEWPAGE
*(--------------- Create variable named Counter)
SET VARIABLE COUNTER TO 1
*(--------------- Repeat loop 10 times)
WHILE Counter <= 10 THEN
        *(--------- Create a prompt and display it)
        SET VARIABLE Progress TO "Loop Number " & CTXT( .Counter)
        WRITE .Progress
        *(--------- Increment Counter variable by 1)
        SET VARIABLE Counter TO .Counter + 1
ENDWHILE *(Bottom of WHILE loop)
*(--------------- End of program)
QUIT
```

■ *Figure 15.6:*
*Sample program
with a While
loop.*

Next, the program increments the Counter variable by one by adding a 1 to its current value:

■   *(– – – – – – – – – – – – – – – – Increment Counter by 1)
     SET VARIABLE Counter TO .Counter + 1

The line below marks the end of the While loop:

■   ENDWHILE *(– – – – – – – – – – – – – – End of WHILE loop)

The last line, QUIT, ends the program and returns control to the R> prompt. R:BASE uses portions of memory to manage While loops, and the Quit command frees up this memory. Therefore, it is a good idea to end a program that contains While loops with the Quit command.

■   *(– End program)
     QUIT

You can use RBEdit to create the command file. When you run the program, you'll see on the screen:

■   Loop Number = 1
     Loop Number = 2
     Loop Number = 3
     Loop Number = 4
     Loop Number = 5
     Loop Number = 6
     Loop Number = 7
     Loop Number = 8
     Loop Number = 9
     Loop Number = 10
     Terminating all WHILE and IF blocks
     Switching INPUT back to KEYBOARD

Notice that the Write command within the While loop repeated ten times, and each time through, the Counter variable incremented by one. The closing remark, "Terminating all WHILE and IF blocks," was produced by the Quit command.

You can use variables to determine how many times the While loop should repeat. For example, the command file Loop2.CMD in Figure 15.7, when run, displays the prompt

■   How high shall I count?

and waits for a response. After you enter a number, the While loop will repeat the appropriate number of times. For example, if you enter a 5, you'll see the following on the screen:

- Loop Number = 1
  Loop Number = 2
  Loop Number = 3
  Loop Number = 4
  Loop Number = 5
  Terminating all WHILE and IF blocks
  Switching INPUT back to KEYBOARD

  Notice in the program that the commands

- SET VARIABLE Done INTEGER
  FILLIN Done USING "How high shall I count?: " AT 9,5

create a variable named Done. The Fillin command displays the prompt "How high shall I count?:" and waits for a response from the user. The user's response is then stored in the Done variable. The While loop repeats as long as the Counter variable is less than or equal to the Done variable, as follows:

- WHILE Counter < = .Done THEN

The Set Pointer Command

With the use of the Set Pointer command, a While loop can also step through a table a single row at a time. The general syntax of the Set Pointer command is

- SET POINTER # <n> <variable name> FOR *table name* +
  SORTED BY *column name(s)* WHERE *conditions*

The Sorted By and Where clauses are optional. The *n* can be any number from 1 to 3. Three pointers, in three separate tables, can be set up simultaneously. The *variable name* is an integer that equals zero until there are no more rows in the table to process. The command

- NEXT # <n> <variable>

is used to move the pointer to the next row in the table. If no Sorted By or Where clause is specified, the Next command simply moves the pointer to the next row in the table. If a Sorted By or Where clause (or both) is included, the pointer moves through the appropriate records in the selected sort order.

Figure 15.8 shows a sample command file that displays the first and last names of individuals in the Names table.

The command

- OPEN Mail

■ *Figure 15.7:*
Program to test
the While
command with
a variable.

```
*(******************************** Loop2.CMD)
*(--------------- Program to test the WHILE loop)
*(------------ Create Counter and Done variables)
SET VARIABLE COUNTER TO 1
SET VARIABLE Done INTEGER
*(------------- Ask how high to count)
NEWPAGE
FILLIN Done USING "How high shall I count?: " AT 9,5
NEWPAGE
*(--------------- Repeat loop until Counter > Done)
WHILE Counter <= .Done THEN
      *(---------- Create a prompt and display it)
      SET VARIABLE Progress TO "Loop Number " & CTXT(.Counter)
      WRITE .Progress
      *(---------- Increment Counter variable by 1)
      SET VARIABLE Counter TO .Counter + 1
ENDWHILE *(Bottom of WHILE loop)
*(--------------- End of program)
QUIT
```

■ *Figure 15.8:*
Sample program
with a While loop
and the Set
Pointer
command.

```
*(****************************** Loop3.CMD)
*(********** Test WHILE loop through a table)
NEWPAGE
*(---------------- Open the Mail database)
OPEN Mail
*(------ Set up pointer into Mail database)
SET POINTER #1 Status FOR Names SORTED BY L:Name F:Name
*(------ Repeat loop until end of table encountered)
WHILE Status = 0 THEN
      SET VARIABLE Name1 TO F:Name IN #1
      SET VARIABLE Name2 TO L:Name IN #1
      SET VARIABLE Name TO .Name1 & .Name2
      WRITE .Name        *(--Display the name)
      NEXT #1 Status     *(--Skip to next row in table)
ENDWHILE
CLOSE        *(-- close the database)
QUIT         *(-- end of program)
```

opens the Mail database. The command

■   SET POINTER #1 Status FOR Names SORTED BY +
     L:Name F:Name

sets up pointer #1 and a variable named Status for the Names table. The While loop continues processing as long as there are still rows in the Names table to process; that is, as long as the Status variable is zero, as below:

■   WHILE Status = 0 THEN

Then the Set Variable and Write commands assign first and last names to variables. Note the use of #1 in the first two Set Variable commands. Since the pointer has been defined as #1, the Names table is now referred to as #1, as follows:

■   SET VARIABLE Name1 TO F:Name IN #1
     SET VARIABLE Name2 TO L:Name IN #1
     SET VARIABLE Name TO .Name1 & .Name2
     WRITE .Name   *(− Display the name)

The following command

■   NEXT #1 Status   *(− Skip to next row in table)

moves the pointer to the next row in the Names table (#1), and the Status variable receives a new value—either zero if there is another row to process or a nonzero number (usually 2406) if there are no more rows to process.

If you key in the command file and run it, the screen will show all the first and last names listed in the Names table, sorted alphabetically, as follows:

■   Bart Adams
     Robin Baker
     Mindy Jones
     Mary Martin
     Anne Miller
     Marie Miller
     Monica Miller
     Sandy Smith
     Trudy Teasdale

End-of-data encountered
Terminating all WHILE and IF blocks
Switching input back to keyboard

We'll see a few more examples of the While and Set Pointer commands in coming chapters.

■ DECISION MAKING WITH IF

Another commonly used programming technique is *decision making* using the If, Then, Else, and Endif commands. The general syntax for the If command is

■   IF *conditions* THEN
       Do *this command*
       and *this command*
   ELSE
       Do *this command*
       and *this command*
   ENDIF

The Else portion is optional, so the If command might also use the following simpler syntax:

■   IF *conditions* THEN
       Do *this command*
       and *this command*
   ENDIF

With either syntax, each If command in a command file *must* have an Endif command associated with it.

There can be any number of commands between the If and Endif commands. The *conditions* portion can have up to ten expressions joined with the AND and OR operators.

Figure 15.9 shows a simple program that makes a decision on whether or not to display information on the printer, based upon the user's response to the question

■   Send message to the printer? (Y/N):

The Fillin command displays the prompt, then waits for the user to enter an answer. This answer is stored in a variable named YesNo. The clause

■   *(— Decide whether to use printer or just screen)
    IF YesNo = Y THEN
       OUTPUT PRINTER WITH SCREEN
    ELSE
       OUTPUT SCREEN
    ENDIF

will channel output to the printer and screen if the YesNo variable contains the letter Y. If this variable contains an N, output will be channeled to the screen only.

Note the use of the Quit command to end the program. Like programs that contain While commands, command files that contain If commands should always end with a Quit command.

■ BRANCHING WITH GOTO

The Goto and Label commands are used to pass over a group of commands in a command file and branch to another group of commands. The basic syntax for the Goto command is

■   GOTO *label name*

```
*(************************ IF1.CMD)
*(----- Program to test the IF command)
NEWPAGE
*(------- Create variable to hold answer)
SET VARIABLE YesNo TEXT
*(------- Display prompt and get answer)
FILLIN YesNo USING "Send message to the printer? (Y/N) " +
    AT 12,2
*(------ Decide whether to use printer or just screen)
IF YesNo = "Y" THEN
    OUTPUT PRINTER WITH SCREEN
ELSE
    OUTPUT SCREEN
ENDIF
*(-- Display message)
WRITE "Here is the message"
OUTPUT SCREEN  *(-- back to normal screen display)
QUIT
```

■ *Figure 15.9:*
Sample program to test the If command.

The syntax for the Label command is the following:

■   LABEL *label name*

The label name may be up to eight characters long. Figure 15.10 shows a sample command file that displays the prompt

■   Do you wish to exit R:base? (Y/N):

If the user answers Yes, the program branches to the routine labeled Done, and control is returned to DOS (or the first R:BASE menu). If the user answers No, all commands between the Goto and Label commands are executed, rather than skipped over, and the Director report from the Mail database is displayed on the screen.

Branching has the disadvantage of slowing down the speed of command file execution considerably, and in most cases a While or If command can be used in place of the Goto and Label commands. You should only resort to using a Goto command when there appears to be no other way to accomplish a programming goal. As you learn more techniques throughout this book, you'll see that the Goto command is rarely necessary.

```
*(******************************** GoTest.CMD)
*(-- Program to test the GOTO and LABEL commands)
NEWPAGE
SET VARIABLE YesNo TEXT
*(------------- Ask if user wants to exit, rather than
                    continuing.  Branch to Done label.)
FILLIN YesNo USING "Do you wish to exit now? (Y/N) " +
    AT 12,1
NEWPAGE
*(------------- If exit requested, skip over all
                    commands before LABEL Done.)
IF YesNo = "Y" THEN
    GOTO Done
ENDIF
*(--- If exit not requested, print Directory report.)
OPEN MAIL
PRINT Director SORTED BY CustNo
CLOSE
QUIT    *(Return to R> prompt)
*(--- Routine to leave R:BASE R> prompt)
LABEL Done
EXIT    *(----- Leave R:BASE)
```

■ *Figure 15.10:*
Sample program
with Goto and
Label commands.

■ SUBROUTINES

Subroutines are command files that can be accessed from other command files. They save programming effort by allowing you to perform a task, which may require several commands, using a single Run command in a command file.

Subroutines (sometimes called *procedures* or *macros*) have the additional advantage of *parameter passing*. This technique leaves certain aspects of the routine open-ended so that it is more flexible.

Figure 15.11 shows a simple subroutine named Area.CMD, which calculates the area of a rectangle using the formula Area = Length × Width. SET VARIABLE Area = %1 × %2 calculates the area by multiplying the first (%1) and second (%2) parameters passed to the subroutine and stores the result in a variable named Area.

The Return command should be placed at the end of every subroutine. This ensures that control is returned either to the R > prompt or to a calling command file after the subroutine is done. Be sure to place the Return command at the bottom of the subroutine (and *not* in the middle of an If or While clause).

After creating and saving a subroutine, using the same technique that is used for creating command files, you can run it and pass parameters to it with the Using option of the Run command.

For example, to calculate the area using a length of 5 and a width of 10, you would enter the command

■   RUN Area.CMD USING 5 10

To see the results of the calculation, enter the command

■   WRITE .Area

and you'll see that the Area variable contains 50.

You also can pass variables to subroutines. For example, if you create

```
*(***************************** Area.CMD
              Subroutine to calculate area)
SET VARIABLE Area REAL
SET VARIABLE Area = %1 * %2
RETURN *(-- return to calling program)
```

■ *Figure 15.11:*
The Area.CMD subroutine.

the variables Length and Width, as below:

- SET VARIABLE Length TO 5.543
  SET VARIABLE Width TO 6.1234

you can use the command

- RUN Area.CMD USING .Length .Width

When you write the Area variable, it will contain the results of the appropriate calculation.

You can pass up to nine parameters to a subroutine. The parameters are assigned numbers (for example, %1, %2, %3, and so on) from left to right. Separate each parameter with a blank space.

In some cases, you might want to pass a parameter to a subroutine that has spaces in it. For example, the subroutine in Figure 15.12 displays a title, the date, and the time at the top of the screen. The title to be printed is passed as a parameter (%1).

To print the title Accounts Receivable Main Menu using the Title subroutine, you would need to enclose the title in quotation marks, as follows:

- RUN Title.CMD USING "Accounts Receivable Main Menu"

If you use the Show Variables command after you've passed parameters to subroutines, you'll notice that R:BASE adds a second digit to the parameters, as in the %1-0 and %2-0 variables below:

Variable	=	Value	Type
#DATE	=	06/21/86	DATE
#TIME	=	4:04:11	TIME
%1-0	=	5.21221	REAL
%2-0	=	6.32994	REAL
Area	=	32.9930	REAL

∎ *Figure 15.12:*
Subroutine to
print a title.

```
*(***************************** Title.CMD
                Subroutine to print a title)
NEWPAGE
WRITE .%1 AT 2,1
WRITE .#DATE AT 2,60
WRITE .#TIME AT 2,70
RETURN
```

R:BASE performs this "housekeeping" task as a means of keeping track of the level at which a parameter was used. The parameters in this example have the extension -0 because they were called from the R> prompt. If they had been called from a command file, the extension would be -1. If they had been called from a command file that had been called from another command file, the extension would be -2. However, you need not concern yourself with these extensions, and you definitely should not add them yourself.

■ DEBUGGING COMMAND FILES

Quite often, when you first run a command file, it will not perform exactly as you had expected. Errors in programs are referred to as *bugs,* and the process of removing them is called *debugging.* There are several techniques that you can use to help debug programs.

Using the Set Echo On Command

If you enter the command Set Echo On at the R> prompt before running a command file, you'll see each line in the program as R:BASE processes it. If an error causes the program to stop running, you'll be able to see the exact line that caused the error. Then, you can use RBEdit to correct the program and try running it again.

To disable the Echo option, use the Set Echo Off command.

Setting Messages

R:BASE will display general-purpose messages, such as "Database exists," while the command file is running. You can suppress messages by entering

■   SET MESSAGES OFF

at the top of a command file. However, if you find that you are having problems getting a command file to run, remove the Set Messages Off command from the command file and enter

■   SET MESSAGES ON

at the R> prompt. After correcting your program, you can replace the Set Messages Off command.

Setting Error Messages

You can enter the following command:

■ SET ERROR MESSAGES OFF

at the top of a command file to suppress the display of R:BASE error messages. However, if your command file has a bug in it that causes control to be returned to the R> prompt, you won't see what the error was. To debug the program, remove the Set Error Messages Off command from the command file. From the R> prompt, enter

■ SET ERROR MESSAGES ON

before you run the command file again. After you find and correct any bugs, you can put the Set Error Messages Off command back into the command file if you wish.

Showing Variables

You can enter the command Show Variables at any time from the R> prompt. If your program uses variables, look closely at the variables displayed. Make sure that all of the variables your program needs have been created and that they are the appropriate data type. If you find that some variables have the incorrect data type, use explicit data typing near the top of your program to specify what type they should be (for example, enter a command like Set Variable YourName Text).

Making a Hard Copy of the Command File

Another method that will help you to debug a command file is to make a printed (hard) copy of it. Use the Output Printer and Type commands at the R> prompt. For example, to print a copy of the IO5.CMD command file, enter the commands

■ OUTPUT PRINTER WITH SCREEN
  TYPE IO5.CMD

at the R> prompt. Enter the Output Screen command after printing the program to return to normal screen mode.

If your program contains While or If commands, you might want to use a pen or pencil to draw connecting lines between all While and Endwhile commands and all If and Endif commands, as shown in Figure 15.13. Make sure that each While and If command has an associated Endwhile and Endif command.

Missing and misplaced Endwhile and Endif commands will definitely cause problems in a program. Drawing connecting lines can help find them, as well as help you see more clearly the commands contained within the While and If clauses.

■ STRUCTURED PROGRAMMING

One of the best debugging techniques is to try to avoid bugs in the first place. The technique of structured programming can help accomplish this feat, and it will greatly aid in the process of debugging, as well as in making future modifications to a program.

The two basic rules of thumb for structured programming are quite simple:

> Use highly visible programmer comments in the command file to make it easy to locate commands that perform a specific task.

```
     *(******************************** Sample3.CMD
                    Test a WHILE loop through a table)
     NEWPAGE
     *(------------ Open the Mail database)
     OPEN Mail
     *(------------ Set a pointer in Names table)
     SET POINTER #1 Status FOR Names SORTED BY L:Name
     *(----------- Continue loop to end of table)
     WHILE Status = 0 THEN
             SET VARIABLE Name1 TO F:Name IN #1
             SET VARIABLE Name2 TO L:Name IN #1
             IF Name2 EXISTS THEN
                 SET VARIABLE Name TO .Name1 & .Name2
                 WRITE .Name
             ENDIF
             NEXT #1 Status
     ENDWHILE
     QUIT
```

■ *Figure 15.13: Sample program with connecting lines drawn in.*

Indent program lines within While loops and If clauses so that you can easily see the beginning and ending points of these specific routines.

The programs we've developed in this chapter have adhered to this basic rule of thumb. Note that the program shown in Figure 15.14 does not follow the basic rules of structured programming. There are no comments and no indentations in the programming. To figure out what the program is supposed to do, you need to read every line in the command file.

As shown in Figure 15.15, the same command file can be made much easier to understand by inserting comments that describe the various tasks that the program performs. Furthermore, the indented lines

■ *Figure 15.14:*
An unstructured program.

```
SET VARIABLE COUNTER TO 1
SET VARIABLE Done INTEGER
NEWPAGE
FILLIN Done USING "How high shall I count?: " AT 9,5
NEWPAGE
WHILE Counter <= .Done THEN
SET VARIABLE Progress TO "Loop Number " & CTXT(.Counter)
WRITE .Progress
SET VARIABLE Counter TO .Counter + 1
ENDWHILE
QUIT
```

■ *Figure 15.15:*
A structured program.

```
*(********************************** Loop2.CMD)
*(--------------- Program to test the WHILE loop)
*(----------- Create Counter and Done variables)
SET VARIABLE COUNTER TO 1
SET VARIABLE Done INTEGER
*(------------- Ask how high to count)
NEWPAGE
FILLIN Done USING "How high shall I count?: " AT 9,5
NEWPAGE
*(--------------- Repeat loop until Counter > Done)
WHILE Counter <= .Done THEN
      *(---------- Create a prompt and display it)
      SET VARIABLE Progress TO "Loop Number " & CTXT(.Counter)
      WRITE .Progress
      *(---------- Increment Counter variable by 1)
      SET VARIABLE Counter TO .Counter + 1
ENDWHILE *(Bottom of WHILE loop)
*(--------------- End of program)
QUIT
```

between the While and Endwhile commands make it easy to see the starting and ending points of the loop, as well as which commands are repeated within the loop. Indenting the program lines between the If and Endif and the While and Endwhile commands is especially beneficial because many program errors are caused by leaving out the necessary Endif and Endwhile commands. If you use indentations, a missing Endif or Endwhile command will be more noticeable.

A missing Endif or Endwhile command in a command file can make R:BASE behave strangely, even after you've returned to the R> prompt. Usually, R:BASE will seem to ignore every command that you enter, simply redisplaying the R> prompt after each command without taking any action. If this happens, first try entering the command Endif right at the R> prompt. Then try some other commands to see if R:BASE is back to normal.

If that doesn't work, enter the Endwhile command at the R> prompt and try again. Things should be back to normal by then, but just to be safe, also enter the Quit command to free the memory used by these commands. Then, use RBEdit to find the missing command and put it into the command file.

■ SUMMARY

In this chapter, we've discussed the following basic programming techniques and commands:

To begin recording keystrokes in an Exec file, press Shift-F7 and enter a valid DOS file name. When you are finished recording keystrokes, press Shift-F7 again.

To play back the keystrokes recorded in an Exec file, press Shift-F8 and enter the name of the Exec file to play back.

Enter the command RBEdit, followed by the name of the command file, at the R> prompt to create or edit a command file.

Use the Run command at the R> prompt to run a command file.

The Write, Pause, and Fillin commands allow a program to interact with a user by displaying messages, pausing for input, and receiving values for variables from the keyboard.

Programmer comments allow a programmer to make notes in a command file. Comments begin with an asterisk and an opening parenthesis and end with a closing parenthesis, *(. . . .).

The While and Endwhile commands set up loops for repeating commands in a command file.

The If, Else, and Endif commands allow for decision making within a command file.

The Quit command should be used to terminate programs that contain While or If commands.

The Goto and Label commands provide a branching capability.

Subroutines are created and stored as are any other command files. However, you can pass information to subroutines using the syntax

■ RUN *command file* USING *parameter list*

The parameters in the subroutine are accessed through the %1, %2, %3, . . ., %9 variables.

The Set Echo, Set Messages, Set Error Messages, and Show Variables commands are valuable aids to the debugging process.

Structured programming techniques help reduce the likelihood of errors in a program, and they also make debugging and future modifications easier.

In later chapters, we'll use these commands and techniques to build sophisticated applications.

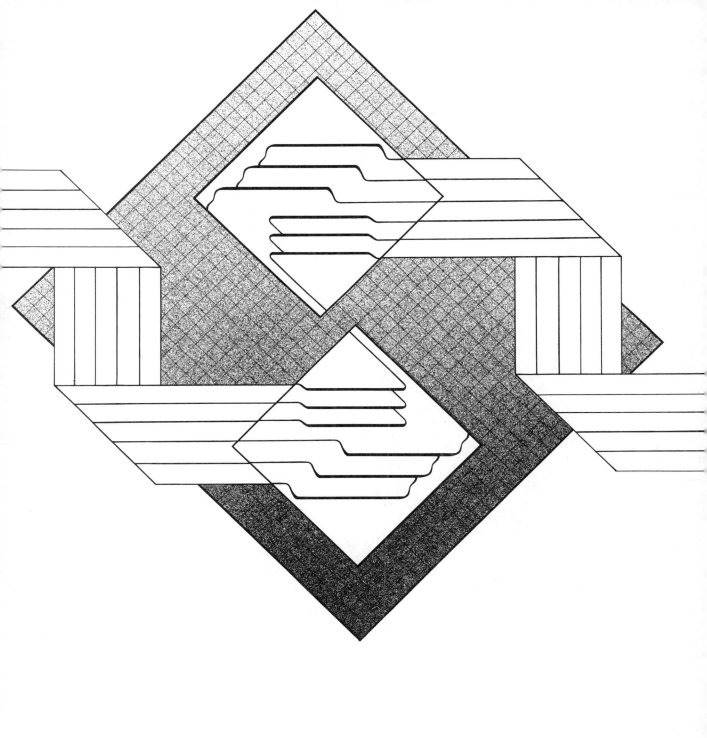

16
AN ACCOUNTS-RECEIVABLE SYSTEM

In this chapter, we'll discuss some advanced programming techniques with the R:BASE programming language and methods for integrating custom routines with applications developed by using the Application Express feature. While learning these new techniques, we'll develop a complete accounts-receivable system with monthly billing.

■ ACCOUNTS-RECEIVABLE/BILLING SYSTEM DESIGN

When developing a large system, it's a good idea to write down your basic goals on paper. Sometimes, an overall goal, such as to develop an accounts-receivable/billing system, is too vague for a starting point. Using an outline, we can break down this overall goal into smaller, more manageable goals, as below:

I. Develop an accounts-receivable/billing system

    A. Maintain a customer list with accounts-receivable balances

    B. Maintain an inventory list of items in stock

    C. Maintain a history of individual charge transactions

    D. Maintain a history of payments

    E. Print monthly bills

From this point, we can further define the tasks required to attain each main goal under the overall goal, as below:

I. Develop an accounts-receivable/billing system

    A. Maintain a customer list with accounts-receivable balances

        1. Add, edit, and delete customers

        2. Print customer list

    B. Maintain an inventory list of items in stock

        1. Add, edit, and delete inventory items

        2. Print inventory list

    C. Maintain a history of individual charge transactions

        1. Add, edit, and delete charges

        2. Print charge transactions

D. Maintain a history of payments

   1. Add, edit, and delete payments

   2. Print payment transactions

E. Print monthly bills

   1. Print the bills

   2. Update customer billing history

Looking at the project from this perspective makes things seem easier. Most tasks simply involve managing data and printing reports from tables.

Once you write down the basic goals of the project, you can begin designing the database structure.

■ DATABASE DESIGN

We'll need several tables in our accounts-receivable system database to meet the goals that we've defined. First, we'll need a table to record basic customer information, including the current, and 30-, 60-, 90-, and 120-day balances, as well as other relevant information. We'll name the database ARSYS, and name the table for recording customer information ARMain. The ARMain table will have the structure shown in Figure 16.1.

Next, we'll develop a table of products with product numbers, product names, prices, and so forth. This table will speed up data entry in the accounts-receivable system. The user will simply enter a product number, and R:BASE will automatically fill in the rest of the information for each charge transaction. The name of the inventory table is Inventry, and its structure is shown in Figure 16.2.

We'll also need a table to record individual charge transactions. This table will have a structure similar to the Charges table in the Mail database. The name of the table is Charges, and its structure is shown in Figure 16.3.

Since accounts-receivable systems typically revolve around a monthly billing cycle, we'll move all transactions that have been billed to a *history* table at the end of each billing period. The CHistory table will hold the historical charge transactions, and its structure will be identical to the structure of the Charges table, as shown in Figure 16.4.

Individual payment transactions will be stored in the Payments table. The structure for the Payments table is shown in Figure 16.5.

As with the Charges table, payments that have already been recorded on a bill at the end of the month will be moved to a history table named PHistory. The structure for the PHistory table is identical to the structure of the Payments table, as shown in Figure 16.6.

Finally, to simplify the printing of bills, a special table named BillTemp will hold records of both the Charges and Payments transactions. (We'll explain the purpose of the BillTemp table later in this chapter.) The structure for the BillTemp table is shown in Figure 16.7.

The hierarchical relationship of the ARMain, Charges, Payments, and two History tables is shown in Figure 16.8. The ARMain table is a *master table* because it maintains ongoing balances of individual customers' credit

Table: ARMain

Column definitions

#	Name	Type	Length	Description
1	CustNo	INTEGER	1 value(s)	Customer number
2	L:Name	TEXT	12 characters	Last name
3	F:Name	TEXT	15 characters	First name
4	Company	TEXT	20 characters	Company
5	Address	TEXT	25 characters	Street address
6	City	TEXT	15 characters	City
7	State	TEXT	2 characters	State
8	Zip	TEXT	10 characters	ZIP code
9	Phone	TEXT	13 characters	Phone number
10	Curr:Bal	CURRENCY	1 value(s)	Current balance
11	Bal:30	CURRENCY	1 value(s)	30-day balance
12	Bal:60	CURRENCY	1 value(s)	60-day balance
13	Bal:90	CURRENCY	1 value(s)	90-day balance
14	Bal:120	CURRENCY	1 value(s)	120-day balance
15	Curr:Chr	CURRENCY	1 value(s)	Last total charge amount
16	Curr:Pay	CURRENCY	1 value(s)	Last payment amount
17	BillDate	DATE	1 value(s)	Last billing date

∎ *Figure 16.1:*
Structure for the ARMain table.

activities. The Charges and Payments tables are *transaction tables* because they record individual transactions during the month. Through *updating*, the ARMain master table receives data from the transaction tables to keep each customer's balances up-to-date. The PHistory and CHistory tables are *history tables*, which record "old" transaction data that have already been through the entire monthly billing cycle.

Table: Inventry

Column definitions

#	Name	Type	Length	Description
1	ProdNo	TEXT	5 characters	Product number
2	PartName	TEXT	20 characters	Product name
3	U:Price	CURRENCY	1 value(s)	Unit price
4	Tax?	INTEGER	1 value(s)	Taxable?
5	OnHand	INTEGER	1 value(s)	Quantity in hand
6	ReOrder	INTEGER	1 value(s)	Reorder point
7	Last:Upd	DATE	1 value(s)	Date of last update

■ *Figure 16.2:*
Structure of the Inventry table.

Table: Charges

Column definitions

#	Name	Type	Length	Description
1	CustNo	INTEGER	1 value(s)	Customer number
2	ProdNo	TEXT	5 characters	Product number
3	Qty	INTEGER	1 value(s)	Quantity purchased
4	U:Price	CURRENCY	1 value(s)	Unit price
5	Tax?	INTEGER	1 value(s)	Taxable?
6	T:Price	CURRENCY	1 value(s)	Total price
7	P:Date	DATE	1 value(s)	Purchase date

■ *Figure 16.3:*
Structure for the Charges table.

Table: CHistory

Column definitions

#	Name	Type	Length	Description
1	CustNo	INTEGER	1 value(s)	Customer number
2	ProdNo	TEXT	5 characters	Product number
3	Qty	INTEGER	1 value(s)	Quantity purchased
4	U:Price	CURRENCY	1 value(s)	Unit price
5	Tax?	INTEGER	1 value(s)	Taxable?
6	T:Price	CURRENCY	1 value(s)	Total price
7	P:Date	DATE	1 value(s)	Purchase date

■ *Figure 16.4:*
Structure for the
CHistory table.

Table: Payments

Column definitions

#	Name	Type	Length	Description
1	CustNo	INTEGER	1 value(s)	Customer number
2	Check:No	INTEGER	1 value(s)	Check number
3	Amount	CURRENCY	1 value(s)	Payment amount
4	Pay:Date	DATE	1 value(s)	Date of payment

■ *Figure 16.5:*
Structure for the
Payments table.

Table: PHistory

Column definitions

#	Name	Type	Length	Description
1	CustNo	INTEGER	1 value(s)	Customer number
2	Check:No	INTEGER	1 value(s)	Check number
3	Amount	CURRENCY	1 value(s)	Payment amount
4	Pay:Date	DATE	1 value(s)	Date of payment

■ *Figure 16.6:*
Structure for the
PHistory table.

If you are following along on-line, go ahead and use Definition Express to create the new database named ARSys. Use option (1), Add a New Table to the Database, from the Tables menu to create each of the tables ARMain, Inventry, Charges, Payments, and BillTemp using the structures shown in the previous figures. (You don't need to define key columns for any of the tables at this point.)

After creating all five tables, exit Definition Express and return to the R> prompt. From the R> prompt, you can easily create the CHistory and PHistory tables by copying the Charges and Payments tables. First, open the new ARSys database by entering the command

■ OPEN ARSys

at the R> prompt. Then enter the two commands below at the R> prompt:

■ PROJECT CHistory FROM Charges USING ALL
   PROJECT PHistory FROM Payments USING ALL

Once you've defined the tables, you can begin developing forms for entering and editing data.

Table: BillTemp

Column definitions

#	Name	Type	Length	Description
1	CustNo	INTEGER	1 value(s)	Customer number
2	ProdNo	TEXT	5 characters	Product number
3	Qty	INTEGER	1 value(s)	Quantity
4	U:Price	CURRENCY	1 value(s)	Unit price
5	Tax?	INTEGER	1 value(s)	Taxable?
6	T:Price	CURRENCY	1 value(s)	Total price
7	P:Date	DATE	1 value(s)	Purchase date
8	Check:No	INTEGER	1 value(s)	Check number
9	Amount	CURRENCY	1 value(s)	Payment amount
10	Pay:Date	DATE	1 value(s)	Payment date

■ *Figure 16.7:*
Structure for the BillTemp table.

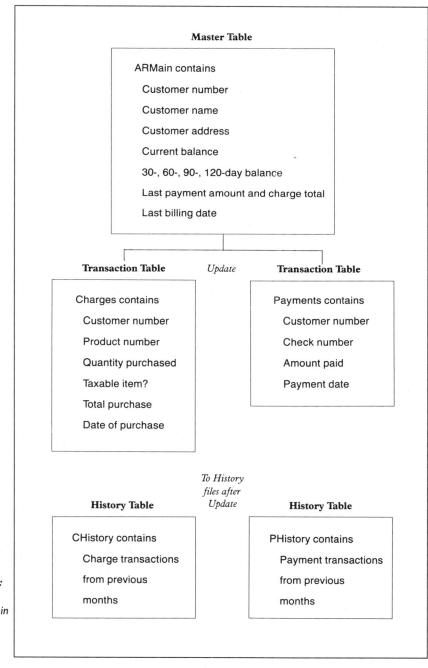

∎ *Figure 16.8:*
Relationship among tables in the accounts-receivable system.

■ *ACCOUNTS-RECEIVABLE SYSTEM FORMS*

After you've created the accounts-receivable system tables, you can begin developing forms for entering and editing data. Enter the Forms Express module, and open the ARSys database if necessary. (Remember, you can enter Forms Express by entering the Forms command at the R> prompt.)

Customer Form

In Forms Express, create a form for entering and editing customer information. Assign the name Main to the form, and attach it to the ARMain table. You don't need to customize the table, form, or field characteristics on this form. Nor do you need to define any expressions for this form. Figure 16.9 shows a suggested format for the form. Column names associated with each start and end location are shown in the figure, but these, of course, will not appear on your screen.

Add/Edit Customers

Customer Number: S *CustNo* E

Last Name: S *L:Name* E		First Name: S *F:Name* E	
Company: S *Company* E		Address: S *Address* E	
City: S *City* E		State: SE	Zip: S *Zip* E
Phone: S E		Date: S *BillDate* E	

State

Current Balance: S *Curr:Bal* E

30 day balance: S *Bal:30* E	60 day balance: S *Bal:60* E
90 day balance: S *Bal:90* E	90 + day balance: S *Bal:120* E
Curr. payment : S *Curr:Pay* E	Curr. charges: S *Curr:Chr* E

■ *Figure 16.9:*
The Main form on the screen.

Press Esc twice after creating the form and select Save Changes to save it.

Inventory Table Form

You can use Forms Express to create a form for entering and editing items in the inventory table. Name this form InvForm, and attach it to the Inventry table. You don't need to define any expression or customize any table or form characteristics for this form. Figure 16.10 shows a suggested format for the form. Once again, column names are shown on the figure, but these will not appear on your screen.

For added convenience, you may want to customize the field characteristics for the Tax? and Last:Upd fields. You can do so either while locating the column names with the F6 key, or by returning the cursor to any place between the S and the E for the column names and pressing F6. Answer Yes to the question about customizing field characteristics. Change the answer to the question about displaying a default value to Yes. For the Tax? field, enter 1 as the default value. For the Last:Upd field, enter #DATE as the default value.

After creating the form, press Esc twice and select Save Changes to save the form.

Charges Form

The form for entering and editing charges will be fancier than the Main and InvForm forms. For convenience, this form will automatically look up the customer name and company from the ARMain table

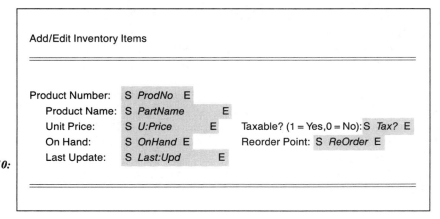

■ *Figure 16.10:*
The InvForm
form on the
screen.

when the user enters a customer number onto the form. These data will be displayed on the form so the user can verify that the correct customer number was entered.

As soon as the user enters a product number for the transaction, the form will look up the product name, unit price, and tax status on the Inventry table. These data will appear on the form immediately and will also be entered into the Charges table automatically. The user only needs to enter the quantity purchased, and the form will calculate and display the total sale.

Use Forms Express to create the form. Assign the name ChrgFrm to the form, and attach it to the Charges table. You don't need to customize any table or form characteristics for this form. From the top menu select Expression Define, and enter each of the expressions below:

■   Name1   = F:Name IN ARMain WHERE CustNo = CustNo
    Name2   = L:Name IN ARMain WHERE CustNo = CustNo
    VName   = Name1 & Name2
    VCompany = Company IN ARMain WHERE CustNo = CustNo
    VPartNm   = PartName IN Inventry WHERE ProdNo = ProdNo
    U:Price   = U:Price IN Inventry WHERE ProdNo = ProdNo
    Tax?   = Tax? IN Inventry WHERE ProdNo = ProdNo
    T:Price   = (IFEQ(Tax?,0,Qty*U:Price,(Qty*U:Price)*1.06))

Notice that the first four expressions look up information in the ARMain table based on the customer number entered onto the form. It stores the customer name and company from the ARMain table in the variables named VName and VCompany.

The last four expressions look up information in the Inventry table. The part name is stored in the variable named VPartNm. The unit price and tax are stored directly in the Charges table (because of the column names Tax? and U:Price, which are the actual column names in the Charges table). The total price (T:Price) is calculated using the IFEQ function to determine whether the item is taxable. T:Price is also a column name in the Charges table, and hence the results of this calculation are stored directly on the Charges table.

After defining the expressions for the form, press Esc twice and select Edit from the top menu to lay out the form. Figure 16.11 shows a suggested format for the ChrgFrm form. Again, column and variable names are displayed on the figure for clarity, but these will not appear on your screen.

For convenience, you can customize the field characteristics for the P:Date column and specify #DATE as the default value for the field.

After creating the ChrgFrm form, press Esc twice and select Save Changes to save your work.

Payments Form

The payments form lets the user enter and edit data on the Payments table. Use Forms Express as usual to create the form. Assign the name PayForm to the form, and attach the form to the Payments table.

From the top menu in Forms Express select Expression Define, and create the following expressions:

■ Name1   = F:Name IN ARMain WHERE CustNo = CustNo
Name2   = L:Name IN ARMain WHERE CustNo = CustNo
VName   = Name1 & Name2
VCompany = Company in ARMain WHERE CustNo = CustNo

Note that these expressions look up customer information in the ARMain table based on the customer number entered onto the form. The form will display this information for the user's convenience when the form is used to record or edit payment transactions.

After defining the expressions, press Esc twice and select Edit from the top menu to lay out the form format. Figure 16.12 shows a suggested format for the PayForm form. Again, column and variable names are included in the figure, but these will not appear on your screen.

For additional convenience, you can customize the field characteristics for the Pay:Date column by entering #DATE as the default date for the column.

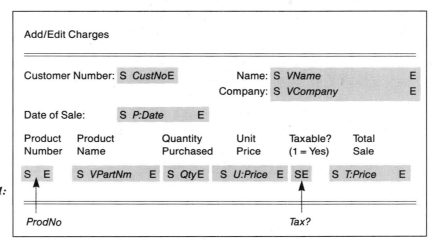

■ *Figure 16.11:*
The ChrgFrm
form on the
screen.

After all four forms are created, you can exit Forms Express to return to the R> prompt.

■ ACCOUNTS-RECEIVABLE SYSTEM RULES

To avoid entering duplicate customer numbers in the ARMain table and duplicate product numbers in the Inventry table, you can create a few rules. Enter Definition Express to define the rules (you can get to Definition Express from the R> prompt by entering the command RBDefine).

From the Definition Express Main menu, select option (2) to modify an existing database definition. Select option (4), Rules, and option (1), Add a New Rule, to create some new rules.

To disallow duplicate customer numbers in the ARMain table, enter the message

■ Duplicate Customer Number!

when requested by the screen. Select ARMain as the table for the rule and CustNo as the column to validate. Select NEA (not equal any) as the operator and ARMain as the table to compare to. Select CustNo as the column to compare to, and select (Done) as the final logical operator.

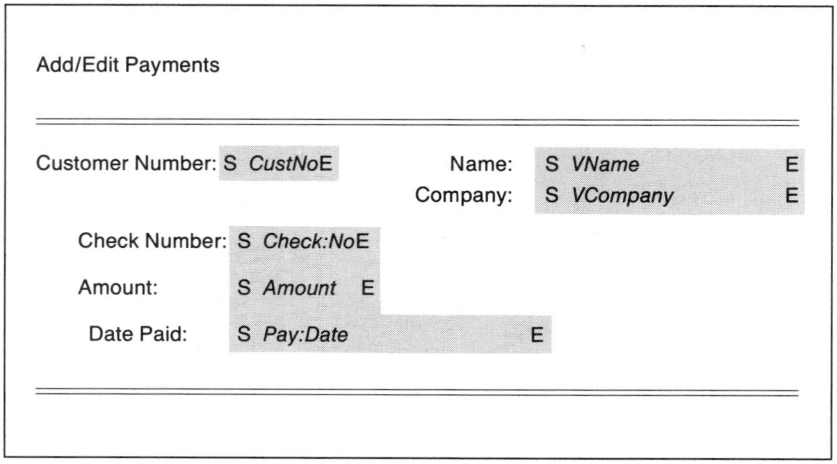

```
Add/Edit Payments
═══════════════════════════════════════════════════

Customer Number: S  CustNoE          Name:     S  VName          E
                                     Company:  S  VCompany       E

   Check Number: S  Check:NoE

        Amount:  S  Amount  E

      Date Paid: S  Pay:Date              E

═══════════════════════════════════════════════════
```

■ *Figure 16.12:*
The PayForm
form on the
screen.

To create a rule to disallow duplicate product numbers in the Inventry table, select option (1) from the menu once again to add a new rule. Enter the message

- Duplicate Product Number!

when requested. Select Inventry as the table for the rule and ProdNo as the column to validate. Select NEA as the operator, Inventry as the table to compare to, and ProdNo as the column to compare to. Select (Done) as the final logical operator. After creating the rules, exit the various menus to return to the R > prompt.

■ ACCOUNTS-RECEIVABLE REPORTS

You can create whatever reports you wish for the accounts-receivable system. In fact, you might want to develop reports similar to the Labels, Letter1, Director, and Sales reports that we developed for the Mail database. Also, simple reports displaying data from the Payments and Inventry table would be useful.

One of the primary reports for the accounts-receivable system will be the Aging report, which is shown in Figure 16.13.

From the R > prompt, enter the command

- REPORTS Aging

■ *Figure 16.13:*
Sample Aging
report from the
accounts-receivable
system.

Accounts Receivable Aging Report

Date: 09/22/86   Page: 1

Current Bal.	30-Days	60-Days	90-Days	120-Days	Payment
Customer Number: 1001	Stewart Smith				
$1,171.00	$56.00	$256.00	$0.00	$203.00	$100.00
Customer Number: 1002	Wanda Watson				
$696.00	$70.00	$80.00	$0.00	$296.00	$200.00
Customer Number: 1003	Zeppo Magillicuddy				
$200.00	$50.00	$85.00	$100.00	$0.00	$0.00

to begin designing the report layout. When prompted, enter the name
ARMain as the table for the report. Select the Expression and Define
options and define the following report variables:

- RepDate   = .#DATE
  PgNo   = .#PAGE
  Name1   = F:Name
  Name2   = L:Name
  FullName = Name1 & Name2

Figure 16.14 shows a suggested format for the Aging report. Note that
the figure includes variable and column names between the S and E locations for your reference, but these will not appear on your screen. Use the
arrow, F7, F8, and F9 keys to enter text and create sections, and use the F6
key to locate column and variable names. Press Esc twice and select Save
Changes when you are finished creating the report format.

The Bills report prints monthly statements, a sample of which is
shown in Figure 16.15.

Enter the command

- REPORTS Bills

to begin designing the Bills report format. The associated table name is
BillTemp. Select the Expression and Define options, and create the

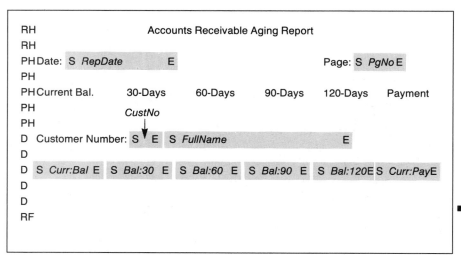

■ **Figure 16.14:**
*Aging report
layout on the
Reports screen.*

report variables listed below:

Name1 = F:Name IN ARMain WHERE CustNo = CustNo

Name2 = L:Name IN ARMain WHERE CustNo = CustNo

FullName = Name1 & Name2

Comp = Company IN ARMain WHERE CustNo = CustNo

Add = Address IN ARMain WHERE CustNo = CustNo

C = City IN ARMain WHERE CustNo = CustNo

S = State IN ARMain WHERE CustNo = CustNo

Z = Zip IN ARMain WHERE CustNo = CustNo

Comma = ","

CSZ = C + Comma & S & Z

B:Date = .#DATE

Andy Adams

ABC Co.

123 A St.

San Diego CA 92111

Customer Number: 1001   Billing Date: 06/26/86   Due Date: 07/26/86

Product	Qty	Unit Price	Tax?	Total	Payment
A-111 Semiconductor	10	$ 1.56	1	$ 16.54	
B-100 RF Modulator	5	$34.56	1	$183.17	
A-111 Semiconductor	90	$ 1.56	1	$148.82	
					$50.00

Previous Balance:	$697.06
Total Charges:	$348.53
Total Payments:	$ 50.00
	———————
Current Balance:	$995.59

■ *Figure 16.15:*
*Sample bill
printed by the
accounts-receivable
system.*

D:Date = B:Date + 30

PartNm = PartName IN Inventry WHERE ProdNo = ProdNo

Prev:Bal = Curr:Bal IN ARMain WHERE CustNo = CustNo

ChrgTot = SUM OF T:Price

PayTot = SUM OF Amount

Sub:Bal = Prev:Bal + ChrgTot

Balance = Sub:Bal − PayTot

Several of these variables warrant discussion. First, note that the Name, Company, Address, City, State, Zip, and Curr:Bal (current balance) variables are all taken from the ARMain table, using the option

■ IN ARMain WHERE CustNo = CustNo

Similarly, the product name is taken from the Inventry table using the expression

■ PartNm = PartName IN Inventry WHERE ProdNo = ProdNo

(We used a technique similar to this when developing the Sales report in the Mail database.)

The B:Date (billing date) variable is assigned the current date (.#DATE), and the D:Date (due date) variable is calculated by adding 30 days to the billing date variable (B:Date + 30).

Balances for each bill are calculated by summing the total charges (**ChrgTot = SUM OF T:Price**) and summing the total payments (**PayTot = SUM OF Amount**), and then adding the total charges to the current balance (**Sub:Bal = Prev:Bal + ChrgTot**) and subtracting the total payments (**Balance = Sub:Bal − PayTot**).

After typing in all the expressions, press Esc and select Configure from the top menu. You'll want to make CustNo the breakpoint for each subtotal (and hence, for each invoice, since one invoice is printed for each customer). To do so, make CustNo the Break column for the Break1 point. Change the Variable Reset column to Yes, and select the following variables to reset:

■ ChrgTot
PayTot
Sub:Bal
Balance

Also, to ensure that each invoice is printed on a separate page, change the Header Before column under FORM FEEDS to [YES], so that the top portion of the screen looks like this:

	BREAKPOINTS		FORM FEEDS			
	Break Column	**Variable Reset**	**Header Before**	**After**	**Footer Before**	**After**
Report			[NO]	[NO]	[NO]	[NO]
Page		[NO]				
Break1	CustNo	[YES]	[YES]			

Press Esc after setting the configurations, and then select Edit to lay out the report format. Figure 16.16 shows a suggested report format. Column and variable names are shown between appropriate S and E locations, although these will not appear on your screen.

Since the Bills report gets its data from the BillTemp table, which is currently empty, we can't test it yet. In the next section we'll develop the appropriate command file to print the bills.

■ ACCOUNTS-RECEIVABLE SYSTEM COMMAND FILES

Most of the command files for the accounts-receivable system can be created by using the Application Express menu. However, a few custom programs and subroutines will help refine the system. In this section, we'll develop these command files and subroutines, and we'll learn some advanced programming techniques along the way.

End-of-Month Procedures

Most accounting systems are based on a monthly schedule, whereby transactions are posted to a ledger at the end of each month. Our accounts-receivable system is no exception, and the tasks performed at the end of each month can be summarized as follows:

1. Print monthy statements (bills or invoices).

2. Shift all current and 30-, 60-, 90-, and 120-day balances back one month.

3. Add new charges to the current balance.

4. Subtract new payments from the current balance.

We can write a single command file to handle all of these tasks, and the user will be able to perform them simply by selecting a menu item. The command file to perform these tasks is named EndMonth.CMD, and it is displayed in Figure 16.17.

When first run, the command file displays the following message:

■   Bills are to be printed once a month only
    Monthly updates are automatically performed after billing
                    Proceed with billing? (Y/N)

```
                                        <  1,  1>   [F3] to list, [ESC] to exit
  H1SFullName               E

  H1SComp                   E

  H1SAdd                    E

  H1SCSZ                    E

  H1

  H1_____

  H1Customer Number:S  CustNo E     Billing Date: S B:Date E  Due Date: S D:Date E

  H1_____

  H1Product                 Qty        Unit Price      Tax?       Total      Payment

  H1

  D  S  ProdNo E  S  PartNm E     S  Qty E  S  U:Price E  S  Tax? E  S  T:Price E  S  Amount E

  F1

  F1

  F1Previous Balance:  S  PrevBal      E

  F1Total Charges:     S  Chrgt       E

  F1Total Payments:    S  PayTot      E

  F1                           _____

  F1Current Balance:   S  lance       E

  F1

  F1
```

■ *Figure 16.16:*
Layout for the
Bills report.

The purpose of this message is to give the user a chance to change his mind, since the procedure is only to be performed once a month. The message is stored in a separate file named Bills.MSG. To create the message file, enter

∎   RBEDIT Bills.MSG

at the R > prompt; then type in the message exactly as it appears above. Save the file in the usual way.

Now let's look at the EndMonth.CMD command file. The first lines include programmer comments and the command to clear the screen. The Display command displays the Bills.MSG file we just created with RBEdit, and the Fillin command waits for a response from the user on whether to proceed with the end-of-month procedures. If the user does not answer Y, control is passed to a routine named Bailout at the bottom of the command file:

∎
```
*(* * * * * * * * * * * * * * * * * * * * * * * * EndMonth.CMD)
*(– – – – – – – – – – – – – Perform monthly billing and update)
NEWPAGE
DISPLAY Bills.MSG
SET VARIABLE YesNo TEXT
FILLIN YesNo USING " " AT 22,1
IF YesNo < > Y THEN
    GOTO Bailout
ENDIF *(yesno < > y)
```

If the user chooses to go ahead with the monthly procedure, the command file displays the following prompt reminding him to prepare the printer and waits for him to press any key to continue:

∎
```
NEWPAGE
WRITE "Prepare printer, then press any key to continue"
PAUSE
```

Next, the command file clears the screen and displays the message "Working . . .." The R:BASE rules and messages are then set off.

∎
```
*(– Set up the BillTemp Table)
NEWPAGE
WRITE "Working . . ."
SET RULES OFF
SET MESSAGES OFF
SET ERROR MESSAGES OFF
```

```
*(***************************************** EndMonth.CMD)
*(------------------ Perform monthly billing and update)
NEWPAGE
DISPLAY Bills.MSG
SET VARIABLE YesNo TEXT
FILLIN YesNo USING " " AT 22,1
IF YesNo <> Y THEN
   GOTO Bailout
ENDIF *(yesno <> y)

NEWPAGE
WRITE "Prepare printer, then press any key to continue"
PAUSE

*(--- Set up the BillTemp Table)
NEWPAGE
WRITE "Working..."
SET RULES OFF
SET MESSAGES OFF
SET ERROR MESSAGES OFF
DELETE ROWS FROM BillTemp WHERE COUNT > 0
APPEND Charges TO BillTemp
APPEND Payments TO BillTemp

*(--- Print the invoices)
SET NULL " "
SET DATE "MM/DD/YY"
CLEAR ALL VARIABLES
OUTPUT PRINTER
NEWPAGE
PRINT Bills
NEWPAGE
OUTPUT SCREEN
SET NULL -0-

*(--- Perform the update)
*(--- First, shift back Current, 30, 60, and 90 day balances)
CHANGE Bal:120 TO (Bal:120+Bal:90) +
 IN ARMain WHERE CustNo EXISTS
CHANGE Bal:90 TO Bal:60 IN ARMain WHERE CustNo EXISTS
CHANGE Bal:60 TO Bal:30 IN ARMain WHERE CustNo EXISTS
CHANGE Bal:30 TO Curr:Bal IN ARMain WHERE CustNo EXISTS

*(--- Set current charges and payments to zero.)
CHANGE Curr:Chr TO 0 IN ARMain WHERE CustNo Exists
CHANGE Curr:Pay TO 0 IN ARMain WHERE CustNo Exists

*(--- Next, update current balance from Charges and Payments)
RUN Update.MAC USING ARMain CustNo Curr:Chr Charges CustNo T:Price PLUS
RUN Update.MAC USING ARMain CustNo Curr:Pay Payments CustNo Amount PLUS

CHANGE Curr:Bal TO (Curr:Bal+(Curr:Chr-Curr:Pay)) +
 IN ARMain WHERE CustNo EXISTS

CHANGE BillDate TO .#DATE IN ARMain WHERE CustNo EXISTS

*(--- Now move transactions to history files)
APPEND Charges TO CHistory
DELETE ROWS FROM Charges WHERE COUNT > 0
APPEND Payments TO PHistory
DELETE ROWS FROM Payments WHERE COUNT > 0
```

■ *Figure 16.17:*
The
EndMonth.CMD
command file.

```
*(---- Now age the balances using the Age.CMD command file.)
RUN Age.CMD

*(--- Update complete)
NEWPAGE
SET MESSAGES ON
SET ERROR MESSAGES ON
WRITE "End of month procedures completed..."
SET RULES ON
RETURN

*(--- Bailout routine for immediate exit)
LABEL Bailout
WRITE "Returning to Main Menu without Update"
RETURN
```

■ *Figure 16.17:*
The
EndMonth.CMD
command file.
(continued)

Next, the command file prepares the BillTemp table for printing bills. The BillTemp table consists of both charges and payments. The two tables are combined into BillTemp for printing reports, because R:BASE only allows a single transaction table in a report. We could have used a single table like BillTemp to record both Charges and Payments throughout the system; but for general data management, it may be preferable to keep the two tables separate, as we have done in this example.

First, the command file deletes any rows currently in the BillTemp table, since any rows there are no doubt from last month's billings. The Delete Rows command below performs the deletions:

■   DELETE ROWS FROM BillTemp WHERE COUNT > 0

Next, the command file appends all rows from the Charges and Payments tables onto the BillTemp table:

■   APPEND Charges TO BillTemp
     APPEND Payments TO BillTemp

Next the command file prints the invoices. To keep null fields from being displayed as -0- symbols, the command file uses the command

■   SET NULL " "

to display all null values as blanks. The date format is set to the MM/DD/YY format. All existing variables are cleared, and output is channeled to the printer. The Newpage command starts the printing on a new page, and the Print Bills command prints the invoices using the report format named Bills. After the invoices are printed, Newpage again ejects the paper in the printer, sets the output back to the screen, and resets the null character to -0-, as follows:

■   *(– Print the invoices)
```
SET NULL " "
SET DATE "MM/DD/YY"
CLEAR ALL VARIABLES
OUTPUT PRINTER
NEWPAGE
PRINT Bills
NEWPAGE
OUTPUT SCREEN
SET NULL -0-
```

Once the bills are printed, a series of Change commands is used to shift the 90-day, 60-day, 30-day, and current balances back one month, as shown below:

■   *(– Perform the update)
```
*(– First, shift back Current, 30, 60, and 90 day balances)
CHANGE Bal:120 TO (Bal:120 + Bal:90) +
IN ARMain WHERE CustNo EXISTS
CHANGE Bal:90 TO Bal:60 IN ARMain WHERE CustNo EXISTS
CHANGE Bal:60 TO Bal:30 IN ARMain WHERE CustNo EXISTS
CHANGE Bal:30 TO (Curr:Chr-Curr:Pay) IN ARMain +
WHERE CustNo EXISTS
```

Since this is the start of a new month, the current charges (Curr:Chr) and current payments (Curr:Pay) are reset to zero in all the rows in the ARMain table, using a couple of Change commands as follows:

■   *(– Set current charges and payments to zero.)
```
CHANGE Curr:Chr TO 0 IN ARMain WHERE CustNo Exists
CHANGE Curr:Pay TO 0 IN ARMain WHERE CustNo Exists
```

Next, a custom macro named Update.MAC (which we'll develop later) adjusts the current charges (Curr:Chr) and current payments (Curr:Pay) columns in the ARMain table to reflect charges and payments currently listed in the Charges and Payments tables:

■   *(– Next, update current balance from Charges and Payments)
```
RUN Update.MAC USING ARMain CustNo Curr:Chr Charges +
```

```
CustNo T:Price PLUS
RUN Update.MAC USING ARMain CustNo Curr:Pay +
Payments CustNo Amount REPLACE
```

Next, a Change command changes the current balance (Curr:Bal) column to reflect the previous month's balance, plus the current charges minus the current payments:

■ CHANGE Curr:Bal TO (Curr:Bal + (Curr:Chr − Curr:Pay)) +
IN ARMain WHERE CustNo EXISTS

The BillDate column in the ARMain table is changed in all rows to reflect the date of the invoices just printed (which is the same as the system date, .#DATE):

■ CHANGE BillDate TO .#DATE IN ARMain WHERE CustNo +
EXISTS

Once all of the updating is done, current transactions from both the Charges and Payments tables are appended onto the CHistory and PHistory tables and deleted from the Charges and Payments tables. This keeps the Charges and Payments tables small, which helps speed general processing.

■ *(− Now move transactions to history tables)
APPEND Charges TO CHistory
DELETE ROWS FROM Charges WHERE CustNo EXISTS
APPEND Payments TO PHistory
DELETE ROWS FROM Payments WHERE CustNo EXISTS

The next step is to age the existing balances by incrementally subtracting the current payment from the current aged balances. This task is handled by a command file named Age.CMD, which we'll develop soon. The EndMonth.CMD calls upon Age.CMD to age the balances in the line below:

■ *(− − Now age the balances using the Age.CMD command file.)
RUN Age.CMD

At this point, the end-of-month procedures are finished. The command file sets the normal messages back on, displays a prompt, and returns control to the calling program, as follows:

- *(– Update complete)
  NEWPAGE
  SET MESSAGES ON
  SET ERROR MESSAGES ON
  WRITE "End of month procedures completed..."
  SET RULES ON
  RETURN

One last routine in the EndMonth.CMD command file is the Bailout routine, which is called if the user does not wish to perform the procedures. The Bailout routine is shown below:

- *(– Bailout routine for immediate exit)
  LABEL Bailout
  WRITE "Returning to Main Menu without Update"
  RETURN

■ AGING THE ACCOUNTS

The EndMonth.CMD command file already performed one aspect involved in aging the accounts receivable; that of shifting all the 30-, 60-, 90-, and over-90-day balances back one month (because, presumably, another 30 days have passed when the EndMonth.CMD command file is run). The EndMonth.CMD command file did so with a series of Change commands, as discussed earlier.

The Bal:120 column actually records (and accumulates) all balances over 90 days past due. (In other words, balances in the Bal:120 column are not shifted off to the right into oblivion.) However, for a true picture of the aged receivables, one should subtract the current payment from the aged balances, starting at the oldest period (Bal:120 in this case) and working toward the Bal:30 balance.

Incrementally subtracting the current payment from the aged balances is a large job and hence is handled separately in a command file named Age.CMD. Recall that the EndMonth.CMD "calls" Age.CMD to perform this task with the command **RUN Age.CMD**.

The entire Age.CMD command file is shown in Figure 16.18. You can use the RBEdit editor to key in this command file exactly as shown in the figure.

Let's briefly discuss how Age.CMD incrementally subtracts the current payment from the existing aged balances. First, numerous

```
*(-------------------------------- Age.CMD
              Ages accounts receivable balances
              by incrementally subtracting current
              payment from existing balances.)

*(----------------- Set up variables.)
SET VARIABLE Remain DOUBLE
SET VARIABLE More INTEGER
SET VARIABLE NextBal INTEGER
SET VARIABLE BAL120 CURRENCY
SET VARIABLE BAL90 CURRENCY
SET VARIABLE BAL60 CURRENCY
SET VARIABLE BAL30 CURRENCY

*(----------------- Display opening messages)
NEWPAGE
WRITE "Aging the balances..." AT 1,1

*(----- Set up pointer for loop through table)
SET POINTER #1 Status FOR ARMain

WHILE Status = 0 THEN

    *(-- 0 is "false", 1 is "true" below)
    SET VARIABLE More TO 0
    SET VARIABLE NextBal TO 1
    SET VARIABLE Remain To 0

    *(------- 90+ day balance)
    SET VARIABLE ThisPay TO Curr:Pay IN #1
    SET VARIABLE Bal120 TO Bal:120 IN #1
    IF Bal120 > 0 THEN
        SET VARIABLE Remain TO .ThisPay - .Bal120
        IF Remain >= 0 THEN
            CHANGE Bal:120 TO 0 IN #1
            SET VARIABLE More TO 1
        ELSE
            CHANGE Bal:120 TO ABS(.Remain) IN #1
            SET VARIABLE NextBal TO 0
        ENDIF
    ENDIF

    *(------- 90 day balance)
    SET VARIABLE Bal90 TO Bal:90 IN #1
    IF NextBal=1 AND Bal90 > 0 THEN
        IF More = 1 THEN
            SET VARIABLE Remain TO .Remain - .Bal90
        ELSE
            SET VARIABLE Remain TO .ThisPay - .Bal90
        ENDIF
        IF Remain >= 0 THEN
            CHANGE Bal:90 TO 0 IN #1
            SET VARIABLE More TO 1

        ELSE
            CHANGE Bal:90 TO ABS(.Remain) IN #1
            SET VARIABLE NextBal TO 0
        ENDIF
    ENDIF
```

∎ *Figure 16.18:*
The Age.CMD
command file.

```
*(------- 60 day balance)
SET VARIABLE Bal60 TO Bal:60 IN #1
IF NextBal=1 AND Bal60 > 0 THEN
   IF More = 1 THEN
      SET VARIABLE Remain TO (.Remain - .Bal60)
   ELSE
      SET VARIABLE Remain TO (.ThisPay - .Bal60)
   ENDIF
   IF Remain >= 0 THEN
      CHANGE Bal:60 TO 0 IN #1
      SET VARIABLE More TO 1
   ELSE
      CHANGE Bal:60 TO ABS(.Remain) IN #1
      SET VARIABLE NextBal TO 0
   ENDIF
ENDIF

*(------- 30 day balance)
SET VARIABLE Bal30 TO Bal:30 IN #1
IF NextBal=1 AND Bal30 > 0 THEN
   IF More = 1 THEN
      SET VARIABLE Remain TO (.Remain - .Bal30)
   ELSE
      SET VARIABLE Remain TO (.ThisPay - .Bal30)
   ENDIF
   IF Remain >= 0 THEN
      CHANGE Bal:30 TO 0 IN #1
      SET VARIABLE More TO 1
   ELSE
      CHANGE Bal:30 TO ABS(.Remain) IN #1
      SET VARIABLE NextBal TO 0
   ENDIF
ENDIF

   NEXT #1 Status
ENDWHILE

NEWPAGE
SET POINTER #1 OFF
WRITE "End of month procedures completed..."
RETURN
```

■ *Figure 16.18:*
The Age.CMD
command file.
(continued)

variables are created with predefined data types. The lines below set up
the variable data types:

```
■  *(- - - - - - - - - - - - - - - - - - - - Set up variables.)
    SET VARIABLE Remain DOUBLE
    SET VARIABLE More INTEGER
    SET VARIABLE NextBal INTEGER
    SET VARIABLE BAL120 CURRENCY
    SET VARIABLE BAL90 CURRENCY
    SET VARIABLE BAL60 CURRENCY
    SET VARIABLE BAL30 CURRENCY
```

A pointer is created, as below, to move through the ARMain table one row at a time. (Whenever a new Set Pointer command is issued, the "pointer" always starts at the first row in the table.)

■　　*(− − Set up pointer for loop through table)
　　　SET POINTER #1 Status FOR ARMain

Then a While loop is set up, as below, to access a row in the table repeatedly until the last row is processed (at which point the Status variable will no longer equal zero):

■　　WHILE Status = 0 THEN

The variable More is used throughout the command file to determine whether the remainder to be subtracted from the next aged balance is greater than zero. (If More is one, then there is more to be subtracted. If More is zero, there is no more to be subtracted.)

The variable NextBal determines whether the next balance needs to be adjusted. (If NextBal is one, then the next balance needs to be adjusted. If NextBal is zero, the next balance does not need to be adjusted.) The Remain variable keeps track of the remainder of the current payment that needs to be subtracted from the next aged balance. These three variables receive their initial values in the commands below:

■　　*(− 0 is "false", 1 is "true" below)
　　　SET VARIABLE More TO 0
　　　SET VARIABLE NextBal TO 1
　　　SET VARIABLE Remain To 0

Now the command file begins incrementally subtracting the current payment from the aged balances, starting at the Bal:120 (or over-90-day) balance. In the line below, a variable named ThisPay receives the value of the current payment in the row being analyzed:

■　　*(− − − 90 + day balance)
　　　SET VARIABLE ThisPay TO Curr:Pay IN #1

A variable named Bal120 receives the column value of the over-90-day balance in the current row, as follows:

■　　SET VARIABLE Bal120 TO Bal:120 IN #1

If there is, indeed, a balance in the over-90-day category (that is, the Bal120 column is greater than zero), then the Remain variable is set to the current payment minus the amount of the Bal:120 balance, as below:

■ IF Bal120 > 0 THEN
     SET VARIABLE Remain TO .ThisPay − .Bal120

If this remainder is greater than or equal to zero, then the balance in the Bal:120 column is set to zero, and the More variable is set to one ("true") to indicate that there is more payment to be subtracted from other balances.

■ IF Remain > = 0 THEN
        CHANGE Bal:120 TO 0 IN #1
        SET VARIABLE More TO 1

If the remainder is not greater than or equal to zero, then the over-90-day balance (Bal:120) is set to the absolute (positive) value of the Remain variable, and the NextBal indicator is set to zero ("false"), as follows:

■   ELSE
        CHANGE Bal:120 TO ABS(.Remain) IN #1
        SET VARIABLE NextBal TO 0
     ENDIF
  ENDIF

The same basic logic is used for the remaining aged balances. First, a variable named Bal90 receives the value of the Bal:90 column for the current row, as below:

■ *(− − − 90 day balance)
  SET VARIABLE Bal90 TO Bal:90 IN #1

If the "Next Balance" indicator is "true," and there is a value greater than zero in the Bal:90 column, as below, then the command file needs to decide what to do based on the status of the More variable.

■ IF NextBal = 1 AND Bal90 > 0 THEN

If the More variable is one ("true"), then the remainder equals itself minus the 90-day balance. If the More variable is not true, then the remainder is the current payment minus the 90-day balance, as follows:

- ```
  IF More = 1 THEN
      SET VARIABLE Remain TO .Remain − .Bal90
  ELSE
      SET VARIABLE Remain TO .ThisPay − .Bal90
  ENDIF
  ```

Once that's decided, the command file decides what to do with the remaining payment amount. If this amount is greater than or equal to zero, then the 90-day balance is set to zero, and the More variable is set to one ("true"), as below:

- ```
  IF Remain > = 0 THEN
      CHANGE Bal:90 TO 0 IN #1
      SET VARIABLE More TO 1
  ```

Otherwise, the 90-day balance is set to the absolute value of the remainder, and the NextBal indicator is set to zero ("false"), as follows:

- ```
      ELSE
          CHANGE Bal:90 TO ABS(.Remain) IN #1
          SET VARIABLE NextBal TO 0
      ENDIF
  ENDIF
  ```

The same process is repeated for the 60- and 30-day balances.

The command below moves the pointer to the next row in the ARMain table and repeats the aging process for the next row in the table:

- ```
  NEXT #1 Status
  ```

After all aged balances in the ARMain table have been aged, the command

- ```
  SET POINTER #1 OFF
  ```

releases the pointer, and the command file prints a closing message and returns control to the EndMonth.CMD command file.

- ```
  WRITE "End of month procedures completed..."
  RETURN
  ```

There is one more command file (which is actually a *procedure* or *macro*) that needs to be written to complete the end-of-month procedures. This macro is the one named *Update.MAC* that updates the current charges and payments in the ARMain table from charges and payments in the Charges and Payments tables. Since updating is applicable to many databases (inventory, general ledger, and accounts payable, to name a few), we'll create this command file as a general-purpose macro that can easily be used in a variety of applications.

■ GENERAL-PURPOSE MACRO

The macro that we'll develop in this section can be used for any type of update. The syntax for using the Update.MAC macro will be the following:

- RUN Update.MAC Using <*master table name*>
  <*master table common column*> <*master table update column*>
  <*transaction table name*> <*transaction table common column*>
  <*transaction table update column*> <*type of update*>

For example, to increment the current charges in the ARMain table by the T:Price amounts in the Charges table, you would use the command

- RUN Update.MAC USING ARMain CustNo Curr:Chr Charges +
  CustNo T:Price PLUS

where ARMain is the name of the table to be updated, CustNo is the name of the common column on which to base the update, and Curr:-Chr is the name of the column in the ARMain table to be updated. Charges is the name of the transaction table, CustNo is the common column, and T:Price is the column to add to the Curr:Chr column. The Plus option tells the macro to add the quantities from the Charges table to the current balance.

To update the ARMain table from the Payments table, use the command

- RUN Update.MAC USING ARMain CustNo Curr:Pay +
  Payments CustNo Amount PLUS

where, once again, ARMain, CustNo, and Curr:Pay are the name, common column, and column to be updated, respectively. Payments, CustNo, and Amount are the table name, common column, and column to perform the update from, respectively. The Plus option tells the macro to add the amounts in the Payments table to the current balance in the ARMain table.

The Update.MAC macro is shown in Figure 16.19. Enter the command

■ RBEDIT Update.MAC

to create and save the macro, just as you would any standard command file.

Looking at the macro line by line, we see that it begins with many comments. When you're writing general-purpose macros, it's a good idea to list the meaning of the various parameters passed to the macro (%1 through %7 in this example), so that you can remember how to use the macro later.

■
```
*(* * * * * * * * * * * * * * * * * * * * * * * * * * UPDATE.MAC)
*(- - - - Update a master table from a transaction table)
*( Parameters are: %1: Master table name
                    %2: Master table common column
                    %3: Master table update column
                    %4: Transaction table name
                    %5: Transaction table common column
                    %6: Transaction table update column
                    %7: PLUS MINUS or REPLACE)
```

The first commands in the macro clear the screen and then erase the variables PassVal and Compare. (Since the data type these variables contain from the most recent update may be incorrect for the current update, they are re-created later with the appropriate data type.)

■
```
NEWPAGE
CLEAR PassVal
CLEAR Compare
```

Next, the command file checks to make sure that the last parameter passed is a valid one. The parameter must be the word PLUS, MINUS, or REPLACE. If it is valid, the command file displays a prompt and sets the R:BASE messages off. If not, the command file displays an error message and branches control to a routine named Bailout, as follows:

■
```
*(- - - Make sure option %7 is valid)
IF %7 = PLUS OR %7 = MINUS OR %7 = REPLACE THEN
   WRITE "Performing update ... Please wait"
```

```
        SET MESSAGES OFF
        SET ERROR MESSAGES OFF
ELSE
        WRITE "Invalid update option"
        WRITE "Must be PLUS, MINUS or REPLACE"
```

```
*(****************************************** UPDATE.MAC)
*(-------- Update a master table from a transaction table)
*(  Parameters are:    %1: Master table name
                       %2: Master table common column
                       %3: Master table update column
                       %4: Transaction table name
                       %5: Transaction table common column
                       %6: Transaction table update column
                       %7: PLUS MINUS or REPLACE)
NEWPAGE
CLEAR PassVal
CLEAR Compare
*(--- Make sure option %7 is valid)
IF %7 = PLUS OR %7 = MINUS OR %7 = REPLACE THEN
    WRITE "Performing update... Please wait"
    SET MESSAGES OFF
    SET ERROR MESSAGES OFF
ELSE
    WRITE "Invalid update option"
    WRITE "Must be PLUS, MINUS or REPLACE"
    WRITE "Press any key to try again..." AT 20 1
    PAUSE
    GOTO Bailout
ENDIF *(%7 option valid)
*(------------------ Set up pointer)
SET POINTER #1 Status1 FOR .%4 SORTED BY .%5
WHILE Status1 = 0 THEN
      SET VARIABLE PassVal TO .%6 IN #1
      SET VARIABLE Compare TO .%5 IN #1
      *(--- Update using PLUS)
      IF %7 = PLUS THEN
         CHANGE .%3 TO .%3 + .PassVal IN .%1 WHERE .%2 = .Compare
      ENDIF (plus)
      *(--- Update using MINUS)
      IF %7 = MINUS THEN
         CHANGE .%3 TO .%3 - .PassVal IN .%1 WHERE .%2 = .Compare
      ENDIF
      *(--- Update using REPLACE)
      IF %7 = REPLACE THEN
         CHANGE .%3 TO .PassVal IN .%1 WHERE .%2 = .Compare
      ENDIF
      NEXT #1 Status1
ENDWHILE
WRITE "Update successful" AT 20 1
SET MESSAGES ON
SET ERROR MESSAGES ON
RETURN
*(------- Error encountered at outset. Return)
LABEL Bailout
CLEAR %7
RETURN
```

■ *Figure 16.19:*
The Update.MAC
macro.

```
        WRITE "Press any key to try again ..." AT 20 1
        PAUSE
        GOTO Bailout
    ENDIF *(%7 option valid)
```

Now the command file begins the actual updating procedure. First, it sets up a pointer in the transaction table (%4 parameter) sorted by the common column (%5 parameter).

∎   *(– – – – – – – – – – – – – – – – – Set up pointer)
    SET POINTER #1 Status1 FOR .%4 SORTED BY .%5

As long as there are still rows in the transaction table (the pointer variable Status1 equals 0), the command file performs the tasks in the While loop below:

∎   WHILE Status1 = 0 THEN

First, the program stores the value to be passed to the master table (%6) to a variable named PassVal. Then, it stores the common column name from the transaction table (%5) to a variable named Compare, as follows:

∎   SET VARIABLE PassVal TO .%6 IN #1
    SET VARIABLE Compare TO .%5 IN #1

If the user specified PLUS in the parameter list, the appropriate column in the master table (%3) is incremented by the amount stored in the PassVal variable, where the common column in the master table (%2) matches the common column in the transaction table (.Compare).

∎   *(– – – Update using PLUS)
    IF %7 = PLUS THEN
        CHANGE .%3 TO .%3 + .PassVal IN .%1 WHERE .%2 +
        = .Compare
    ENDIF (plus)

If the user specified MINUS in the parameter list, the PassVal value is subtracted from the appropriate column in the master table, as below:

∎   *(– – – Update using MINUS)
    IF %7 = MINUS THEN
        CHANGE .%3 TO .%3 – .PassVal IN .%1 WHERE .%2 +
        = .Compare
    ENDIF

If the user specified REPLACE, the item in the master table is replaced with the item in the transaction table, as follows:

- ```
  *( – – – Update using REPLACE)
  IF %7 = REPLACE THEN
      CHANGE .%3 TO .PassVal IN .%1 WHERE .%2 = .Compare
  ENDIF
  ```

Next, the pointer is moved to the next row in the transaction table, and the procedure is repeated until all the rows from the transaction table have been updated.

- ```
  NEXT #1 Status1
  ENDWHILE
  ```

When the macro is done, it returns to the calling command file below:

- ```
  SET MESSAGES ON
  SET ERROR MESSAGES ON
  RETURN
  ```

The last routine in the Update.MAC macro is the Bailout routine, which is called in the event of an error at the beginning of the program. Before returning to the calling program, the routine clears the faulty update option (%7) from memory, as follows:

- ```
  *( – – – Error encountered at outset. Return)
  LABEL Bailout
  CLEAR %7
  RETURN
  ```

The Update.MAC macro is flexible, and it can be used for inventory-system updating, as well as for updating our accounts-receivable system. For example, to subtract the items that have been sold in the Charges table from the OnHand quantities in the Inventry table, you could simply enter the command

- ```
  RUN Update.MAC USING Inventry ProdNo OnHand Charges +
  ProdNo Qty MINUS
  ```

That's the real benefit of a general-purpose macro. You need only write the macro once, and then you can use it repeatedly, just as though it were a regular R:BASE command.
  ```

■ *TESTING THE ACCOUNTS-RECEIVABLE SYSTEM*

Before integrating all of the parts of the accounts-receivable system through menus, you should check to see that all the parts work as expected directly from the R> prompt. You should also create whatever additional reports you want for the various tables using Reports Express. As mentioned earlier, you might want to add a directory listing, mailing labels, and perhaps form letters for the ARMain table, similar to the Director, Labels, and Letter1 report formats we developed in Chapter 6. You can also develop reports for displaying information from the Charges, Payments, and Inventry tables.

To enter some practice data for the system, enter the command

■　OPEN ARSys

at the R> prompt to open the database. Then use the command

■　ENTER Main

to enter a couple of sample customers. Use customer numbers that are easy to remember for the practice data, such as 1001 and 1002. You can fill in zeros for all the balances on the bottom half of the screen, because the system will automatically take care of these balances. Press Esc and select Quit after entering a couple of customers.

Enter a few sample records in the Inventry table as well. To do so, enter the command

■　ENTER InvForm

Use part numbers that will be easy to remember for the practice data, such as A-111 and B-222. You don't need to worry about the In Stock quantities, because the AR system, as designed, does not work on these directly. The column is only included in case you want to develop an inventory module later to manage the inventory database. Remember to enter either a 1 (for taxable) or 0 (for nontaxable) into the Tax? column.

After entering a couple of inventory records, press Esc and select Quit to return to the R> prompt.

Enter a few Charge transactions for each customer. To do so, first enter the command

■　ENTER ChrgFrm

Be sure to use only valid customer numbers and product numbers that you've already entered on the ARMain and Inventry tables. After entering a few Charge transactions, press Esc and select Quit.

Enter the command

■   ENTER PayForm

at the R> prompt to enter some payment transactions. Again, be sure to use only valid customer numbers from the ARMain table. Press Esc and select Quit after entering a couple of payment transactions.

To test the EndMonth.CMD, UpDate.MAC, and Age.CMD files, enter the command

■   DO EndMonth.CMD

at the R> prompt. The files should print the invoices and then take a few minutes to perform all of the updating. If all runs smoothly, you'll be returned to the R> prompt without any error messages. At this point, all transactions from the Charges and Payments tables should be empty. To verify this, enter the commands

■   SELECT ALL FROM Charges
     SELECT ALL FROM Payments

To verify that the old transactions were copied to the history files, enter the commands

■   SELECT ALL FROM CHistory
     SELECT ALL FROM PHistory

These two tables should contain the data that were originally on the Charges and Payments tables.

If the Charges, Payments, and history tables do not contain the data you expected, then perhaps there is an error in the EndMonth.CMD command file, or in the UpDate.MAC or Age.CMD command file. Make sure you've keyed in the command files exactly as described in this chapter. You'll want to be sure to remove all the bugs from any command files, as well as from any forms or reports, before proceeding to the final step of integrating the accounts-receivable system through Application Express.

■ *INTEGRATING THE ACCOUNTS-RECEIVABLE SYSTEM*

The final step in creating a working accounts-receivable system is to link all the modules together through menus generated by Application Express. To start Application Express, enter the command

- ■ EXPRESS

at the R> prompt, or select Application Express from the RBSystem Main menu. From the Application Express Main menu, select option (1) to define a new application.

The screen will ask that you select a database for the new application. Select ARSys. The screen will ask that you enter a name for the application. Type in AR and press Enter. When the screen asks you to enter the name of the main menu, press Enter to use the suggested name, Main. Select Vertical for the menu type.

Accounts-Receivable System Main Menu

Type in the menu title and options for the Main menu. Figure 16.20 shows a suggested format for the Main menu. Press Esc after filling in the menu title and options.

For this menu (and all subsequent submenus), you can select Yes after the prompt

- ■ Do you want [ESC] to exit this menu?

You can select No in response to the prompt

- ■ Do you want a help screen for this menu?

Furthermore, for each submenu that you create in the following paragraphs, select Vertical as the menu type.

Now you can begin assigning menu actions to items. For the action to menu option (1), select Menu from the list of choices, and enter the menu name CustMenu. Figure 16.21 shows a suggested format for the CustMenu menu.

Press Esc after filling in the submenu title and options. Select No in response to the last prompt about assigning additional actions.

To assign actions to menu option (2), select Menu from the choices on the screen. Type InvMenu as the submenu name, and press Enter.

```
    Enter or change the menu choices

    ┌─────────────────Accounts Receivable Main Menu──────────────────┐
    │   (1)   Manage Customer List                                    │
    │   (2)   Manage Inventory Data                                   │
    │   (3)   Manage Charges                                          │
    │   (4)   Manage Payments                                         │
    │   (5)   Print Reports                                           │
    │   (6)   Do End-of-Month Procedures                             │
    │   (7)   Exit                                                    │
    │   (8)   ███████████████████████████████████████████████        │
    │                                                                │
    └────────────────────────────────────────────────────────────────┘




    [ESC] Done   [PgUp] Title   [F3] Actions   [F5] Reset value   [F10] Help
    Application AR       --- Database ARSYS   --- Menu Main
```

■ *Figure 16.20:*
Accounts-
Receivable
Main menu

```
    Enter or change the menu choices

    ┌──────────────────────Manage Customer List─────────────────────┐
    │   (1)   Add New Customers                                       │
    │   (2)   Edit/Delete Customers                                   │
    │   (3)   Look Up Customer Data                                   │
    │   (4)   Return to Main Menu                                     │
    │   (5)   ███████████████████████████████████████████████        │
    │                                                                │
    │                                                                │
    └────────────────────────────────────────────────────────────────┘




    [ESC] Done   [PgUp] Title   [F3] Actions   [F5] Reset value   [F10] Help
    Application AR       --- Database ARSYS   --- Menu CustMenu
```

■ *Figure 16.21:*
The CustMenu
submenu.

Figure 16.22 shows a suggested format for the InvMenu submenu. Press Esc and select No after filling in the submenu title and options.

When asked to assign actions to Main menu option (3), once again select Menu from the list of options, and then enter ChrgMenu as the submenu name. Figure 16.23 shows a suggested format for the ChrgMenu submenu. Press Esc and select No after entering the menu title and options.

Next you'll be asked to assign actions to Main menu option (4). Once again, select Menu, and type in the name PayMenu for the submenu. Figure 16.24 shows a suggested format for the submenu. Press Esc and select No after filling in the menu title and options.

Next you can assign actions to menu option (5). Select Menu from the list of options, and enter ReptMenu as the submenu name. Create a menu to access the various reports that you've created for your accounts-receivable system (except for printing invoices, which are printed automatically by the EndMonth.CMD command file). Figure 16.25 shows suggested options for the ReptMenu submenu. Press Esc and select No after creating this submenu.

Main menu option (6) performs the end-of-month procedures. These are all handled by the EndMonth.CMD command file and the other command files that EndMonth.CMD accesses. When asked to assign an action to Main menu option (6), select Macro from the list of options. (The Macro option will run an existing command file.) Type

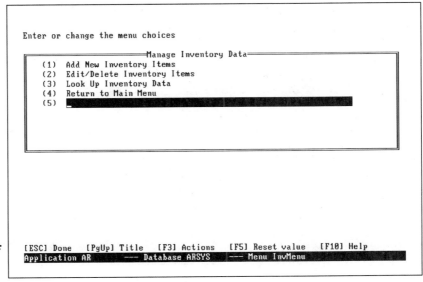

■ Figure 16.22:
The InvMenu submenu.

in the command file name EndMonth.CMD, and press Enter. Select No to continue.

Finally, you'll be asked to assign an action to Main menu option (7). Select Exit from the list of options, since this menu option allows the user to exit the accounts-receivable system.

Customers Submenu Actions

Next you'll be asked to select menu actions for the CustMenu submenu. For CustMenu option (1), select Load from the list of choices. Select ARMain as the table to load, and select Main as the name of the form to use. Choose No in response to the questions about editing the form and adding more actions.

When assigning menu actions to CustMenu option (2), select Edit from the list of choices. Select ARMain as the table to edit and Main as the form to use. When asked about sort orders, select CustNo and Ascending and press Esc. When asked for a column to validate, select CustNo as the column name and EQ (equal) as the operator. When asked if the user should enter the comparison value, select Yes. Type in the prompt message

■   Enter customer number

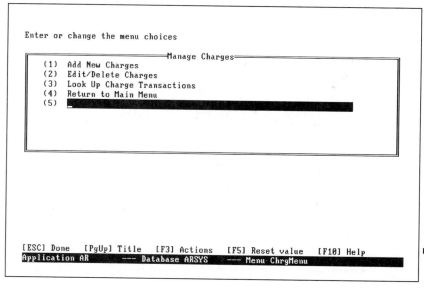

```
Enter or change the menu choices

                              ═Manage Charges═
        (1)  Add New Charges
        (2)  Edit/Delete Charges
        (3)  Look Up Charge Transactions
        (4)  Return to Main Menu
        (5)  ████████████████████████████████████████




 [ESC] Done   [PgUp] Title   [F3] Actions   [F5] Reset value   [F10] Help
 Application AR       --- Database ARSYS   --- Menu ChrgMenu
```

■ *Figure 16.23:*
The ChrgMenu submenu.

when requested, and press Enter. Select (Done) as the final logical operator. Choose No when asked about adding more actions.

To assign actions to CustMenu option (3), Look Up Customer Data, choose Select from the list of options and ARMain as the table to display data from. You can then choose columns to display. Select the particular columns you wish to display, or select (All) to display all columns. Of course, all the columns from the ARMain table will not fit on the screen simultaneously, so you might want to select a few important columns to display, such as CustNo, L:Name, F:Name, and Curr:Bal.

You can select CustNo and Ascending as the sort columns, and then press Esc. Select CustNo as the column to validate, EQ as the operator, and Yes in response to the question about having the user enter a comparison value. When prompted, type in the prompt message

■   Enter customer number

and press Enter. Select (Done) as the final logical operator, and select No when asked about assigning additional actions to the menu option.

To assign actions to CustMenu option (4), select Exit from the list of actions.

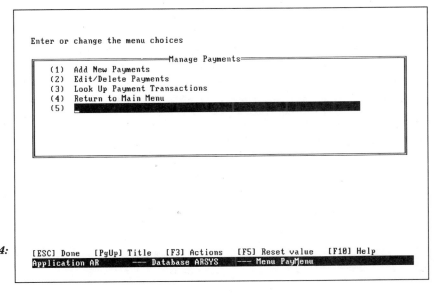

```
Enter or change the menu choices

                              ═══════════Manage Payments══════════
      (1)  Add New Payments
      (2)  Edit/Delete Payments
      (3)  Look Up Payment Transactions
      (4)  Return to Main Menu
      (5)  ████████████████████████████████████████████





 [ESC] Done   [PgUp] Title   [F3] Actions   [F5] Reset value   [F10] Help
 Application AR      --- Database ARSYS   --- Menu PayMenu
```

■ *Figure 16.24:*
The PayMenu
submenu.

Inventory Submenu Actions

The action for the Inventory submenu option (1) is Load, with Inventry as the name of the table to load and InvForm as the form to use. Select No to the prompts about editing the form and adding more menu actions.

For Inventory submenu option (2), select Edit as the action. Select Inventry as the table to edit and InvForm as the form to use. Select No when asked about editing the form. Select ProdNo and Ascending as sorting characteristics, and press Esc. For the column to validate, select ProdNo as the column, EQ as the operator, and Yes for having the user enter the comparison value. Enter the prompt message

■   Enter product number

when requested, and press Enter. Select (Done) as the last logical operator, and then select No.

For Inventory submenu option (3), choose Select from the list of possible actions. Specify Inventry as the table to display, and then select columns to display and a sort order. When requested, select ProdNo as the column to validate, EQ as the operator, and Yes in response to the user entering the comparison value. Enter the prompt

■   Enter product number

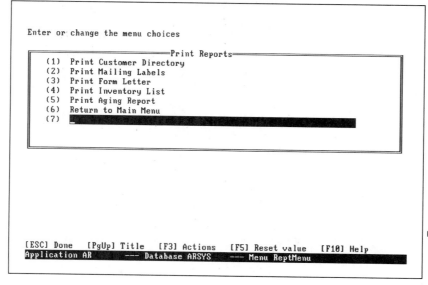

■ *Figure 16.25:*
Suggested format
for the ReptMenu
submenu.

when requested, and then select (Done) as the final logical operator. Select No for additional actions.

For the Inventory submenu option (4), select Exit from the list of actions.

Charges Submenu Actions

For the action to Charges submenu option (1), select Load and select Charges as the table to load. Select ChrgFrm as the form to use, and select No when asked to edit the form. Select No when asked about adding more actions.

The action for Charges SubMenu option (2) is Edit, with Charges as the table to edit and ChrgFrm as the form for editing. Select CustNo and Ascending as the sort order. Select CustNo as the column to validate, EQ as the operator, and Yes. Enter the prompt message

■   Enter customer number

when requested. Select (Done) as the final operator, and say No to the last prompt.

For Charges submenu option (3), choose Select as the action. Select Charges as the table to display, and then select the columns to display and a sort order to your liking. Select CustNo as the column to validate, EQ as the operator, and Yes, and then enter the prompt message

■   Enter customer number

Select (Done) as the final operator and then No.

For the last Charges submenu option, select Exit from the list of actions.

Payments Submenu Actions

The Payments submenu is similar to the previous submenus. For option (1), select Load as the action, Payments as the table to load, and PayForm as the form to use.

For Payments submenu option (2), select Edit as the action, Payments as the table to edit, and PayForm as the form to use. Select CustNo and Ascending for the sort order. Select CustNo as the column to validate, EQ as the operator, and Yes. Enter the prompt

■   Enter customer number

and press Enter. Select (Done) and then select No.

For Payments submenu option (3), choose Select as the action, Payments as the table, (All) as columns to display, and CustNo and Ascending as the sort order. Select CustNo as the column to validate, EQ as the operator, and Yes. Enter the prompt message

■   Enter customer number

and press Enter. Select (Done) and No from the next prompts.

For Payments submenu option (4), select Exit.

Reports Submenu Actions

Next you can assign actions to the Reports submenu. Select Print as the action for each of the menu options (except the last option), and select the appropriate report name for each menu option. You can, of course, select sort orders and search criteria for each report. (Generally, you'll want to leave the search comparisons blank for all the reports.)

For the last menu option on the Reports submenu, select Exit.

Finishing Up

After you've defined all the actions for all the menu options, the screen will ask

■   Do you want to change default express settings?

Select No. Then you'll see the message

■   Writing application files—Please wait...

After all the application files are written, you'll see the prompt

■   Do you want to create an initial command file?

Select No.

From this point you'll be returned to the Application Express Main menu. Select option (4) to exit from Application Express.

■ USING THE ACCOUNTS-RECEIVABLE SYSTEM

To use the accounts-receivable system in the future, enter the command

■   **RUN AR IN AR.APX**

at the R > prompt. You'll see the Accounts-Receivable Main menu.

At any time during the month, you can enter new data or edit existing data. Before assigning charges or payments to a customer, the customer should be entered into the customer list with a unique customer number. To do so, select option (1), Manage Customer List, from the Accounts Receivable Main menu and option (1), Add New Customers, from the Customers submenu. You should enter zeros in all the balances on the bottom half of the screen when first entering a new customer.

You also need to add products to the inventory table before entering charges for that product. To enter or edit products, select option (2), Manage Inventory Data, from the Main menu and option (1), Add New Items, from the inventory submenu. Each item you enter must have a unique product number.

As customers charge items and make payments, record each transaction on the Charges and Payments tables. To record charges, select option (3), Manage Charges, from the Main menu and option (1), Add New Charges, from the submenu. To record payments, select option (4), Manage Payments, from the Main menu and option (1), Add New Payments, from the submenu.

You can make changes and corrections to the Charges and Payments tables any time *prior to performing the end-of-the-month procedures.* The Charges and Payments submenus each have options for editing and deleting transactions. (We'll discuss techniques for editing after the end-of-the-month procedures shortly.)

End-of-the-Month Procedures

At the end of the month (or whenever you normally send bills), you can select option (6), Do End-Of-Month Procedures, from the Main menu to print the invoices and update all the balances in the ARMain file. Be sure you have plenty of paper in the printer and that the printer is ready. Then select option (6) from the Main menu, and wait until the Main menu reappears. (If you add a report format for mailing labels, you can print mailing labels for the invoices as well.)

Once the end-of-the-month procedures are complete, you can no longer change that information on the Charges and Payments tables, because those transactions have now moved to the history files to make room for next month's charges and payments. The Inventry file is unchanged, and the ARMain table has updated balances for the start of the new month.

Adjustment Transactions

Of course, errors will sneak through the end-of-month procedures from time to time. To fix those, you can add *adjustment transactions,* which not only correct the error, but also leave an *audit trail* to explain the change.

For example, if you overcharge a customer or a customer returns some merchandise for which she has already been billed, you can simply enter a payment transaction to credit the account. (In fact, you could add a "comment" column to the Payments table to add comments to each transaction to explain the reason for the adjustment.)

If you overcharged the customer $200.00 or the customer returned $200.00 worth of merchandise, just add a payment transaction in the amount of $200.00. The next time the end-of-month procedures are performed, the $200.00 will automatically be credited to the customer's account, and it will appear on the next invoice as a credit and be stored in the history file for future reference.

■ SUMMARY

We've covered much advanced material in this chapter, and unless you are already a programmer who is fluent in some other database-management language, the techniques discussed in this chapter will probably take some study and practice to master. The time and effort you invest will be worthwhile—the techniques that we've used in this chapter are similar to the ones that you'll be using to develop your own custom applications.

The new techniques and commands we've discussed are summarized below:

When you're designing custom applications, create an outline of the system to break down the overall goal into smaller, more manageable goals.

In the accounts-receivable system, the *master table* maintains a list of customers and their current balances.

In the accounts-receivable system, individual charges and payments are stored on *transaction tables.*

Through a process known as *updating,* balances in the master table are adjusted to reflect current charges and payments in the transaction tables.

The accounts-receivable system uses *history* tables to store "old" transactions that have been billed on a previous billing cycle.

To access custom command files or macros from menus developed using Application Express, select Macro as the action for the menu option.

17

USING CODELOCK

In this chapter, we'll discuss CodeLock, an R:BASE feature that converts command files, which are normally stored as ASCII files, into binary format. ASCII files are stored in the format that you used to create the command file. Binary files are stored using special codes that are easily read by the computer (but not by people). One of the advantages of a command file stored in binary format is that it runs faster because the computer does not have to perform the work of converting the program from "English" (ASCII) to computer language (binary).

You can convert the following four different types of files with CodeLock:

Command files and macros created with RBEdit (or any other text editor that provides an unformatted mode)

Screen files, which display screens from within command files (such as the Bills.MSG file that we created in the last chapter)

Menu files, which display menus

Application files created with the Application Express Main menu

You can also combine up to 42 different files in a single procedure file using CodeLock. In this chapter, we'll experiment with converting the various types of files.

∎ CONVERTING COMMAND FILES

The simplest use of CodeLock is to convert a command file to binary format. In Chapter 15, we created a command file named Loop2.CMD to test the While and Endwhile commands. Figure 17.1 shows the Loop2.CMD command file. Let's convert this program to a binary file.

As with most modules in R:BASE System V, you can enter Code-Lock via several methods. From the RBSystem Main menu, select the CodeLock option. From the R > prompt, enter the command

∎ CODELOCK

The CodeLock Main menu will appear on the screen, as shown in Figure 17.2.

Select option (1) to convert the command file. CodeLock asks for the

■ Name of the ASCII command file to convert:

```
*(************************************* Loop2.CMD)
*(--------------- Program to test the WHILE loop)
*(------------ Create Counter and Done variables)
SET VARIABLE COUNTER TO 1
SET VARIABLE Done INTEGER

*(------------ Ask how high to count)
NEWPAGE
FILLIN Done USING "How high shall I count?: " AT 9,5
NEWPAGE

*(--------------- Repeat loop until Counter > Done)
WHILE Counter <= .Done THEN
       *(--------- Create a prompt and display it)
       SET VARIABLE Progress TO "Loop Number " & CTXT(.Counter)
       WRITE .Progress
       *(--------- Increment Counter variable by 1)
       SET VARIABLE Counter TO .Counter + 1
ENDWHILE *(Bottom of WHILE loop)

*(--------------- End of program)
QUIT
```

■ *Figure 17.1:*
The Loop2.CMD
command file.

```
                           CODELOCK
      Copyright (C) 1983,1984,1985,1986 by Microrim, Inc. (Ver. 1.00 PC-DOS)

              ===========CODELOCK Main Menu===========
          (1)  Convert an ASCII command file to a binary command file
          (2)  Add an ASCII command file to a procedure file
          (3)  Add an ASCII screen file to a procedure file
          (4)  Add an ASCII menu file to a procedure file
          (5)  Convert an ASCII application file to a binary application file
          (6)  Display directory
          (7)  Display the contents of an ASCII file
          (8)  Exit
```

■ *Figure 17.2:*
The CodeLock
Main menu.

For this example, enter the name **Loop2.CMD**. CodeLock then asks for the

∎ Name of back-up file [Loop2.ASC]

This is the file that will contain the original, unconverted command file. CodeLock suggests the name Loop2.ASC (ASC is short for ASCII). To use the suggested name, press Enter. Next, CodeLock asks for the

∎ Name of the binary command file [Loop2.CMD]:

CodeLock suggests the name Loop2.CMD. Press Enter to use the suggested name. As CodeLock converts the command file, it displays each line on the screen. When it's done, CodeLock displays the following prompt:

∎ Press any key to continue

When you press any key, you'll be returned to the CodeLock Main menu.

To run the converted command file, return to the R> prompt. Then use the Run command, as below:

∎ RUN Loop2.CMD

You may not notice a major increase in speed when you're running this small command file, but as you begin converting larger command files, you will notice a significant improvement in your processing time.

You should always fully test and debug a command file before converting it. However, if you need to make changes to a command file, be sure to use the unconverted backup. In this example, you would use RBEdit to modify the Loop2.ASC command file. Then, when reconverting with CodeLock, enter **Loop2.ASC** as the ASCII file to convert, **Loop2.ASC** as the backup file, and **Loop2.CMD** as the name of the binary file.

If you need to check which version of a command file is the ASCII version and which is the converted version, you can use the Type command from either the DOS prompt or the R> prompt. For example, after you've converted a command file, if you enter the command

∎ TYPE Loop2.ASC

you'll see the ASCII file in its normal state. However, if you enter the command

■ TYPE Loop2.CMD

you'll see the binary file, which appears as a group of strange-looking characters including happy faces and umlauts. Never attempt to edit the binary file. Again, if you must make changes, edit the ASCII file and then reconvert it into a revised binary file.

■ PROCEDURE FILES

A *procedure file* is one that contains a group of previously separate files in a single binary file. The files within the procedure file can be command files, screen files, menu files, or macros. In this section, we'll develop a procedure file named TestProc.CMD for practice.

Adding Command Files to Procedure Files

To add a command file to a procedure file, select option (2) from the CodeLock Main menu. CodeLock will display this prompt:

■ Name of ASCII file to add:

Enter the name of the command file. (Be sure to use the name of the ASCII backup file if you've previously converted the command file.) For this example, enter the file name **Loop2.ASC**. CodeLock asks for the

■ Name of procedure file:

Enter the name **TestProc.CMD**. CodeLock displays the prompt

■ Name of the binary command block [Loop2]

suggesting the name Loop2. (Since the command file will be contained within a procedure file, you do not want to use file-name extensions.) Press Enter to use the suggested name.

CodeLock displays the command file as it converts the file and adds it to the procedure file. When it's done, you are prompted to press any key to continue. Before we try out the procedure file, let's add a screen file to it.

Adding Screen Files to Procedure Files

In the last chapter, we created a screen file named Bills.MSG. Let's add that screen file to the TestProc.CMD procedure file. Select option (3) from the CodeLock Main menu to add an ASCII screen file to a procedure file. CodeLock displays the prompt

■ Name of ASCII screen file to add:

Enter the name **Bills.MSG** and press Enter. CodeLock displays the prompt

■ Name of the procedure file [TestProc.CMD]:

suggesting the TestProc procedure file. Press Enter to use the suggested file name. CodeLock displays the following prompt:

■ Current blocks in the procedure file:
  Loop2
  Name of the binary screen block [Bills]:

Since each block in a procedure file must have a unique name, Code-Lock displays the names of the blocks already in the file. Furthermore, CodeLock suggests the name Bills for the new block. Press Enter to accept the suggested name. You'll see the screen file displayed on the screen, and then you'll be prompted to press any key to continue. Press a key to return to the CodeLock Main menu.

We'll see how to access the screen in the procedure file shortly. First let's try adding a menu file to the procedure file.

Adding Menu Files to Procedure Files

A menu file is one that uses a specific format to display a menu. To create a menu file, you need to use the RBEdit text editor (or word processor with a nondocument mode). If you're following along on-line, you'll need to exit CodeLock and then run the RBEdit editor.

Figure 17.3 shows a sample menu file typed in with RBEdit. Notice that the name of the menu, MENU1, is the first line in the file. The menu name must always be the first line, in the far-left column, of the menu file, and it cannot be more than eight characters long or contain spaces or punctuation marks.

The second line of the menu file contains the word COLUMN, which specifies a vertical menu display. (Use the word ROW for a horizontal menu display.)

Next to COLUMN is the title of the menu, which is Sample Menu in this example. The menu title must always appear next to the menu type (COLUMN or ROW).

The last three lines in the menu file are menu options. When displayed on a vertical menu, the menu options will be numbered automatically.

After you've created the menu file, save it with any file name (**Menu1.ASC** in this example). Then, exit RBEdit and return to the CodeLock Main menu.

To add the menu file to the TestProc.CMD procedure file, select option (4) from the CodeLock Main menu. CodeLock displays the prompt

■   Name of the ASCII menu file to add:

Enter the name of the menu file, which is **Menu1.ASC** in this example. CodeLock then displays the prompt

■   Name of the procedure file:

Enter the name of the procedure file, which is **TestProc.CMD** in this example. CodeLock displays the following:

■   Current blocks in the procedure file:
    Loop2   Bills
    Name of the binary menu block: [Menu1]:

to remind you of existing blocks in the procedure file. Press Enter to use the suggested block name, Menu1. CodeLock will display the menu file and ask you to press any key to continue. Press a key to return to the CodeLock Main menu, and then select option (8) to exit CodeLock.

```
MENU1

COLUMN Sample Menu

Add New Data

Edit/Delete data

Print Reports
```

■ *Figure 17.3:*
Sample menu file.

■ ACCESSING PROCEDURES

Now that we've created a procedure file, let's look at ways to access the procedures within it. First, you'll need to return to the R > prompt. Then, use the Run command with the procedure block name and the procedure file name in the following syntax:

■   RUN *command file block* IN *procedure file name*

To run the Loop2 procedure, enter the command

■   RUN Loop2 IN TestProc.CMD

The Loop2 command file will run its course, and you'll be returned to the R > prompt.

To display a screen block in a procedure file, use the Display command with the following syntax:

■   DISPLAY *screen block name* IN *procedure file name*

For this example, enter the command

■   DISPLAY Bills IN TestProc.CMD

You'll see the screen display appear, and then you'll be returned to the R > prompt.

If you were accessing this screen from within another command file, you'd probably use the commands

■   NEWPAGE
    DISPLAY Bills IN TestProc.CMD

to clear the screen prior to displaying the screen block.

To access the menu in the procedure file, use the Choose command with this syntax:

■   CHOOSE *variable name* FROM *menu block name* IN +
    procedure file

For this example, enter the command

■   CHOOSE MChoice FROM Menu1 IN TestProc.CMD

MChoice is an arbitrary variable name that will record the menu selection. You'll see the menu appear on the screen, as shown in Figure 17.4.

Select an item from the menu to return to the R> prompt. If you enter the command

■   SHOW VARIABLES

after returning to the R> prompt, you'll see that the MChoice variable contains your menu selection.

The variable used for storing the menu selection is always of the Integer data type. If you had pressed the Esc key, rather than selected a menu item, the variable would contain a zero. If you had pressed F10 rather than selected a menu item, the variable would contain − 1. Figure 17.5 shows a sample command file, named MenuTest.CMD, that can be used to respond to a user's menu choice.

Note that if the user presses F 10, the command file displays a screen named MenuHelp.SCN. (**Note:** We have not created such a screen file yet. If you want to test the MenuTest.CMD command file fully, use RBEdit to create a screen file named MenuHelp.SCN.) Also, notice that the While loop repeats as long as the MChoice variable does not equal zero. This means that the menu will be redisplayed until the user chooses to exit by pressing the Esc key.

If you develop the MenuHelp.SCN and MenuTest.CMD files, these, too, can be converted in the procedure file. You'll just need to

```
R>CHOOSE MChoice FROM Menu1 IN TestProc.CMD
                          ═Sample Menu═
                   (1)  Add New Data
                   (2)  Edit/Delete Data
                   (3)  Print Reports
```

■ *Figure 17.4:*
*Sample menu
displayed on the
screen.*

change the line in the MenuTest.CMD command file that reads

- DISPLAY MenuHelp.SCN

to the following:

- DISPLAY MenuHelp IN TestProc.CMD

   If you add the MenuTest.CMD command file to the TestProc procedure file and you want to run it, enter the command

- RUN MenuTest IN TestProc.CMD

at the R> prompt.

```
*(********************************************* MenuTest.CMD)
*(-- Test the menul block in the TestProc.CMD procedure file)
OPEN Mail

*(--- Set up loop for displaying menu)

SET VARIABLE MChoice TO 1
WHILE MChoice <> 0 THEN

    *(--- Clear screen and display menu. Store choice in MChoice)
    NEWPAGE
    CHOOSE MChoice FROM Menul IN TestProc.CMD

    *(--- Respond to menu selection)
    IF MCHoice = 1 THEN
        ENTER NamesFrm
    ENDIF

    IF MChoice = 2 THEN
        EDIT ALL From Names
    ENDIF

    IF MChoice = 3 THEN
        PRINT Director
    ENDIF

    *(--- Display help screen if F10 selected)
    IF MChoice = -1 THEN
        NEWPAGE
        DISPLAY MenuHelp.SCN
        PAUSE
    ENDIF

ENDWHILE

NEWPAGE
WRITE "Exit Selected"
```

■ *Figure 17.5:*
The
MenuTest. CMD
command file.

■ *CONVERTING APPLICATION FILES*

When you create an application file, such as the MailSys application that we created earlier, R:BASE generates three files with the extensions .APP, .API, and .APX, as below:

MailSys.APP
MailSys.API
MailSys.APX

When you're converting with CodeLock, use the .APP file as the name of the ASCII application file to convert.

To convert an application file, select option (5) from the CodeLock Main menu. When CodeLock asks for the

- Name of ASCII application file to convert:

enter the name of the .APP file (**MailSys.APP**, for example). Code-Lock will then display the prompt

- Name of the procedure file:

You can add the application file to an existing procedure file if you wish. In this example, we'll create a new application file named MailSys-.CMD. Enter the procedure file name **MailSys.CMD.**
CMD.

CodeLock will display each line of the application file as it converts. When it's done, you can press any key to return to the CodeLock Main menu.

From the R> prompt, use the syntax

- RUN *application name* IN *procedure file*

to run the converted application. In this example, you would enter the command

- RUN MailSys IN MailSys.CMD

to run the converted MailSys application.

■ CONVERTING MACROS

Macros are particularly good candidates for procedure files. By combining (or *compiling*) macros, you can develop a library of general-purpose routines, stored together in a single file, that are readily accessible when you need them.

Figure 17.6 shows a macro named Summary.MAC, which you can use with the following syntax to summarize the data in a table:

■ RUN Summary.MAC USING <*source table name*> +
    <*Break Column*> <*column to sum*> <*destination table name*>

For example, look at the data from the Mail database in the Charges table below:

CustNo	ProdNo	Qty	U:Price	Tax?	Total
1001	A-111	12	$ 10.00	Y	$127.20
1001	B-222	5	$ 12.50	Y	$ 66.25
1001	C-434	2	$100.00	Y	$212.00
1004	A-111	5	$ 10.00	Y	$ 53.00
1004	Z-128	10	$ 12.80	N	$128.00
1007	A-111	10	$ 10.00	Y	$106.00
1007	Z-128	10	$ 12.80	N	$128.00
1002	B-222	12	$ 12.50	Y	$159.00
1002	A-111	10	$ 10.00	Y	$106.00

The Summary.MAC macro can create a table from these data that displays the sum of the Total column for each customer. In this example, the *source table name* is Charges, the *break column* is CustNo (since we're summarizing for individual customers), and the *column to sum* can be any numeric column. (We'll use the Total column in this example.) The table that you are creating for the summary (the *destination table name* portion of the command) can have any table name. However, if a table with the same name already exists, it will be overwritten—so be sure to use a unique table name unless you want to replace an existing table.

Let's look at an example. Suppose that you open the Mail database and then wish to see a summary of totals for each customer in the Charges table. From the R> prompt, you could enter the command

■ RUN Summary.MAC USING Charges CustNo Total SumTable

The macro will create a table named SumTable that summarizes the totals for each customer, as below:

CustNo	Total
1001	$405.45
1002	$265.00
1004	$181.00
1007	$234.00

To verify that the summary table exists, enter the command

■   SELECT ALL FROM SumTable

at the R> prompt.

Now suppose that you wish to put the Summary.MAC macro and the Update.MAC macro that we created in the last chapter into a single procedure file. From the CodeLock Main menu, select option (2) to add an ASCII command file to a procedure file. Enter the name of the macro (**Summary.MAC**, for this example), and name the procedure file when prompted (**GenProcs.CMD**, for this example). Use the default block name (Summary) when prompted.

After returning to the CodeLock Main menu, select option (2) again. Enter **Update.MAC** as the name of the ASCII command file and **Gen-Procs.CMD** as the procedure file. Use the suggested block name, Update.

Once the macros have been added to the GenProcs.CMD procedure file, they can be accessed from the R> prompt using the following syntax:

■   RUN *block name* IN *procedure file name* USING *parameter list*

For example, to run the Summary.Mac macro in the Gen-Procs.CMD procedure file to summarize the Total column by customer number in the Charges table, thereby creating a new table named SumTable, you would enter the command

■   RUN Summary IN GenProcs.CMD USING Charges CustNo +
     Total SumTable

To run the Update.Mac macro in the GenProcs.CMD procedure file, you would enter a command such as

■   RUN Update IN GenProcs.CMD USING ARMain CustNo +
     Curr:Bal Payments CustNo Amount MINUS

Of course, the parameters will vary depending on the tables involved and the type of update (PLUS, MINUS, or REPLACE). Also, be sure the appropriate database is open before you run the macro.

Remember, you can add up to 42 blocks to a procedure file, so you could develop a good collection of general-purpose macros and have them all readily accessible from a single file.

```
*(---------------------------------------- SUMMARY.MAC)
*(-------------------------- Summarize a table column)
*(Parameters:            %1: Name of table to summarize
                         %2: Key field to summarize on
                         %3: Column to sum [summarize]
                         %4: Name of summary table name)
NEWPAGE
SET MESSAGES OFF
SET ERROR MESSAGES OFF
WRITE "Summarizing... Please wait" AT 1,1
CLEAR SubTot

*(--------- Create empty table for summary data)
REMOVE .%4
PROJECT .%4 FROM .%1 USING .%2 .%3 WHERE .%2 FAILS
DELETE ROWS FROM .%4 WHERE LIMIT = 10000

*(--- Set up pointer for moving through table)
SET POINTER #1 Status1 FOR .%1 SORTED BY .%2
SET VAR SubTot TO .%3 IN #1

*(--- Loop through all rows until end of table)
WHILE Status1 = 0 THEN
     SET VAR SubTot TO 0
     SET VAR ThisNo TO .%2 IN #1
     SET VAR NextNo TO .%2 IN #1

     *(-------------- Loop through rows with common value)
     WHILE ThisNo = .NextNo THEN
          Set Var ThisRow TO .%3 IN #1
          Set Var SubTot To .Subtot + .ThisRow
          NEXT #1 Status1
          IF Status1 <> 0 THEN
               BREAK
          ENDIF
          SET VAR NextNo TO .%2 IN #1
     ENDWHILE

     *(------------ Load Summary Table)
     LOAD .%4
          .ThisNo .SubTot
     END *(--- End load)

ENDWHILE   *(checker = 0)
WRITE "Finished summarizing..." AT 21,1
SET MESSAGES ON
SET ERROR MESSAGES ON
RETURN
```

■ *Figure 17.6:*
The
Summary.MAC
macro.

■ *MODIFYING PROCEDURES*

At some point, you may need to make changes to a file that has already been converted into a procedure file. To do so, use RBEdit to change the *original* file. (Don't attempt to modify the procedure file.) Then, use CodeLock to add the file to the procedure file once again. When you specify the name of the modified file, CodeLock will display the warning

■   Duplicate name–overwrite (Y or N):

If you answer yes, the modified file will be added to the procedure file, and the existing procedure will be erased.

■ *DISPLAYING THE DIRECTORY*

Option (6) from the CodeLock Main menu allows you to view the files stored on disk. When you select this option, you'll see the prompt

■   Enter DOS drive and subdirectory:

Press Enter to display files on the current drive and directory.

To view the files on a separate drive or directory, include the drive specification and directory name; for example, enter B:\Newdbs or C:\Newdbs.

■ *DISPLAYING CONTENTS OF ASCII FILES*

To view the contents of a file before you compile it, select option (7) from the CodeLock Main menu. CodeLock will display the following prompt:

■   Enter the name of the file to be displayed:

Enter the name of the file (and the drive specification and directory name if necessary). For example, enter **Loop2.ASC** to display the contents of the Loop2.ASC file on the current drive and directory. Enter the file name **B:Loop2.ASC** to look for and display the Loop2.ASC file on drive B.

■ *SUMMARY*

The CodeLock option allows you to convert ASCII command files to binary command files, as well as to group command, screen, and menu files into a single procedure file. The options from the CodeLock Main menu are summarized below:

Option (1) converts an ASCII command file to binary format.

Option (2) converts an ASCII command file to binary format and adds it to a procedure file. The **RUN** *block name* **IN** *procedure file name* syntax runs the compiled command file in the procedure file from the R > prompt or from a command file.

You can also use option (2) to compile macros into procedure files. To run a compiled macro from the R > prompt or from a command file, use the syntax **RUN** *macro name* **IN** *procedure file name* **USING** *parameter list*.

Option (3) adds a screen file to a procedure file. The **DISPLAY** *screen block* **IN** *procedure file* syntax displays the screen from the R > prompt or from a command file.

Option (4) adds menu files to a procedure file. The syntax **CHOOSE** *variable name* **FROM** *menu name* **IN** *procedure file name* displays the menu from the R > prompt or from a command file, and stores the user's selection in the specified variable name.

Option (5) converts an application file (created by Application Express) into a procedure file. Specify the file name with the .APP extension when you're using this option.

18

INTERFACING R:BASE WITH OTHER SOFTWARE SYSTEMS

R:BASE includes many commands, as well as the FileGateway and Convert.EXE programs, that can be used to transfer data to and from a variety of formats for interfacing with other software systems. In this chapter, we'll explore general techniques for creating and transferring ASCII-format files into and out of R:BASE, and we'll discuss the options available in the FileGateway program. First, we'll explain how to convert R:BASE 5000 data to the R:BASE System V format using the Convert.EXE program.

R:BASE System V comes with two programs that can help you transfer data to and from other software systems. Convert.EXE is a small program that converts R:BASE 5000 databases to the R:BASE System V database format. FileGateway lets you transfer data to and from other popular microcomputer software systems such as Lotus 1-2-3, dBASE, and WordStar.

You can also use the Output <file name> command to store copies of reports on disk files. These can then be embedded in word-processing documents. In this chapter we'll look at basic techniques for all types of data transfers.

∎ CONVERTING R:BASE 5000 DATA TO R:BASE SYSTEM V

If you have an R:BASE 5000 database that you wish to use with R:BASE System V, you'll need to convert the original database to the new R:BASE System V format. Converting the database is simple, because R:BASE System V performs the conversion automatically with the Convert.EXE program.

Let's suppose that you have an R:BASE 5000 database named MyData that you want to convert to the R:BASE System V format. Here are the steps necessary to make the conversion:

1. First use R:BASE 5000 to view all the column names and variable names in the original R:BASE 5000 database, and check to see if any of the column names (or variable names in reports) match any R:BASE System V *reserved words*. (Reserved words are listed in Table 1-9 in the R:BASE Fundamentals chapter of the R:BASE System V *User's Manual*.) If you find any reserved words in the column names or

variable names, change the names to nonreserved words in the R:BASE 5000 database.

2. Copy the entire R:BASE 5000 database to the hard disk on which you keep R:BASE System V. The original database will be stored in three files, each with the file name you assigned followed by the number 1, 2, or 3. Each file will also have the extension .RBS, as in the examples below:

■   MyData1.RBS
        MyData2.RBS
        MyData3.RBS

To copy the files from a a floppy disk in drive A to your hard disk, you could use the DOS Copy command at the C> prompt with the ? wildcard character, as follows:

■   COPY A:MyData?.RBS

3. If you have not already done so, copy the file Convert.EXE from the R:BASE System V System Disk III onto the same directory on your hard disk where R:BASE System V is stored. To do so, enter the command

■   COPY A:Convert.EXE

at the DOS C> prompt.

4. At the DOS C> prompt, enter the Convert command followed by the name of the file to convert. In this example, you would enter the command

■   CONVERT MyData

at the DOS C> prompt.

The converted files will be stored under the same file name, but with the extension .RBF, as below:

■   MyData1.RBF
    MyData2.RBF
    MyData3.RBF

The original files will still be stored under the original file names. (To conserve disk space, you might want to erase the original .RBS files from your hard disk.)

If you do not have enough space left on your hard disk to convert the R:BASE 5000 databases, you can leave the R:BASE 5000 files in the floppy disk in drive A. With the Convert.EXE program on the hard disk and directory on which you normally store your R:BASE System V disks, enter the command

◼ CONVERT A:MyData

(substituting the appropriate file name in place of *MyData*) at the DOS C> prompt. The original R:BASE 5000 files will still be stored on the floppy disks, and the converted R:BASE System V files will be stored on the hard disk.

Once the conversion is complete, you can use the R:BASE Open command to open the converted database, using the original database name (that is, **OPEN MyData** in this example).

To convert exceptionally large files, you can use the Unload and Load techniques discussed below. The *Conversion Guide* booklet that came with your R:BASE System V package discusses additional techniques for converting large R:BASE files. The *Conversion Guide* also discusses techniques for converting applications written in R:BASE 5000 to R:BASE System V. But in most cases, the application created in R:BASE 5000 will run well in R:BASE System V without any conversion.

◼ *FILEGATEWAY*

The FileGateway program can copy data from tables to a variety of formats and can also import data from external formats into R:BASE tables. To run FileGateway, either select the FileGateway option from the R:BASE System V Main menu, or enter the command

◼ GATEWAY

directly at the R> prompt. The FileGateway Main menu will appear on the screen, as in Figure 18.1. As the menu shows, you can import data, export data, get help on the screen, or exit FileGateway.

Getting Help

If you need help while using FileGateway, select option (3), or press the F10 key at any time. After viewing the help screen, press Esc to return to FileGateway.

Importing Options

Selecting option (1) from the FileGateway Main menu presents options for importing data into R:BASE tables. Figure 18.2 shows the Import Options menu on the screen. We'll discuss some specific examples for importing data later in the chapter.

Exporting Options

Option (2) from the FileGateway Main menu presents options for exporting R:BASE tables to other file formats. Figure 18.3 shows the Export Options menu. (Again, we'll look at specific examples later in the chapter.)

Other FileGateway Options

You can also call up the Options menu at any time while using File-Gateway by pressing Shift-F6. This menu, shown in Figure 18.4, lets

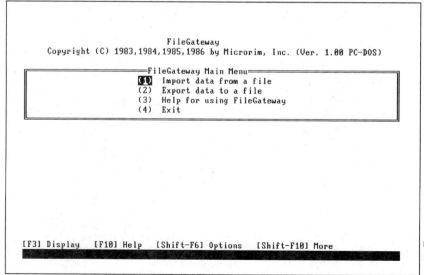

```
                         FileGateway
      Copyright (C) 1983,1984,1985,1986 by Microrim, Inc. (Ver. 1.00 PC-DOS)

      ╔═══════════════════════FileGateway Main Menu════════════════╗
      ║                     ▓1▓  Import data from a file            ║
      ║                     (2)  Export data to a file              ║
      ║                     (3)  Help for using FileGateway         ║
      ║                     (4)  Exit                               ║
      ╚═════════════════════════════════════════════════════════════╝




      [F3] Display    [F10] Help   [Shift-F6] Options   [Shift-F10] More
```

■ *Figure 18.1:*
The FileGateway Main menu.

you perform basic file maintenance, change and view directories, run external programs (Zip), and set rule checking and passwords.

The first option is used for basic DOS file maintenance such as copying, erasing, renaming, and viewing the contents of ASCII files with

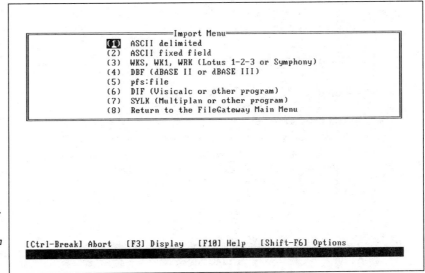

```
                         ════════Import Menu════════
                    (1)  ASCII delimited
                    (2)  ASCII fixed field
                    (3)  WKS, WK1, WRK (Lotus 1-2-3 or Symphony)
                    (4)  DBF (dBASE II or dBASE III)
                    (5)  pfs:file
                    (6)  DIF (Visicalc or other program)
                    (7)  SYLK (Multiplan or other program)
                    (8)  Return to the FileGateway Main Menu




    [Ctrl-Break] Abort   [F3] Display   [F10] Help   [Shift-F6] Options
```

∎ *Figure 18.2:*
Options for
importing data
into R:BASE
tables.

```
                         ════════Export Menu════════
                    (1)  ASCII delimited
                    (2)  ASCII fixed field
                    (3)  WKS (Lotus 1-2-3 or Symphony)
                    (4)  DIF (Visicalc or other program)
                    (5)  SYLK (Multiplan or other program)
                    (6)  Return to the FileGateway Main Menu




    [Ctrl-Break] Abort   [F3] Display   [F10] Help   [Shift-F6] Options
```

∎ *Figure 18.3:*
Options for
exporting R:BASE
tables.

the Type command (a topic we'll discuss in the section on ASCII files in this chapter). The second option lets you change, create, view, and remove directories from your hard disk, using the basic DOS CHDIR, DIR, MKDIR, and RMDIR commands. Option (3) lets you change drives and check the disk status with the basic DOS CHDRV and CHKDSK commands.

Option (4) allows you to run an external program. When you select this option, the screen asks that you

- Enter the name of the program to execute:

Type in the name of the program in the same way that you would to run the program from the DOS C> prompt. For example, to run dBASE, type in dBASE and press Enter. To run WordStar, type in WS and press Enter. If the program that you wish to run is not on the current directory, include the drive specification and directory name. For example, if WordStar is stored on a directory named WP, you would enter the name of the program to execute as follows:

- C:\WP\WS

The external program will run only if it is small enough to fit into memory along with FileGateway. If not, you'll only see the message

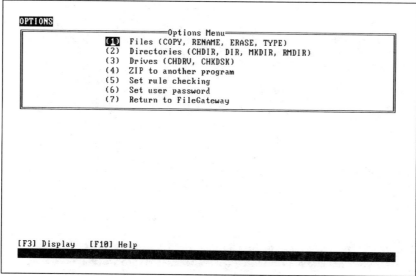

```
OPTIONS
                    ═Options Menu═
              (1)  Files (COPY, RENAME, ERASE, TYPE)
              (2)  Directories (CHDIR, DIR, MKDIR, RMDIR)
              (3)  Drives (CHDRV, CHKDSK)
              (4)  ZIP to another program
              (5)  Set rule checking
              (6)  Set user password
              (7)  Return to FileGateway




    [F3] Display   [F10] Help
```

■ *Figure 18.4:*
Options menu.

"Press any key to continue" and be returned immediately to the Options menu.

If the external program does fit into memory, you can use it in the usual way. When you exit the program, you'll automatically be returned to the Options menu.

Option (5), Set Rule Checking, can be used when importing files into R:BASE tables. When you select this option from the Options menu, the screen asks whether to

∎ Check data against entry rules?

If you select Yes, incoming data will be validated against whatever rules you defined for the table that is receiving the data. If you select No, all of the imported data from the external file will be imported, regardless of whether it meets the requirements of the rules.

Option (6) lets you enter the password necessary to add data to the table (assuming that you've created a password for the table). Chapter 19 discusses passwords. For now, suffice it to say that if you've created passwords for a database or table, you must use this option to enter the appropriate password before you can import or export table data.

In Chapter 15 we discussed techniques for recording and playing back keystrokes with Exec files. You can record and use Exec files in FileGateway using the same keys discussed earlier: Shift-F7 to start and stop recording keystrokes, and Shift-F8 to play back the keystrokes.

∎ A NOTE ON ASCII FILES

Before discussing specific file transfer techniques, you should become familiar with basic ASCII file structures. Many software systems accept data that are stored in ASCII format. In fact, you can accomplish almost any data transfer imaginable, including many minicomputer and mainframe transfers, with some knowledge of ASCII file formats. Let's discuss those now.

ASCII (American Standard Code for Information Interchange) data files are generally stored in one of two formats: *delimited* or *structured*.

Delimited ASCII Files

The most common format is the delimited ASCII file, also called the *sequential access* file. In this file, individual *fields* (columns) are separated by commas (or another delimiting character). Character (text)

fields are usually surrounded by quotation marks. Many data files passed from minicomputers and mainframe computers to microcomputers are stored as delimited ASCII files. Figure 18.5 shows a sample delimited ASCII file.

Structured ASCII Files

Structured ASCII files (also called *random-access* or *fixed-field* data files) store data with fixed-*field* (column) and *record* (row) lengths, with no delimiting characters between the fields. Often, information captured from other computers via a modem is stored in the structured format. Figure 18.6 shows a sample structured data file.

ASCII files generally contain only data and delimiters, with no special formatting codes or header information. Therefore, if you use the DOS or R:BASE Type command to view the file, you can quickly see the file displayed on the screen. When importing an ASCII file, you

```
1003,"Tape Backup",1.00,1250.00,"7/8/86"

1000,"Ram Disk",1.00,1100.00,"7/8/86"

1001,"Floppy Disks",10.00,2.11,"7/8/86"

1001,"Color Card",1.00,101.00,"7/8/86"

1001,"Video Cable",2.00,16.00,"7/8/86"

1001,"8 Mhz Clock",2.00,16.39,"7/8/86"

1001,"Ram Disk",1.00,1100.00,"7/8/86"

1002,"8 Mhz Clock",2.00,16.39,"7/8/86"

1002,"Ram Disk",1.00,1100.00,"7/8/86"

1003,"8 Mhz Clock",1.00,16.39,"7/8/86"

1003,"Tape Backup",1.00,1250.00,"7/8/86"

1003,"40 Meg. Disk",1.00,450.00,"7/8/86"

1003,"Floppy Disks",5.00,2.11,"7/8/86"

1003,"Color Card",1.00,101.00,"7/8/86"

1004,"Video Cable",10.00,16.00,"7/8/86"

1004,"8 Mhz Clock",1.00,16.39,"7/8/86"

1004,"Tape Backup",2.00,1250.00,"7/8/86"
```

■ *Figure 18.5:*
A sample delimited ASCII file.

need only use the Type command to see whether the file is structured or delimited. The Type command uses the following syntax:

■   TYPE *<d:>* *<file name>*

Hence, if you enter the command

■   TYPE NewData.DAT

at the DOS prompt or R:BASE R> prompt, you'll see the contents of a file named NewData.DAT stored on the currently logged drive. The command

■   ·TYPE A:Transfer.DAT

displays the contents of a file named Transfer.DAT on drive A.

1000 Turbo Board	1	550.00	07/08/86
1000 Ram Disk	1	1100.00	07/08/86
1001 Floppy Disks	10	2.11	07/08/86
1001 Color Card	1	101.00	07/08/86
1001 Video Cable	2	16.00	07/08/86
1001 8 Mhz Clock	2	16.39	07/08/86
1001 Ram Disk	1	1100.00	07/08/86
1002 8 Mhz Clock	2	16.39	07/08/86
1002 Ram Disk	1	1100.00	07/08/86
1003 8 Mhz Clock	1	16.39	07/08/86
1003 Tape Backup	1	1250.00	07/08/86
1003 40 Meg. Disk	1	450.00	07/08/86
1003 Floppy Disks	5	2.11	07/08/86
1003 Color Card	1	101.00	07/08/86
1004 Video Cable	10	16.00	07/08/86
1004 8 Mhz Clock	1	16.39	07/08/86
1004 Tape Backup	2	1250.00	07/08/86

■ *Figure 18.6:*
A structured data file.

■ TECHNIQUES FOR TRANSFERRING FILES

Chapter 8 from the R:BASE System V *User's Manual* discusses all the details of transferring files using FileGateway. Rather than repeat all of that information here, we'll look at specific examples of transferring R:BASE table data. We'll look at some creative ways to perform transfers with ASCII files that are not discussed in the R:BASE manuals.

■ CREATING A WORDSTAR FORM-LETTER FILE

WordStar's MailMerge option (and most other word processors) allow you to print form letters using data stored in delimited ASCII data files. You can easily create such files from any R:BASE table using FileGateway.

For example, suppose you want to print form letters with WordStar using names and addresses from the Names table in the Mail database we created earlier in this book. Begin by starting FileGateway, and select (2), Export Data to a File, from the Main menu. Select (1), ASCII Delimited, from the Export menu. When the screen asks for the name of the database to use, select Mail. When the screen asks for the name of the table to export, select Names.

Next, you'll be given the opportunity to select columns to export. For this example, you'll need only the following columns:

■
    L:Name
    F:Name
    Company
    Address
    City
    State
    Zip

Press Esc after selecting the column names.

Next, select a sort order for the exported file. You can select any of the columns to sort on, although for bulk mailing, Zip would be the best choice. Select either Ascending or Descending order, and press Esc twice.

From the next screen, you can specify that only particular rows be exported, such as rows with CA in the State column, or rows with ZIP codes in the range 90000 to 99999. For this example, just press Esc to export all the rows. FileGateway will verify the request by asking

■   Export all rows?

For this example, you can select Yes.

Next the screen asks for the name of the file to export and suggests Names.DEL as the name. You can enter a more descriptive name if you like, such as WS.DAT, and press Enter to proceed.

Next the screen asks that you

■   Enter the character to separate fields in your output file:

In almost every situation, you'll want to use a comma to separate fields, so type in a comma and press Enter.

Next the screen asks

■   Add a carriage return/line feed at the end of each row?

Virtually all ASCII files need a carriage return/line feed at the end of each row, so you'll want to select Yes in response to this question.

At this point, FileGateway begins creating the ASCII file and displays its progress. (The original data in the Names table is left unchanged; the new file named WS.DAT will contain a copy of the table data in ASCII delimited format.) When exporting is complete, you can press any key to return to the FileGateway menu.

When the Import Options menu reappears, select option (6) to return to the Main menu, and select option (4) to exit from FileGateway. If the R> prompt reappears, enter the Exit command to work your way back to the DOS C> prompt.

To verify that the exportation was successful, you can enter the command

■   TYPE WS.DAT

at the DOS C> prompt. The delimited ASCII file will appear on your screen as in Figure 18.7.

Next you'll want to make sure that the WS.DAT file is accessible to your word processor. You can either copy the word processor to the directory containing WS.DAT or copy WS.DAT to the directory containing your word processor, using the DOS Copy command.

Assuming that you are using WordStar as the word processor, run WordStar in the usual way. Create a document file by selecting D from the WordStar opening menu. Give it a file name, such as FORM.LET. Then type in the appropriate dot commands and the body of the letter, which is shown in Figure 18.8.

"Martin","Mary","Atomic Ovens","321 Microwave St.","Lassiter","OH","12121"

"Teasdale","Trudy","Atomic Ovens","321 Microwave St.","Lassiter","OH","12121"

"Miller","Monica","Acme Development","355 Torrey Pines St.","Newark","NJ",

"54821"

"Miller","Marie","Zeerox Inc.","234 C St.","Los Angeles","CA","91234"

"Adams","Bart","Dataspec Inc.","P.O. Box 2890","Malibu","CA","92111"

"Jones","Mindy","ABC Co.","123 A St.","San Diego","CA","92122"

"Baker","Robin","Peach Computers","2311 Coast Hwy","San Diego","CA","92122"

"Miller","Anne","Golden Gate Co.","2313 Sixth St.","Berkeley","CA","94711"

"Smith","Sandy","Hi Tech, Inc.","456 N. Rainbow Dr.","Berkeley","CA","94721"

■ *Figure 18.7:*
ASCII delimited version of the Names table.

```
        C:FORM.LET  PAGE 1 LINE 18 COL 16           INSERT ON
L----!----!----!----!----!----!----!----!----!----!--------R
.DF WS.DAT                                                    M
.RV LNAME FNAME COMPANY ADDRESS CITY STATE ZIP                M
.OP                                                           <
                                                              <
&FNAME& &LNAME&                                               <
&COMPANY/O&                                                   <
&ADDRESS&                                                     <
&CITY&, &STATE&  &ZIP&                                        <
                                                              <
Dear &FNAME&:                                                 <
                                                              <
This is a sample form letter that I've written to test the
interface between R:BASE System V data and WordStar's MailMerge
option.  The data for this form letter are stored in a file named
WS.DAT, which I created using the FileGateway options to export a
delimited ASCII file.  So what do you think of that?          <
                                                              <
Sincerely,                                                    <
                                                              <
Susita Maria                                                  <
.pa                                                           .
```

■ *Figure 18.8:*
Sample form letter created with WordStar.

You use the .DF (data file) dot command to name the MailMerge file of names and addresses. The .RV (Read Variable) command assigns a name to each column in the data file. It is important to assign a name to every column in the table, even if you do not plan to use the column in your form letter. In this example, we've listed column names that match the columns we exported to the ASCII file. The .OP command omits page numbers, and .PA ensures that each form letter starts on a new page.

Variable names used within the letter are surrounded by ampersands, such as &LNAME& and &FNAME&. The /O option used with the &COMPANY/O& column tells WordStar to omit this line if there are no company data for an individual. This will ensure that a blank line doesn't appear between the name and the address if an individual does not have a company.

After you create and save the form letter using the WordStar Ctrl-KD command (hold down the Ctrl key and type K, then D), you need to merge print it using the Merge Print command. That is, select Word-Star option M from the WordStar menu, and when it asks for the name of the file to merge print, type in the file name of the form-letter file (not the WS.DAT data file). A letter for each individual in the Members database will then be printed.

Other Tips for Interfacing with WordStar

You can send R:BASE reports to WordStar for further editing or inclusion in other documents. To do so, design a report format using Reports Express in R:BASE. Then, print the data using the syntax **OUTPUT** *file name* and **PRINT** *report name*. Exit R:BASE and load WordStar to read in the text file.

The commands below, when entered at the R> prompt, will create an ASCII file named Transfer.TXT, which you can read directly into WordStar:

■
```
OPEN Mail
OUTPUT Transfer.TXT
PRINT Sales
OUTPUT Screen
EXIT
```

At this point, the Transfer.TXT file contains a copy of the data displayed by the Sales report format.

Now you can load WordStar. Let's say that you want to pull the R:BASE report into a document called MANUAL.TXT. At the DOS prompt, type in the command

■ WS MANUAL.TXT

When the document appears on the screen, position the cursor where you want the R:BASE report to appear. Then enter Ctrl-KR (hold down the Ctrl key and type K, then R). WordStar asks for the

■ NAME OF FILE TO READ?

Type in the name of the transfer file (**Transfer.TXT**, for this example), and press Enter. That's all there is to it.

You can use WordStar to create and edit R:BASE command files. Just be sure to use the nondocument mode at all times when you're creating and editing the command file.

■ dBASE II AND dBASE III INTERFACING

You can import data from dBASE II, III, and III PLUS data files into R:BASE System V tables, as well as export data from R:BASE tables to dBASE.

Importing dBASE Files into R:BASE

Importing dBASE files into R:BASE is a simple task. Figure 18.9 shows a dBASE III PLUS database named Sample.DBF that we'll import into R:BASE in this example.

First, you'll need to make a copy of the dBASE database available to FileGateway. The easiest way to do this is to copy the dBASE database to your R:BASE directory using the DOS Copy command. (Remember that dBASE database files have the extension .DBF, so in this example you would want to use the file name Sample.DBF in the DOS Copy command.)

When the file is on the same directory as FileGateway, run FileGateway in the usual way. Select option (1) from the FileGateway Main menu to import a file, and option (4) from the Import menu to import a

DBF file. The screen will ask that you select the file to import. (In this example, let's assume that you want to import the file named Sample.DBF.)

Next, the screen asks that you specify the name of the R:BASE database in which to import the dBASE data. In lieu of importing the data into an existing database, you can select (Other) to create a new database. Then you need to assign a name to the new database. In this example, type in the name Sample. (You don't need to add an extension to the R:BASE database name.)

The screen asks that you enter the name of the table to import the data into and suggests the name Sample. Press the Enter key to accept the suggested table name.

Next the screen asks if you want to

■   Import deleted records from dBASE file?

Record#	PARTNO	PARTNAME	QTY	U_PRICE	DATE
1	A-123	MicroProcessor	100	55.55	01/01/86
2	B-222	Laser Engine	2	1234.56	02/01/86
3	C-333	Color Terminal	5	400.00	02/01/86
4	D-444	Hard Disk	25	500.00	03/02/86
5	E-555	Disk Controller	50	200.00	04/15/86
6	F-666	Graphics Board	20	249.00	05/15/86
7	G-777	Modem	5	249.00	05/15/86
8	H-888	SemiDisk	25	600.00	06/15/86
9	A-123	MicroProcessor	10	55.55	07/30/86
10	B-222	Laser Engine	8	1234.56	07/31/86
11	A-123	MicroProcessor	10	55.00	08/30/86
12	E-555	Disk Controller	25	200.00	09/01/86
13	E-555	Disk Controller	100	180.00	10/01/86
14	F-666	Graphics Board	5	200.00	11/01/86
15	A-123	MicroProcessor	20	51.00	11/15/86
16	H-888	SemiDisk	15	600.00	12/15/86

■ *Figure 18.9: dBASE database named Sample.DBF.*

dBASE allows you to mark records for deletion without actually deleting them. If you want to exclude these records that are marked for deletion, select No. If you want to import all the records, select Yes.

Next, the screen shows a suggested structure for the table that will receive the imported data, as in Figure 18.10. You can use the suggested structure or change field names and data types. For this example, you'd want to change the data type for the U_PRICE column from Text to Currency. Use the arrow keys to position the cursor to the data type for the U_PRICE column, and type in the new data type, Currency. Press Enter after changing the data type; then press Esc when you are finished making changes on the screen.

Next you'll see the Data Loading menu. Select option (1) to load data into the database. If the file being imported contains dates, you'll see a screen presenting several possible formats for dates in the imported file. For dBASE, the suggested format (MM/DD/(YY)YY) is fine, so press Esc to use the suggested format.

Finally, FileGateway will begin importing data from the dBASE file, and it will present a counter to show its progress. When the importation is complete, you can press any key to proceed and then select menu options to exit FileGateway.

To verify that the data have been imported, run R:BASE to get to the R> prompt. Then open the database and select rows from the newly imported table. In this example, we named the new R:BASE

```
══════════════════════File Conversion Editor══════════════
  To change the name, type, or length of a field, move the cursor to the
  field and type in the new information. Do not change sample values.
   Up, Dn, Lt, Rt, PgUp, PgDn, Home, End  Move the cursor between fields
   + . . . . . . . . . . . . . . . . . Get next record of sample data
   ESC . . . . . . . . . . . . . . . . When changes are complete


  Field name   Data type    Maximum length   Sample values
  ----------   ---------    --------------   -------------

  PARTNO       TEXT                 5        A-123
  PARTNAME     TEXT                15        MicroProcessor
  QTY          INTEGER                       100
  U_PRICE      CURRENCY                          55.55
  DATE         DATE                          01/01/1986




  [F3] Display   [F10] Help   [Shift-F6] Options
  DATABASE: Sample  TABLE: SAMPLE   IMPORT FILE: SAMPLE.DBF
```

■ *Figure 18.10:*
Suggested structure for new R:BASE table.

database Sample, and we also assigned the name Sample to the new table. Therefore, to view the imported data, enter the commands

■   OPEN Sample
    SELECT ALL FROM Sample

at the R:BASE R > prompt.

Exporting Files to dBASE

To send data from an R:BASE System V table to a dBASE database, you first need to create an ASCII delimited copy of the table data. To do so, use FileGateway and the same techniques we used to create the WordStar MailMerge file in the previous section.

Run dBASE and create a file with the same fields as the R:BASE table. The Names table has the following structure:

Table: Names

Column definitions

#	Name	Type	Length
1	CustNo	INTEGER	1 value(s)
2	L:Name	TEXT	15 characters
3	F:Name	TEXT	15 characters
4	Company	TEXT	25 characters
5	Address	TEXT	25 characters
6	City	TEXT	15 characters
7	State	TEXT	5 characters
8	Zip	TEXT	10 characters
9	Ent:Date	DATE	1 value(s)
10	Phone	TEXT	13 characters

In dBASE III, you would create a database with the following structure:

Structure for database : C:dbfile.dbf

Field	Field name	Type	Width	Dec
1	CUSTNO	Numeric	4	
2	LNAME	Character	20	

3	FNAME	Character	20
4	COMPANY	Character	25
5	ADDRESS	Character	25
6	CITY	Character	15
7	STATE	Character	5
8	ZIP	Character	10
9	ENT_DATE	Date	8
10	PHONE	Character	13

In dBASE II, you could create a database with the structure below:

STRUCTURE FOR FILE: C:DBFILE .DBF

FLD	NAME	TYPE	WIDTH	DEC
001	CUSTNO	N	004	
002	LNAME	C	020	
003	FNAME	C	020	
004	COMPANY	C	025	
005	ADDRESS	C	025	
006	CITY	C	015	
007	STATE	C	005	
008	ZIP	C	010	
009	ENT:DATE	C	008	
010	PHONE	C	013	

In either case, you would then use the database you created and enter the command

- APPEND FROM RbtoDB.DAT DELIMITED

After the dot prompt reappears, use the List command to verify the accuracy of the transfer.

■ INTERFACING WITH SPREADSHEETS

FileGateway includes options for directly transferring data to and from Lotus 1-2-3 (Version 2.0), Symphony, Multiplan SYLK files, and Visi-Calc DIF files. (The SYLK and DIF file formats can also be used by other spreadsheet packages.) Keep in mind, however, that databases store tables in a fixed column and row format, while spreadsheets allow you to place data randomly around the screen. Therefore, when importing data from spreadsheets, you'll need to import only those areas that are stored in a fixed tabular format (columns and rows), such as with 1-2-3 and Symphony databases.

As an alternative to using the options for directly importing and exporting spreadsheet data, you can use intermediate ASCII files to help with the conversion (although you may never need to). For example, you can use FileGateway to create a delimited ASCII file from an R:BASE table and assign a file name to the exported file with the extension .PRN. Then, you can use the /FIN (File Import Numbers) options in Lotus 1-2-3 to read the ASCII file directly into a spreadsheet.

You can export ASCII fixed-field files from almost any spreadsheet. For example, the /PF (Print File) options will allow you to highlight any portion of a Lotus 1-2-3 spreadsheet and write that portion of the spreadsheet to an ASCII file. Then, you can use FileGateway to import the ASCII fixed-field file into an R:BASE table.

∎ *SUMMARY*

In this chapter we've looked at some basic techniques for transferring data to and from R:BASE tables to other file formats, focusing mainly on ASCII file transfers.

The Convert.EXE program that came with your R:BASE System V package can convert R:BASE 5000 databases to the new R:BASE System V format.

You can export R:BASE table data to word-processed form-letter files using the ASCII Delimited option in FileGateway.

FileGateway includes options for importing dBASE files directly. To export dBASE files, use the ASCII Delimited option in FileGateway, and use the Append From <file name> Delimited command in dBASE to read in the ASCII file.

FileGateway includes numerous options for importing and exporting spreadsheet data, although you can also use ASCII files to interface with most spreadsheet packages.

19
ADDITIONAL
TECHNIQUES

In this chapter, we'll discuss some additional techniques that you can use with R:BASE. These include techniques for reducing processing time, conserving disk space, tailoring system parameters, protecting your files with passwords, using word wrap, and others.

∎ REDUCING PROCESSING TIME

As your R:BASE databases and applications grow, you will need to think about techniques for maximizing the speed of managing data.

The Build Key Command

The Build Key command can speed up processing relational commands and some searches. It is used to create a key column, or *index*, which speeds up the process of looking up data. In general, you might want to build a key for those columns that relate two tables to one another and for columns that you often use to look up data that is unique to each row.

The general syntax for the Build Key command is

∎   BUILD KEY FOR *column name* IN *table name*

For example, to build keys for the CustNo columns of the Names and Charges tables in the Mail database, you would separately enter the commands

∎   BUILD KEY FOR CustNo IN Names
       BUILD KEY FOR CustNo IN Charges

You can find out if a table has a key column when you use the List command to view the contents of the table. For example, if you built a key for the Charges table and entered the command

∎   LIST Charges

you would see the word **yes** under the Key column of the display, as below:

Table: Charges   No lock(s)
Read Password: No
Modify Password: No

Column definitions

#	Name	Type	Length	Key	Expression
1	CustNo	INTEGER		yes	
2	ProdNo	TEXT	8 characters		
3	Qty	INTEGER			
4	U:Price	CURRENCY			
5	Tax?	INTEGER			
6	Total	CURRENCY			(IFEQ('Tax?',0,'Qty' ★ 'U:Price',('Qty'★'U :Price')★1.06))
7	P:Date	DATE			

As an alternative to using the Build Key command to create an index, you can enter Definition Express and select options to modify an existing table. When the table structure appears on the screen, move the highlighter to the column name that you want to make into a key. Press Enter, and the screen will ask

■   Do you want this column to be a key?

Select Yes. All keyed columns will be displayed on the Definition Express screen with an asterisk in front of them.

Since all relational commands take advantage of key columns automatically, it's a good idea to build keys for all the columns in database tables that you use to relate tables to one another.

Searches with a Where clause can profit from the increased speed of a key column, if the Where clause conforms to the following conditions:

The last condition in the Where clause refers to the key column.

The last operator in the Where clause is an EQ or = (for "equal to").

The last logical operator in the Where clause is an AND.

For example, the command below would fit all of these criteria:

■   SELECT ALL FROM Names WHERE City = ''Newark'' +
    AND CustNo = 1007

You can delete keys using the Delete Key command with the general syntax

■   DELETE KEY FOR *column name* IN *table name*

Optionally, use Definition Express to modify the existing table, and press Enter when the highlighter is on the keyed column name. Select No in response to the question about making the column a key.

∎ CONSERVING DISK SPACE

When you delete rows from a table or remove tables, R:BASE does not automatically free the disk space that was used by the data. To make that space available, you use the Pack command. The general syntax for the Pack command is

∎ PACK *database name*

If you don't include a database name, the Pack command works on the currently open database.

If an error or machine malfunction occurs during a Pack procedure, the database may be destroyed. Therefore, it's a good idea to back up your database using the R:BASE or DOS Copy command before using the Pack command. Also, avoid using the Pack command in the multi-user mode.

∎ CUSTOM CONFIGURATIONS

You can tailor some general parameters in R:BASE by creating a file named RBASE.DAT on the same directory as the R:BASE program.

Specifying Screen Colors

You can specify foreground screen colors for color monitors using the syntax **SET COLOR FORE** *color*, and you can specify background colors using the syntax **SET COLOR BACK** *color*. To set colors, you create or edit the RBASE.DAT file with RBEdit. For example, to run R:BASE with yellow letters on a blue background, you would enter the following command at the R > prompt:

∎ RBEDIT Rbase.DAT

Then, type in the commands

∎ SET COLOR FORE YELLOW
SET COLOR BACK BLUE

and press Esc. Save the file to return to the R > prompt, and then exit R:BASE. The next time you enter R:BASE, the colors you specified will appear on the screen.

Background colors that you can use in R:BASE are black, blue, brown, cyan (blue-green), gray, green, magenta, and red. Foreground colors include all of the background colors plus light black, light blue, light cyan, light green, light magenta, light red, yellow, and white.

Automatic Program Execution at Start-up

You can also have R:BASE automatically run an application or command file when you start it up by using the Run command in the RBASE.DAT file. For example, the RBASE.DAT file below:

```
SET COLOR FORE YELLOW
SET COLOR BACK BLUE
RUN MailSys IN MailSys.APX
```

sets up colors and immediately runs the MailSys application. Note that the colors are set before the Run command.

■ PASSWORD PROTECTION

You can use Definition Express to assign various passwords to data in tables to limit the number of users who can access the information. At the highest level, you can assign an *owner* password. This type of password allows anyone to view data and change *information* in the database, but it allows only individuals who know the password to change the database *structure* (such as renaming, adding, or deleting columns).

After assigning an owner password, you can also define passwords for individual tables in the database. Individual table passwords are of two types:

Read password	The user can view data in the table, but cannot change it.
Modify password	The user can read and modify data in the table.

We can work through an exercise with our trusty Mail database to test these passwords.

Begin by entering Definition Express either from the RBSystem Main menu or by entering the command RBDefine at the R> prompt. Select option (2) to modify an existing database definition. When the screen asks for the name of the database to modify, select Mail. From the next menu, select option (3), Passwords.

The screen will ask that you choose a table or view or select (Owner). You'll always want to define the Owner password first, so select (Owner). The screen asks that you

■   **Enter the database owner password:**

You can enter any password with up to eight characters. When doing so, be *sure* to write down the password on a piece of paper as well, and store that password in a safe place. If you forget the password in the future, even though you are the owner, you will not be able to modify your database. In this example, enter the word SESAME as the owner password.

Next you can assign passwords to individual tables. Select Charges, in this example, as the table to assign passwords to. The screen provides prompts for entering Read and Modify passwords, as follows:

■   **Read password: NONE**
     Modify password: NONE

Currently, no passwords are defined. To assign passwords, type them into the appropriate prompts. In this example, enter LOOK as the Read password and BOSS as the Modify password. Press Esc twice and exit the Definition Express menus to work your way back to the RBSystem Main menu or to the R> prompt.

From the R> prompt, open the Mail database by entering the command

■   **OPEN Mail**

You can interact freely with the Names table, since no passwords were assigned to it. For example, both the Select All From Names and Edit All From Names commands work in the usual way.

If you enter the command

■   **SELECT ALL FROM Charges**

you'll see the following message:

■   **– WARNING – Unauthorized access to the table**

You need to enter a password with the User command to view this table. At the R > prompt, enter the command

■   USER Look

Then enter the following command:

■   SELECT ALL FROM Charges

and you'll see the data in the Charges table.
   If you enter the command

■   EDIT ALL FROM Charges

you'll see the unauthorized access message. To have access to the Charges table and make changes, you need to know the Modify password. Hence, if you enter the command

■   USER Boss

you can then enter the command

■   EDIT ALL FROM Charges

to make changes to the Charges table. (You can still use the Select All From Charges command, because the right to modify data assumes the right to view it.)
   You will not need to use the owner password until you attempt to change the database structure or the passwords. When you enter Definition Express, you will be required to enter the owner password (SESAME in this example) before having access to the Mail database. From there, you can change anything in the table, including any existing passwords. To remove existing passwords, change them to the word NONE.

■ BROWSING WITHOUT EDITING

As we've seen earlier in the book, the Edit All command allows you to scroll through columns and rows in a table with the Tab key and the arrow keys. If you assign a modify password to a table, users who do not know the password will not be able to take advantage of the scrolling capability of the Edit command. Therefore, R:BASE System V includes the Browse command, which allows any user to scroll through the database in a way similar to the Edit command, but without the ability to make changes.

The general syntax for the Browse command, from the R> prompt, is the following:

- BROWSE <column names or ALL> FROM <table name> +
  SORTED BY <columns> WHERE <condition>

where <column names or ALL> lists the specific column names to display or all columns, and <table name> is the name of the table (or view) to scroll through. The Sorted By and Where clauses use the customary syntax.

For example, the command

- BROWSE ALL FROM Names

displays all data from the Names table in the Mail database on the screen in a format identical to that used by the Edit All From Names command. You can use the arrow and Tab keys to scroll through the table and view data, but no changes are allowed.

The command that follows displays the CustNo, ProdNo, and Total columns (with the Total column displayed 12 characters wide) from the Charges table, sorted by the CustNo column, on the screen in the browse mode:

- BROWSE CustNo ProdNo Total = 12 FROM Charges +
  SORTED BY CustNo

∎ WORD WRAP

When defining reports, you can use *word wrap* to display long lines of text. Word wrap ensures that any breaks in a line are made between words instead of in the middle of them.

Suppose that you have a database with a table to record bibliographic references. This table has Author, Title, Publisher, City, Date, and Abstract columns, as in the Refs table below:

Table: Refs

Column definitions

#	Name	Type	Length
1	Author	TEXT	30 characters
2	Title	TEXT	70 characters
3	Pub	TEXT	25 characters
4	City	TEXT	15 characters
5	Date	DATE	1 value
6	Abstract	TEXT	500 characters

Notice that in the Abstract column we allow 500 characters for a Text column.

When you locate the Abstract column in the reports mode, mark the start location with an S, as usual. Then, move the cursor to the end location on the same row, but type a **W** rather than an E to specify word wrap. That sets up the width for the column.

R:BASE will then display the prompt

■ Press [T] for end line or [ESC]

If you press Esc, the entire text string will be displayed. To truncate the text, move the cursor to the row and column position where you want the text string cut off, and type the letter **T.**

Next, R:BASE will display the prompt

■ Press [I] for indentation or [ESC]

To indent the text, move the cursor to the indentation column and press **I.** Figure 19.1 shows a row from the Refs table printed on a report with word wrap and an indentation in the 11th column.

■ *NOTE FIELDS*

In the last section, we defined a column named Abstract that was 500 characters long. Using the Text data type, we could have assigned a maximum length of 1500 characters to the Abstract column. For longer columns, you can assign the Note data to the column, which automatically allocates up to 4092 characters for the field.

There is nothing tricky about using Note fields, except that you should use word wrap, as we discussed in the last section, to locate the column on a report and also to locate the column on a form.

Figure 19.2 shows the Refs table from the Library database with the Abstract column defined as the Note data type. Notice that you don't need to specify a length with the Note data type.

Author: Hunter, Bruce H.
Title: Understanding C
Publisher: SYBEX   Berkeley   6/1/84
Abstract:
          Tutorial on the C programming language, especially
          geared toward microcomputers and the CP/M and MS-DOS
          operating systems. Topics include data types and
          storage classes, memory management, UNIX-like utilities,
          C library functions, number crunching, and comparisons
          of various C compilers.

■ *Figure 19.1:*
Sample row from the Refs table.

Change the name for this table

┌──────────────┐   An asterisk (*) identifies key columns
│ Refs   │   A plus sign (+) identifies computed columns
└──────────────┘

Author	Title	Pub	City	Date	Abstract	
TEXT 30	TEXT 70	TEXT 25	TEXT 15	DATE	NOTE	

[ESC] Done   [F3] Review   [F5] Reset value   [F10] Help   [Shift-F10] More
Database LIBRARY --- Table Refs

■ *Figure 19.2:*
Sample table with Note data type.

Figure 19.3 shows a form defined for entering and editing data on the Refs database. The field for entering and editing data in the Abstract column was created by pressing F6 and specifying Abstract as the column to locate. The S location was marked in column 1, and the W (for *wrap*) location was marked near the right column. The E location for the field was marked in the lower-right corner of the screen to provide as much room as possible for the abstract.

Figure 19.4 shows the form for the Refs table in use. Note that if the text inside the highlighted Abstract field does not fit in the space provided on the screen, the text in the screen will automatically scroll the text within the area as you move the cursor.

When typing information into the Abstract column on the form, don't press the Enter key until all of the text is typed in. Pressing Enter moves you to the next field or brings up the top menu. You'd need to select Edit again from the menu or use the Tab key or the arrow keys to move the cursor back into the Abstract field on the form.

As you type in sentences, the cursor will automatically move down to the next line when you attempt to type past the right margin. Even though the text will be broken in the middle of words on the screen, the sentences will all wrap around when you print the data with a report format that uses word wrapping. To put blank lines between paragraphs of text, press the down arrow key.

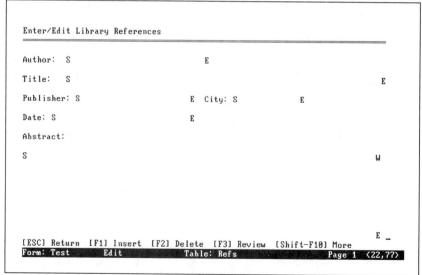

■ *Figure 19.3:*
Form for entering
data into sample
Refs table.

You can use the CONTAINS operator to access rows in the table that only contain a particular word or words. For example, to view references to rows that mention DOS, using a report format named Refernc, you could enter the command

■ PRINT Refernc WHERE Abstract CONTAINS "DOS"

■ THE CROSSTAB COMMAND

A powerful feature of R:BASE System V is the Crosstab command, which counts or calculates values based on two existing columns. For example, suppose the Charges table in the Mail (or ARSys) database contains the data shown in Figure 19.5.

To see the total number of items that each customer purchased, you could enter the command

■ CROSSTAB SUM Qty FOR ProdNo BY CustNo FROM Charges

The resulting output is shown in Figure 19.6.

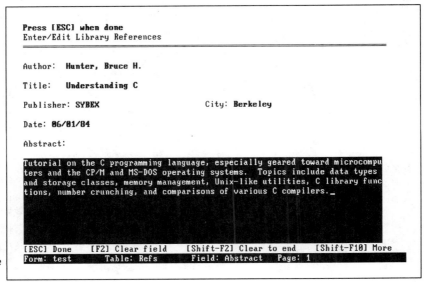

■ *Figure 19.4: Sample data on a form with a Note column.*

The general syntax for the Crosstab command is

■ CROSSTAB <operation> <column> FOR <columns> BY +
   <rows> WHERE <conditions>

```
R>SELECT ALL FROM Charges
CustNo      ProdNo   Qty        U:Price          Tax?        Total
---------   -------- ---------  ----------------  ---------   ----------------
     1001 A-111          12       $10.00            1           $127.20
     1001 B-222           5       $12.50            1            $66.25
     1001 C-434           2      $100.00            1           $212.00
     1004 A-111           5       $10.00            1            $53.00
     1004 Z-128          10       $12.80            0           $128.00
     1007 A-111          10       $10.00            1           $106.00
     1007 Z-128          10       $12.80            0           $128.00
     1002 B-222          12       $12.50            1           $159.00
     1002 A-111          10       $10.00            1           $106.00
R>_
```

■ *Figure 19.5:*
Sample data in
the Charges
table.

```
R>CROSSTAB SUM Qty FOR ProdNo BY CustNo FROM Charges
CustNo   │ A-111       B-222       C-434       Z-128       (Total)
-------- │ ---------   ---------   ---------   ---------   ---------
    1001 │     12           5           2           0          19
    1002 │     10          12           0           0          22
    1004 │      5           0           0          10          15
    1007 │     10           0           0          10          20
-------- │ ---------   ---------   ---------   ---------   ---------
         │     37          17           2          20          76
R>_
```

■ *Figure 19.6:*
Results of the
Crosstab
command.

where <operation> is any of the operators COUNT, MAXIMUM, MINIMUM, AVERAGE, or SUM; <column> is the name of the column being analyzed; <columns> is the name of the column containing data to be placed across the top of the resulting Crosstab display; and <rows> is the column name of values to be placed in the rows in the Crosstab display. The Where clause is optional.

You can use the Output command to send the results of the Crosstab command to the printer or to a file. Of course, the results of the command could produce a huge number of rows and columns if a large table were in use. In that case, R:BASE will only display as much data as will fit on the screen. One way around this is to use the Where clause with the Crosstab command. For example, the command

■   CROSSTAB SUM Qty FOR ProdNo BY CustNo FROM +
     Charges WHERE ProdNo = "A-111" .OR. ProdNo = "B-222"

will display the total of the Qty field for each customer for product numbers A-111 and B-222.

If the resulting display produces far more columns than rows, you can reverse the order of the column names surrounding the By portion of the command. That way you'll probably be able to see more data.

■ BACKING UP TO FLOPPY DISKS

You can store backup copies of R:BASE System V databases in a condensed format on floppy disks using the Backup command. Although R:BASE cannot use the backup file directly, you can use the Restore command to "uncondense" the backup and bring it back to the hard disk for normal use in R:BASE. It's a good idea to back up databases often onto floppy disks, in case someone accidentally erases or in some other way corrupts the original database on the hard disk.

To make a backup, first open the database that you wish to back up. Then use the Output command to specify the drive and a file name for the backup. Then use the Backup command to make the backup. For example, the following commands, entered at the R> prompt, make a backup copy of the ARSys database on the floppy disk in drive A.

■   OPEN ARSys
     OUTPUT A:ARSys.BAK
     BACKUP ALL

The resulting backup file is given the extension .BAK, so that it becomes ARSys.BAK.

If R:BASE needs more than a single floppy disk to make the backup, it will inform you when to place a new diskette in drive A. If several diskettes are required for the backup, *you should label the diskettes in the order that they were filled* (for example, label the first diskette filled 1, the second diskette filled 2, and so forth). It may take several diskettes (and several minutes) to back up a large R:BASE database.

When the R> prompt reappears, remember to enter the Output Screen command once again so that no additional data are accidentally stored on the backup diskette.

Should a disaster cause you to lose your database on the hard disk, use the Restore command to bring a copy of the backup from the floppy disks to the hard disk. Start by placing the first backup diskette (number 1) in drive A. If there are any remaining portions of the original database on the hard disk (that is, files with the extension .RBF), erase them using the DOS or R:BASE Erase command. Then, at the R:BASE R> prompt, enter the Restore command followed by the drive and the name of the backup file. In this example, you would enter the command

■   RESTORE A:ARSys.BAK

R:BASE will keep you informed of its progress and ask you to change diskettes in drive A when, and if, necessary. Be sure to place the diskettes back into drive A in the appropriate order (that is, insert diskette number 1 first, diskette number 2 second, and so forth, as requested on the screen).

You can also back up portions of databases by specifying certain tables, columns, or rows in the Backup command, although you'll usually want to use the Backup All command to make backups. See Chapter 9 on system maintenance in the R:BASE System V *User's Manual* for instructions on backing up portions of databases.

■ *RUNNING EXTERNAL PROGRAMS*

You can run programs outside of R:BASE System V using the Zip command at the R> prompt. For example, you would normally enter the command

■   WS

at the DOS C> prompt to run WordStar. To run WordStar directly from the R:BASE R> prompt, you would enter the command

■ **ZIP WS**

When you exit WordStar, you'll automatically be returned to the R> prompt, with your original database still open.

If the program that you are attempting to run with the Zip command requires more memory than is available with R:BASE still running, you'll see a message that tells you so, and then the R> prompt will reappear. To make more memory available for the external program, use the Rollout option in the Zip command, as follows:

■ **ZIP ROLLOUT WS**

As before, when you leave the external program, you'll be returned to the R> prompt. However, when Rollout is used to suspend R:BASE temporarily, it will take longer for the R> prompt to reappear when you exit the external program. As an extra protection against the slim chance of losing data while using the Zip command, you can first enter the Close command at the R> prompt to save all data to disk. Later, use the Open command to reopen the database.

■ *WHERE DO I GO FROM HERE?*

R:BASE System V is a large and powerful database-management system for microcomputers. A single book on the subject can hardly do justice to its many capabilities. However, we've covered the basic concepts using practical examples, and I hope that these examples have helped you to understand the basic workings of R:BASE System V and enabled you to manage your own databases.

If you bought this book because the manuals that came with R:BASE seemed too technical or too abstract, this tutorial text should have given you sufficient practical background to make the more technical material in the manuals understandable. The *User's Manual* that came with the R:BASE package should be particularly helpful in expanding your knowledge and skills in using R:BASE System V.

I should mention that, as I finish this book, I'm already preparing to write a companion book entitled *Power User's Guide to R:BASE System V,* which will continue where this book left off and present examples of more complex business applications. That book will also be published by SYBEX.

But perhaps the most important element in fully mastering any software package, including R:BASE System V, is practice. Hands-on experimentation (with some printed reference material nearby to back you up) will provide the experience that leads to complete mastery. Experimenting and working in a comfortable place will make your learning experience enjoyable and productive.

■ SUMMARY

The additional techniques for use with R:BASE that we've discussed in this chapter include the following:

The Build Key command creates an index or key column, which will speed up locating information in that column. Using Build Key is identical to marking columns as keys in Definition Express.

The Pack command reclaims unused disk space left by deleted records, and therefore conserves disk space.

The Set Color commands allow you to define colors for a color monitor.

R:BASE always checks the contents of a file named RBASE.DAT when first loading. If you place the Run command in the RBASE.DAT file, the program specified in the Run command will run automatically when R:BASE is loaded.

In Definition Express, you can define passwords to limit access to data to certain users. A modify password (MPW) prevents unauthorized persons from changing data in a database. A read password restricts viewing data to those persons who know the password.

The Browse command lets users view table data in a tabular form, similar to the display produced by the Edit command, but it does not allow any changes to the data.

Long character fields can be *word wrapped* on forms and reports by locating the field with a W rather than an E.

Note-field columns are similar to Character columns in a database, except that they allow over 4000 characters to be entered.

The Crosstab command cross-tabulates values in a column, based on values in two other columns.

The Backup command allows you to store condensed copies of database data on floppy disks. The Restore command retrieves the backup and puts it back into uncondensed R:BASE format.

The Zip command allows you to run external programs without exiting R:BASE.

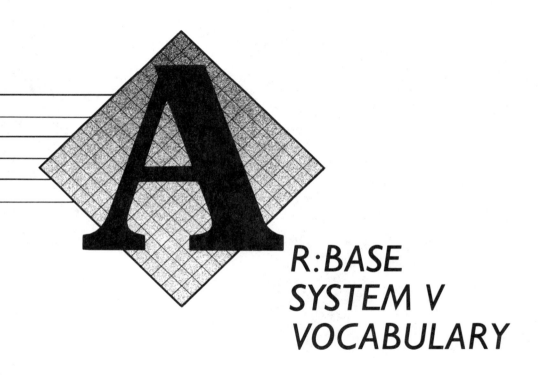

R:BASE
SYSTEM V
VOCABULARY

This appendix lists and defines the vocabulary used with R:BASE System V.

■ Entry   Function

*(Marks the start of a programmer comment in a command file. A closing parenthesis marks the end of the comment. Example: ★(− − This is a programmer comment).

ALL   Usually specifies all columns, rather than specific columns, when displaying or copying data. Example: SELECT ALL FROM Names.

AND   Used with a Where clause to specify multiple conditions that must be simultaneously true. Example: SELECT ALL FROM Names WHERE L:Name = Smith AND State = CA displays all Smiths in the state of California.

APPEND   Copies rows from an existing table onto the bottom of another existing table. Syntax is APPEND *table name* TO *table name* WHERE *conditions*. The Where clause is optional. Example: APPEND Charges TO History WHERE Date > = 3/1/86 AND Date < = 3/31/86.

AUTOSKIP   Determines whether the highlighting automatically moves to the next item on a custom form as each field is filled. The commands Set Autoskip On and Set Autoskip Off control automatic skipping. The Show command displays the current status.

AVE   Used with the Compute command to specify an average. Example: COMPUTE AVE Qty FROM Charges WHERE ProdNo = A-111.

BACKUP   Creates condensed backup files of R:BASE databases on floppy disks. Use the Output command to specify a drive and a file name for the backup, and use the Backup All command to back up the entire database. The Restore command returns backup files to the hard disk. Syntax is BACKUP *option1* FOR *table name* USING *columns* SORTED BY *column names* WHERE *conditions*. *Option1* can be ALL, DATA, or STRUCTURE. Example: BACKUP ALL FOR Mail USING ALL.

■ *Entry   Function*

BEEP   Makes a beeping sound. Most often used in custom command files to bring attention to a message on the screen. Syntax is simply BEEP.

BELL   Used with the Set command to determine whether a beep is sounded with R:BASE error messages. The commands Set Bell On and Set Bell Off control the bell. The Show command displays the current status.

BREAK   Used in command files within While and Endwhile loops to terminate a loop. Most often used within an If and Endif clause to terminate a loop under special circumstances.

BROWSE   Allows the user to scroll through a table in a fashion similar to the Edit command, but does not allow any changes to be made. Syntax is the same as the Edit command; that is, BROWSE *column names* FROM *table name* SORTED BY *column names* WHERE *conditions*. Example: BROWSE ALL FROM Names SORTED BY L:Name WHERE State = "CA".

BUILD KEY   Creates an index, or a key column, for a table to speed up searches with a Where clause and relational processing. Syntax is BUILD KEY FOR *column name* IN *table name*. Example: BUILD KEY FOR CustNo IN Charges. The Delete Key command removes an index.

CASE   Determines whether uppercase and lowercase are taken into consideration in a Where clause. The commands Set Case On and Set Case Off determine case distinction. The Show command displays the current status.

CHANGE   Globally modifies the contents of a column in a table. Syntax is CHANGE *column name* TO *value* IN *table name* WHERE *conditions*. Example: CHANGE City TO "San Diego" IN Names WHERE City = S.D.

CHANGE COLUMN   Redefines a column in a table. General syntax is CHANGE COLUMN *column name* TO < *column name* > < *data type* > < *length* >. Example: CHANGE COLUMN Company TO TEXT 35. The second *column name* option allows you to change the column name.

■ *Entry*	*Function*
CHDIR	Changes the directory; most often used on hard-disk systems. Syntax is CHDIR *<drive>* *<path>*. Example: CHDIR C:\dbs makes the dbs directory on drive C the current directory. The abbreviated form, CD, is also acceptable.
CHDRV	Displays the default drive, or changes it. The command CHDRV B: makes drive B the default drive. You can omit the command and use only the command B:. CHDRV without a drive specification displays the name of the current drive (for example, C:).
CHECK/ NOCHECK	Entered at the L> prompt to turn rule checking on and off in the load mode. Unless it is changed, rule checking is normally on. Nocheck turns rule checking off. If an owner password has been defined, the password must be entered for Nocheck to be effective.
CHKDSK	Displays the total number of bytes available on a drive. Syntax is CHKDSK *drive*. Example: CHKDSK B:.
CHOOSE	Displays a custom menu and records user's selection. Syntax is CHOOSE *variable name* FROM *menu name* IN *file name*. Example: CHOOSE MChoice FROM Main IN ARsys.
CLEAR	Removes currently active variables. Syntax is CLEAR *variable name* or CLEAR ALL VARIABLES. Example: CLEAR SubTotal.
CLOSE	Closes the currently open database and stores all current modifications on disk. The Exit and Open commands also close the currently active database and save all modifications.
CLS	Clears the screen or a portion of the screen. To clear a portion of the screen, use From and To with the command. Syntax is either CLS or CLS FROM *screen row* TO *screen row*. Example: CLS FROM 5 TO 10 clears the screen from row 5 to row 10.
CODELOCK	Enters the CodeLock module of R:BASE System V. Syntax is simply CODELOCK.

■ *Entry*	*Function*
COLOR	Used with the Set command to determine the color of displays. Colors are black, blue, brown, cyan, gray, green, magenta, red, yellow, white, and light versions of most colors. The command Set Color displays choices.
COMPUTE	Performs calculations on column data. Options are Ave, Count, Max, Min, and Sum. Syntax is COMPUTE *variable* AS *<option>* *<column name>* FROM *table name* WHERE *condition*. Example: COMPUTE GrandTot AS SUM Qty FROM Charges WHERE Qty EXISTS.
COMPUTE ALL	Displays the average, count, highest value, lowest value, and sum of a numeric column. Syntax is COMPUTE ALL *column name* FROM *table name* WHERE *condition*. Example: COMPUTE ALL Total FROM Charges WHERE P:Date > 06/01/86.
COMPUTE ROWS	Counts the number of rows in a table, optionally storing the result in a variable. Syntax is COMPUTE *variable name* AS ROWS FROM *table name*. Example: COMPUTE Row-Count AS ROWS FROM Charges.
CONTAINS	Used with a Where clause to specify rows in which a column contains a text value. Example: SELECT ALL FROM Names WHERE Address CONTAINS Maple.
COPY	Copies one or more files on disk to other files. Syntax is COPY *<file name1>* *<file name2>*. DOS wildcard characters, ? and ★, are allowed. Example: COPY Mail?.RBS Mail?.BAK copies all Mail?.RBS files to Mail?.BAK files (where ? stands for any character).
COUNT	Used with the Compute command to count how many rows contain a value. Example: COMPUTE COUNT ProdNo FROM Charges WHERE ProdNo = A-111.
CROSSTAB	Calculates sums or other values for a single column based on data in two other columns. Can be used to cross-tabulate data from two tables if the two tables are united in a view. Syntax is CROSSTAB *option 1 column name 3* FOR *column name 1* BY

■ *Entry*   *Function*

column name 2 FROM *table/view name* WHERE *conditions*. The *option 1* argument can be COUNT, MINIMUM, MAX-IMUM, AVERAGE, or SUM. Example: CROSSTAB SUM Qty FOR ProdNo BY CustNo FROM Charges.

DATE

Used with the Set command to display the formats of dates. Months may be MM (1–12) or MMM (Jan–Dec). Years may be YY (86) or YYYY (1986). Examples: SET DATE MM/DD/YY or SET DATE MMM/DD/YYYY. The Show command displays the current setting.

DELETE DUPLICATES

Deletes duplicate rows from a table. A duplicate row is defined as one that is identical in every column. Syntax is DELETE DUPLICATES FROM *table name*. Example: DELETE DUP-LICATES FROM Names.

DELETE KEY

Deletes an index created using the Build Key command. Syntax is DELETE KEY FOR *column name* IN *table name*. Example: DELETE KEY FOR CustNo IN Charges.

DELETE ROWS

Deletes rows from a table that meet a specific criterion. Syntax is DELETE ROWS FROM *table name* WHERE *condition*. Example: DELETE ROWS FROM Names WHERE L:Name FAILS AND Company FAILS.

DIR

Displays files on the directory. Supports DOS wildcard characters ? and ⋆. Example: DIR ⋆.RBS shows all the R:BASE database files on the current drive and directory.

DISPLAY

Displays a screen stored in a procedure file or screen file. Syntax is DISPLAY *screen name* IN *procedure file*. Example: DIS-PLAY Help1 IN Procfile displays the Help1 screen from the Procfile procedure file.

DRAW

Used to display a variable form. Syntax is DRAW *form name* WITH VARIABLE *variable list* AT *row*. The optional With portion displays the current value of variables. The At portion is also optional. Example: DRAW MyForm WITH ALL AT 3.

DUPLICATES

Used with the Delete command to delete duplicate rows from a table. Example: DELETE DUPLICATES FROM Names.

■ Entry	Function
ECHO	Used with the Set command primarily as a debugging tool. The command Set Echo On echoes all commands from a command file as they are processed. Set Echo Off turns the echo off. The Show command displays the current status.
EDIT	Displays a full edit screen for modifying data in a table. Syntax is EDIT *column names* FROM *table name* SORTED BY *column names* WHERE *conditions*. Sorted By and Where are optional. Example: EDIT ALL FROM Charges SORTED BY CustNo.
EDIT USING	Provides full editing of a table through a predefined form. Syntax is EDIT USING *form name* SORTED BY *column name* WHERE *conditions*. Sorted By and Where are optional. Example: EDIT USING ChrgFrm SORTED BY CustNo.
ENTER	Adds data to a table using a predefined form. Syntax is ENTER *form name* FROM *file name* FOR *n* ROWS. From and For are optional. FROM *file name* indicates an external ASCII file; FOR *n* ROWS limits the number of new rows added. Example: ENTER NamesFrm.
EQ	Used in a Where clause to specify equals (same as using =). Example: SELECT ALL FROM Names WHERE L:Name EQ Smith. EQA is the equivalent form for comparing data from two columns.
ERASE	Erases files from the disk (same as the DOS Erase command). Syntax is ERASE *file name*. Wildcard characters ? and ★ are supported. Example: ERASE ★.BAK erases all .BAK files from the current drive and directory.
ESCAPE	Determines whether pressing the Esc key will abort a command file or database access. The commands Set Escape On and Set Escape Off control this option.
EXISTS	Used with a Where clause to specify only rows that do not contain null data in a specific column. Example: SELECT ALL FROM Names WHERE CustNo EXISTS.

∎ Entry   Function

EXIT
Leaves the R:BASE R> prompt and returns to the first menu or DOS C> prompt.

EXPAND
Adds a new column to a table. Syntax is EXPAND *table name* WITH *<column name>* *<data type>* *<length>*. Length should be defined for Text data only. Example: EXPAND Names WITH Phone TEXT 13.

FAILS
Used with a Where clause to specify rows that contain null data in a specified column. Example: DELETE ROWS FROM Names WHERE CustNo FAILS AND L:Name FAILS.

FILL/
NOFILL
Does or does not automatically fill empty columns with the null character when in load mode. Nofill suppresses automatic filling; Fill activates it. Unless Nofill is specified, Fill is automatically on.

FILLIN
Used to get input from the user from within a command file and store that input in a variable. Syntax is FILLIN *variable name* USING *"message"* AT *<row>* *<column>*. Example: FILLIN YesNo USING "Send report to printer?" AT 12,1.

FORMS
Used to create and modify forms for entering and editing table and variable data. Syntax is FORMS *form name*. Example: FORMS NamesFrm creates or edits a form named NamesFrm.

GATEWAY
Enters the FileGateway module of R:BASE System V for transferring data to and from other software systems. Syntax is simply GATEWAY.

GE
Specifies greater than or equal to in a Where clause (same as using >=). Example: SELECT ALL FROM Names WHERE Ent:Date GE 3/1/86. GEA is the equivalent form for comparing data from two columns.

GOTO
Branches control in a command file to a labeled group of commands. Syntax is GOTO *label name*. Requires a Label command in the same command file with matching *label name*. Example: GOTO PrinChek.

■ *Entry*   *Function*

GT   Specifies greater than in a Where clause (same as using >). Example: SELECT ALL FROM Charges WHERE Total GT 1000. GTA is the equivalent form for comparing data from two columns.

HELP   Enters the help mode from the R> prompt. The syntax is HELP *command name*. When used with a command name, Help displays information on a particular command. Example: HELP SELECT.

IF   Used in a command file to make decisions. Requires the Then and Endif commands and allows an optional Else command. Syntax is IF *conditions* THEN *command lines* ELSE *command lines* ENDIF. Up to ten conditions may be included with the If command. Example:

> IF Total > 5000 THEN
>   *perform these commands*
> ELSE
>   *perform these commands*
> ENDIF

INPUT   Like the Run command, changes the source of input from the keyboard to a command file. Syntax is INPUT *command file name*. Example: INPUT Sample1.CMD.

INTERSECT   Relational command that creates a new third table from two existing tables with a common column. Syntax is INTERSECT *table name 1* WITH *table name 2* FORMING *new table name 3* USING *column names*. Example: INTERSECT Names WITH Charges FORMING Temp.

JOIN   Creates a third table from two existing tables by including in the new table rows from table 1 that are in a specified relation to rows in table 2. Syntax is JOIN *table name 1* USING *column name* WITH *table name 2* USING *column name* FORMING *new table name 3* WHERE *operator*. Optional operator allows value comparisons.

KEY   Used with the Build and Delete Key commands to create and remove indexes for faster processing. Examples: BUILD

∎ *Entry* *Function*

	KEY FOR CustNo IN Charges; DELETE KEY FOR CustNo IN Charges.
LABEL	Used in conjunction with the Goto command to assign a name to a group of commands in a command file. Syntax is LABEL *label name*. Example: LABEL PrinChek.
LE	Specifies less than or equal to in a Where clause (same as using < =). Example: SELECT ALL FROM Names WHERE Ent:Date LE 12/31/86. LEA is the equivalent form for comparing data from two columns.
LIMIT	Used in a Where clause to limit the number of rows displayed. Example: To display 20 rows from the Names table, enter the command SELECT ALL FROM Names WHERE LIMIT = 20.
LINES	Determines the number of lines displayed on the screen or printer (except for Reports displays, which use the Set option on the Reports menu). The Show command displays the current setting.
LIST	Displays the names of tables (when used with All), column names, databases, forms, reports, rules, or tables. LIST *table name* displays the structure of the named table. Syntax is LIST *item*. Examples: LIST ALL, LIST Names, LIST RULES, LIST Tables.
LOAD	Allows data entry from within the R:BASE command mode without the use of a predefined form. Syntax is LOAD *table name* WITH PROMPTS FROM *file name* USING *column names*. From and Using are optional. Example: LOAD Names WITH PROMPTS.
LT	Specifies less than in a Where clause (same as using <). Example: SELECT ALL FROM Charges WHERE Total LT 1000. LTA is the equivalent form for comparing data from two columns.

■ *Entry*   *Function*

MAX   Used with the Compute command to find the highest value in a column. Example: COMPUTE MAX Total FROM Charges WHERE P:Date > = 3/31/86 AND P:Date < = 5/31/86.

MESSAGE   Used with the Set command, usually in command files, to determine whether R:BASE messages are displayed during program execution. The Show command displays the current status.

MIN   Used with the Compute command to find the smallest value in a column. Example: COMPUTE MIN Total FROM Charges WHERE P:Date > = 3/1/86 AND P:Date < = 5/31/86.

MKDIR   Creates a new directory on the currently logged drive (same as the DOS MKDIR command). May be abbreviated MD. Syntax is MKDIR *<drive>* *<path>* *<directory>*. Example: MKDIR C:\Newdbs creates a directory on drive C named Newdbs.

NE   Used in a Where clause to specify not equal (same as using < >). Example: SELECT ALL FROM Names WHERE State NE Ca. NEA is the equivalent form for comparing data from two columns.

NEWPAGE   Clears the screen. If the printer is active, advances paper to the top of the next page.

NEXT   Used in conjunction with the Set Pointer command to advance a row pointer to the next row in a table. Syntax is NEXT *#n variable name* where *#n* is the route (1–3) and *variable name* is the variable assigned with the Set Pointer command. Example: NEXT #1 Status.

NULL   Used with the Set command to change the null character (-0-) to another symbol. Example: SET NULL − . The Show command displays the current character.

OPEN   Makes a database on disk accessible to all commands. Syntax is OPEN *database name*. Example: OPEN Mail. The

∎ *Entry* *Function*

Close command closes that database and saves any current modifications.

OR   Used with a Where clause to expand a search to multiple conditions. Example: SELECT ALL FROM Names WHERE L:Name = Smith OR L:Name = Jones displays everyone with either the last name Smith or Jones.

OUTPUT   Redirects output from the screen to the printer, a file, or any combination. Syntax is OUTPUT *device 1* WITH *device 2*. The With clause is optional. Example: OUTPUT C:follow.txt WITH BOTH stores output to a file named Follow.TXT and displays output on both the screen and the printer.

PACK   Recovers extraneous disk space after a Remove or Delete command. Syntax is PACK *database name*. Examples: PACK packs the currently open database; PACK Mail packs the Mail database.

PAUSE   Halts execution of a command file until the user presses any key. Most often used with a prompt displayed by the Write command. Example: WRITE "Press any key to continue" AT 23,1; PAUSE.

PLAYBACK   Plays back keystrokes recorded in an Exec file with the Shift-F7 key. The Shift-F8 keystroke combination can be used instead of the Playback command. Syntax is PLAYBACK *file name* where *file name* is the name of a previously created "exec" file. Example: PLAYBACK ManyKeys.EXC.

PRINT   Displays table data using report formats designed with the Reports option. Syntax is PRINT *report name* SORTED BY *column names* WHERE *conditions*. Sorted By and Where are optional. Example: PRINT Director SORTED BY L:Name F:Name WHERE State = CA.

PRINTER   Used with the Output command to send displays to the printer. Example: OUTPUT PRINTER WITH SCREEN.

■ Entry   Function

PROJECT   Copies data from an existing table to a new table, using all or some of the data from the existing table. Syntax is PROJECT *new table* FROM *table name* USING *column names* SORTED BY *column names* WHERE *conditions*. Example: PROJECT Temp FROM Names.

PROMPT   Enters the prompt mode (P >) and displays helpful prompts for entering commands. Syntax is PROMPT *command name*. Example: PROMPT SELECT provides a prompt screen for entering a Select command.

QUIT   Terminates a command file and closes all If and While blocks. Should always be used to terminate a command file that contains While or If commands. Syntax is QUIT TO *file name*, where the To portion is optional.

RBDEFINE   Enters Definition Express from the R > prompt for creating or modifying databases. Syntax is simply RBDEFINE.

RBEDIT   A text editor used for creating and editing command files. Syntax is RBEDIT *file name*. If a file name is not included, RBEDIT prompts for one. Example: RBEDIT Sample1.CMD.

RECORD   Records a series of keystrokes in an Exec file (same as pressing Shift-F7). The Record Off command stops recording keystrokes. Syntax is RECORD *file name* where *file name* is the name of the file to record keystrokes in. Example: RECORD ManyKeys.EXC.

REDEFINE   Lets you change the data structure of a column in a table outside of Definition Express. Syntax is REDEFINE *column name* TO *data type length* IN *table name*. Example: REDEFINE Company TO TEXT 30 IN Names converts the Company column in the Names table to Text data, 30 characters wide.

RELOAD   Copies an existing database without unusable disk space occupied by deleted rows, keys, or tables. Syntax is RELOAD *database name*. Similar to PACK, but creates a new copy of the database with a new name.

■ *Entry*   *Function*

REMOVE   Removes a table from the currently open database. Syntax is REMOVE *table name*. Example: REMOVE Temp.

REMOVE   Removes a column from a table in the currently open data-
COLUMN   base. Syntax is REMOVE COLUMN *column name* FROM *table name*. Example: REMOVE COLUMN Phone FROM Names.

RENAME   Changes the name of a file on disk using the syntax RENAME <*file name*> <*new file name*> (same as the DOS Rename command). Accepts DOS ? and ★ wildcard characters. Example: RENAME Mail?.RBS Test?.RBS.

RENAME   Changes the name of a column in a table in the currently open
COLUMN   database. Syntax is RENAME COLUMN *column name* TO *column name* IN *table name*. Example: RENAME COLUMN Phone TO PhoneNo IN Names.

RENAME   Changes the owner password for a database. Syntax is
OWNER   RENAME OWNER *password* TO *new password*. Example: RENAME OWNER Andy TO Betty.

RENAME   Changes the name of a table in the currently open database.
TABLE   Syntax is RENAME TABLE *table name* TO *new table name*. Example: RENAME Temp TO Charges.

REPORTS   Begins the report definition that allows the user to create a customized report format. Syntax is REPORTS *report name*. Example: REPORTS Labels.

RESTORE   Brings condensed files from floppy disks, which were created with the Backup command, back to the hard disk as complete R:BASE System V databases. Syntax is RESTORE *file name* where *file name* is the name of the file containing the backed-up database. Example: RESTORE MyBack.BAK.

RETURN   Used at the end of a subroutine or subordinate command file to return control to the command file that called it.

■ Entry   Function

REVERSE	Used with the Set command to determine whether data-entry fields are displayed in reverse video. Controlled by the Set Reverse On and Set Reverse Off commands. The Show command displays the current settings.
RMDIR	Removes a directory from the specified drive. Syntax is RMDIR *<drive>* *<path>* *<directory>*. The abbreviated form, RD, is also acceptable. Example: RMDIR C:\Newdbs removes the Newdbs directory from drive C.
RUN	Executes all the commands in a command file. Syntax is RUN *command file name* IN *procedure file* USING *parameter list*. The In clause works only with compiled procedure files and application files. The Using clause passes parameters to subroutines. Example: RUN Area.CMD IN MyProcs.CMD USING 20 50.
SCREEN	Used with the Output command to specify the screen as the output device. Example: OUTPUT SCREEN.
SELECT	Displays data from a table. Syntax is SELECT *<column names>* *<=w>* *<=S>* FROM *table name* SORTED BY *column names* WHERE *conditions*. Optional *=w* specifies a column width and *=S* specifies summation. Example: SELECT ALL FROM Names SORTED BY L:Name.
SET	Modifies special characters and key words. Syntax is SET *<key word>* *<value>*. The key words are Autoskip, Bell, Blank, Case, Color, Comma, Date, Dollar, Echo, Escape, Lines, Message, Null, Plus, Quotes, Reverse, Rules, Scratch, Semi, User, and Width. The Show command displays the current status of most characters and key words.
SET ERROR	Allows programmers to modify error procedures and handle errors independently of R:BASE. The command Set Error Messages Off suppresses error message display. The syntax Set Error Variable *variable name* stores the error code in *variable name*.

∎ *Entry*   *Function*

SET POINTER	Sets up a pointer (1, 2, or 3) in a table, which is moved with the Next command. Syntax is SET POINTER *variable name* FOR *table name* SORTED BY *column name* WHERE *condition*. Example: SET POINTER #1 Status FOR Names SORTED BY L:Name.
SET VARIABLE	Defines a type or value for a variable. The syntax SET VARIABLE *<variable name> <type>* creates an empty variable with an explicit data type. The syntax SET VARIABLE *variable name* TO *value* assigns a value to a variable. Example: SET VARIABLE X TO 10.
SHOW	Displays the status of numerous parameters that can be modified through the Set command. The parameters are Autoskip, Bell, Case, Clear, Date, Echo, Escape, Lines, Messages, Null, Reverse, Rules, User, Width, Blank, Comma, Dollar, Plus, Quotes, Semi.
SHOW ERROR	Displays the status of a variable created by the Set Error Variable command. Syntax is SHOW ERROR *variable name* AT *<row> <column>*, where the At clause is optional. Example: SHOW ERROR Status AT 12,1.
SHOW VARIABLES	Shows the current value of all variables. The syntax SHOW VARIABLE *variable name* shows the contents of the named variable. Examples: SHOW VARIABLES, SHOW VARIABLE Status.
SORTED BY	Used with most commands that display data to determine a sort order. Syntax is ...SORTED BY *<column name>* *<=A> <=D>*, where =A is ascending and =D is descending sort order. Up to ten columns may be specified. Example: PRINT Labels SORTED BY ZIP=D.
SUBTRACT	Creates a new table with nonmatching rows from two existing tables. Syntax is SUBTRACT *table name 1* FROM *table name 2* FORMING *new table name 3* USING *column names*. Example: SUBTRACT Charges FROM Names FORMING Temp USING CustNo.

■ *Entry*   *Function*

SUM   Used with the Compute command to calculate the total of a numeric column. Example: COMPUTE SUM Total FROM Charges WHERE ProdNo = A-111.

TALLY   Calculates and displays a frequency distribution of data in a table. Syntax is TALLY *column name* FROM *table name* WHERE *conditions*. The Where clause is optional. Example: TALLY Zip FROM Names displays all of the ZIP codes in the Names table and the number of occurrences of each one.

TYPE   Displays the contents of an ASCII file stored on disk (same as the DOS Type command). Syntax is TYPE *file name*. Example: TYPE Sample1.CMD. With the Output Printer command, can be used to make a hard copy of a command file.

UNION   Combines the rows and columns from two existing tables into a new third table. Syntax is UNION *table name 1* WITH *table name 2* FORMING *table name 3* USING *column names*. The Using clause is optional. Example: UNION Names WITH Charges FORMING Temp.

USER   Used for operator identification to get through password restrictions. Syntax is USER *password*. Example: USER Betty.

VIEW   Defines a pseudotable (view file), displaying data from multiple tables simultaneously. (This can be accomplished in Definition Express, as well as from the R > prompt using the View command.) Syntax is VIEW *view name* WITH *columns* FROM *table names* WHERE *conditions*. Example: VIEW Manyfile WITH L:Name F:Name Qty U:Price Date FROM Customer Charges WHERE State EQ "NY".

WHERE   Clause used with most commands that display data to restrict display to rows that meet specific criteria. Syntax is WHERE *<column name>* *<operator>* *<value>* AND/OR . . . Example: SELECT ALL FROM Names WHERE L:Name = Smith AND State = NE.

■ Entry   Function

WHILE   Sets up a loop in a command file. Syntax is WHILE *conditions*
THEN . . . commands . . . ENDWHILE. Up to ten condi-
tions may be defined. Every While must have associated Then
and Endwhile commands. Example:
WHILE Status = 0 THEN
    perform these commands . . .
ENDWHILE

WIDTH   Used with the Set command to determine the width of the
screen or the printed page, from 39 to 132 characters.
Example: SET WIDTH 131. The Show command displays
the current width.

WRITE   Displays a message on the screen, using the syntax WRITE
"*message*" AT <*row*> <*column*>. The At clause is optional.
The "*message*" can be a variable name preceded by a period.
Examples: WRITE "My name is Ralph"; WRITE .Prompt
(where Prompt is a defined variable).

ZIP   Temporarily suspends R:BASE and executes an external program. When the external program is done, control is returned
directly to R:BASE. Syntax is ZIP *rollout program name,* where
rollout is an optional command used when an external program
will not fit into memory with R:BASE, and *program name* is the
name of the program to run. Example: ZIP ROLLOUT WS.

INDEX

SYBEX Computer Books
are different.

Here is why . . .

At SYBEX, each book is designed with you in mind. Every manuscript is carefully selected and supervised by our editors, who are themselves computer experts. We publish the best authors, whose technical expertise is matched by an ability to write clearly and to communicate effectively. Programs are thoroughly tested for accuracy by our technical staff. Our computerized production department goes to great lengths to make sure that each book is well-designed.

In the pursuit of timeliness, SYBEX has achieved many publishing firsts. SYBEX was among the first to integrate personal computers used by authors and staff into the publishing process. SYBEX was the first to publish books on the CP/M operating system, microprocessor interfacing techniques, word processing, and many more topics.

Expertise in computers and dedication to the highest quality product have made SYBEX a world leader in computer book publishing. Translated into fourteen languages, SYBEX books have helped millions of people around the world to get the most from their computers. We hope we have helped you, too.

For a complete catalog of our publications:

SYBEX, Inc. 2021 Challenger Drive, #100, Alameda, CA 94501
Tel: (415) 523-8233/(800) 227-2346   Telex: 336311

UNDERSTANDING
R: BASE SYSTEM V

If you'd like to ... book
but don't want to ... tain-
ing all the examp ... order
form and return ... Cali-
fornia residents a ...

SMS Softw
P.O. Box 28
La Jolla, CA

Name_____

Company____

City/State/Z

Enclosed is m
(Make check

Understanding R:

SYBEX is not affiliated w... assumes no responsibility for any defect in the
disk or program.